PENGUIN MODERN CLASSICS

Good-bye to All That

ROBERT GRAVES was born in Wimbledon in 1895 and educated at Charterhouse School, where he began to write poetry. On 4 August 1914 England declared war on Germany; Graves enlisted in the Royal Welch Fusiliers in the same month and was drafted to France. During the war he became close friends with the poet Siegfried Sassoon, published his first book of poetry and, in July 1916, was seriously wounded at the Battle of the Somme. He married his first wife, Nancy Nicholson, in 1918 and the couple had four children, born while Graves was studying English at St John's College, Oxford. In 1926 he went to Egypt with his family and the poet Laura Riding to take up a position as Professor of English Literature at Cairo University, but resigned after six months. He returned briefly to England and then, three years later, left for Deià, Majorca, which was to remain his home for most of the rest of his life. Graves wrote his autobiography, *Good-bye to All That*, in 1929 and it was soon established as a modern classic. *The Times Literary Supplement* acclaimed it as 'one of the most candid self-portraits of a poet, warts and all, ever painted'. Graves's many books in the succeeding years included the novels *I, Claudius* and *Claudius the God* (both 1934), *Count Belisarius* (1938), *Sergeant Lamb of the Ninth* (1940), *The Story of Mary Powell, Wife to Mr. Milton* (1943) and *The Golden Fleece* (1944), as well the non-fiction work *The White Goddess: A Historical Grammar of Poetic Myth* (1948), collections of poetry and translations of ancient writers. He married his second wife, Beryl Hodge, in 1950 and together they had four children. Graves died on 7 December 1985 in Majorca.

FRAN BREARTON was educated at the University of Durham and is currently Professor of Modern Poetry at Queen's University, Belfast. In 2004 she gave the Chatterton lecture on the subject of Graves's *The White Goddess*, and she has written several articles on Graves's poetry and prose, and on the literature of the Great War. She is President of the Robert Graves Society. Her books include *The Great War in Irish Poetry* (2000), *Reading Michael Longley* (2006) and, as co-editor, *The Oxford Handbook of Modern Irish Poetry* and *Incorrigibly Plural: Louis MacNeice and his Legacy* (both 2012).

ANDREW MOTION was Poet Laureate from 1999 to 2009 and is currently Professor of Creative Writing at Royal Holloway, University of London. He is also the founder and co-director of the Poetry Archive and the current President of the Campaign to Protect Rural England. His books include acclaimed biographies of the poets Philip Larkin and John Keats; a memoir, *In the Blood* (2006); and *Silver* (2012), a sequel to *Treasure Island*. His most recent poetry collections are *The Customs House* (2012), which features a sequence of war poems, and *The Cinder Path* (2009), shortlisted for the Ted Hughes Award for New Work in Poetry. He was knighted for his services to poetry in 2009.

ROBERT GRAVES

Good-bye to All That
An Autobiography

The Original Edition

Edited and annotated by FRAN BREARTON
with an Introduction by ANDREW MOTION

PENGUIN BOOKS

PENGUIN CLASSICS

Published by the Penguin Group
Penguin Books Ltd, 80 Strand, London WC2R ORL, England
Penguin Group (USA) Inc., 375 Hudson Street, New York, New York 10014, USA
Penguin Group (Canada), 90 Eglinton Avenue East, Suite 700, Toronto, Ontario,
Canada M4P 2Y3 (a division of Pearson Penguin Canada Inc.)
Penguin Ireland, 25 St Stephen's Green, Dublin 2, Ireland
(a division of Penguin Books Ltd)
Penguin Group (Australia), 707 Collins Street, Melbourne, Victoria 3008, Australia
(a division of Pearson Australia Group Pty Ltd)
Penguin Books India Pvt Ltd, 11 Community Centre,
Panchsheel Park, New Delhi – 110 017, India
Penguin Group (NZ), 67 Apollo Drive, Rosedale, Auckland 0632, New Zealand
(a division of Pearson New Zealand Ltd)
Penguin Books (South Africa) (Pty) Ltd, Block D, Rosebank Office Park,
181 Jan Smuts Avenue, Parktown North, Gauteng 2193, South Africa

Penguin Books Ltd, Registered Offices: 80 Strand, London WC2R ORL, England

www.penguin.com

First published by Jonathan Cape in 1929
This edition first published in Penguin Classics 2014
001

Set in 10.25/12.5pt Adobe Sabon
Typeset by Jouve (UK), Milton Keynes
Printed in England by Clays Ltd, St Ives plc

ISBN: 978-0-141-39266-0

www.greenpenguin.co.uk

Penguin Books is committed to a sustainable
future for our business, our readers and our planet.
This book is made from Forest Stewardship
Council™ certified paper.

Contents

Introduction

When Robert Graves first wrote his autobiography *Good-bye to All That* in 1929, at the age of thirty-three, he began by claiming that its three main 'objects' were 'simple enough: an opportunity for a formal good-bye to you and to you and to you and to me and to all that; forgetfulness, because once all this has been settled in my mind and written down and published it need never be thought about again; money'.

As far as money was concerned, his intentions were soon fulfilled. The memoir caused a good deal of controversy and sold strongly.

As far as 'forgetfulness' went, he did less well: the traumas resulting from his experiences in the First World War, which fill the centre of the book, remained with him for the rest of his life and continued to terrify, disturb and inspire him; indeed, the very next book he published was called *But It Still Goes On* (1930).

As for bidding 'a formal good-bye to you and to you and to you and to me and to all that' – well, it's complicated. Because part of what Graves is referring to here is his private life at the time, which was itself extremely complicated.

In January 1926, when Graves had already been married to his wife Nancy for eight years and was about to take up an appointment as Professor of English at the University of Cairo, Graves met the American poet Laura Riding: Riding travelled with the family to Egypt as Graves's 'lady-secretary'. By the time they returned later the same year, he and Riding were in love, and soon afterwards the whole lot of them set up in Hammersmith, London, and embarked on what they called a 'three-life', in which the eccentric and domineering Riding was established as the central figure, announcing (as Graves's biographer Richard Perceval Graves says) 'that historical time had effectively come to an end, and referring to herself as "Finality"'. In 1929 this ménage à trois became a 'four-life', when the young Irish writer Geoffrey Phibbs also fell in love with Riding, which soon brought matters to a crisis. In the spring of the same year Riding swallowed disinfectant before jumping from an upper window – provoking Graves into leaping from another window a storey below. Both survived, and soon afterwards Phibbs set up with Nancy, leaving Graves and Riding to one another for a while.

It was during this period that Graves wrote *Good-bye to All That*, working very fast and completing the manuscript in less than four months, when he was most intensely under Riding's influence. Although she is not named in the main text of the book, her presence is established in the prefatory poem 'World's End' (which she wrote), and she is addressed directly in the strange and moving 'Dedicatory Epilogue', where Graves admits 'the silence [of not mentioning her previously] is false if it makes the book seem to have been written forward from where I was instead of backward from where you are'. Furthermore, her determination that Graves should refashion himself according to her beliefs and standards, and therefore 'say good-bye to you and to you and to you and to me and to all that', informs every page and gives the entire text its main impetus and determination. It is, in fact, a memoir written to an invisible love, whose ideas and ideals it adopts almost wholesale.

Predictably enough, the Graves/Riding ménage à deux soon ended in acrimony and estrangement. So much so that, when Graves was invited by an American editor to revise his book for republication in 1957, twenty-eight years after it had first appeared, he gratefully seized the chance to remove from it as many traces of Riding as he could, including the prefatory poem and the 'Dedicatory Epilogue', and eradicated his iteration of her ideas as well as her cadences wherever possible. In this way, the book's hidden mentor was effaced or gagged or driven underground.

Ever since then the 1957 edition of the memoir has been printed as the standard edition of the text. There are several good reasons for this, not the least of them being that the first edition contains a great many inaccuracies, one of which was flagged from the start: Graves suggested there was a Rupert Brooke Fund administered by Edward Marsh that doled out money to impecunious poets, and immediately before publication, at Marsh's insistence, an erratum slip had to be inserted in the book to say that no such fund existed. More woundingly, Graves also included a good deal of material about his friends Siegfried Sassoon and Edmund Blunden, which offended them either because it breached their copyright (including and especially in the case of a long verse-letter Sassoon had written about the war, which he had not given Graves permission to publish); or because it presented 'fiction[alized]' accounts of episodes in the war as reliable truth; or because it insulted sensitive feelings (Graves tells a story, for instance, about Sassoon's mother's use of a spiritualist to contact one of her other sons, who was killed in the war, which Sassoon thought was 'unforgiveable'); or because it indulged in 'self-glorification' by promoting his own role in protecting Sassoon from the consequences of his – Sassoon's – famous public letter protesting that the war had changed from being a matter of 'defence and liberation' into one of 'aggression and conquest'.

Some of these hurts had already been addressed by the time the book first appeared: Sassoon was enraged when he saw an advance copy and contacted the publisher, who then printed cancel pages that blanked out his verse-letter and eleven lines of the prose relating to his mother. As if these kinds of damage weren't enough, the first edition also caused difficulties within Graves's own family – since it manages (as a part of the Riding-inspired business of 'saying good-bye' to 'historical time') to slight most of them in turn: his high-minded German mother, who taught him to 'speak the truth and shame the devil'; his poetry-writing Irish father (whose work and personality he humorously patronized – including by saying at one point 'Some of his songs I sing without prejudice; when washing up after meals or shelling peas or on similar occasions'); his remoter ancestors in Ireland and Germany; and his brothers. Especially his brothers, who were so upset by Graves describing himself as being 'the only one of my father's five sons of military age who had seen active service' – which seemed to imply that he was 'accusing them of dodging the draft', which was very far from being the case – that he was obliged to issue a correction the following year (1930).

It would be reasonable to describe all these things as

flaws in the 1929 edition of *Good-bye to All That*. And when they are combined with Graves's changed feelings about Riding, as well as his distaste for some of the 'ragged' and hurried aspects of his prose, it's equally easy to see why he took the chance to revise it. Among other things, he alters a great many of his recollections of episodes at the front line; he softens several of the references to family members; and he modifies his own image (including making some important changes to the way he recounted his early homoerotic experiences). The effect, combined with many other small alterations, is to rework the book at a local level while also re-presenting it in a fundamental way.

Despite these changes, which can be called improvements in accuracy and fairness, a comparison of the two versions makes it difficult not to think that more was lost than gained in the revisions. Lost because a kind of controlling tidiness is imposed on the originally headstrong, impulsive, galvanized, energetic, tumbling (and, yes, sometimes, 'ragged') prose, and also because the changes, while they cannot be said entirely to mask Graves's first intention, are at odds with it. Which is to say: his first intention was to produce a version of events that told the poetic truth about his experiences, the emotional truth, rather than being primarily fact-driven.

This means we do best to read the 1929 edition of the book as one in which the personnel are handled as 'characters' and events are treated as dramas or farces. Paul Fussell has written well about this in *The Great War and Modern Memory* (1975), reminding us that the American critic Randall Jarrell described Graves as 'the true heir of Ben Jonson', and himself describing the author as 'a tongue-in-cheek neurasthenic farceur whose material is "facts"'.

We can see Fussell's point on almost any page of the book, starting with the first nine chapters, in which he describes his family background and schooling at Charterhouse. Each of what he later calls 'the caricature scenes of my life' is populated by men and women who come close to being cartoons, including his close family and himself, whom he describes as someone who 'began playing games seriously, was quarrelsome, boastful, and talkative, won prizes, and collected things'. In the same way, themes and subjects which appear throughout the book (and make school-experience not simply a prelude to war-experience, but a pre-echo of it) are introduced as a reliable means of joking or joshing. Even poetry, which he admits gives his mind its focus, and which is repeatedly shown to be life-shaping, life-saving and life-giving, is not immune; when he remembers Swinburne peering into his infant eyes, it is not to describe him as a vintage bard but 'an inveterate pram-stopper and patter and kisser'; when he describes his own early efforts in verse it is to deprecate one of the most successful as 'silly [and] quaint'.

The point, obviously, is to cut everything pretentious down to size and to shake complacency. But his strategy is also designed to create a vision of life as farce, which becomes even more intense and purposeful when the beam of his attention switches to the war. Here the critique of often-ridiculous routines, languages and minor cruelties of school becomes enormously amplified and deepened – initially in his descriptions of regimental behaviour. Virtually the first fellow-soldier we meet is Jackie Barrett, 'a Kipling character'; the camp staff includes 'a fatherly colonel' and a doctor who is 'the mess buffoon'; and Graves himself has to be threatened by the adjutant 'that he would not send me to France until I had entirely overhauled my ward-robe and looked more like a soldier'.

Once he has made it to France and is involved in trench fighting, the same sort of cartooning and carica-turing becomes even more resonant. Very soon, in fact, we discover that all the previous examples have been a clever preparation for this central part of the book – which shows the whole story of the war as a series of 'bloody balls-ups' organized by fools and blunderers who appear to lack any proper skill or subtlety of feel-ing. Stupid priorities are preserved, wrong judgements are made, silly traditions are upheld – and all with quite appalling consequences. It's like reading a ver-sion of the final episode of *Blackadder*, some eighty years before that show was written. And a far cry from the patient accumulation of paradoxes (war/peace, pastoral/brutal, regenerative/nihilistic) that we find in war memoirs by Sassoon and Blunden, and in many of Wilfred Owen's finest poems.

The effect, of course, is to make Graves seem highly critical of everything he sees – and so he is in many obvious respects. But his comic manner has a stylistic counterpart that gives the book a different and associated power. This derives from its passion for plain-dealing and plain-speaking. For finding a way to record mater-ial that is in itself so horrible, anything fancy or ornamental would seem a kind of betrayal. Once again, examples are legion. The wounded soldier Graves hears 'making a snoring noise mixed with animal groans. At my feet was the cap he had worn, splashed with his brains. I had never seen human brains before; I had somehow regarded them as a poetical figment'; the two rats he sees 'tussling for the possession of a severed hand', which his fellows consider to be 'a great joke'; the dead body who has 'forced his knuckles into his mouth to stop himself crying out and attracting any more men to their death'.

The point about all these scenes, and many other instances of deadpan description, is not to show that Graves and other soldiers are unfeeling. It is to show that war has de-sensitized them – that its relentless mutilations and explosions and killings have deprived them of their proper responsiveness, and so also of their humanity. In this way, its effect is opposite to its appearance. Just as Graves's farcical writing registers a horrified amusement at its subjects as well as tenderness (because the black comedy of living has turned them into stereotypes), so the simplicity of his horror-descriptions reveals the deep complexity of his response. It amounts to a very ingenious trick of style – one that is both calculating and instinctive, in the same way that the great Second World War poet Keith Douglas was both calculating and instinctive when he adopted a similar tone (surely influenced by Graves) in his memoir of desert fighting *Alamein to Zem Zem* (1946), where he dispassionately – but feelingly – describes casualties as looking like 'sun bathers'.

The double climax of these two linked methods arrives near the centre of *Good-bye to All That*. The first involves a report, sent back to England and, of course, devastating his family, that Graves had been killed in action, when in fact he had 'only' been very seriously wounded. This is the memoir's supreme moment of farce, and Graves does not hesitate to decorate it with other and smaller examples of the ridiculous. 'I cannot tell you how pleased I am you are alive,' his colonel writes to him once the mistake has been discovered, consciously twisting together pathos and absurdity.

The other involves Sassoon's letter of protest about the prolongation of the war. For all the 'self-glorification' that Graves indulges in during this episode (which is, in fact, rather less than Sassoon – understandably – feels), the integrity of the letter is never in doubt, because it is so absolutely lucid in its condemnation, and so thoroughly disbelieved and rebuffed by the military. Exactly as Graves uses his sense of the ridiculous to puncture illusions and his cold eye to express warm feeling, so Sassoon makes his protest 'On behalf of those who are suffering [. . .] against the deception which is being practised on them.' By very different routes they arrive at the same point. The memoir and the letter that stands at its centre are absolutely complementary to one another.

And one more thing. Graves's book, which was denounced by several of its original readers as unreliable, is full of documents that themselves are unreliable in one way or another. Either because they are presented out of sequence, edited or misquoted, or because they contain propaganda (like the 'Message to the Pacifists' which is written by 'a Little Mother'). Or because they are somehow or other mistaken. But there is a difference between Graves's text and those he lampoons. *Good-bye to All That*, like Sassoon's letter and despite the difference in their language, is determined to shake itself free of illusions. To withdraw a little from 'literature' and even from the experience of all and sundry, in order to give itself breathing space and announce that mankind is irredeemably foolish, that good sense is likely to be disbelieved, that death and destruction, along with hurtfulness and stupidity, are as strong, if not stronger, than love and kindness. This is the dark heart of the book. And we see it even more clearly, and hear it beating even more loudly, in this original edition than we do in the comparatively careful and considered terms of the later one.

Andrew Motion, 2014

Chronology

1895 24 July: Robert von Ranke Graves is born in Wimbledon, the third child of Alfred Perceval Graves and Amy Graves. Graves has two elder sisters, Clarissa and Rosaleen, and two younger brothers, Charles and John. He also has five elder half-siblings: Philip, Mary (Mollie), Richard (Dick), Alfred and Susan.

1909–14 Attends Charterhouse School, Surrey.

1914 August: Enlists in the Royal Welch Fusiliers, following England's declaration of war on Germany (4 August).

1915 May: Drafted to northern France.

1916 1 May: First volume of poems, *Over the Brazier*, is published.

1916 July: Wounded at the Battle of the Somme and reported 'died of wounds'.

1918 January: Marries Nancy Nicholson, with whom he has four children: Jenny (b. 1919), John David (b. 1920), Catherine (b. 1922) and Samuel (b. 1924).

1925 June: Awarded a BLitt from St John's College, Oxford.

1926 January: Meets the American poet Laura Riding, with whom he and Nancy establish a 'trinity of friendship'.

1927 Publication of the (best-selling) *Lawrence and the Arabs* and, co-authored with Riding, *A Survey of Modernist Poetry*.

1929 April: Laura Riding jumps from the fourth-floor window of their London flat, with Graves following her from the floor below.

October: Graves and Riding leave England for Majorca, settling in the village of Deià. *Good-bye to All That* is published in November.

1934 Publication of *I, Claudius* and *Claudius the God*.

1936 The Spanish Civil War forces Graves and Riding to leave Majorca.

1938 Publication of *Collected Poems* and *Count Belisarius*.

1939 April: Graves and Riding sail to America, where Riding begins a relationship with the American poet Schuyler Jackson.

August: Graves returns to England, followed, in October, by Beryl Hodge (whom he marries in 1950, following his divorce from Nancy Nicholson). They settle in Galmpton, South Devon, for the war years, where three of their four children are born: William (b. 1940), Lucia (b. 1943) and Juan (b. 1944).

1940 Publication of *Sergeant Lamb of the Ninth*.

1943 March: Graves's eldest son, (John) David, is killed in action in Burma. Publication of *The Story of Mary Powell, Wife to Mr. Milton*.

1944 Publication of *The Golden Fleece*.

1946 The Graveses return to Majorca, where their fourth child, Tomás, is born in 1953.

1948 Publication of *The White Goddess: A Historical Grammar of Poetic Myth*.

1950 Graves meets Judith Bledsoe, the first of the 'muses' – the others being Margot Callas, Cindy Lee and the dancer Juli Simon – who would inspire much of his love poetry through the 1950s and 1960s.

1954 Graves delivers the Clark lectures in Cambridge (collected in *The Crowning Privilege*, 1955).

1955 Publication of *The Greek Myths*.

1957 First (and highly successful) lecture tour of the United States, to be followed by several others over the next decade.

1959 Publication of *Collected Poems 1959*.

1961 Elected Professor of Poetry at Oxford. Lectures published in *Oxford Addresses on Poetry* (1962) and *Mammon and the Black Goddess* (1965).

1964 Sudden death of his eldest daughter, the journalist Jenny Nicholson, from a cerebral aneurysm.

1974 Publication of his last individual volume of poems, *At the Gate*.

1976 BBC TV adaptation of *I, Claudius* broadcast.

1985 December: Graves dies at his home in Deià, aged 90, after many years of failing health.

Good-bye to All That
[1929]

My Dedication Is
An Epilogue

World's End[1]

The tympanum is worn thin.
The iris is become transparent.
The sense has overlasted.
Sense itself is transparent.
Speed has caught up with speed.
Earth rounds out earth.
The mind puts the mind by.
Clear spectacle: where is the eye?

All is lost, no danger
Forces the heroic hand.
No bodies in bodies stand
Oppositely. The complete world
Is likeness in every corner.
The names of contrast fall
Into the widening centre.
A dry sea extends the universal.

No suit and no denial
Disturb the general proof.
Logic has logic, they remain
Quiet in each other's arms,
Or were otherwise insane,
With all lost and nothing to prove
That even nothing can be through love.

LAURA RIDING
(From *Love as Love, Death as Death*)

I

The objects of this autobiography, written at the age of thirty-three, are simple enough: an opportunity for a formal good-bye to you and to you and to you and to me and to all that; forgetfulness, because once all this has been settled in my mind and written down and published it need never be thought about again; money. Mr. Bentley once wrote:

> The science of geography
> Is different from biography:
> Geography is about maps,
> Biography is about chaps.[1]

The rhyme might have been taken further to show how closely, nevertheless, these things are linked. For while maps are the biographical treatment of geography, biography is the geographical treatment of chaps. Chaps who are made the subjects of biography have by effort, or by accident, put themselves on the contemporary map as geographical features; but seldom have reality by themselves as proper chaps. So that *Who's Who?* though claiming to be a dictionary of biography, is hardly less of a geographical gazetteer than *Burke's Peerage* . . . One of the few simple people I have known who have had a philosophic contempt for such gazetteering

5

was Old Joe, a battalion quartermaster in France. He
was a proper chap. When he had won his D.S.O. for
being the only quartermaster in the Seventh Division to
get up rations to his battalion in the firing line at, I think,
the Passchendaele show, he was sent a slip to complete
with biographical details for the appropriate directory.
He looked contemptuously at the various headings. Disregarding 'date and place of birth', and even 'military
campaigns', he filled in two items only:

Issue . . Rum, rifles, etc.
Family seat . My khaki pants.

And yet even proper chaps have their formal geography, however little it may mean to them. They have
birth certificates, passports, relatives, earliest recollections, and even, sometimes, degrees and publications
and campaigns to itemize, like all the irrelevant people,
the people with only geographical reality. And the less
that all these biographical items mean to them the
more particularly and faithfully can they fill them in, if
ever they feel so inclined. When loyalties have become
negligible and friends have all either deserted in alarm
or died or been dismissed or happen to be chaps to
whom geography is also without significance, the task
is easy for them. They do not have to wait until they
are at least ninety[2] before publishing, and even then
only tell the truth about characters long dead and
without influential descendants.[3]

As a proof of my readiness to accept biographical
convention, let me at once record my two earliest recollections. The first is being held up to the window to
watch a carnival procession for the Diamond Jubilee in

1897 (this was at Wimbledon, where I had been born on 24th July 1895). The second, an earlier recollection still, is looking up with a sort of despondent terror at a cupboard in the nursery, which stood accidentally open and which was filled to the ceiling with octavo volumes of Shakespeare. My father was organizer of a Shakespeare reading circle. I did not know until long afterwards that it was the Shakespeare cupboard, but I, apparently, had then a strong instinct against drawing-room activities. It is only recently that I have overcome my education and gone back to this early intuitional spontaneousness.

When distinguished visitors came to the house, like Sir Sidney Lee with his Shakespearean scholarship, and Lord Ashbourne, not yet a peer, with his loud talk of 'Ireland for the Irish', and his saffron kilt, and Mr. Eustace Miles with his samples of edible nuts, I knew all about them in my way. I had summed up correctly and finally my Uncle Charles of the *Spectator* and *Punch*, and my Aunt Grace, who came in a carriage and pair, and whose arrival always caused a flutter because she was Lady Pontifex, and all the rest of my relations. And I had no illusions about Algernon Charles Swinburne, who often used to stop my perambulator when he met it on Nurses' Walk, at the edge of Wimbledon Common, and pat me on the head and kiss me; he was an inveterate pram-stopper and patter and kisser. Nurses' Walk lay between 'The Pines', Putney (where he lived with Watts-Dunton) and the Rose and Crown public-house, where he went for his daily pint of beer; Watts-Dunton allowed him twopence for that and no more. I did not know that Swinburne was a poet, but I knew that he was no good. Swinburne, by the way, when a very young man, went to Walter Savage Landor, then a very old man, and asked

for and was given a poet's blessing; and Landor when a
child had been patted on the head by Dr. Samuel Johnson; and Johnson when a child been taken to London to
be touched by Queen Anne for scrofula, the King's evil;
and Queen Anne when a child . . .

But I mentioned the Shakespeare reading circle. It
went on for years, and when I was sixteen curiosity
finally sent me to one of the meetings. I remember the
vivacity with which my mother read the part of Kather-
ine in the *Taming of the Shrew* to my father's Petruchio,
and the compliments on their performance which the
other members gave me. Mr. and Mrs. Maurice Hill
were two of the most popular members of the circle.
This meeting took place some years before they became
Mr. Justice Hill and Lady Hill, and some years, too,
before I looked into *The Shrew*. I remember the lemon-
ade glasses, the cucumber sandwiches, the *petits fours*,
the drawing-room knick-knacks, the chrysanthemums
in bowls, and the semi-circle of easy chairs around the
fire. The gentle voice of Mr. Maurice Hill as Hortentio
was admonishing my father: 'Thou go thy ways, thou
hast tamed a cursed shrew.' I myself as Lucio was ending the performance with: ''Tis a wonder by your leave
she will be tamed so.' I must go one day to hear him
speak his lines as Judge of the Divorce Courts; his
admonishments have become famous.

After earliest recollections I should perhaps give a
passport description of myself and let the items enlarge
themselves. Date of birth . . . Place of birth . . . I have
given those. Profession. In my passport I am down as
'university professor'. That was a convenience for 1926,
when I first took it out. I thought of putting 'writer', but
people who are concerned with passports have complicated reactions to the word. 'University professor' wins a

simple reaction – dull respect. No questions asked. So also with 'army captain (pensioned list)'.

My height is given as six feet two inches, my eyes as grey, and my hair as black. To 'black' should be added 'thick and curly'. I am described as having no special peculiarity. This is untrue. For a start, there is my big, once aquiline, now crooked nose. I broke it at Charterhouse playing Rugger with Soccer players. (I broke another player's nose myself in the same game.) That unsteadied it, and boxing sent it askew. Finally, it was operated on. It is very crooked. It was once useful as a vertical line of demarcation between the left and right sides of my face, which are naturally unassorted – my eyes, eyebrows, and ears being all set noticeably crooked and my cheek-bones, which are rather high, being on different levels. My mouth is what is known as 'full' and my smile is crooked; when I was thirteen I broke two front teeth and became sensitive about showing them. My hands and feet are large. I weigh about twelve stone four. My best comic turn is a double-jointed pelvis; I can sit on a table and rap like the Fox sisters with it. One shoulder is distinctly lower than the other, but that is because of a lung wound in the war. I do not carry a watch because I always magnetize the main-spring; during the war, when there was an army order that officers should carry watches and synchronize them daily, I had to buy two new ones every month. Medically, I am a thoroughly 'good life'.

My passport gives my nationality as 'British subject'. Here I might parody Marcus Aurelius, who begins his Golden Book with the various ancestors and relations to whom he owes the virtues of a worthy Roman Emperor. Something of the sort about myself, and why I am not a Roman Emperor or even, except on occasions, an English gentleman. My mother's father's family, the von Ranke's, was a family of Saxon country pastors, not anciently noble. Leopold von Ranke, the first modern historian, my great-uncle, brought the 'von' into the family. To him I owe my historical method. It was he who wrote, to the scandal of his contemporaries: 'I am a historian before I am a Christian; my object is simply to find out how the things actually occurred,' and of Michelet the French historian: 'He wrote history in a style in which the truth could not be told.' Thomas Carlyle decried him as 'Dry-as-Dust'; to his credit. To Heinrich von Ranke, my grandfather, I owe my clumsy largeness, my endurance, energy, seriousness, and my thick hair. He was rebellious and even atheistic in his youth. As a medical student at a Prussian university he was involved in the political disturbances of 1848. He and a number of student friends demonstrated in favour of Karl Marx at the time of his trial for high treason. Like Marx, they had to leave the country. He came to London and finished his medical course there. In 1859[4] he went to the Crimea with the British forces as a regimental surgeon. All I know about this is a chance remark that he made to me as a child: 'It is not always the big bodies that are the strongest. When I was at Sevastopol in the trenches I saw the great British Guards crack up and die by the score, while the little sappers took no harm.' Still, his big body carried him very well.

He married, in London, my grandmother, a Schleswig-Dane. She was the daughter of Tiarks, the Greenwich astronomer. She was tiny, saintly, frightened. Before her father took to astronomy the Tiarks family had, it seems, followed the Danish country system, not at all a bad one, of alternate professions for father and son. The odd generations were tinsmiths and the even generations were pastors. My gentler characteristics trace back to my grandmother. She had ten children; the eldest of these was my mother, who was born in London. My grandfather's atheism and radicalism sobered down. He eventually returned to Germany, where he became a well-known children's doctor at Munich. He was about the first doctor in Europe to insist on clean milk for his child patients. When he found that he could not get clean milk to the hospitals by ordinary means he started a model dairy-farm himself. His agnosticism grieved my grandmother; she never ceased to pray for him, but concentrated more particularly on saving the next generation. She was a Lutheran. My grandfather did not die entirely unregenerate; his last words were: 'The God of my fathers, to Him at least I hold.' I do not know exactly what he meant by that, but it was a statement consistent with his angry patriarchal moods, with his acceptance of a prominent place in Bavarian society as Herr Geheimrat Ritter von Ranke, and with his loyalty to the Kaiser, with whom once or twice he went deer-shooting. It meant, practically, that he was a good Liberal in religion as in politics, and that my grandmother need not have worried. I prefer my German relations to my Irish relations;[5] they have high principles, are easy, generous, and serious. The men have fought duels not for cheap personal honour, but in the public interest – called out, for example, because they have protested publicly against the scandalous behaviour of some superior officer or official. One of them who was in the German consular service lost seniority, just before the war, I was told, because he refused to use the consulate as a clearing-place for secret-service reports. They are not heavy drinkers either. My grandfather, as a student at the regular university 'drunks', was in the habit of pouring his beer down into his eighteen-fortyish riding-boots. His children were brought up to speak English in their home, and always looked to England as the home of culture and progress. The women were noble and patient, and kept their eyes on the ground when they went out walking.

At the age of eighteen my mother was sent to England as companion to a lonely old woman who had befriended my grandmother when she was an orphan. For seventeen years she waited hand and foot on this old lady, who for the last few years was perfectly senile. When she finally died, my mother determined to go to India, after a short training as a medical missionary. This ambition was baulked by her meeting my father, a widower with five children; it was plain to her that she could do as good work on the home-mission field.

About the other side of my family. The Graves' have a pedigree that dates back to the Conquest, but is good as far as the reign of Henry VII. Colonel Graves, the regicide, who was Ireton's chief of horse, is claimed as the founder of the Irish branch of the family. Limerick was its centre. There were occasional soldiers and doctors in it, but they were collaterals; in the direct male line was a sequence of rectors, deans, and bishops. The Limerick Graves' have no 'hands' or mechanical sense; instead they have a wide reputation as conversationalists. In those of my relatives who have the family characteristics most strongly marked, unnecessary talk is a nervous disorder. Not bad talk as talk goes; usually informative, often witty, but it goes on and on and on and on and on. The von Ranke's have, I think, little mechanical aptitude either. It is most inconvenient to have been born into the age of the internal-combustion engine and the electric dynamo and to have no sympathy with them; a push bicycle, a primus stove, and an army rifle mark the bounds of my mechanical capacity.

My grandfather, on this side, was Protestant Bishop of Limerick. He had eight, or was it ten, children. He was a little man and a remarkable mathematician; he first formulated some theory or other of spherical conics. He was also an antiquary, and discovered the key to ancient Irish Ogham script. He was hard and, by reputation, far from generous. A gentleman and a scholar, and respected throughout the countryside on that account. He and the Catholic Bishop were on the very best terms. They cracked Latin jokes at each other, discussed fine points of scholarship, and were unclerical enough not to take their religious differences too seriously.

When I was in Limerick as a soldier of the garrison some twenty-five years after my grandfather's death, I heard a lot about Bishop Graves from the townsfolk. The Catholic Bishop had once joked him about the size of his family, and my grandfather had retorted warmly with the text about the blessedness of the man who has his quiver full of arrows, to which the Catholic answered briefly and severely: 'The ancient Jewish quiver only held six.' My grandfather's wake, they said, was the longest ever seen in the town of Limerick; it stretched from the cathedral right down O'Connell Street and over Sarsfield Bridge, and I do not know how many miles Irish beyond. He blessed me when I was a child, but I do not remember that.

Of my father's mother, who was a Scotswoman, a Cheyne from Aberdeen, I have been able to get no information at all beyond the fact that she was 'a very beautiful woman'. I can only conclude that most of what she said or did passed unnoticed in the rivalry of family conversations. The Cheyne pedigree was better than the Graves'; it was flawless right back to the medieval Scottish kings, to the two Balliols, the first and second Davids, and the Bruce. In later times the Cheynes had been doctors and physicians. But my father is engaged at the same time as myself on his autobiography, and no doubt he will write at length about all this.

My father, then, met my mother some time in the early 'nineties. He had previously been married to one of the Irish Coopers, of Cooper's Hill, near Limerick. The Coopers were an even more Irish family than the Graves'. The story is that when Cromwell came to Ireland and ravaged the country, Moira O'Brien, the last surviving member of the great clan O'Brien, who were the paramount chiefs of the country round Limerick, came to him one day and said: 'General, you have killed my father and my uncles, my husband and my brothers. I am left as the sole heiress of these lands. Do you intend to confiscate them?' Cromwell is said to have been struck by her magnificent presence and to have answered that that certainly had been his intention. But that she could keep her lands, or a part of them, on condition that she married one of his officers. And so the officers of the regiment which had taken a leading part in hunting down the O'Briens were invited to take a pack of cards and cut for the privilege of marrying Moira and succeeding to the estate. The winner was one Ensign Cooper. Moira, a few weeks after her marriage, found herself pregnant. Convinced that it was a male heir, as indeed it proved, she kicked her husband to death. It is said that she kicked him in the pit of the stomach after making him drunk. The Coopers have always been a haunted family and *Hibernicis ipsis Hibernicores*. Jane Cooper, whom my father married, died of consumption.

The Graves family was thin-nosed and inclined to petulance, but never depraved, cruel, or hysterical. A persistent literary tradition; of Richard, a minor poet and a friend of Shenstone; and John Thomas, who was a mathematician and jurist and contributed to Sir William Hamilton's discovery of quaternions; and Richard, a divine and regius professor of Greek; and James, an archaeologist; and Robert, who invented the disease called after him and was a friend of Turner's; and Robert, who was a classicist and theologian and a friend of Wordsworth's; and Richard, another divine; and Robert, another divine; and other Robert's, James's, Thomas's and Richard's, and Clarissa, one of the toasts of Ireland, who married Leopold von Ranke (at Windermere Church) and linked the Graves and von Ranke families a couple of generations before my father and mother married. See the British Museum catalogue for an eighteenth and nineteenth-century record of Graves' literary history.

It was through this Clarissa-Leopold relationship that my father met my mother. My mother told him at once that she liked *Father O'Flynn*, for writing which my father will be chiefly remembered. He put the words to a traditional jig tune, *The Top of Cork Road*, which he remembered from his boyhood. Sir Charles Stanford supplied a few chords for the setting. My father sold the complete rights for a guinea. The publisher made thousands. Sir Charles Stanford, who drew a royalty as the composer, also made a very large sum. Recently my father has made a few pounds from gramophone rights. He has never been bitter about all this, but he has more than once impressed on me almost religiously never to sell for a sum down the complete rights of any work of mine whatsoever.

I am glad in a way that my father was a poet. This at least saved me from any false reverence of poets, and his work was never an oppression to me. I am even very pleased when I meet people who know his work and not mine. Some of his songs I sing without prejudice; when washing up after meals or shelling peas or on similar occasions. He never once tried to teach me how to write, or showed any understanding of my serious work; he was always more ready to ask advice about his own work than to offer it for mine. He never tried to stop me writing and was glad of my first successes. His light-hearted early work is the best. His *Invention of Wine*, for instance, which begins:

> Ere Bacchus could talk
> Or dacently walk,
> Down Olympus he jumped
> From the arms of his nurse,
> And though ten years in all
> Were consumed by the fall
> He might have fallen further
> And fared a dale worse.[6]

After he married my mother and became a convinced teetotaller he lost something of this easy playfulness.

He broke the ecclesiastical sequence. His great-grandfather had been a dean, his grandfather a rector, his father a bishop, but he himself was never more than a lay-reader. And he broke the geographical connection with Ireland, for which I cannot be too grateful to him. I am much harder on my relations and much more careful of associating with them than I am with strangers. But I can in certain respects admire my father and mother. My father for his simplicity and persistence and my mother for her seriousness and strength. Both for their generosity. They never bullied me or in any way exceeded their ordinary parental rights, and were grieved rather than angered by my default from formal religion. In physique and general characteristics my mother's side is stronger in me on the whole. But I am subject to many habits of speech and movement characteristic of the Graves', most of them eccentric. Such as finding it difficult to walk straight down a street, getting tired of sentences when half-way through and leaving them in the air, walking with the hands folded in a particular way behind the back, and being subject to sudden and most disconcerting spells of complete amnesia. These fits, so far as I can discover, serve no useful purpose, and the worst about them is that they tend to produce in the subject the same sort of dishonesty that deaf people have when they miss the thread of conversation. They dare not be left behind and rely on their intuition and bluff to get them through. This disability is most marked in very cold weather. I do not now talk too much except when I have been drinking or when I meet someone who was with me in France. The Graves' have good minds for purposes like examinations, writing graceful Latin verse, filling in forms, and solving puzzles (when we children were invited to parties where guessing games and brain-tests were played we never failed to win). They have a good eye for ball games, and a graceful style. I inherited the eye, but not the style; my mother's family are entirely without style and I went that way. I have an ugly but fairly secure seat on a horse. There is a coldness in the Graves' which is anti-sentimental to the point of insolence, a necessary check to the goodness of heart from which my mother's family suffers. The Graves', it is fair to generalize, though loyal to the British governing class to which they belong, and so to the Constitution, are individualists; the von Ranke's regard their membership of the corresponding class in Germany as a sacred trust enabling them to do the more responsible work in the service of humanity. Recently, when a von Ranke entered a film studio, the family felt itself disgraced.

The most useful and at the same time most dangerous gift that I owe to my father's side of the family – probably more to the Cheynes than the Graves' – is that I am always able, when it is a question of dealing with officials or getting privileges from public institutions which grudge them, to masquerade as a gentleman. Whatever I happen to be wearing; and because the clothes I wear are not what gentlemen usually wear, and yet I do not seem to be an artist or effeminate, and my accent and gestures are irreproachable, I have even been 'placed' as the heir to a dukedom, whose perfect confidence in his rank would explain all such eccentricity. In this way I have been told that I seem, paradoxically, to be more of a gentleman even than one of my elder brothers who spent a number of years as a consular official in the Near East. His wardrobe is almost too carefully a gentleman's, and he does not allow himself the pseudo-ducal privilege of having disreputable acquaintances and saying on all occasions what he really means. About this being a gentleman business: I paid so heavily for the fourteen years of my gentleman's education that I feel entitled occasionally to get some sort of return.

II

My mother married my father largely, it seems, to help him out with his five motherless children. Having any herself was a secondary consideration. But first she had a girl, then she had another girl, and it was very nice of course to have them, but slightly disappointing, because she belonged to the generation and the tradition that made a son the really important event; then I came and I was a fine healthy child. She was forty when I was born and my father was forty-nine. Four years later she had another son and four years later she had still another son. The desired preponderance of male over female was established and twice five made ten. The gap of two generations between my parents and me was easier in a way to bridge than a single generation gap. Children seldom quarrel with their grandparents, and I have been able to think of my mother and father as grandparents. Also, a family of ten means a dilution of parental affection; the members tend to become indistinct. I have often been called: 'Philip, Richard, Charles, I mean Robert.'

My father was a very busy man, an inspector of schools for the Southwark district of London, and we children saw practically nothing of him except during the holidays. Then he was very sweet and playful and told us stories with the formal beginning, not 'once upon a time', but always 'and so the old gardener blew his nose on a red pocket handkerchief'. He occasionally played games with us, but for the most part when he was not doing educational work he was doing literary work or being president of literary or temperance societies. My mother was so busy running the household and conscientiously carrying out her social obligations as my father's wife that we did not see her continuously, unless on Sunday or when we happened to be ill. We had a nurse and we had each other and that was companionship enough. My father's chief part in our education was to insist on our speaking grammatically, pronouncing words correctly, and using no slang. He left our religious instruction entirely to my mother, though he officiated at family prayers, which the servants were expected to attend, every morning before breakfast. Punishments, such as being sent to bed early or being stood in the corner, were in the hands of my mother. Corporal punishment, never severe and given with a slipper, was my father's business. We learned to be strong moralists and spent a great deal of our time on self-examination and good resolutions. My sister Rosaleen put up a printed notice in her corner of the nursery – it might just as well have been put up by me: 'I must not say bang bust or pig bucket, for it is rude.'

We were given very little pocket-money – a penny a week with a rise to twopence at the age of twelve or so, and we were encouraged to give part at least of any odd money that came to us from uncles or other visitors to Dr. Barnardo's Homes and (this frightened us a bit) to beggars. There was one blind beggar at Wimbledon who used to sit on the pavement reading the Bible aloud in Braille; he was not really blind, but able to turn his eyes up and keep the pupils concealed for minutes at a time under drooping lids which were artificially inflamed. We often gave to him. He died a rich man and had been able to provide his son with a college education. The first distinguished writer that I remember meeting after Swinburne was P. G. Wodehouse, a friend of one of my brothers; he was then in the early twenties, on the staff of the *Globe*, and was writing school stories in *The Captain* magazine. He gave me a penny, advising me to get marsh-mallows with it. I was too shy to express my gratitude at the time; and have never since permitted myself to be critical about his work.

I had great religious fervour which persisted until shortly after my confirmation at the age of sixteen. I remember the incredulity with which I first heard that there actually were people, people baptized like myself into the Church of England, who did not believe in Jesus. I never met an unbeliever in all these years. As soon as I did, it was all over with my simple faith in the literal fundamentalist interpretation of the Bible. This was bad luck on my parents, but they were doomed to it. One married couple that I know, belonging to the same generation, decided that the best way in the end to ensure a proper religious attitude in their children, was not to teach them any religion at all until they were able to understand it in some degree of fulness. The children were sent to schools where no religious training was given. At the age of thirteen the eldest boy came indignantly to his father and said: 'Look here, father, I think you've treated me very badly. The other chaps laugh at me because I don't know anything about God. And who's this chap Jesus? When I ask them they won't tell me, they think I am joking.' So the long-hoped-for moment had arrived. The father told the boy to call his sister, who was a year younger than him, because he had something very important to tell them both. Then very reverently and carefully he told them the Gospel story. He had always planned to tell it to them in this way. The children did not interrupt him. When finally he had finished there was a silence. Then the girl said, rather embarrassed: 'Really father, I think that is the silliest story I've heard since I was a kid.' The boy said: 'Poor chap. But what about it, anyhow?'[1]

I have asked many of my acquaintances at what point in their childhood or adolescence they became class-conscious, but have never been given a satisfactory answer. I remember when it happened to me. When I was four and a half I caught scarlet fever; my younger brother had just been born, and it was impossible for me to have scarlet fever in the house, so I was sent off to a public fever hospital. There was only one other bourgeois child in the ward; the rest were all proletarians. I did not notice particularly that the attitude of the nurses or the other patients to me was different; I accepted the kindness and spoiling easily, because I was accustomed to it. But I was astonished at the respect and even reverence that this other little boy, a clergyman's child, was given. 'Oh,' the nurses would cry after he had gone; 'Oh,' they cried, 'he did look a little gentleman in his pretty white pellisse when they came to take him away.' 'He was a fair toff,' echoed the little proletarians. When I came home from hospital, after being there about two months, my accent was commented on and I was told that the boys in the ward had been very vulgar. I did not know what 'vulgar' meant; it had to be explained to me. About a year later I met Arthur, a boy of about nine, who had been in the ward and taught me how to play cricket when I was getting better; I was then at my first preparatory school and he was a ragged errand-boy. In hospital we had all worn the same hospital nightgown, and I had not realized that we came off such different shelves. But now I suddenly recognized with my first shudder of gentility that there were two sorts of people – ourselves and the lower classes. The servants were trained to call us children, even when we were tiny, Master Robert, Miss Rosaleen, and Miss Clarissa, but I had not realized that these were titles of respect. I had thought of 'Master' and 'Miss' merely as vocative prefixes used when addressing other people's children. But now I realized that the servants were the lower classes, and that we were ourselves.

I accepted this class separation as naturally as I had accepted religious dogma, and did not finally discard gentility until nearly twenty years later. My mother and father were never of the aggressive, shoot-'em-down type. They were Liberals or, more strictly, Liberal-Unionists. In religious theory, at least, they treated their employees as fellow-creatures. But social distinctions remained clearly defined. That was religion too:

> He made them high or lowly,
> And ordered their estates.

I can well recall the tone of my mother's voice when she informed the maids that they could have what was left of the pudding, or scolded the cook for some carelessness. It was a forced hardness, made almost harsh by embarrassment. My mother was *gemütlich* by nature. She would, I believe, have given a lot to be able to dispense with servants altogether. They were a foreign

23

body in the house. I remember what the servants' bedrooms used to look like. By a convention of the times they were the only rooms in the house that had no carpet or linoleum; they were on the top landing on the dullest side of the house. The gaunt, unfriendly-looking beds, and the hanging-cupboards with faded cotton curtains, instead of wardrobes with glass doors as in the other rooms. All this uncouthness made me think of the servants as somehow not quite human. The type of servant that came was not very good; only those with not particularly good references would apply for a situation where there were ten in the family. And because it was such a large house, and there was hardly a single tidy person in the household, they were constantly giving notice. There was too much work they said. So that the tendency to think of them as only half human was increased; they never had time to get fixed as human beings.

The bridge between the servants and ourselves was our nurse. She gave us her own passport on the first day she came: 'Emily Dykes is my name; England is my nation; Netheravon is my dwelling-place, and Christ is my salvation.' Though she called us Miss and Master she spoke it in no servant tone. In a practical way she came to be more to us than our mother. I began to despise her at about the age of twelve – she was then nurse to my younger brothers – when I found that my education was now in advance of hers, and that if I struggled with her I was able to trip her up and bruise her quite easily. Besides, she was a Baptist and went to chapel; I realized by that time that the Baptists were, like the Wesleyans and Methodists, the social inferiors of the members of the Church of England.

I was brought up with a horror of Catholicism and

this remained with me for a very long time. It was not a case of once a Protestant always a Protestant, but rather that when I ceased to be Protestant I was further off than ever from being Catholic. I discarded Protestantism in horror of its Catholic element. My religious training developed in me a great capacity for fear (I was perpetually tortured by the fear of hell), a superstitious conscience and a sexual embarrassment. I was very long indeed in getting rid of all this. Nancy Nicholson and I (later on in this story) were most careful not to give our four children an early religious training. They were not even baptized.

The last thing that is discarded by Protestants when they reject religion altogether is a vision of Christ as the perfect man. That persisted with me, sentimentally, for years. At the age of nineteen I wrote a poem called 'In the Wilderness'. It was about Christ meeting the scapegoat – a silly, quaint poem – and has appeared in at least seventy anthologies. Its perpetual recurrence. Strangers are always writing to me to say what a beautiful poem it is, and how much strength it has given them, and would I, etc.? Here, for instance, is a letter that came yesterday:

Sir, – I heard with great delight your beautiful poem 'In the Wilderness', broadcast from 2LO last night, and am writing to you because your poem has given me strength and hope. I am a gentlelady in need – in great need – not of a gift, but of a *loan* on interest of 5 per cent. I also need a kind friend to show me human sympathy and to help me if possible by an introduction to a really upright and conscientious London solicitor who will fight my cause, not primarily for the filthy lucre, but because it is waging the battle of Right against the most infamous

Wrong. First of all I ask you to believe that I am writing you the simple truth. I also am gifted as a writer, but as my physical health has always been a great struggle, and poverty from my childhood has been my lot, and I will not stoop to write down to the popular taste, and perhaps, also, because I have no influential friends to give me a helping hand, I earn very little by my pen. But I know how to wield a pen, and I am going to put myself into this letter just as I am – I am not apt to deceive, I hate lies and every form of deception. This letter is 'a bow sent at a venture' – to see if you would like to help a literary sister who is being gravely wronged by her only near relative, an abnormal woman, who has hated her for years without any cause. To be very direct – I need £10 for one year at 5 per cent. – to be repaid £10, 10s. od. I need it *at once, very urgently* – to pay arrears of furnished digs – £3, 13s. od. – Milk Bill 16s. 8d., Grocery Bill 10s. 6d. and coal 1s. 8d. – then to leave Bolton (the black town of mills which fogs incessantly) and go for a change to Blackpool: then to go up to Town to put my legal business into a London solicitor's hands. I will sign a Promissory Note for £10, 10s. od., to repay a year hence. I am cultured and highly educated and well-born. I was trained to teach on the higher schools and I hold high testimonials for teaching. But I overworked and at last became consumptive, and had tuberculosis of both lungs. It was taken early and I am relatively cured. But my teaching career is broken, and I do so love teaching. In consequence of this I have a monthly pension from a Philanthropic Society of £2, 11s. 8d. But it is so tiny, I cannot possibly *live* on it, squeeze as I may. But an inheritance of over £1,000 is mine, which is being wrongly withheld from me by the rogue of a solicitor in whose hands it is. I had one brother and one sister. The brother had saved money, and insured himself in many ways against his old age. The sister was well married to a man in good position; heartless, and hardened with her worldly life, and abnormally unnatural. She was expelled from two schools. She contracted an insane hatred of me, her little sister, and being full of cupidity, has tried to rob me of the little I have. My brother intended me to be his heir and inherit all his money. He wrote her this. But he was not a good brother and I did not visit him. He was a widower without offspring. Then he died suddenly in 1926, Xmas. She got to his house and wired me the death. Afterwards she wrote a few lines *but never told me the date of the funeral and has hid everything about his affairs from me* – his declared heir! She declared there was no Will to be found, and when I arrived in the Midlands from Yorkshire and got to his Vicarage *she, with her woman friend, had locked me out of the house, to prevent my search for the Will!* Upon advice I issued a Caveat and they at once *violated the Caveat*, and began to arrange for the sale of furniture! I heard of it by chance and stopped the sale. Then I was taken ill with my lungs in Derbyshire, whither I had returned after engaging a lawyer to safeguard my interests on the spot. They then corrupted my solicitor, who let me down badly, and I was ill in Derby. They warned the Caveat, and I could not enter an appearance, so it became abortive. Then my sister got herself made sole Administratrix. I had intended to apply to be joint Administratrix. Then began a series of fraudulent acts and maladministration. Her solicitor is a rogue and he is trying to force me to '*approve*' his unsatisfactory accounts by withholding my share until I sign an undertaking not to proceed against them afterwards. *One* item in accounts is falsified which I can prove, and other gross acts of fraud can be proved. *Foul play* has been pursued throughout, and they are now shadowing me everywhere by hired agents who find out the solicitors I employ and buy them off, or otherwise prevent their acting against them for me. It is the *grossest* case imaginable. I hold all my documents and can prove everything. I have a clear and strong case. But I need a *London* solicitor – away from the North where my sister lives in Northumberland – and I will not sink my moral principle to accept, not my lawful Half-Share, but what they choose to offer me, namely £919, 13s. 3d. and 18 months' interest. I want the Court to take over the administration. I have applied to the solicitor for an advance upon my share and he refuses again in order to *compel* me to sign this infamous agreement. I had £50 in advance in 1926 which is shown in accounts. I just need this £10 now so as to pay up here and get to Blackpool – for I have been ill again with my lungs, and I *badly* need a change.

Will you help a stranger with this not very big loan, and on interest? I would bring all the accounts and papers to show you when I come to town. And if I have found a friend in you, I shall indeed thank God. You can trust me. I *am* worthy, though I can give no references, because the people are dead. But I think you do not like being 'bullied' with such things. I am middle-aged, but a child in heart – original – and just myself, and look rather ridiculously young, without any artifice or make-up.

But apart from the loan, I need a *friend*. The family used to sneer at me that I 'never made friends for what I could get out of them'. Truly I never did. I like rather to help others myself. I should like to help *you* if I could in any way. I just love to serve. My life has been lonely, and both parents are dead, and I don't make friends lightly. So that is all. But I won't finish without telling you that I love the Master, the Lord Jesus Christ, as you love Him, and trust Him in all this darkness. I always like to bring His Name in – and so good night – I would be thankful if you will write to me in a *registered* letter. Some of my letters have gone astray, I fear I do not trust the woman in these lodgings, and my letters are going to a shop to be called for.

I am, dear Sir,
Yours very truly
***** (Miss).

P.S. – Do you think you could get a letter to me by *Saturday?* I do so love your poems.

I put this in here because it is not a letter to answer, nor yet somehow a letter to throw away. The style reminds me of one of my Irish female cousins. And that again reminds me of the ancient Irish triad – 'Three ugly sisters: Chatter, Poverty and Chastity.'[2]

III

I went to six preparatory schools.[1] The first was a dame's school at Wimbledon. I went there at the age of six. My father, as an educational expert, did not let me stay here long. He found me crying one day at the difficulty of the twenty-three-times table, and there was a Question and Answer History Book that we used which began:

Question: Why were the Britons so called?
Answer: Because they painted themselves blue.

My father said it was out of date. Also I was made to do mental arithmetic to a metronome. I once wet myself for nervousness at this torture. So I went to the lowest class of King's College School, Wimbledon. I was just seven years old, the youngest boy there, and they went up to nineteen. I was taken away after a couple of terms because I was found to be using naughty words. I was glad to leave that school because I did not understand a word of the lessons. I had started Latin and I did not know what Latin was or meant; its declensions and conjugations were pure incantations to me. For that matter so were the strings of naughty words. And I was oppressed by the huge hall, the enormous boys, the frightening rowdiness of the corridors, and compulsory

Rugby football of which nobody told me the rules. I went from there to another preparatory school of the ordinary type, also at Wimbledon, where I stayed for about three years. Here I began playing games seriously, was quarrelsome, boastful, and talkative, won prizes, and collected things. The only difference between me and the other boys was that I collected coins instead of stamps. The value of coins seemed less fictitious to me than stamp values. My first training as a gentleman was here. I was only once caned, for forgetting to bring my gymnastic shoes to school, and then I was only given two strokes on the hand with the cane. Yet even now the memory makes me hot with fury. The principal outrage was that it was on the hand. My hands have a great importance for me and are unusually sensitive. I live a lot in them; my visual imagery is defective and so I memorize largely by sense of touch.

I seem to have left out a school. It was in North Wales, right away in the hills behind Llanbedr. It was the first time I had been away from home. I went there just for a term, for my health. Here I had my first beating. The headmaster was a parson, and he caned me on the bottom because I learned the wrong collect one Sunday by mistake. This was the first time that I had come upon forcible training in religion. (At my dame's school we learned collects too, but were not punished for mistakes; we competed for prizes – ornamental texts to take home and hang over our beds.) There was a boy at this school called Ronny, and he was the greatest thing that I had ever met. He had a house at the top of a pine tree that nobody else could climb, and a huge knife, made from the top of a scythe that he had stolen; and he killed pigeons with a catapult and cooked them up in the tree. He was very kind to me; he went into the

Navy afterwards and deserted on his first voyage and was never heard of again. He used to steal rides on cows and horses that he found in the fields. And I found a book that had the ballads of 'Chevy Chace' and 'Sir Andrew Barton' in it; they were the first two real poems that I remember reading. I saw how good they were. But, on the other hand, there was an open-air swimming bath where all the boys bathed naked, and I was overcome by horror at the sight. There was one boy there of nineteen with red hair, real bad, Irish, red hair all over his body. I had not known that hair grew on bodies. And the headmaster had a little daughter with a little girl friend, and I was in a sweat of terror whenever I met them; because, having no brothers, they once tried to find out about male anatomy from me by exploring down my shirt-neck when we were digging up pig-nuts in the garden.

Another frightening experience of this part of my life was when I had once to wait in the school cloakroom for my sisters, who went to the Wimbledon High School. We were going on to be photographed together. I waited about a quarter of an hour in the corner of the cloakroom. I suppose I was about ten years old, and hundreds and hundreds of girls went to and fro, and they all looked at me and giggled and whispered things to each other. I knew they hated me, because I was a boy sitting in the cloakroom of a girls' school, and when my sisters arrived they looked ashamed of me and quite different from the sisters I knew at home. I realized that I had blundered into a secret world, and for months and even years afterwards my worst nightmares were of this girls' school, which was always filled with coloured toy balloons. 'Very Freudian,' as one says now. My normal impulses were set back for years by these two experiences. When I was about seventeen we spent our Christmas holidays in Brussels. An Irish girl staying at the same *pension* made love to me in a way that I see now was really very sweet. I was so frightened I could have killed her.

In English preparatory and public schools romance is necessarily homo-sexual. The opposite sex is despised and hated, treated as something obscene. Many boys never recover from this perversion. I only recovered by a shock at the age of twenty-one. For every one born homo-sexual there are at least ten permanent pseudo-homo-sexuals made by the public school system. And nine of these ten are as honourably chaste and sentimental as I was.

I left that day-school at Wimbledon because my father decided that the standard of work was not good enough to enable me to win a scholarship at a public school. He sent me to another preparatory school in the Midlands; because the headmaster's wife was a sister of an old literary friend of his. It proved later that these were inadequate grounds. It was a queer place and I did not like it. There was a secret about the headmaster which a few of the elder boys shared. It was somehow sinister, but I never exactly knew what it was. All I knew was that he came weeping into the classroom one day beating his head with his fists and groaning: 'Would to God I hadn't done it! Would to God I hadn't done it!' I was taken away suddenly a few days later, which was the end of the school year. The headmaster was said to be ill. I found out later that he had been given twenty-four hours to leave the country. He was succeeded by the second master, a good man, who had taught me how to write English by eliminating all phrases that could be done without, and using verbs and nouns instead of adjectives and adverbs wherever possible. And where to start new paragraphs, and the difference between O and Oh. He was a very heavy man. He used to stand at his desk and lean on his thumbs until they bent at right angles. (The school he took over was now only half-strength because of the scandal. A fortnight later he fell out of a train on to his head and that was the end of him; but the school is apparently going on still; I am occasionally asked to subscribe to Old Boys' funds for chapel windows and miniature rifle ranges and so on.) I first learned rugger here. What surprised me most at this school was when a boy of about twelve, whose father and mother were in India, was told by cable that they had both suddenly died of cholera. We all watched him sympathetically for weeks after, expecting him to die of grief or turn black in the face, or do something to match the occasion. Yet he seemed entirely unmoved, and since nobody dared discuss the tragedy with him he seemed to forget what had happened; he played about and ragged as he had done before. We found that rather monstrous. But he could not have been expected to behave otherwise. He had not seen his parents for two years. And preparatory schoolboys live in a world completely dissociated from home life. They have a different vocabulary, different moral system, different voice, and though on their return to school from the holidays the change over from home-self to school-self is almost instantaneous, the reverse process takes a fortnight at least. A preparatory-school boy, when off his guard, will often call his mother, 'Please, matron', and will always address any man relation or friend of the family as 'Sir', as though he were a master. I used to do it. School life becomes the reality and home life the illusion.

In England parents of the governing classes virtually finish all intimate life with their children from about the age of eight, and any attempt on their part to insinuate home feeling into school life is resented.

Next I went to a typically good school in Sussex. The headmaster was chary of admitting me at my age, particularly from a school with such a bad recent history. Family literary connections did the trick, however, and the headmaster saw that I was advanced enough to win a scholarship and do the school credit. The depressed state I had been in since the last school ended the moment I arrived. My younger brother followed me to this school, being taken away from the day-school at Wimbledon, and, later, my youngest brother went there straight from home. How good and typical the school was can best be seen in the case of my youngest brother, who is a typical good, normal person, and, as I say, went straight from home to the school without other school influences. He spent five or six years there – and played in the elevens – and got the top scholarship at a public school – and became head boy with athletic distinctions – and won a scholarship at Oxford and further athletic distinctions – and a degree – and then what did he do? Because he was such a typically good normal person he naturally went back as a master to his old typically good preparatory school, and now that he has been there some years and wants a change he is applying for a mastership at his old public school and, if he gets it and becomes a housemaster after a few years, he will at last, I suppose, become a headmaster and eventually take the next step and become the head of his old college at Oxford. That is the sort of typically good preparatory school it was. At this school I learned to keep a straight

bat at cricket and to have a high moral sense, and my
fifth different pronunciation of Latin, and my fifth or
sixth different way of doing simple arithmetic. But I
did not mind, and they put me in the top class and I got
a scholarship – in fact I got the first scholarship of the
year. At Charterhouse. And why Charterhouse? Because
of ἵστημι and ἵημι.[2] Charterhouse was the only public
school whose scholarship examination did not contain
a Greek grammar paper and, though I was good enough
at Greek Unseen and Greek Composition, I could not
conjugate ἵστημι and ἵημι conventionally. If it had not
been for these two verbs I would almost certainly have
gone to the very different atmosphere of Winchester.

IV

My mother took us abroad to stay at my grandfather's house in Germany five times between my second and twelfth year. After this he died and we never went again. He had a big old manor-house ten miles from Munich;[1] it was called 'Laufzorn', which means 'Begone, care!' Our summers there were easily the best things of my early childhood. Pine forests and hot sun, red deer and black and red squirrels, acres of blue-berries and wild strawberries; nine or ten different kinds of edible mushrooms that we went into the forest to pick, and unfamiliar flowers in the fields – Munich is high up and there are outcrops of Alpine flowers here and there – and the farm with all the usual animals except sheep, and drives through the countryside in a brake behind my grandfather's greys. And bathing in the Iser under a waterfall; the Iser was bright green and said to be the fastest river in Europe. We used to visit the uncles who had a peacock farm a few miles away, and a granduncle, Johannes von Ranke, the ethnologist, who lived on the lake-shore of Tegensee, where every one had buttercup-blonde hair. And occasionally my Aunt Agnes, Baronin von Aufsess, who lived some hours away by train, high up in the Bavarian Alps, in Aufsess Castle.

This castle was a wonder; it was built in the ninth

century and had been in the von Aufsess family ever
since. The original building was a keep with only a
ladder-entrance half-way up. A medieval castle had
been added. Aufsess was so remote that it had never
been sacked, and its treasures of plate and armour
were amazing. Each baron added to the treasure and
none took away. My Uncle Siegfried was the heir. He
showed us children the chapel with its walls hung with
enamelled shields of each Aufsess baron, impaled with
the arms of the family into which he married. These
families were always noble. He pointed to a stone in
the floor which pulled up by a ring and said: 'That is
the family vault where all we Aufsesses go when we
die. I'll go there one day.' He scowled comically. (But
he was killed in the war as an officer of the Imperial
German Staff and I believe that they never found his
body.) He had a peculiar sense of humour. One day we
children found him on the pebbled garden path, eating
the pebbles. He told us to go away, but, of course, we
would not. We sat down and tried to eat pebbles too.
He told us very seriously that eating pebbles was not a
thing for children to do; we should break our teeth. We
agreed after trying one or two; so to get rid of us he
found us each a pebble which looked just like all the
other pebbles, but which crushed easily and had a
chocolate centre. But this was only on condition that
we went away and left him to his picking and crunch-
ing. When we came back later in the day we searched
and searched, but only found the ordinary hard pebbles. He never once let us down in a joke.

Among the treasures of the castle were a baby's lace
cap that had taken two years to make, and a wine
glass that my uncle's old father, the reigning baron, had
found in the Franco-Prussian War standing upright in

the middle of the square in an entirely ruined village. For dinner when we were there we had enormous trout. My father, who was a fisherman, was astonished and asked the baron how they came to be that size. The baron said that there was an underground river that welled up close to the castle and the fish that came out with it were quite white from the darkness, of enormous size and stone-blind. They also gave us jam, made of wild roseberries, which they called 'Hetchi-Petch'.

The most remarkable thing in the castle was an iron chest in a small thick-walled white-washed room at the top of the keep. It was a huge chest, twice the size of the door, and had obviously been made inside the room – there were no windows but arrow-slits. It had two keys. I could not say what its date was, but I recall it as twelfth or thirteenth century work. There was a tradition that it should never be opened unless the castle were in the most extreme danger. One key was held by the baron and one by the steward; I believe the stewardship was a hereditary office. The chest could only be opened by using both keys, and nobody knew what was inside; it was even considered unlucky to speculate. Of course we speculated. It might be gold, more likely it was a store of corn in sealed jars, or even some sort of weapon – Greek fire, perhaps. From what I know of the Aufsesses and their stewards, it is inconceivable that the chest ever got the better of their curiosity. The castle ghost was that of a former baron known as the Red Knight; his terrifying portrait hung half-way up the turret staircase that took us to our bedrooms. We slept for the first time in our lives on feather beds.

Laufzorn, which my grandfather had bought and restored from a ruinous state, had nothing to compare with the Aufsess tradition, though it had for a time been a shooting-lodge of the kings of Bavaria. Still, there were two ghosts that went with the place; the farm labourers used to see them frequently. One of them was a carriage which drove furiously along without any horses, and before the days of motor-cars this was frightening enough. And the banqueting hall was magnificent. I have not been there since I was a child, so it is impossible for me to recall its true dimensions. It seemed as big as a cathedral, and its bare boards were only furnished at the four corners with little islands of tables and chairs. The windows were of stained glass, and there were swallows' nests all along where the walls joined the ceiling. Roundels of coloured light from the stained-glass windows, the many-tined stags' heads (that my grandfather had shot) mounted on the wall, swallow-droppings on the floor under the nests and a little harmonium in one corner where we sang German songs; these concentrate my memories of Laufzorn. It was in three divisions. The bottom storey was part of the farm. A carriage-drive went right through it, and there was also a wide, covered courtyard – originally these had served for driving the cattle to safety in times of baronial feud. On one side of the drive was the estate steward's quarters, on the other the farm servants' inn and kitchen. In the middle storey lived my grandfather and his family. The top storey was a store-place for corn and apples and other farm produce. It was up here that my cousin Wilhelm, who was killed in an air-fight during the war, used to lie for hours shooting mice with an air-gun. (I learned that he was shot down by a schoolfellow of mine.)

The best part of Germany was the food. There was a richness and spiciness about it that we missed in

England. We liked the rye bread, the black honey (black, I believe, because it came from the combs of the previous year), the huge ice-cream puddings made with fresh raspberry juice, and the venison, and the honey cakes, and the pastries, and particularly the sauces made with different sorts of mushrooms. And the bretzels, and carrots cooked with sugar, and summer pudding of cranberries and blue-berries. There was an orchard close to the house, and we could eat as many apples, pears, and greengages as we liked. There were rows of blackcurrant and gooseberry bushes. The estate, in spite of the recency of my grandfather's tenure, and his liberalism and experiments in modern agricultural methods, was still feudalistic. The farm servants, because they talked a dialect that we could not understand and because they were Catholics and poor and sweaty and savage-looking, frightened us. They were lower even than the servants at home; and as for the colony of Italians settled about half a mile from the house, imported from Italy by my grandfather as cheap labour for his brick-making factory, we associated them in our minds with the 'gypsies in the wood' of the song. My grandfather took us over the factory one day; he made me taste a lump of Italian *polenta*. My mother told us afterwards (when a milk pudding at Wimbledon came to table burnt and we complained about it), 'Those poor Italians at the factory used to burn their *polenta* on purpose sometimes just for a change of flavour.'

There were other unusual things at Laufzorn. There was a large pond full of carp; it was netted every three or four years. The last year we were there we were allowed to help. It was good to see the net pulled closer and closer to the shallow landing corner. It bulged with wriggling carp, and a big pike was threshing about among them. I was allowed to wade in to help, and came out with six leeches, like black rubber tubes, fastened to my legs; salt had to be put on them to make them leave go. I do not remember that it hurt much. The farm labourers were excited, and one of them, called The Jackal, gutted a fish with his thumbs and ate it raw. And there was the truck line between the railway station, two miles away, and the brick-yard. There was a fall of perhaps one in a hundred from the factory to the station. The Italians used to load up the trucks with bricks, and a squad of them would give the trucks a hard push and run along the track pushing for about twenty or thirty yards; and then the trucks used to sail off all by themselves to the station. There was a big haybarn where we were allowed to climb up on the rafters and jump down into the springy hay; we gradually increased the height of the jumps. It was exciting to feel our insides left behind us in the air. Then the cellar, not the ordinary beer cellar, but another that you went down into from the courtyard. It was quite dark there except for a little slit-window; and there was a heap of potatoes on the floor. To get to the light they had put out long white feelers – a twisted mass. In one corner there was a dark hole closed by a gate; it was a secret passage out of the house to a ruined monastery, a mile or two away. My uncles had once been down some way, but the air got bad and they had to come back. The gate had been put up to prevent anyone else trying it and being overcome.

When we drove out with my grandfather he was acclaimed by the principal personages of every village we went through. At each village there was a big inn with a rumbling skittle-alley and always a tall Maypole banded like a barber's pole with blue and white, the Bavarian national colours. The roads were lined with fruit trees. The idea of these unguarded public fruit trees astonished us. We could not understand why there was any fruit left on them. Even the horse-chestnut trees on Wimbledon Common were pelted with sticks and stones, long before the chestnuts were ripe and in defiance of an energetic common keeper. The only things that we could not quite get accustomed to in Bavaria were the wayside crucifixes with the realistic blood and wounds, and the *ex-voto* pictures, like sign-boards, of naked souls in purgatory, grinning with anguish in the middle of high red and yellow flames. We had been taught to believe in hell, but did not like to be reminded of it. Munich we found sinister – disgusting fumes of beer and cigar smoke and intense sounds of eating, the hotly dressed, enormously stout population in the trams and trains, the ferocious officials, the wanton crowds at the art shops and picture galleries. Then there was the Morgue. We were not allowed inside because we were children, but it was bad enough to be told about it. Any notable who died was taken to the Morgue and put in a chair, sitting in state for a day or two, and if he was a general he had his uniform on, or if she was a burgomaster's wife she had on her silks and jewels; and strings were tied to their fingers and the slightest movement of one of the strings would ring a great bell, in case there was any life left in the corpse after all. I have never verified the truth of all this, but it was true enough to me. When my grandfather died about a year after our last visit I thought of him there in the Morgue with his bushy white hair, and his morning coat and striped trousers and his decorations and his stethoscope, and perhaps,

I thought, his silk hat, gloves, and cane on a table beside the chair. Trying, in a nightmare, to be alive but knowing himself dead.

The headmaster who caned me on the hand was a lover of German culture, and impressed this feeling on the school, so that it was to my credit that I could speak German and had been to Germany. At my other preparatory schools this German connection was regarded as something at least excusable and perhaps even interesting. It was not until I went to Charterhouse that I was made to see it as a social offence. My history from the age of fourteen, when I went to Charterhouse, to just before the end of the war, when I began to realize things better, was a forced rejection of the German in me. In all that first period I used to insist indignantly that I was Irish and deliberately cultivate Irish sentiment. I took my self-protective stand on the technical point that it was the father's nationality that counted. Of course I also accepted the whole patriarchal system of things. It is difficult now to recall how completely I believed in the natural supremacy of male over female. I never heard it even questioned until I met Nancy, when I was about twenty-two, towards the end of the war. The surprising sense of ease that I got from her frank statement of equality between the sexes was among my chief reasons for liking her.[2] My mother had always taken the 'love, honour, and obey' contract literally; my sisters were brought up to wish themselves boys, to be shocked at the idea of woman's suffrage, and not to expect as expensive an education as their brothers. The final decision in any domestic matter always rested with my father. My mother would say: 'If two ride together one must ride behind.' Nancy's crude summary, 'God is a man, so it must be all rot,' took a load off my shoulders.[3]

We children did not talk German well; our genders and minor parts of speech were shaky, and we never learned to read Gothic characters or script. Yet we had the feel of German so strongly that I would say now that I know German far better than French, though I can read French almost as fast as I can read English and can only read a German book very painfully and slowly, with the help of a dictionary. I use different parts of my mind for the two languages. French is a surface acquirement and I could forget it quite easily if I had no reason to use it every now and then.

V

I spent a good part of my early life at Wimbledon. My mother and father did not get rid of the house, a big one near the Common, until some time about the end of the war; yet of all the time I spent in it I can recall little or nothing of significance. But after the age of eleven or twelve I was away at school, and in the spring and summer holidays we were all in the country, so that I was only at Wimbledon in the Christmas holidays and for a day or two at the beginning and end of the other holidays. London was only a half-hour away and yet we seldom went there. My mother and father never took us to the theatre, not even to pantomimes, and until the middle of the war I had only been to the theatre twice in my life, and then only to children's plays, taken by an aunt. My mother wished to bring us up to be serious and to benefit humanity in some practical way. She allowed us no hint of its dirtiness and intrigue and lustfulness, believing that innocence was the surest protection against them. Our reading was carefully censored by her. I was destined to be 'if not a great man at least a good man'. Our treats were educational or æsthetic, to Kew Gardens, Hampton Court, the Zoo, the British Museum, or the Natural History Museum. I remember my mother, in the treasure room at the British Museum, telling us with shining eyes that all these treasures were ours. We looked at her astonished. She said: 'Yes, they belong to us as members of the public. We can look at them, admire them, and study them for as long as we like. If we had them back at home we couldn't do more.'

We read more books than most children do. There must have been four or five thousand books in the house. They consisted of an old-fashioned scholar's library bequeathed to my father by my namesake, whom I have mentioned as a friend of Wordsworth, but who had a far more tender friendship with Felicia Hemans; to this was added my father's own collection of books, mostly poetry, with a particular cupboard for Anglo-Irish literature; devotional works contributed by my mother; educational books sent to my father by their publishers in the hope that he would recommend them for use in Government schools; and novels and adventure books brought into the house by my elder brothers and sisters.

My mother used to tell us stories about inventors and doctors who gave their lives for the suffering, and poor boys who struggled to the top of the tree, and saintly men who made examples of themselves. There was also the parable of the king who had a very beautiful garden which he threw open to the public. Two students entered; and one, who was the person of whom my mother spoke with a slight sneer in her voice, noticed occasional weeds even in the tulip-beds, but the other, and there she brightened up, found beautiful flowers growing even on rubbish heaps. She kept off the subject of war as much as possible; she always had difficulty in explaining to us how it was that God

permitted wars. The Boer War clouded my early childhood; Philip, my eldest brother (who also called himself
a Fenian), was a pro-Boer and there was great tension
at the breakfast-table between him and my father,
whose political views were always orthodox.

The sale of the Wimbledon house solved a good
many problems; it was getting too full. My mother
hated throwing away anything that could possibly, in
the most remote contingency, be of any service to anyone. The medicine cupboard was perhaps the most
significant corner of the house. Nobody could say that
it was untidy, exactly; all the bottles had stoppers, but
they were so crowded together that it was impossible
for anybody except my mother, who had a long memory, to know what was at the back. Every few years, no
doubt, she went through this cupboard. If there was
any doubtful bottle she would tentatively re-label it.
'This must be Alfred's old bunion salve,' and another,
'Strychnine – query?' Even special medicines prescribed
for scarlet-fever or whooping-cough were kept, in case
of re-infection. She was always an energetic labeller.
She wrote in one of my school prizes: 'Robert Ranke
Graves won this book as a prize for being first in his
class in the term's work and second in examinations.
He also won a special prize for divinity, though the
youngest boy in the class. Written by his affectionate
mother, Amy Graves. Summer, 1908.' Home-made jam
used always to arrive at table well labelled; one small
pot read: 'Gooseberry, lemon and rhubarb – a little
shop gooseberry added – Nelly re-boiled.'

In a recent book, *Mrs. Fisher*, I moralized on three
sayings and a favourite story of my mother's. I ascribed
them there for the argument's sake to my Danish grandmother. They were these:

Children, I command you, as your mother, never to swing objects around in your hands. The King of Hanover put out his eye by swinging a bead purse.

Children, I command you, as your mother, to be careful when you carry your candles up to bed. The candle is a little cup of grease.

There was a man once, a Frenchman, who died of grief because he could never become a mother.

And the story told in candlelight:

There was once a peasant family living in Schleswig-Holstein, where they all have crooked mouths, and one night they wished to blow out the candle. The father's mouth was twisted to the left, so! and he tried to blow out the candle, so! but he was too proud to stand anywhere but directly before the candle, and he puffed and he puffed, but could not blow the candle out. And then the mother tried, but her mouth was twisted to the right, so! and she tried to blow, so! and she was too proud to stand anywhere but directly before the candle, and she puffed and puffed, but could not blow the candle out. Then there was the brother with mouth twisted outward, so! and the sister with the mouth twisted downward, so! and they tried each in their turn, so! and so! and the idiot baby with his mouth twisted in an eternal grin tried, so! And at last the maid, a beautiful girl from Copenhagen with a perfectly formed mouth, put it out with her shoe. So! Flap!

These quotations make it clear how much more I owe, as a writer, to my mother than to my father.[1] She also taught me to 'speak the truth and shame the devil!' Her favourite biblical exhortation was 'My son, whatever thy hand findeth to do, do it with all thy might.'

I always felt that Wimbledon was a wrong place, neither town nor country. It was at its worst on Wednesdays, my mother's 'At Home' day. Tea was in the drawing-room. We were called down in our Sunday clothes to eat cakes, be kissed, and be polite. My sisters were made to recite. Around Christmas, celebrated in the German style, came a dozen or so children's parties; we used to make ourselves sick with excitement. I do not like thinking of Wimbledon. Every spring and summer after my third year, unless we happened to go to Germany, or to France as we did once, we went to Harlech in North Wales. My mother had built a house there.

In the days before motor traffic began around the North Welsh coast, Harlech was a very quiet place and little known, even as a golf centre. It was in three parts. First, the village itself, five hundred feet up on a steep range of hills; it had granite houses with slate roofs and ugly windows and gables, chapels of seven or eight different denominations, enough shops to make it the shopping centre of the smaller villages around, and the castle, a favourite playground of ours. Then there was the Morfa, a flat plain from which the sea had receded; part of this was the golf links, but to the north was a stretch of wild country which we used to visit in the spring in search of plovers' eggs. The sea was beyond the links – good hard sand stretching for miles, safe bathing, and sandhills for hide and seek.

The third part of Harlech, which became the most important to us, was never visited by golfers or the few other summer visitors or by the village people themselves; this was the desolate rocky hill-country at the back of the village. As we grew older we spent more and more of our time up there and less and less on the beach and the links, which were the most obvious attractions of the place. There were occasional farms, or rather crofts, in these hills, but one could easily walk fifteen or twenty miles without crossing a road or passing close to a farm. Originally we went up there with some practical excuse. For the blue-berries on the hills near Maesygarnedd; or for the cranberries at Gwlawllyn; or to find bits of Roman hypocaust tiling (with the potter's thumbmarks still on them) in the ruined Roman villas by Castell Tomenymur; or for globe-flowers in the upper Artro; or to catch a sight of the wild goats that lived at the back of Rhinog Fawr, the biggest of the hills of the next range; or to eat raspberries from the thickets near Cwmbychan Lake; or to find white heather on a hill that we did not know the name of away to the north of the Roman Steps. But after a time we walked about those hills simply because they were good to walk about on. They had a penny plain quality about them that was even better than the twopence coloured quality of the Bavarian Alps. My best friend at the time was my sister Rosaleen, who was one year older than myself.

I suppose what I liked about this country (and I know no country like it) was its independence of formal nature. The passage of the seasons was hardly noticed there; the wind always seemed to be blowing and the grass always seemed to be withered and the small streams were always cold and clear, running over black stones. Sheep were the only animals about, but they were not nature, except in the lambing season; they were too close to the granite boulders covered with grey lichen that lay about everywhere. There were few trees except a few nut bushes, rowans, stunted oaks and thorn bushes in the valleys. The winters were always mild, so that last year's bracken and last year's heather lasted in a faded way through to the next spring. There were almost no birds except an occasional buzzard and curlews crying in the distance; and wherever we went we felt that the rocky skeleton of the hill was only an inch or two under the turf. Once, when I came home on leave from the war, I spent about a week of my ten days walking about on these hills to restore my sanity. I tried to do the same after I was wounded, but by that time the immediate horror of death was too strong for the indifference of the hills to relieve it.

I am glad that it was Wales and not Ireland. We never went to Ireland, except once when I was an infant in arms. We had no Welsh blood in us and did not like the Harlech villagers much. We had no temptation to learn Welsh or to pretend ourselves Welsh. We knew that country as a quite ungeographical region; any stray sheep-farmers that we met who belonged to the place we resented somehow as intruders on our privacy. Clarissa, Rosaleen and I were once out on the remotest hills and had not seen a soul all day. At last we came to a waterfall and two trout lying on the bank beside it; ten yards away was the fisherman. He was disentangling his line from a thorn-bush and had not seen us. So we crept up quietly to the fish and put a sprig of white bell-heather (which we had found that afternoon) in the mouth of each. We hurried back to cover, and I said: 'Shall we watch?' but Clarissa said: 'No, don't spoil it.' So we came home and never spoke of it again even to each other: and never knew the sequel ... If it had been Ireland we would have self-consciously learned Irish and the local legends. Instead we came to know the country more purely, as a place whose history was too old for local legends; when we were up walking there we made our own. We decided who was buried under the Standing Stone and who had lived in the ruined round-hut encampment and in the caves of the valley where the big rowans were. On our visits to Germany I had felt a sense of home in my blood in a natural human way, but on the hills behind Harlech I found a personal harmony independent of history or geography. The first poem I wrote as myself concerned that hill-country. (The first poem I wrote as a Graves was a free translation of a satire by Catullus.)

My father was always too busy and absent-minded to worry much about us children; my mother did worry. Yet she allowed us to go off immediately after breakfast into the hills and did not complain much when we came back long after supper-time. Though she had a terror of heights herself she never restrained us from climbing about in dangerous places; so we never got hurt. I had a bad head for heights and trained myself deliberately and painfully to overcome it. We used to go climbing in the turrets and towers of Harlech Castle. I have worked hard on myself in defining and dispersing terrors. The simple fear of heights was the most obvious to overcome. There was a quarry-face in the garden of our Harlech house. It provided one or two easy climbs, but gradually I invented more and more difficult ones for myself. After each new success I had to lie down, shaking with nervousness, in the safe meadow grass at the top. Once I lost my foothold on a ledge and should have been killed; but it seemed as though I improvised a foothold in the air and kicked myself up to safety from it. When I examined the place afterwards it was almost as if the Devil had given me what he had offered Christ in the Temptation, the freedom to cast myself down from the rock and be restored to safety by the angels. Yet such events are not uncommon in mountain climbing. George Mallory, for instance, did an inexplicable climb on Snowdon once. He had left his pipe on a ledge half-way down one of the precipices and scrambled back by a short cut to retrieve it, then up again by the same way. No one saw just how he did the climb, but when they came to examine it the next day for official record, they found that it was an impossible overhang nearly all the way. The rule of the Climbers' Club was that climbs should not be called after their inventors, but after natural features. An exception was made in this case; the climb was recorded something like this: '*Mallory's Pipe*, a variation on Route 2; see adjoining map. This climb is totally impossible. It has been performed once, in failing light, by Mr. G. H. L. Mallory.'

VI

About Charterhouse. Let me begin by recalling my feelings on the day that I left, about a week before the outbreak of war. I discussed them with a friend[1] who felt much as I did. First we said that there were perhaps even more typical public schools than Charterhouse at the time, but that this was difficult to believe. Next, that there was no possible remedy, because tradition was so strong that if one wished to break it one would have to dismiss the whole school and staff and start all over again. But that even this would not be enough, for the school buildings were so impregnated with what was called the public school spirit, but what we felt as fundamental badness, that they would have to be demolished and the school rebuilt elsewhere and its name changed. Next, that our only regret at leaving the place was that for the last year we had been in a position as members of Sixth Form to do more or less what we pleased. Now we were both going on to St. John's College, Oxford, which seemed by reputation to be merely a more boisterous repetition of Charterhouse. We would be freshmen there, and would naturally refuse to be hearty and public school-ish, and there would be all the stupidity of having our rooms raided and being forced to lose our temper and hurt somebody and be hurt ourselves. And there would be no peace probably until we got into our third year, when we would be back again in the same sort of position as now, and in the same sort of position as in our last year at our preparatory school. 'In 1917,' said Nevill, 'the official seal will be out on all this dreariness. We'll get our degrees, and then we'll have to start as new boys again in some dreary profession. My God,' he said, turning to me suddenly, 'I can't stand the idea of it. I must put something in between me and Oxford. I must at least go abroad for the whole vacation.' I did not feel that three months was long enough. I had a vague intention of running away to sea. 'Do you realize,' he said to me, 'that we have spent fourteen years of our life principally at Latin and Greek, not even competently taught, and that we are going to start another three years of the same thing?' But, when we had said our very worst of Charterhouse, I said to him or he said to me, I forget which: 'Of course, the trouble is that in the school at any given time there are always at least two really decent masters among the forty or fifty, and ten really decent fellows among the five or six hundred. We will remember them, and have Lot's feeling about not damning Sodom for the sake of ten just persons. And in another twenty years' time we'll forget this conversation and think that we were mistaken, and that perhaps everybody, with a few criminal exceptions, was fairly average decent, and we'll say "I was a young fool then, insisting on impossible perfection," and we'll send our sons to Charterhouse sentimentally, and they'll go through all we did.' I do not wish this to be construed as an attack on my old school, but merely as a record of my feelings at the time. No doubt I was unappreciative of the hard knocks and character-training that public schools are supposed to provide, and as a typical Old Carthusian remarked to me recently: 'The whole moral tone of the school has improved out of all recognition since those days.'

As a matter of fact I did not go up to Oxford until five years later, in 1919, when my brother, four years younger than myself, was already in residence, and I did not take my degree until 1926, at the same time as the brother[2] who was eight years younger than myself. Oxford was extraordinarily kind to me. I did no Latin or Greek there, though I had a Classical Exhibition. I did not sit for a single examination. I never had rooms at St. John's, though I used to go there to draw a Government grant for tuition fees. I lived outside the University three-mile radius. For my last two undergraduate years I did not even have a tutor. I have a warm feeling for Oxford. Its rules and statutes, though apparently cast-iron, are ready for emergencies. In my case, at any rate, a poet was an emergency.

Whenever I come to the word 'Charterhouse' in this story I find myself escaping into digressions, but I suppose that I must get through with it. From the moment I arrived at the school I suffered an oppression of spirit that I hesitate now to recall in its full intensity. It was something like being in that chilly cellar at Laufzorn among the potatoes, but being a potato out of a different bag from the rest. The school consisted of about six hundred boys. The chief interests were games and romantic friendships. School-work was despised by every one; the scholars, of whom there were about fifty in the school at any given time, were not concentrated in a single dormitory-house as at Winchester, but divided among ten. They were known as 'pro's', and unless they were good at games and willing to pretend that they hated work as much as or more than the non-scholars, and ready whenever called on to help these with their work, they usually had a bad time. I was a scholar and really liked work, and I was surprised and disappointed at the apathy of the class-rooms. My first term I was left alone more or less, it being a school convention that new boys should be neither encouraged nor baited. The other boys seldom spoke to them except to send them on errands, or to inform them of breaches of school convention. But my second term the trouble began. There were a number of things that naturally made for my unpopularity. Besides being a scholar and not outstandingly good at games, I was always short of pocket-money. I could not conform to the social custom of treating my contemporaries to food at the school shop, and because I could not treat them I could not accept their treating. My clothes were all wrong; they conformed outwardly to the school pattern, but they were ready-made and not of the best-quality cloth that the other boys all wore. Even so, I had not been taught how to make the best of them. Neither my mother nor my father had any regard for the niceties of modern dress, and my elder brothers were abroad by this time. The other boys in my house, except for five scholars, were nearly all the sons of business men; it was a class of whose interests and prejudices I knew nothing, having hitherto only met boys of the professional class. And I talked too much for their liking. A further disability was that I was as prudishly innocent as my mother had planned I should be. I knew nothing about simple sex, let alone the many refinements of sex constantly referred to in school conversation. My immediate reaction was one of disgust. I wanted to run away.

The most unfortunate disability of all was that my

name appeared on the school list as 'R. von R. Graves'. I had only known hitherto that my second name was Ranke; the 'von', discovered on my birth certificate, was disconcerting. Carthusians were secretive about their second names; if these were fancy ones they usually managed to conceal them. Ranke, without the 'von' I could no doubt have passed off as monosyllabic and English, but 'von Ranke' was glaring. The business class to which most of the boys belonged was strongly feeling at this time the threat and even the necessity of a trade war; 'German' meant 'dirty German'. It meant 'cheap shoddy goods competing with our sterling industries', and it also meant military menace, Prussianism, sabre-rattling. There was another boy in my house with a German name, but English by birth and upbringing. He was treated much as I was. On the other hand a French boy in the house was very popular, though he was not much good at games; King Edward VII had done his *entente* work very thoroughly. There was also considerable anti-Jewish feeling (the business prejudice again) and the legend was put about that I was not only a German but a German-Jew.

Of course I always maintained that I was Irish. This claim was resented by an Irish boy who had been in the house about a year and a half longer than myself. He went out of his way to hurt me, not only by physical acts of spite, like throwing ink over my school-books, hiding my games-clothes, setting on me suddenly from behind corners, pouring water over me at night, but by continually forcing his bawdy humour on my prudishness and inviting everybody to laugh at my disgust; he also built up a sort of humorous legend of my hypocrisy and concealed depravity. I came near a nervous breakdown. School morality prevented me from informing the House-Master of my troubles. The house-monitors were supposed to keep order and preserve the moral tone of the house, but at this time they were not the sort to interfere in any case of bullying among the juniors. I tried violent resistance, but as the odds were always heavily against me this merely encouraged the ragging. Complete passive resistance would probably have been better. I only got accustomed to bawdy-talk in my last two years at Charterhouse, and it was not until I had been some time in the army that I got hardened to it and could reply in kind to insults.

A former headmaster of Charterhouse, an innocent man, is reported to have said at a Headmasters' Conference: 'My boys are amorous but seldom erotic.' Few cases of eroticism indeed ever came to his notice; there were not more than five or six big rows all the time I was at Charterhouse and expulsions were rare. But the house-masters knew little about what went on in their houses; their living quarters were removed from the boys'. There was a true distinction between 'amorousness', by which the headmaster meant a sentimental falling in love with younger boys, and eroticism, which was adolescent lust. The intimacy, as the newspapers call it, that frequently took place was practically never between an elder boy and the object of his affection, for that would have spoilt the romantic illusion, which was hetero-sexually cast. It was between boys of the same age who were not in love, but used each other coldly as convenient sex-instruments. So the atmosphere was always heavy with romance of a very conventional early-Victorian type, yet complicated by cynicism and foulness.

VII

Half-way through my second year I wrote to my parents to tell them that I must leave Charterhouse, because I could not stand life there any longer. I told them that the house was making it plain that I did not belong and that it did not want me. I gave them details, in confidence, to make them take my demand seriously. They were unable to respect this confidence, considering that it was their religious duty to inform the House-Master of all I had written them. They did not even tell me what they were doing; they contented themselves with visiting me and giving me assurances of the power of prayer and faith; telling me that I must endure all for the sake of . . . I have forgotten what exactly. Fortunately I had not given them any account of sex-irregularities in the house, so all that the House-Master did was to make a speech that night after prayers deterrent of bullying in general; he told us that he had just had a complaint from a boy's parents. He made it plain at the same time how much he disliked informers and outside interference in affairs of the house. My name was not mentioned, but the visit of my parents on a day not a holiday had been noticed and commented on. So I had to stay on and be treated as an informer. I was now in the upper school and so had a study of my own. But this was no security; studies had no locks. It was always being wrecked. After my parents' visit to the House-Master it was not even possible for me to use the ordinary house changing-room; I had to remove my games-clothes to a disused shower-bath. My heart went wrong then; the school doctor said I was not to play football. This was low water. My last resource was to sham insanity. It succeeded unexpectedly well. Soon nobody troubled about me except to avoid any contact with me.

I must make clear that I am not charging my parents with treachery; they were trying to help me. Their honour is beyond reproach . . . One day I went down to Charterhouse by the special train from Waterloo to Godalming. I was too late to take a ticket; I just got into a compartment before the train started. The railway company had not provided enough coaches, so I had to stand up all the way. At Godalming station the crowd of boys rushing out into the station-yard to secure taxis swept me past the ticket collectors, so I had got my very uncomfortable ride free. I mentioned this in my next letter home, just for something to say, and my father sent me a letter of reproach. He said that he had himself made a special visit to Waterloo Station, bought a ticket to Godalming, and torn it up . . . My mother was even more scrupulous. A young couple on their honeymoon once happened to stop the night with us at Wimbledon, and left behind them a packet of sandwiches, some of which had already been eaten. My mother sent them on.

Being thrown entirely on myself I began to write poetry. This was considered stronger proof of insanity than the formal straws I wore in my hair. The poetry I wrote was not the easy showing-off witty stuff that all the Graves' write and have written for the last couple of centuries. It was poetry that was dissatisfied with itself. When, later, things went better with me at Charterhouse, I became literary once more.

I sent one of my poems to the school magazine, *The Carthusian*. On the strength of it I was invited to join the school Poetry Society. This was a most anomalous organization for Charterhouse. It consisted of seven members. The meetings, for the reading and discussion of poetry, were held once a month at the house of Guy Kendall, then a form-master at the school, now head-master of University College School at Hampstead. The members were four sixth-form boys and two boys a year and a half older than myself, one of whom was called Raymond Rodakowski. None of them were in the same house as myself. At Charterhouse no friend-ship was permitted between boys of different houses or of different years beyond a formal acquaintance at work or organized games like cricket and football. It was, for instance, impossible for boys of different houses, though related or next-door neighbours at home, even to play a friendly game of tennis or squash-racquets together. They would never have heard the last of it. So the friendship that began between me and Raymond was most unconventional. Coming home one evening from a meeting of the society I told Raymond about life in the house; I told him what had happened a week or two before. My study had been raided and one of my more personal poems had been discovered and pinned up on the public notice board in 'Writing School'. This was the living-room of the members of the lower school, into which, as a member of the upper school, I was not allowed to go, and so could not rescue the poem. Raymond was the first person I had been able to talk to humanly. He was indignant, and took my arm in his in the gentlest way. 'They are bloody barbarians,' he said. He told me that I must pull myself together and do something about it, because I was a good poet he said, and a good person. I loved him for that. He said: 'You're not allowed to play football; why don't you box? It's supposed to be good for the heart.' So I laughed and said I would. Then Raymond said: 'I expect they rag you about your initials.' 'Yes,' I said, 'they call me a dirty German.' 'I had trouble, too,' he said, 'before I took up boxing.' Raymond's mother was Scottish, his father was an Austrian Pole.

Very few boys at Charterhouse boxed and the boxing-room, which was over the school confectionery shop, was a good place to meet Raymond, whom, otherwise, I would not have been able to see often. I began boxing seriously and savagely. Raymond said to me: 'You know these cricketers and footballers are all afraid of boxers, almost superstitious. They won't box themselves for fear of losing their good looks – the inter-house competitions every year are such bloody affairs. But do you remember the Mansfield, Waller and Taylor show? That's a good tradition to keep up.'

Of course I remembered. Two terms previously there had been a meeting of the school debating society which I had attended. The committee of the debating society was usually made up of sixth-form boys; the debates were formal and usually dull, but in so far as there was any intellectual life at Charterhouse, it was represented by the debating society – and by *The Carthusian*, always edited by two members of this committee; both institutions were free from influence of the masters. Debates were always held in the school library on Saturday night. One debate night the usual decorous conventions were broken by an invasion of 'the bloods'.

The bloods were the members of the cricket and football elevens. They were the ruling caste at Charterhouse; the eleventh man in the football eleven, though a member of the under-fourth form, had a great deal more prestige than the most brilliant classical scholar in the sixth. Even 'Head of the School' was an empty title. There was not, however, an open warfare between the sixth-form intellectuals and the bloods. The bloods were stupid and knew it, and had nothing to gain by a clash; the intellectuals were happy to be left alone. So this invasion of the bloods, who had just returned from winning a match against the *Casuals*, and had probably been drinking, caused the debating society a good deal of embarrassment. The bloods disturbed the meeting by cheers and cat-cries and slamming the library magazine-folders on the table. Mansfield, as president of the society, called them to order, but they continued the disturbance; so Mansfield closed the debate. The bloods thought the incident finished, but it was not. A letter appeared in *The Carthusian* a few days later protesting against the bad behaviour in the debating society of 'certain First Eleven babies'. Three sets of initials were signed and they were those of Mansfield, Waller and Taylor. The school was astonished by this suicidally daring act; it waited for Korah, Dathan and Abiram to be swallowed up. The captain of football is said to have sworn that he'd chuck the three signatories into the fountain in Founder's Court. But somehow he did not. The fact was that this happened early in the autumn term and there were only two other First Eleven colours left over from the preceding year; new colours were only given gradually as the football season advanced. The other rowdies had only been embryo bloods. So it was a matter entirely between

these three sixth-form intellectuals and the three colours of the First Eleven. And the First Eleven were
uncomfortably aware that Mansfield was the
heavy-weight boxing champion of the school, Waller
the runner-up for the middleweights, and that Taylor
was also a person to be reckoned with (a tough fellow,
though not perhaps a boxer – I forget). While the First
Eleven were wondering what on earth to do their three
opponents decided to take the war into the enemy's
country.

The social code of Charterhouse was based on a very
strict caste system; the caste-marks were slight distinctions in dress. A new boy had no privileges at all; a boy
in his second term might wear a knitted tie instead of a
plain one; a boy in his second year might wear coloured
socks; third year gave most of the privileges – turned
down collars, coloured handkerchiefs, a coat with a
long roll, and so on; fourth year, a few more, such as
the right to get up raffles; but very peculiar and unique
distinctions were reserved for the bloods. These
included light grey flannel trousers, butterfly collars,
coats slit up the back, and the privilege of walking
arm-in-arm. So the next Sunday Mansfield, Waller and
Taylor did the bravest thing that was ever done at
Charterhouse. The school chapel service was at eleven
in the morning, but the custom was for the school to be
in its seats by five minutes to eleven and to sit waiting
there. At two minutes to eleven the bloods used to
stalk in; at one and a half minutes to came the masters;
at one minute to came the choir in its surplices; then
the headmaster arrived and the service started. If any
boy was accidentally late and sneaked in between five
minutes to and two minutes to the hour, he was followed by six hundred pairs of eyes; there was nudging

and giggling and he would not hear the last of it for a long time; it was as though he were pretending to be a blood. On this Sunday, then, when the bloods had come in with their usual swaggering assurance, an extraordinary thing happened.

The three sixth-formers slowly walked up the aisle magnificent in grey flannel trousers, slit coats, First Eleven collars, and with pink carnations in their buttonholes. It is impossible to describe the astonishment and terror that this spectacle caused. Everyone looked at the captain of the First Eleven; he had gone quite white. But by this time the masters had come in, followed by the choir, and the opening hymn, though raggedly sung, ended the tension. When chapel emptied it always emptied according to 'school order', that is, according to position in work; the sixth form went out first. The bloods were not high in school order, so Mansfield, Waller and Taylor had the start of them. After chapel on Sunday the custom in the winter terms was for people to meet and gossip in the school library; so it was here that Mansfield, Waller and Taylor went. They had buttonholed a talkative master and drawn him with them into the library, and there they kept him talking until dinner-time. If the bloods had had courage to do anything desperate they would have had to do it at once, but they could not make a scene in the presence of a master. Mansfield, Waller and Taylor went down to their houses for dinner still talking to the master. After this they kept together as much as possible and the school, particularly the lower school, which had always chafed under the dress regulations, made heroes of them, and began scoffing at the bloods as weak kneed.

Finally the captain of the eleven was stupid enough

to complain to the headmaster about this breach of school conventions, asking for permission to enforce First Eleven rights by disciplinary measures. The headmaster, who was a scholar and disliked the games tradition, refused his request. He said that the sixth form deserved as distinctive privileges as the First Eleven. The sixth form would therefore in future be entitled to hold what they had assumed. After this the prestige of the bloods declined greatly.

At Raymond's encouragement I pulled myself together and my third year found things very much easier for me. My chief persecutor, the Irishman, had left. It was said that he had had a bad nervous breakdown. He wrote me a hysterical letter, demanding my forgiveness for his treatment of me, saying at the same time that if I did not give this forgiveness, one of his friends (whom he mentioned) was still in the house to persecute me. I did not answer the letter. I do not know what happened to him. The friend never bothered.

VIII

I still had no friends except among the junior members of the house, to whom I did not disguise my dislike of the seniors; I found the juniors were on the whole a decent lot of fellows. Towards the end of this year, in the annual boxing and gymnastic display, I fought three rounds with Raymond. There is a lot of sex feeling in boxing – the dual play, the reciprocity, the pain not felt as pain. This exhibition match to me had something of the quality that Dr. Marie Stopes would call sacramental.[1] We were out neither to hurt nor win though we hit each other hard.

This public appearance as a boxer improved my position in the house. And the doctor now allowed me to play football again and I played it fairly well. Then things started going wrong in a different way. It began with confirmation, for which I was prepared by a zealous evangelical master. For a whole term I concentrated all my thoughts on religion, looking forward to the ceremony as a spiritual climax. When it came, and the Holy Ghost did not descend in the form of a dove, and I did not find myself gifted with tongues, and nothing spectacular happened (except that the boy whom the Bishop of Zululand was blessing at the same time as myself slipped off the narrow footstool on which we were both kneeling), I was bound to feel a reaction.

Raymond had not been confirmed, and I was astonished to hear him admit and even boast that he was an
atheist. I argued with him about the existence of God
and the divinity of Christ and the necessity of the Trinity. He said, of the Trinity, that anybody who could
agree with the Athanasian creed that 'whoever will be
saved must confess that there are not Three Incompre-
hensibles but One Incomprehensible' was saying that a
man must go to Hell if he does not believe something
that is by definition impossible to understand. He said
that his respect for himself as a reasonable being did
not allow him to believe such things. He also asked me
a question: 'What's the good of having a soul if you
have a mind. What's the function of the soul? It seems
a mere pawn in the game.' I was shocked, but because
I loved him and respected him I felt bound to find an
answer. The more I thought about it the less certain I
became that he was wrong. So in order not to prejudice
religion (and I put religion and my chances of salvation
before human love) I at first broke my friendship with
Raymond entirely. Later I weakened, but he would not
even meet me, when I approached him, with any
broad-church compromise. He was a complete and
ruthless atheist and I could not appreciate his strength
of spirit. For the rest of our time at Charterhouse we
were not as close as we should have been. I met Raymond in France in 1917, when he was with the Irish
Guards; I rode over to see him one afternoon[2] and felt
as close to him as I had ever felt. He was killed at Cam-
brai not long after.

My feeling for Raymond was more comradely than
amorous. In my fourth year an even stronger relationship started. It was with a boy three years younger
than myself, who was exceptionally intelligent and

fine-spirited. Call him Dick,[3] because his real name was the same as that of another person in the story. He was not in my house, but I had recently joined the school choir and so had he, and I had opportunities for speaking to him occasionally after choir practice. I was unconscious of sexual feeling for him. Our conversations were always impersonal. Our acquaintance was commented on and I was warned by one of the masters to end it. I replied that I would not have my friendships in any way limited. I pointed out that this boy was interested in the same things as myself, particularly in books; that the disparity in our ages was unfortunate, but that a lack of intelligence among the boys of my own age made it necessary for me to find friends where I could. Finally the headmaster took me to task about it. I lectured him on the advantage of friendship between elder and younger boys, citing Plato, the Greek poets, Shakespeare, Michael Angelo and others, who had felt the same way as I did. He let me go without taking any action.

In my fifth year I was in the sixth form and was made a house-monitor. There were six house-monitors. One of them was the house games-captain, a friendly, easy-going fellow. He said to me one day: 'Look here, Graves, I have been asked to send in a list of competitors for the inter-house boxing competition; shall I put your name down?' I had not boxed for two terms. I had been busy with football and played for the house-team now. And since my coolness with Raymond boxing had lost its interest. I said: 'I'm not boxing these days.' 'Well,' he said, 'young Alan is entering for the welter-weights. He's got a very good chance. Why don't you enter for the welter-weights too? You might be able to damage one or two of the stronger men and make it easier for him.' I did not particularly like the idea of making things easier for Alan, but I obviously had to enter the competition. I had a reputation to keep up. I knew, however, that my wind, though all right for football, was not equal to boxing round after round. I decided that my fights must be short. The night before the competition I smuggled a bottle of cherry-whisky into the house. I would shorten the fights on that.

I had never drank anything alcoholic before in my life. When I was seven years old I was prevailed on to sign the pledge. My pledge card bound me to abstain by the grace of God from all spirituous liquors so long as I retained it. But my mother took the card from me and put it safely in the box-room with the Jacobean silver inherited from my Cheyne grandmother, Bishop Graves' diamond ring which Queen Victoria gave him when he preached before her, our christening mugs, and the heavy early-Victorian jewellery bequeathed to my mother by the old lady whom she had looked after. And since box-room treasures never left the box-room, I regarded myself as permanently parted from my pledge. I liked the cherry-whisky a lot.

The competitions started about one o'clock on a Saturday afternoon and went on until seven. I was drawn for the very first fight and my opponent by a piece of bad luck was Alan. Alan wanted me to scratch. I said I thought that it would look bad to do that. We consulted the house games-captain and he said: 'No, the most sporting thing to do is to box it out and let the decision be on points; but don't either of you hurt each other.' So we boxed. Alan started showing off to his friends, who were sitting in the front row. I said: 'Stop that. We're boxing, not fighting,' but a few seconds later he hit me again unnecessarily hard. I got angry and knocked him out. This was the first time I had ever knocked anyone out and I liked the feeling. I had drunk a lot of cherry-whisky. I rather muzzily realized that I had knocked him out with a right swing on the side of the neck and that this blow was not part of the ordinary school-boxing curriculum. Straight lefts; lefts to body, rights to head; left and right hooks; all these were known, but the swing was somehow neglected, probably because it was not so 'pretty'.

I went to the changing-room for my coat, and stout Sergeant Harris, the boxing instructor, said: 'Look here, Mr. Graves, why don't you put down your name for the middle-weight competition too?' I cheerfully agreed. Then I went back to the house and had a cold bath and more cherry-whisky. My next fight was to take place in about half an hour for the first round of the middle-weights. This time my opponent, who was a stone heavier than myself but had little science, bustled me about for the first round, and I could see that he would tire me out unless something was done. In the second round I knocked him down with my right swing, but he got up again. I was feeling tired, so hastened to knock him down again. I must have knocked him down four or five times that round, but he refused to take the count. I found out afterwards that he was, like myself, conscious that Dick was watching the fight. He loved Dick too. Finally I said to myself as he lurched towards me again: 'If he doesn't go down and stay down this time, I won't be able to hit him again at all.' This time I just pushed at his jaw as it offered itself to me, but that was enough. He did go down and he did stay down. This second knock-out made quite a stir. Knock-outs were rare in the inter-house boxing competition. As I went back to the house for another cold bath and some more cherry-whisky I noticed the fellows looking at me curiously.

The later stages of the competition I do not remember well. The only opponent that I was now at all concerned about was Raymond, who was nearly a stone heavier than myself and was expected to win the middle-weights; but he had also tried for two weights, the middle and the heavy, and had just had such a tough fight with the eventual winner of the heavy-weights that he was in no proper condition to fight. So he scratched his fight with me. I believe that he would have fought all the same if it had been against someone else; but he was still fond of me and wanted me to win. His scratching would give me a rest between my bouts. A semi-finalist scratched against me in the welter-weights, so I only had three more fights, and I let neither of these go beyond the first round. The swing won me both weights, for which I was given two silver cups. But it had also broken both my thumbs; I had not got my elbow high enough over when I used it.

The most important thing that happened to me in my last two years, apart from my attachment to Dick, was that I got to know George Mallory. He was twenty-six or twenty-seven then, not long up from Cambridge. He was so young looking that he was often mistaken for a member of the school. From the first he treated me as an equal, and I used to spend my spare time reading books in his room or going for walks with him in the country. He told me of the existence of modern authors. My father being two generations older than myself and my only link with books, I had never heard of people like Shaw, Samuel Butler, Rupert Brooke, Wells, Flecker, or Masefield, and I was greatly interested in them. It was at George Mallory's rooms that I first met Edward Marsh, who has always been a good friend to me, and with whom, though we seldom see each other now, I have never fallen out: in this he is almost unique among my pre-war friends. Marsh said that he liked my poems, which George had showed him, but pointed out that they were written in the poetic vocabulary of fifty years ago and that, though the quality of the poem was not necessarily impaired by this, there would be a natural prejudice in my readers against work written in 1913 in the fashions of 1863.

George Mallory, Cyril Hartmann, Raymond, and I published a magazine in the summer of 1913 called *Green Chartreuse*. It was only intended to have one number; new magazines at a public school always sell out the first number and lose heavily on the second. From *Green Chartreuse* I quote one of my own contributions, of autobiographical interest, written in the school dialect:

MY NEW-BUG'S EXAM.

When lights went out at half-past nine in the evening of the second Friday in the Quarter, and the faint footfalls of the departing House-Master were heard no more, the fun began.

The Head of Under Cubicles constituted himself examiner and executioner, and was ably assisted by a timekeeper, a question-recorder, and a staff of his disreputable friends. I was a timorous 'newbug' then, and my pyjamas were damp with the perspiration of fear. Three of my fellows had been examined and sentenced before the inquisition was directed against me.

'It's Jones' turn now,' said a voice. 'He's the little brute that hacked me in run-about to-day. We must set him some tight questions!'

'I say, Jones, what's the colour of the House-Master – I mean what's the name of the House-Master of the House, whose colours are black and white? One, two, three . . .'

'Mr. Girdlestone,' my voice quivered in the darkness.

'He evidently knows the simpler colours. We'll muddle him. What are the colours of the Clubs to which Block Houses belong? One, two, three, four . . .'

I had been slaving at getting up these questions for days, and just managed to blurt out the answer before being counted out.

'Two questions. No misses. We must buck up,' said someone.

'I say, Jones, how do you get to Farncombe from Weekites? One, two, three . . .'

I had only issued directions as far as Bridge before being counted out.

'Three questions. One miss. You're allowed three misses out of ten.'

'Where is Charterhouse Magazine? One, two, three, four . . .'

'Do you mean *The Carthusian* office?' I asked.

Everyone laughed.

'Four questions. Two misses. I say, Robinson, he's answered far too many. We'll set him a couple of stingers.'

Much whispering.

'What is the age of the horse that rolls Under Green? One, two, three . . .'

'Six!' I said, at a venture.

'Wrong; thirty-eight. Six questions. Three misses! Think yourself lucky you weren't asked its pedigree.'

'What are canoeing colours? One, two, thr . . .'

'There aren't any!'

'You'll get cocked-up for festivity; but you can count it. Seven questions. Three misses. Jones?'

'Yes!'

'What was the name of the girl to whom rumour stated that last year's football secretary was violently attached? One, two, three, four . . .'

'Daisy!' (It sounded a likely name.)

'Oh really! Well, I happen to know last year's football secretary; and he'll simply kill you for spreading scandal. You're wrong anyhow. Eight questions. Four misses!'

'You'll come to my "cube" at seven to-morrow morning. See? Good night!'

Here he waved his hair-brush over the candle, and a colossal shadow appeared on the ceiling.

The Poetry Society died about this time – and this is how it died. Two of its sixth-form members came to a meeting and each read a rather dull and formal poem about love and nature; none of us paid much attention to them. But the following week they were published in *The Carthusian*, and soon every one was pointing and giggling. Both poems, which were signed with pseudonyms, were acrostics, the initial letters spelling out a 'case'. 'Case' meant 'romance', a formal coupling of two boys' names, with the name of the elder boy first. In these two cases both the first names mentioned were those of bloods. It was a foolish act of aggression in the feud between sixth form and the bloods. But nothing much would have come of it had not another of the sixth-form members of the Poetry Society been in love with one of the smaller boys whose names appeared in the acrostics. In rage and jealousy he went to the head-master and called his attention to the acrostic – which otherwise neither he nor any other of the masters would have noticed. He pretended that he did not know the authors; but though he had not been at the particular meeting where the poems were read, he could easily have guessed them from the styles. Before things had taken this turn I had incautiously told some-one who the authors were; so I was now dragged into the row as a witness against them. The headmaster took a very serious view of the case. The two poets were deprived of their monitorial privileges; the editor of *The Carthusian*, who, though aware of the acros-tics, had accepted the poems, was deprived of his editorship and of his position as head of the school. The informer, who happened to be next in school order, succeeded him in both capacities; he had not expected this development and it made him most unpopular. His consolation was a real one, that he had done it all for love, to avenge the public insult done to the boy. And he was a decent fellow, really. The Poetry Society was dissolved in disgrace by the headmaster's orders. Guy Kendall was one of the few masters who insisted on treating the boys better than they deserved, so I was sorry for him when this happened; it was an 'I told you so' for the other masters, who did not believe either in poetry or in school uplift societies. I owe a great debt of gratitude to Kendall; the meetings of the Poetry Society were all that I had to look forward to when things were at their worst for me.

My last year at Charterhouse I devoted myself to doing everything I could to show how little respect I had for the school tradition. In the winter of 1913 I won a classical exhibition at St. John's College, Oxford, so that I could go slow on school work. Nevill Barbour and I were editing the *Carthusian*, and a good deal of my time went in that. Nevill, who as a scholar had met the same sort of difficulties as myself, also had a dislike of most Charterhouse traditions. We decided that the most objectionable tradition of all was compulsory games. Of these cricket was the most objectionable, because it wasted most time in the best part of the year. We began a campaign in favour of tennis. We were not seriously devoted to tennis, but it was the best weapon we had against cricket – the game, we wrote, in which the selfishness of the few was supposed to excuse the boredom of the many. Tennis was quick and busy. We asked Old Carthusian tennis internationalists to contribute letters proposing tennis as the manlier and more vigorous game. We even got the famous Anthony Wilding to write. The games-masters were scandalized at this assault on cricket; to them tennis was 'pat ball', a game for girls. But the result of our campaign was surprising. Not only did we double our sales, but a fund was started for providing the school with a number of tennis-courts and making Charterhouse the cradle of public-school tennis. Though delayed by the war, these courts actually appeared. I noticed them recently as I went past the school in a car; there seemed to be plenty of them. I wonder, are there tennis-bloods at Charterhouse now?

Poetry and Dick were now the only two things that really mattered. My life with my fellow house-monitors was one of perpetual discord. I had grudges against them all except the house-captain and the head-monitor. The house-captain, the only blood in the house, spent most of his time with his fellow bloods in other houses. The head-monitor was a scholar who, though naturally a decent fellow, had been embittered by his first three years in the house and was much on his dignity. He did more or less what the other monitors wanted him to do, and I was sorry that I had to lump him in with the rest. My love for Dick provoked a constant facetiousness, but they never dared to go too far. I once caught one of them in the bathroom scratching up a pair of hearts conjoined, with Dick's initials and mine on them. I pushed him into the bath and turned the taps on. The next day he got hold of a manuscript note-book of mine that I had left on the table in the monitors' room with some other books. It had poems and essay notes in it. He and the other monitors, except the house-captain, annotated it critically in blue chalk and all signed their initials. The house-captain would have nothing to do with this: he thought it ungentlemanly. I was furious when I found what had been done. I made a speech. I demanded a signed apology. I said that if I were not given it within an hour I would choose one of them as solely responsible and punish him. I said that I would now have a bath and that the first monitor that I met after my bath I would knock down.

Whether by accident or whether it was that he thought his position made him secure, the first monitor I met in the corridor was the head-monitor. I knocked him down. It was the time of evening preparation, which only the monitors were free not to attend. But a fag happened to pass on an errand and saw the blow and the blood; so it could not be hushed up. The head-monitor went to the house-master and the house-master sent for me. He was an excitable, elderly man who had some difficulty in controlling his spittle when angry. He made me sit down in a chair in his study, then stood over me, clenching his fists and crying in his high falsetto voice: 'Do you realize you have done a very brutal action?' His mouth was bubbling. I was as angry as he was. I jumped up and clenched my fists too. Then I said that I would do the same thing to anyone who, after scribbling impertinent remarks on my private papers, refused to apologize. 'Private papers. Filthy poems,' said the house-master.

I had another difficult interview with the headmaster over this. But it was my last term, so he allowed me to finish my five years without ignominy. He was puzzled by the frankness of my statement of love for Dick. He reopened the question. I refused to be ashamed. I heard afterwards that he had said that this was one of the rare cases of a friendship between boys of unequal ages which he felt was essentially moral. I went through one of the worst quarters of an hour of my life on Dick's account in this last term. When the master had warned me about exchanging glances with Dick in chapel I had been infuriated. But when I was told by one of the boys that he had seen the master surreptitiously kissing Dick once, on a choir-treat or some such occasion, I went quite mad. I asked for no details or confirmation. I went to the master and told him he must resign or I would report the case to the headmaster. He already had a reputation in the school for this sort of thing, I said. Kissing boys was a criminal offence. I was morally outraged. Probably my sense of outrage concealed a murderous jealousy. I was surprised when he vigorously denied the charge; I could not guess what was going to happen next. But I said: 'Well, come to the headmaster and deny it to him.' He asked: 'Did the boy tell you this himself?' I said 'No.' 'Well then,' he said, 'I'll send for him here and he shall tell us the truth.' So Dick was sent for and arrived looking very frightened, and the house-master said menacingly: 'Graves tells me that I once kissed you. Is that true?' Dick said: 'Yes, it is true.' So Dick was dismissed and the master collapsed, and I felt miserable. He said he would resign at the end of the term, which was quite near, on grounds of ill-health. He even thanked me for speaking directly to him and not going to the headmaster. That was in the summer of 1914; he went into the army and was killed the next year. I found out much later from Dick that he had not been kissed at all. It may have been some other boy.

One of the last events that I remember at Charterhouse was a debate with the motion that 'this House is in favour of compulsory military service'. The Empire Service League, or whatever it was called, of which Earl Roberts of Kandahar, V.C., was the President, sent down a propagandist to support the motion. There were only six votes out of one hundred and nineteen cast against it. I was the principal speaker against the motion, a strong anti-militarist. I had recently resigned from the Officers' Training Corps, having revolted against the theory of implicit obedience to orders. And during a fortnight spent the previous summer at the O.T.C. camp at Tidworth on Salisbury Plain, I had been frightened by a special display of the latest military fortifications, barbed-wire entanglements, machine-guns, and field artillery in action. General, now Field-Marshal Sir William Robertson, whose son was a member of the school, had visited the camp and impressed upon us that war against Germany was inevitable within two or three years, and that we must be prepared to take our part in it as leaders of the new forces that would assuredly be called into being. Of the six voters against the motion Nevill Barbour and I are, I believe, the only ones who survived the war.

My last memory was the headmaster's good-bye. It was this: 'Well, good-bye, Graves, and remember this, that your best friend is the waste-paper basket.'

I used to speculate on which of my contemporaries would distinguish themselves after they left school. The war upset my calculations. Many dull boys had brief brilliant military careers, particularly as air-fighters, becoming squadron and flight commanders. 'Fuzzy' McNair, the head of the school, won the V.C. as a Rifleman; young Sturgess, who had been my study fag, distinguished himself more unfortunately by flying the first heavy bombing machine of a new pattern across the Channel on his first trip to France and making a beautiful landing (having mistaken the land-marks) at an aerodrome behind the German lines. A boy whom I admired very much during my first year at Charterhouse was the Hon. Desmond O'Brien. He was the only Carthusian in my time who cheerfully disreg-arded all school rules. He had skeleton keys for the school library, chapel and science laboratories and used to break out of his house at night and carefully disarrange things there. The then headmaster was fond of O'Brien and forgave him much. O'Brien had the key of the headmaster's study too and, going there one night with an electric torch, carried off a memorandum which he showed me – 'Must expel O'Brien.' He had a wireless receiving-station in one of the out-of-bounds copses on the school grounds, and he discovered a vent-ilator shaft down which he could hoot into the school library from outside and create great disturbance with-out detection. One day we were threatened with the

83

loss of a Saturday half-holiday because some member of the school had killed a cow with a catapult, and nobody would own up. O'Brien had fired the shot; he was away at the time on special leave for a sister's wedding. A friend wrote to him about the half-holiday. He sent the headmaster a telegram: 'Killed cow sorry coming O'Brien.' At last, having absented himself from every lesson and chapel for three whole days, he was expelled. He was killed early in the war while bombing Bruges.

At least one in three of my generation at school was killed. This was because they all took commissions as soon as they could, most of them in the infantry and flying corps. The average life of the infantry subaltern on the Western front was, at some stages of the war, only about three months; that is to say that at the end of three months he was either wounded or killed. The proportions worked out at about four wounded to every one killed. Of the four one was wounded seriously and the remaining three more or less lightly. The three lightly wounded returned to the front after a few weeks or months of absence and were again subject to the same odds. The flying casualties were even higher. Since the war lasted for four and a half years, it is easy to see why the mortality was so high among my contemporaries, and why most of the survivors, if not permanently disabled, were wounded at least two or three times.

Two well-known sportsmen were contemporaries of mine: A. G. Bower, captain of England at soccer, who was only an average player at Charterhouse, and Woolf Barnato, the Surrey cricketer (and millionaire racing motorist), who also was only an average player. Barnato was in the same house as myself and we had not a word to say to each other for the four years we were

together. Five scholars have made names for themselves: Richard Hughes as a B.B.C. playwright; Richard
Goolden as an actor of old-man parts; Vincent Selig-
man as author of a propagandist life of Venizelos; Cyril
Hartmann as an authority on historical French scan-
dals; and my brother Charles as society gossip-writer
on the middle page of *The Daily Mail*. Occasionally
I see another name or two in the newspapers. There
was one the other day – M . . . who was in the news for
escaping from a private lunatic asylum. I remembered
that he had once offered a boy ten shillings to hold his
hand in a thunderstorm and that he had frequently
threatened to run away from Charterhouse

IX

George Mallory did something better than lend me books, and that was to take me climbing on Snowdon in the school vacations. I knew Snowdon very well from a distance, from my bedroom window at Harlech. In the spring its snow cap was the sentimental glory of the landscape. The first time I went with George to Snowdon we stayed at the Snowdon Ranger Hotel at Quellyn Lake. It was January and the mountain was covered with snow. We did little rock-climbing, but went up some good snow slopes with rope and ice-axe. I remember one climb the objective of which was the summit; we found the hotel there with its roof blown off in the blizzard of the previous night. We sat by the cairn and ate Carlsbad plums and liver-sausage sandwiches. Geoffrey Keynes, the editor of the *Nonesuch Blake*, was there; he and George, who used to go drunk with excitement at the end of his climbs, picked stones off the cairn and shied them at the chimney stack of the hotel until they had sent it where the roof was.

George was one of the three or four best climbers in climbing history. His first season in the Alps had been spectacular; nobody had expected him to survive it. He never lost his almost foolhardy daring; yet he knew all that there was to be known about climbing technique. One always felt absolutely safe with him on the rope.

George went through the war as a lieutenant in the artillery, but his nerves were apparently unaffected – on his leaves he went rock-climbing.

When the war ended he was more in love with the mountains than ever. His death on Mount Everest came five years later. No one knows whether he and Irvine actually made the last five hundred yards of the climb or whether they turned back or what happened; but anyone who had climbed with George felt convinced that he did get to the summit, that he rejoiced in his accustomed way and had not sufficient reserve of strength left for the descent. I do not think that it was ever mentioned in the newspaper account of his death that George originally took to climbing when he was a scholar at Winchester as a corrective to his weak heart.

George was wasted at Charterhouse, where, in my time at least, he was generally despised by the boys because he was neither a disciplinarian nor interested in cricket or football. He tried to treat his classes in a friendly way and that puzzled and offended them. There was a tradition in the school of concealed warfare between the boys and the masters. It was considered no shame to cheat, to lie, or to deceive where a master was concerned; yet to do the same to a member of the school was immoral. George was also unpopular with the house-masters because he refused to accept this state of war and fraternized with the boys whenever he could. When two house-masters who had been unfriendly to him happened to die within a short time of each other he joked to me: 'See, Robert, how mine enemies flee before my face.' I always called him by his Christian name, and so did three or four more of his friends in the school. This lack of dignity in him put him beyond the pale both with the boys and the masters. Eventually the falseness of his position told on his temper; yet he always managed to find four or five boys in the school who were, like him, out of their element, and befriended them and made life tolerable for them. Before the final Everest expedition he had decided to resign and do educational work at Cambridge with, I believe, the Workers' Educational Association. He was tired of trying to teach gentlemen to be gentlemen.

I spent a season with George and a large number of climbers at the hotel at Pen-y-Pass on Snowdon in the spring of 1914. This time it was real precipice-climbing, and I was lucky enough to climb with George, with H. E. L. Porter, a renowned technician of climbing, with Kitty O'Brien and with Conor O'Brien, her brother, who afterwards made a famous voyage round the world in a twenty-ton or five-ton or some even-less-ton boat. Conor climbed principally, he told us, as a corrective to bad nerves. He used to get very excited when any slight hitch occurred; his voice would rise to a scream. Kitty used to chide him: 'Ach, Conor, dear, have a bit of wit,' and Conor would apologize. Conor, being a sailor, used to climb in bare feet. Often in climbing one has to support the entire weight of one's body on a couple of toes – but toes in stiff boots. Conor said that he could force his naked toes farther into crevices than a boot would go.

But the most honoured climber there was Geoffrey Young. Geoffrey had been climbing for a number of years and was president of the Climbers' Club. I was told that his four closest friends had all at different times been killed climbing; this was a comment on the extraordinary care with which he always climbed. It was not merely shown in his preparations for a climb –

the careful examination, foot by foot, of the alpine rope, the attention to his boot-nails and the balanced loading of his knapsack – but also in his cautiousness in the climbing itself. Before making any move he thought it out foot by foot, as though it were a problem in chess. If the next handhold happened to be just a little out of his reach or the next foothold seemed at all unsteady he would stop and think of some way round the difficulty. George used sometimes to get impatient, but Geoffrey refused to be hurried. He was short, which put him at a disadvantage in the matter of reach. He was not as double-jointed and prehensile as Porter or as magnificent as George, but he was the perfect climber. And still remains so. This in spite of having lost a leg while serving with a Red Cross unit on the Italian front. He climbs with an artificial leg. He has recently published the only satisfactory text-book on rock-climbing. I was very proud to be on a rope with Geoffrey Young. He said once: 'Robert, you have the finest natural balance that I have ever seen in a climber.' This compliment pleased me far more than if the Poet Laureate had told me that I had the finest sense of rhythm that he had ever met in a young poet.

It is quite true that I have a good balance; once, in Switzerland, it saved me from a broken leg or legs. My mother took us there in the Christmas holidays of 1913–14, ostensibly for winter sports, but really because she thought that she owed it to my sisters to give them a chance to meet nice young men of means. About the third day that I put on skis I went up from Champéry, where we were staying and the snow was too soft, to Morgins, a thousand feet higher, where it was like sugar. Here I found an ice-run for skeleton-toboggans. Without considering that skis have no purchase on ice at all, I launched myself down it. After a few yards my speed increased alarmingly and I suddenly realized what I was in for. There were several sharp turns in the run protected by high banks, and I had to trust entirely to body-balance in swerving round them. I reached the terminus still upright and had my eyes damned by a frightened sports-club official for having endangered my life on his territory.

In an essay on climbing that I wrote at the time, I said it was a sport that made all others seem trivial. 'New climbs or new variations of old climbs are not made in a competitive spirit, but only because it is satisfactory to stand somewhere on the earth's surface where nobody else has stood before. And it is good to be alone with a specially chosen band of people – people that one can trust completely. Rock-climbing is one of the most dangerous sports possible, unless one keeps to the rules; but if one does keep to the rules it is reasonably safe. With physical fitness in every member of the climbing team, a careful watch on the weather, proper overhauling of climbing apparatus, and with no hurry, anxiety or stunting, climbing is much safer than fox-hunting. In hunting there are uncontrollable factors, such as hidden wire, holes in which a horse may stumble, caprice or vice in the horse. The climber trusts entirely to his own feet, legs, hands, shoulders, sense of balance, judgment of distance.'

The first climb on which I was taken was up Crib-y-ddysgel. It was a test climb for beginners. About fifty feet up from the scree, a height that is really more frightening than five hundred, because death is almost as certain and much more immediate, there was a long sloping shelf of rock, about the length of an ordinary room, to be crossed from right to left. It was without handholds or footholds worth speaking of and too steep to stand upright or kneel on without slipping. It shelved at an angle of, I suppose, forty-five or fifty degrees. The accepted way to cross it was by rolling in an upright position and trusting to friction as a maintaining force. Once I got across this shelf without disaster I felt that the rest of the climb was easy. The climb was called The Gambit. Robert Trevelyan, the poet, was given this test in the previous season, I was told, and had been unlucky enough to fall off. He was pulled up short, of course, after a few feet by the rope of the leader, who was well belayed; but the experience disgusted him with climbing and he spent the rest of his time on the mountains just walking about.

Belaying means making fast on a projection of rock a loop of the rope which is wound round one's waist, and so disposing the weight of the body that, if the climber above or below happens to slip and fall, the belay will hold and the whole party will not go down together. Alpine rope has a breaking point of a third its own length. Only one member of the climbing team is moving at any given time, the others are belayed. Sometimes on a precipice it is necessary to move up fifty or sixty feet before finding a secure belay as a point from which to start the next upward movement, so that if the leader falls and is unable to put on a brake in any way he must fall more than twice that length before being pulled up. On the same day I was taken on a spectacular though not unusually difficult climb on Crib Goch. At one point we traversed round a knife-edge buttress. From this knife-edge a pillar-like bit of rock, technically known as a monolith, had split away. We scrambled up the monolith, which overhung the valley with a clear five hundred feet drop, and each in turn stood on the top and balanced. The next thing was to make a long, careful stride from the top of the monolith to the rock face; here there was a ledge just wide enough to take the toe of a boot, and a handhold at convenient height to give an easy pull-up to the next ledge. I remember George shouting down from above: 'Be careful of that foothold, Robert. Don't chip the edge off or the climb will be impossible for anyone who wants to do it again. It's got to last another five hundred years at least.'

I was only in danger once. I was climbing with Porter on an out-of-the-way part of the mountain. The climb, known as the Ribbon Track and Girdle Traverse, had not been attempted for about ten years. About half-way up we came to a chimney. A chimney is a vertical fissure in the rock wide enough to admit the body; a crack is only wide enough to admit the boot. One works up a chimney sideways with back and knees, but up a crack with one's face to the rock. Porter was leading and fifty feet above me in the chimney. In making a spring to a handhold slightly out of reach he dislodged a pile of stones that had been wedged in the chimney. They rattled down and one rather bigger than a cricket ball struck me on the head and knocked me out. Fortunately I was well belayed and Porter was already in safety. The rope held me up; I recovered my senses a few seconds later and was able to continue.

The practice of Pen-y-Pass was to have a leisurely breakfast and lie in the sun with a tankard of beer before starting for the precipice foot in the late morning. Snowdon was a perfect mountain for climbing. The rock was sound and not slippery. And once you came to the top of any of the precipices, some of which were a thousand feet high, but all just climbable one way or another, there was always an easy way to run down. In the evening when we got back to the hotel we lay and stewed in hot baths. I remember wondering at my body – the worn fingernails, the bruised knees, and the lump of climbing muscle that had begun to bunch above the arch of the foot, seeing it as beautiful in relation to this new purpose. My worst climb was on Lliwedd, the most formidable of the precipices, when at a point that needed most concentration a raven circled round the party in great sweeps. This was curiously unsettling, because one climbs only up and down, or left and right, and the raven was suggesting all the diverse possibilities of movement, tempting us to let go our hold and join him.

X

I was at Harlech when war was declared; I decided to
enlist a day or two later.[1] In the first place, though only
a very short war was expected – two or three months
at the very outside – I thought that it might last just
long enough to delay my going to Oxford in October,
which I dreaded. I did not work out the possibilities of
being actively engaged in the war. I thought that it
would mean garrison service at home while the regular
forces were away. In the second place, I entirely believed
that France and England had been drawn into a war
which they had never contemplated and for which they
were entirely unprepared. It never occurred to me that
newspapers and statesmen could lie. I forgot my
pacifism – I was ready to believe the worst of the Germans. I was outraged to read of the cynical violation of
Belgian neutrality. I wrote a poem promising vengeance
for Louvain. I discounted perhaps twenty per cent of
the atrocity details as war-time exaggeration. That was
not, of course, enough. Recently I saw the following
contemporary newspaper cuttings quoted somewhere
in chronological sequence:

> 'When the fall of Antwerp got known the church bells
> were rung' (*i.e.*, at Cologne and elsewhere in Germany).
> – *Kölnische Zeitung.*

'According to the *Kölnische Zeitung*, the clergy of Antwerp were compelled to ring the church bells when the fortress was taken.' – *Le Matin* (Paris.)

'According to what *The Times* has heard from Cologne, via Paris, the unfortunate Belgian priests who refused to ring the church bells when Antwerp was taken have been sentenced to hard labour.' – *Corriere della Sera* (Milan.)

'According to information to the *Corriere della Sera* from Cologne, via London, it is confirmed that the barbaric conquerors of Antwerp punished the unfortunate Belgian priests for their heroic refusal to ring the church bells by hanging them as living clappers to the bells with their heads down.' – *Le Matin* (Paris.)

When I was in the trenches a few months later I happened to belong to a company mess in which four of us young officers out of five had, by a coincidence, either German mothers or naturalized German fathers. One of them said: 'Of course I'm glad I joined when I did. If I'd put it off for a month or two they'd have accused me of being a German spy. As it is I have an uncle interned at Alexandra Palace, and my father's only been allowed to retain the membership of his golf club because he has two sons in the trenches.' I said: 'Well, I have three or four uncles sitting somewhere opposite, and a number of cousins too. One of my uncles is a general. But that's all right. I don't brag about them. I only advertise the uncle who is a British admiral commanding at the Nore.'

Among my enemy relatives was my cousin Conrad, who was the same age as myself, and the son of the German consul at Zurich. In January 1914 I had gone ski-ing with him between the trees in the woods above

the city. We had tobogganed together down the Dolder-
strasse in Zurich itself, where the lampposts were all
sandbagged and family toboggans, skidding broadside
on at the turns, were often crashed into by single-seater
skeletons; arms and legs were broken by the score and
the crowds thought it a great joke. Conrad served with
a crack Bavarian regiment all through the war, and won
the 'Pour le Mérite' Order, which was more rarely
awarded than the British Victoria Cross. He was killed
by the Bolsheviks after the war in a village on the Baltic
where he had been sent to make requisitions. He was a
gentle, proud creature, whose chief interest was natural
history. He used to spend hours in the woods studying
the habits of wild animals; he felt strongly against
shooting them. Perhaps the most outstanding military
feat was that of an uncle who was dug out at the age of
sixty or so as a lieutenant in the Bavarian artillery. My
youngest brother met him a year or two ago and happened to mention that he was going to visit Rheims. My
uncle nudged him: 'Have a look at the cathedral. I was
there with my battery in the war. One day the divisional
general came up to me and said: "Lieutenant, I understand that you are a Lutheran, not a Catholic?" I said
that this was so. Then he said: "I have a very disagreeable service for you to perform, Lieutenant. Those
misbegotten swine, the French, are using the cathedral
for an observation post. They think they can get away
with it because it's Rheims Cathedral, but this is war
and they have our trenches taped from there. So I call
upon you to dislodge them." I only needed to fire two
rounds and down came the pinnacle and the Frenchmen with it. It was a very neat bit of shooting. I was
proud to have limited the damage like that. Really, you
must go and have a look at it.'

The nearest regimental depot was at Wrexham: the Royal Welch Fusiliers.[2] The Harlech golf secretary suggested my taking a commission instead of enlisting. He rang up the adjutant and said that I was a public-school boy who had been in the Officers' Training Corps at Charterhouse. So the adjutant said: 'Send him right along,' and on 11th August I started my training. I immediately became a hero to my family. My mother, who said to me: 'My race has gone mad,' regarded my going as a religious act; my father was proud that I had 'done the right thing'. I even recovered, for a time, the respect of my uncle, C. L. Graves, of *The Spectator* and *Punch*, with whom I had recently had a tiff. He had given me a sovereign tip two terms previously and I had written my thanks, saying that with it I had bought Samuel Butler's *Note Books*, *The Way of all Flesh* and the two *Erewhons*. To my surprise this had infuriated him.

The fellows who applied for commissions at the same time as myself were for the most part boys who had recently failed to pass into the Royal Military College at Sandhurst, and were trying to get into the regular army by the old militia door – which was now known as the Special Reserve. There were only one or two fellows who had gone into the army, like myself, for the sake of the war and not for the sake of a career. There were about a dozen of us recruit officers on the Square learning to drill and be drilled. My Officers' Training Corps experience made this part easy, but I knew nothing about army traditions and made all the worst mistakes; saluting the bandmaster, failing to recognize the colonel when in mufti, walking in the street without a belt and talking shop in the mess. But I soon learned to conform. My greatest difficulty was to talk to men of the company[3] to which I was posted with the necessary air of authority. Many of them were old soldiers re-enlisted, and I disliked bluffing that I knew more than they did. There were one or two very old soldiers employed on the depot staff, wearing the ribbon of Burma, 1885, and of even earlier campaigns, and usually also the ribbon of the 'Rooti' or good service medal awarded for eighteen years of undetected crime. There was one old fellow called Jackie Barrett, a Kipling character, of whom it was said: 'There goes Jackie Barrett. He and his mucking-in chum deserted the regiment in Quetta and went across the north-west frontier on foot. Three months later he gave himself up as a deserter to the British consul at Jerusalem. He buried his chum by the way.'

I was on the square only about three weeks before being sent off on detachment duty to Lancaster to a newly-formed internment camp for enemy aliens. The camp was a disused wagon-works near the river, a dirty, draughty place, littered with old scrap-metal and guarded with high barbed-wire fences. There were about three thousand prisoners already there and more and more piled in every day; seamen arrested on German vessels in Liverpool harbour, waiters from big hotels in the north, an odd German band⁴ or two, harmless German commercial travellers and shopkeepers. The prisoners were resentful at being interned, particularly those who were married and had families and had lived peaceably in England for years. The only comfort that we could give was that they were safer inside than out; anti-German feeling was running high, shops with German names were continually being raided and even German women were made to feel that they were personally responsible for the Belgian atrocities. Besides, we said, if they were in Germany they would be forced

into the army. At this time we made a boast of our voluntary system. We did not know that there would
come a time when these internees would be bitterly
envied by forcibly-enlisted Englishmen because they
were safe until the war ended.

In the summer of 1915, *The Times* reprinted in the
daily column, *Through German Eyes*,[5] a German newspaper account by Herr Wolff, an exchanged prisoner,
of his experiences at Lancaster in 1914. *The Times*
found very amusing Herr Wolff's allegations that he
and forty other waiters from the Midland Hotel, Manchester, had been arrested and taken, handcuffed *and
fettered*, in special railway carriages to Lancaster under
the escort of fifty Manchester policemen armed with
carbines. But it was true, because I was the officer who
took them over from the chief inspector. He was a fine
figure in frogged uniform and gave me a splendid
salute. I signed him a receipt for his prisoners and he
gave me another salute. He had done his job well and
was proud of it. The only mishap was the accidental
breaking of two carriage windows by the slung carbines. Wolff also said that even children were interned
in the camp. This was true. There were a dozen or so
little boys from the German bands who had been
interned because it seemed more humane to keep them
with their friends than to send them to a workhouse.
Their safety in the camp caused the commandant great
concern.

I had a detachment of fifty Special Reservists, most
of them with only about six weeks' service. They had
joined the army just before war started as a cheap way
of getting a holiday at the training camp; to find themselves forced to continue beyond the usual fortnight
annoyed them. They were a rough lot, Welshmen from

the border counties, and were constantly deserting and having to be fetched back by the police. They made nervous sentries, and were probably more frightened of the prisoners than the prisoners were of them. Going the round of sentries on a dark night about 2 a.m. was dangerous. Very often my lantern used to blow out and I would fumble to light it again in the dark and hear the frightened voice of a sentry roar out, 'Halt! Who goes there?' and know that he was standing with his rifle aimed and his magazine charged with five live rounds. I used to gasp out the password just in time. Rifles were often being fired off at shadows. The prisoners were a rowdy lot; the sailors particularly were always fighting. I saw a prisoner spitting out teeth and blood one morning. I asked him what was wrong. 'Oh, sir, one no-good friend give me one clap on the chops.' Frequent deputations were sent to complain of the dullness of the food; it was the same ration food that was served to the troops. But after a while they realized the war and settled down to sullen docility; they started hobbies and glee parties and games and plans for escape. I had far more trouble with my men. They were always breaking out of their quarters. I could never find out how they did it. I watched all the possible exits, but caught no one. Finally I discovered that they used to crawl out through a sewer. They boasted of their successes with the women. Private Kirby said to me: 'Do you know, sir? On the Sunday after we arrived, all the preachers in Lancaster took as their text, "Mothers, take care of your daughters; the Royal Welch have come to town."'

The camp staff consisted of:

A fatherly colonel of the Loyal North Lancashire Regiment, the commandant.

His secretary, by name C. B. Gull, one of the best-known pre-war figures in Oxford, owner of the *Isis*, and combined divinity, athletics and boxing coach. We used to box together to keep fit. He also sponsored me as a candidate for the local lodge of The Royal Antediluvian Order of Buffaloes. The Grand Marshal who officiated at my initiation had drunk four or five pints of 'bitter-gatter' and a glass or two of 'juniper' (these were secret words) and continually short-circuited in the ritual. He kept on returning to the part where they intone:

Grand Marshal: Spirit of true Buffaloism hover around us!
Response: Benevolence and joy ever attend us!

The assistant-commandant, who alleged that he had ten years more seniority than any other major in the British army and made wistful jokes about his lost virility. His recurrent theme was: 'If you only knew how much that would mean to an old man like me.'

The adjutant, an East Lancashire lieutenant, by name Deane. The day after war was declared a German armed cruiser had held up the neutral liner in which he was sailing home from the Cape and taken him off. He was forced to give his parole not to fight against Germany in the war. The cruiser was subsequently sunk by a British ship, the *High-flyer*, and Deane was rescued; but the signed parole was saved by the German captain, who escaped in a boat and gave it in charge of the German consul at Las Palmas. So Deane was forbidden the trenches, and when I met him in 1917 he was a staff-colonel.

A doctor who was the mess buffoon. I broke the scabbard of my sword on his back one night.

The interpreter, a Thomas Cook man who could speak every European language but Basque. He admitted to a weakness in Lithuanian, and when asked what his own nationality was would answer, 'I am Wagon-Lits.'[6]

I had an inconvenient accident. The telephone bell was constantly going from Western Command Headquarters; it was installed in an office-room where I slept on a sloping desk. One night Pack-Saddle (the code-name for the Chief Supply Officer of the Western Command) rang up shortly after midnight with orders for the commandant. They were about the rationing of a batch of four hundred prisoners who were being sent up to him from Chester and North Wales. I was half asleep and not clever at the use of the telephone. In the middle of the conversation, which was difficult because a storm was going on at the time and Pack-Saddle was irritable, the line was, I suppose, struck by lightning somewhere. I got a bad electric shock, and was unable to use a telephone properly again until some twelve years later.

Guarding prisoners seemed an unheroic part to be playing in the war, which had now reached a critical stage; I wanted to be abroad fighting. My training had been interrupted, and I knew that even when I was recalled from detachment duty I would have to wait a month or two at least before being sent out. When I got back to the depot in October I found myself stale. The adjutant, a keen soldier, decided that there were two things wrong with me. First of all, I dressed badly. I had apparently gone to the wrong tailor, and had also had a soldier-servant palmed off on me who was no good. He did not polish my buttons and shine my belt and boots as he should have done, and neglected me generally; as I had never had a valet before I did not know how to manage him or what to expect of him. The adjutant finally summoned me to the Orderly Room and threatened that he would not send me to France until I had entirely overhauled my wardrobe and looked more like a soldier. My company commander, he said, had reported me to him as 'unsoldierlike and a nuisance'. This put me in a fix, because my pay only just covered the mess bills, and I knew that I could not ask my parents to buy me another outfit so soon after I had assured them that I had everything necessary. The adjutant next decided that I was not a sportsman. This was because on the day that the Grand National (I think) was run all the young officers applied for leave to see the race except myself, and I volunteered to take the job of Orderly Officer of the Day for someone who wanted to go.

I saw my contemporaries one by one being sent out to France to take the place of casualties in the First and Second Battalions, while I remained despondently at the depot. But once more boxing was useful. Johnny Basham, a sergeant in the regiment, was training at the time for his fight (which he won) with Boswell for the Lonsdale Belt, welter-weight. I went down to the training camp one evening, where Basham was offering to fight three rounds with any member of the regiment, the more the merrier. One of the officers put on the gloves and Basham got roars of laughter from the crowd as soon as he had taken his opponent's measure, by dodging about and playing the fool with him. I asked Basham's manager if I could have a go. He gave me a pair of shorts and I stepped into the ring. I pretended that I knew nothing about boxing. I led off with my right and moved about clumsily. Basham saw a chance of getting another laugh; he dropped his guard and danced about with a you-can't-hit-me challenge. I caught him off his balance and knocked him across the ring. He recovered and went for me, but I managed to keep on my feet; I laughed at him and he laughed too. We had three very brisk rounds, and he was decent in making it seem that I was a much better boxer than I was by accommodating his pace to mine. As soon as the adjutant heard the story he rang me up at my billet and told me that he was very pleased to hear of my performance, that for an officer to box like that was a great encouragement to the men, that he was mistaken about my sportsman-ship, and that to show his appreciation he had put me down for a draft to go to France in a week's time.

Of the officers who had been sent out before me several had already been killed or wounded. Among the killed was Second-Lieutenant W. G. Gladstone, whom we called Glad Eyes. He was in his early thirties; a grandson of old Gladstone, whom he resembled in fea-ture, a Liberal M.P., and lord-lieutenant of his county. When war was hanging in the balance he had declared himself against it. His Hawarden tenantry were ashamed on his account, and threatened, he told us, to duck him in the pond. Realizing, once war was declared, that further protest was useless, he immediately joined the regiment as a second-lieutenant. His political convic-tions remained. He was a man of great integrity and refused to take the non-combative employment as a staff-colonel offered him at Whitehall. When he went to France to the First Battalion he took no care of himself. He was killed by a sniper when unnecessarily exposing himself. His body was brought home for a military funeral at Hawarden; I attended it.

I have one or two random memories of this training

period at Wrexham. The landlord of my billet was a Welsh solicitor, who greatly overcharged us while pretending amicability. He wore a wig – or, to be more exact, he had three wigs, with hair of progressive lengths. When he had worn the medium-sized hair for a few days he would put on the wig with long hair, and say that, dear him, it was time to get a hair-cut. Then he would go out of the house and in a public lavatory perhaps or a wayside copse would change into the short-haired wig, which he wore until it was time to change to the medium one again. This deception was only discovered when one of the officers billeted with me got drunk and raided his bedroom. This officer, whose name was Williams, was an extreme example of the sly border Welshman. The drunker he got the more shocking his confessions. He told me one day about a girl he had got engaged to in Dublin, and even slept with on the strength of a diamond engagement ring. 'Only paste really,' he said. The day before the wedding she had had a foot cut off by a Dalkey tram, and he had hurriedly left the city. 'But, Graves, she was a lovely, lovely girl before that happened.' He had been a medical student at Trinity College, Dublin. Whenever he went to Chester, the nearest town, to pick up a prostitute, he not only used to appeal to her patriotism to charge him nothing, but he always gave her my name. I knew of this because these women used to write to me. One day I said to him in mess: 'In future you are going to be distinguished from all the other Williams' in the regiment by being called Dirty Williams.' The name stuck. By one shift or another he escaped all trench-service except for a short spell in a quiet sector, and lasted the war out safely.

Private Robinson.[7] He was from Anglesey, and had

joined the Special Reserve before the war for his health. In September the entire battalion volunteered for service overseas except Robinson. He said he would not go, and that he could be neither coaxed nor bullied. Finally he was brought before the colonel, who was genuinely puzzled at his obstinacy. Robinson explained that he was not afraid. 'I have a wife and pigs at home.' The battalion was, in September, rigged out in a temporary navy-blue uniform until khaki might be available. All but Robinson. They decided to shame him. So he continued, by order, to wear the peace-time scarlet tunic and blue trousers with a red stripe; a very dirty scarlet tunic (they had put him on the kitchen staff). His mates called him Cock Robin and sang a popular chorus at him:

> And I never get a knock
> When the boys call Cock
> Cockity ock, cock,
> Cock Robin!
> In my old red vest I mean to cut a shine . . .

But Robinson did not care:

> For the more they call me Robin Redbreast
> I'll wear it longer still.
> I will wear a red waistcoat, I will,
> I will, I will, I will, I will, I will!*

---

* 'Why,' said the cobbler, 'what should I do? Will you have me to go in the King's wars and to be killed for my labour?' 'What, knave,' said Skelton, 'art thou a coward, having so great bones?' 'No,' said the cobbler, 'I am not afeared: it is good to sleep in a whole skin.' – MERRY TALES OF SKELTON (*Early sixteenth century*). [RG]

So in October he was discharged as medically unfit: 'Of under-developed intelligence, unlikely to be of service in His Majesty's Forces,' and went home to his wife and pigs. While, of the singers, those who survived Festubert in the following May did not survive Loos in the following September.[8]

Recruit officers spent a good deal of their time at Company and Battalion Orderly Room, learning how to deal with crime. Crime, of course, meant any breach of army regulations; and there was plenty of it. In these days Battalion Orderly Room would last four or five hours every day, at the rate of one crime dealt with every three or four minutes. This was apart from the scores of less serious offences tried by company commanders. The usual Battalion Orderly Room crimes were desertion, refusing to obey an order, using obscene language to a non-commissioned officer, drunk and disorderly, robbing a comrade, and so on. On pay-nights there was hardly a man sober; and no attention was paid so long as there was silence as soon as the company officer came on his rounds just before Lights Out. (Two years later serious crime had diminished to a twentieth of that amount, though the battalion was treble its original strength, and though many of the cases that the company officers had dealt with summarily now came before the colonel; and there was practically no drunkenness.)

There was a boy called Taylor in my company. He had been at Lancaster, and I had bought him a piccolo to play when the detachment went out on route-marches; he would give us one tune after another for mile after mile. The other fellows carried his pack and rifle. At Wrexham, on pay-nights, he used to sit in the company billet, which was a drill-hall near the station, and play jigs for the drunks to dance to. He never drank himself. The music was slow at first, but he gradually quickened it until he worked them into a frenzy. He would delay this climax until my arrival with the company orderly-sergeant. The sergeant would fling open the door and bellow: 'F Company, Attention!' Taylor would break off, thrust the piccolo under his blankets, and spring to his feet. The drunks were left frozen in the middle of their capers, blinking stupidly.

In the first Battalion Orderly Room that I attended I was surprised to hear a private soldier charged with a nursery offence, about the committal of which expert evidence was given and heard without a smile. I have an accurate record of the trial but my publishers advise me not to give it here.[9]

Orderly Room always embarrassed and dispirited me. I never got used to it even after sentencing thousands of men myself. There was something shameful about it. The only change that the introduction of the civilian element into the army brought was that about half-way through the war an army order came out that henceforth the word of command was to be 'Accused and escort, right turn, quick march,' etc., instead of 'Prisoner and escort, right turn, quick march,' etc. It was only very seldom that an interesting case came up. Even the obscene language, always quoted verbatim, was drearily the same; the only variation I remember from the four stock words was in the case of a man charged with using threatening and obscene language to an N.C.O. The man had, it appeared, said to a lance-corporal who had a down on him: 'Corporal Smith, two men shall meet before two mountains.' Humour only came from the very Welsh Welshmen from the hills who had an imperfect command of English.

One of them, charged with being absent off ceremonial parade and using obscene language to the sergeant, became very indignant in Orderly Room and cried out to the colonel: 'Colonel, sir, sergeant tole me wass I for guard; I axed him no, and now the bloody bastard says wass I.'

The greatest number of simultaneous charges that I ever heard preferred against a soldier was in the case of Boy Jones at Liverpool in 1917. He was charged with, first, using obscene language to the bandmaster; the bandmaster, who was squeamish, reported it as: 'Sir, he called me a double effing c—.' Next, with breaking out of the detention that was awarded for this crime. Third, with 'absenting himself from the regiment until apprehended in the Hindenburg Line, France'. Fourth, with resisting an escort. Fifth, with being found in possession of regimental property of the Cheshire Regiment. Boy Jones, who was only fourteen and looked thirteen, had wriggled through the bars of his detention-cell and, after getting a few things together at his hut, had gone to Liverpool Exchange Station to wait for a victim. The victim was a private in a Bantam Battalion[10] just returning to France from leave. He treated the Bantam to a lot of drink and robbed him of his rifle, equipment, badges and papers. He then went off in his place. Arrived in France he was posted to the Bantam Battalion; but this did not suit him. He wanted to be with his own regiment. He deserted the Bantams, who were somewhere north of Arras, and walked south along the trenches looking for his regiment, having now resumed his proper badges. After a couple of days' walk he found the Second Battalion and reported and was immediately sent home, though he had a struggle with the escort at the railhead. The punishment for all these offences was ten days confined to camp and a spanking from the bandmaster.

The most unusual charge was against the regimental goat-major (a corporal); it was first framed as *Lese majesty*, but this was later reduced to 'disrespect to an officer: in that he, at Wrexham – on such and such a date – did prostitute the Royal Goat, being the gift of His Majesty the Colonel-in-Chief from His royal herd at Windsor, by offering his stud-services to ———, Esq., farmer and goat breeder, of Wrexham'. The goat-major pleaded that he had done this out of kindness to the goat, to which he was much attached. He was reduced to the ranks and the charge of the goat given to another.

The regular battalions of the regiment, though officered mainly by Anglo-Welshmen of county families, did not normally contain more than about one Welshman in fifty in the ranks. They were mainly recruited in Birmingham. The only man at Harlech besides myself who had joined the regiment at the start was a poor boy, a golf-caddie, who had got into trouble a short time before for shoplifting. The chapels held soldiering to be sinful, and in Merioneth the chapels were supreme. Prayers were offered for me in the chapels, not because of the dangers I ran in the war, but because I was in the army. Later, Lloyd George persuaded the chapels that the war was a crusade. So there was a sudden tremendous influx of Welshmen from North Wales. They were difficult soldiers; they particularly resented having to stand still while the N.C.O.'s swore at them. A deputation of North Welshmen came to me once and said: 'Captain Graves, sir, we do not like our sergeant-major; he do curse and he do swear, and he do drink, and he is a maan of lowly origin, too.'

At Wrexham we learned regimental history, drill,

musketry, Boer War field-tactics, military law and organization, how to recognize bugle calls, how to work a machine-gun, and how to conduct ourselves as officers on formal occasions. We dug no trenches, handled no bombs and came to think of the company, not of the platoon, still less of the section, as the smallest independent tactical unit. There were only two wounded officers back from the front at the time; both had left the Second Battalion on the retreat from Mons. Neither would talk much of his experiences. All that one of them, Emu Jones, would tell us was: 'The first queer sight I saw in France was three naked women hanging by their feet in a butcher's shop.' The other would say: 'The shells knock hell out of a man, especially the big black ones. Just hell. And that fellow Emu; he wasn't any good. We marched and marched and he had a weak heart and used to faint and expect his poor, bloody platoon to carry him as well as the rest of their load. We used to swear he was shamming. Don't believe what old Emu tells you of the retreat.'

XI

I will try to recall my war-time feelings about the Royal Welch Fusiliers. I used to congratulate myself on having chosen, quite blindly, this of all regiments. 'Good God!' I used to think, 'suppose that when the war broke out I had been living in Cheshire and had applied for a commission in the Cheshire Regiment.' I thought how ashamed I should have been to find in the history of that regiment (which was the old Twenty-second Foot, just senior in the line to the Royal Welch, which was the Twenty-third) that it had been deprived of its old title 'The Royal Cheshires' as a punishment for losing a battle.[1] Or how lucky not to have joined the Bedfords. Though the Bedfords had made a name for themselves in this war, they were still called 'The Peacemakers'. For they only had four battle-honours on their colours and none of these more recent than the year 1711; it was a sneer that their regimental motto was:[2] 'Thou shalt not kill.' Even the Black Watch, the best of the Highland regiments, had a stain on its record; and everyone knew about it. If a Tommy of another regiment went into a public bar where men of the Black Watch were drinking, and felt brave enough to start a fight, he would ask the bar-maid not for 'pig's ear', which is rhyming-slang for beer, but for a pint of 'broken square'. Then belts would be unbuckled.

The Royal Welch record was beyond reproach. There

were twenty-nine battle-honours on its colours, a number only equalled by two other two-battalion regiments. And the Royal Welch had the advantage of these since they were not single regiments, but recent combinations[3] of two regiments each with its separate history. The First Battalion of the Royal Welch Fusiliers had twenty-six battle-honours of its own, the remaining three having been won by the Second Battalion in its short and interrupted existence. They were all good bloody battle-honours, none of them like that battle of the Argyll and Sutherland Highlanders into which, it was said, they had gone with nine hundred men and from which they had come out with nine hundred and one – no casualties, and a band-boy come of age and promoted a private. For many hard battles, such as The Boyne and Aughrim and the capture of Lille, the Royal Welch had never been honoured. The regiment had fought in each of the four hardest fought victories of the British army, as listed by Sir John Fortescue. My regimental history is rusty, but I believe that they were The Boyne, Malplaquet, Albuhera and Inkerman. That is three out of four. It may have been Salamanca or Waterloo instead of The Boyne. It was also one of the six Minden regiments and one of the front-line regiments at that. They performed the unprecedented feat of charging a body of cavalry many times their own strength and driving it off the field. The surrender at York Town in the American War of Independence was the regiment's single disaster, but even that was not a disgrace. It was accorded the full honours of war. Its conduct in the hard fighting at Lexington, at Guildford Court House, and in its suicidal advance up Bunker's Hill, had earned it them.

I caught the sense of regimental tradition a day or two after I arrived at the depot. In a cupboard in the junior anteroom at the mess, I came across a big leather-bound ledger and pulled it out to see what it was about. It was the Daily Order-book of the First Battalion in the trenches before Sebastopol. I opened it at the page giving orders for the attack on the Redan Fort. Such and such a company was desired to supply volunteers for the storming party under Lieutenant So-and-so. There followed details of their arms and equipment, the number of ladders they were to carry, and the support to be afforded by other companies. Then details of rations and supply of ammunition, with an earnest Godspeed from the commanding officer. (A sketch of the commanding officer was on the wall above my head, lying sick in his tent at Scutari, wearing a cap-comforter for the cold.) And the next entries were about clearing up after an unsuccessful attack – orders for the burial of the dead, thanks from headquarters for the gallantry vainly displayed, and a notice that the effects of the late Lieutenant So-and-so, who had led the storming party, would be sold at public auction in the trenches next day. In another day's orders was the notice of the Victoria Cross awarded to Sergeant Luke O'Connor. He had lived to be Lieutenant-General Sir Luke O'Connor and was now colonel of the regiment.

The most immediate piece of regimental history that I met as a recruit-officer was the flash. The flash is a fan-like bunch of five black ribbons, each ribbon two inches wide and seven and a half inches long; the angle at which the fan is spread is exactly regulated by regimental convention. It is stitched to the back of the tunic collar. Only the Royal Welch are privileged to wear it. The story is that the Royal Welch were abroad on foreign service for several years in the 1830's, and by some chance never received the army order abolishing the queue. When the regiment returned and paraded at Plymouth the inspecting general rated the commanding officer because his men were still wearing their hair in the old fashion. The commanding officer, angry with the slight, immediately rode up to London and won from King William IV, through the intercession of some Court official, the regimental privilege of continuing to wear the bunch of ribbons in which the end of the queue was tied – the flash. It was to be a distinctive badge worn by all ranks in reward for the regiment's exemplary service in the Napoleonic wars.

The Army Council, which is usually composed of cavalry, engineer, and artillery generals, with the infantry hardly represented, had never encouraged regimental peculiarities, and perhaps could not easily forget the irregularity of the colonel's direct appeal to the Sovereign in the matter of the flash. The flash was, at any rate, not sanctioned by the Army Council on the new khaki service dress. None the less, the officers and warrant-officers continued to wear it. There was a correspondence in the early stages of the war, I was told, between the regiment and the Army Council. The regiment maintained that since the flash was a distinctive mark won in war it should be worn with service dress and not merely with peace-time scarlet. The Army Council put forward the objection that it was a distinctive mark for enemy marksmen and particularly dangerous when worn only by officers. The regiment retorted by inquiring on what occasion since the retreat from Corunna, when the regiment was the last to leave Spain, with the key of the town postern in the pocket of one of its officers, had any of His Majesty's enemies seen the back of a Royal Welch Fusilier? The Army Council was firm, but the regiment was obstinate, and the matter was in abeyance throughout the war.

Once in 1917, when an officer of my company went to Buckingham Palace to be decorated with the Military Cross, the King, as colonel-in-chief of the regiment, showed a personal interest in the matter. He asked: 'You are serving in one of the line battalions?' 'The Second Battalion, Your Majesty.' So the King gave him the order: 'About turn,' and looked at the flash, and then 'About turn' again. 'Good,' he said, 'you're still wearing it, I see,' and then, in a stage whisper: 'Don't ever let anyone take it from you.' The regiment was delighted. After the war, when scarlet was abandoned on the grounds of expense, the Army Council saw that it could reasonably sanction the flash on service dress for all ranks. As an additional favour it consented to recognize another defiant regimental peculiarity, the spelling of the word 'Welch' with a 'c'. The permission was published in a special Army Order in 1919. The *Daily Herald* commented 'Strewth!' as if it were unimportant. That was ignorance. The spelling with a 'c' was as important to us as the miniature cap-badge worn at the back of the cap was to the Gloucesters (a commemoration of the time when they fought back to back: was it at Quatre Bras?).[4] I have seen a young officer sent off battalion parade because his buttons read Welsh instead of Welch. 'Welch' referred us somehow to the antique North Wales of Henry Tudor and Owen Glendower and Lord Herbert of Cherbury, the founder of the regiment; it dissociated us from the modern North Wales of chapels, liberalism, the dairy and drapery business, Lloyd George, and the tourist trade.

The regiment was extremely strict on the standard measurements of the flash. When new-army battalions were formed and rumours came to Wrexham that in, I think, the Eighteenth Battalion officers were wearing flashes nearly down to their waists, there was great consternation. The adjutant sent off the youngest sub-altern on a special mission to the camp of the Eighteenth Battalion, the colonel of which was not a Royal Welch Fusilier, but a loan from one of the Yorkshire regiments. He was to present himself at the Battalion Orderly Room with a large pair of shears.

The new-army battalions were as anxious to be regimental as the line battalions. It once happened in France that a major of the Royal Fusiliers entered the mess of the Nineteenth (Bantam) Battalion of the Royal Welch Fusiliers. He greeted the mess with 'Good afternoon, gentlemen', and called for a drink from the mess sergeant. After he had talked for a bit he asked the senior officer present: 'Do you know why I ordered that drink from the mess sergeant?' The Welch Fusilier said: 'Yes, you wanted to see if we remembered about Albuhera.' The Royal Fusilier answered: 'Well, our mess is just along behind that wood there. We haven't forgotten either.' After Albuhera the few survivors of the Royal Welch Fusiliers and the Royal Fusiliers had messed together on the captured hill. It was then decided that henceforth and for ever the officers of each regiment were honorary members of the other's mess, and the N.C.O.'s the same.

Perhaps the most legendary item was Thomas Atkins. He was a private soldier in the First Battalion who had served under Wellington in the Peninsular War. It is said that when, many years later, Wellington at the War Office was asked to approve a specimen form for military attestation, he had ordered it to be amended from: 'I, Private John Doe of the blank regiment, do hereby, etc.,' to 'I, Private Thomas Atkins of the Twenty-third Foot, do hereby, etc.' And now I am going to spoil the story, because I cannot for the life of me remember what British grenadierish conduct it was that made Wellington remember. And so here ends my very creditable (after eleven years) lyrical passage.

I was, as a matter of fact, going on to St. David's Night. To the raw leeks eaten to the roll of the drum with one foot on a chair and one on the mess table enriched with spoils of the Summer Palace at Pekin. (They are not at all bad to eat raw, despite Shakespeare.) And to the Royal Goat with gilded horns that once leapt over the mess table with the drummer-boy on its back. And Major Toby Purcell's Golden Spurs. And Shenkin Ap Morgan, the First Gentleman of Wales. And 'The British Grenadiers', the regimental march-past. I was going to explain that British grenadiers does not mean, as most people think, merely the Grenadier Guards. It includes all regiments, the Royal Welch among them, which wear a bursting grenade as a collar and cap-badge to recall their early employment as storm troops armed with bombs.

In the war the Royal Welch Fusiliers grew too big; this damaged regimental *esprit de corps*. Before the war there were the two line battalions and the depot; the affiliated and flash-less territorials, four battalions recruited for home service, could be disregarded, in spite of their regular adjutants. The Third Battalion, which trained at the depot, was a poor relation. Now more and more new-army battalions were added (even a Twenty-fifth Battalion was on service in 1917, and was as good a battalion as the Eighth). So the regiment (that is, consensus of opinion in the two line battalions) only tentatively accepted the new-army battalions one by one as they proved themselves worthy, by service in the field. The territorials it never accepted, disowning them contemptuously as 'dog-shooters'. The fact was that three of the four territorial battalions failed signally in the Suvla Bay landing at Gallipoli. One battalion, it was known, had offered violence to its officers; the commanding officer, a regular, had not cared to survive that day. Even the good work that these battalions did later in Palestine could not cancel this disgrace. The remaining territorial battalion was attached to the First Division in France early in 1915, where, at Givenchy, it quite unnecessarily lost its machine-guns. Regimental machine-guns in 1915 were regarded almost as sacred. To lose one's machine-guns before the annihilation of the entire battalion was considered as bad as losing the regimental colours would have been in any eighteenth or nineteenth-century battle. The machine-gun officer had congratulated himself on removing the machine-gun bolts before abandoning the guns; it would make them useless to the enemy. But he had forgotten to take away the boxes of spare-parts. The Second Battalion made a raid in the same sector a year and a half later and recaptured one of the guns, which had been busy against the British trenches ever since.

As soon as we arrived at the depot we Special Reserve officers were reminded of our great good fortune. We were to have the privilege of serving with one or the other of the line battalions. In peace-time a candidate for a commission in the regiment had not only to distinguish himself in the passing-out examination at the Royal Military College, Sandhurst, and be strongly recommended by two officers of the regiment, but he had to have a guaranteed independent income that enabled him to play polo and hunt and keep up the social reputation of the regiment. These requirements were not insisted on; but we were to understand that we did not belong to the 'regiment' in the special sense. To be allowed to serve with it in time of war should satisfy our ambitions. We were not temporary officers, like those of the new army, but held permanent commissions in the Special Reserve battalion. We were reminded that the Royal Welch considered themselves second to none, even to the Guards. Representations had been made to the regiment after the South African War, inquiring whether it was willing to become the Welsh Guards, and it had indignantly refused; such a change would have made the regiment junior, in the Brigade of Guards, even to the Irish Guards only so recently formed. We were warned that while serving with a line battalion we were none of us to expect to be recommended for orders or decorations. An ordinary campaigning medal inscribed with a record of service with the battalion should be sufficient reward. Decorations were not regarded in the regiment as personal awards, but as representative awards for the whole battalion. They would therefore be reserved for the professional soldiers, to whom they would be more useful than to us as helps to extra-regimental promotion. And this was what happened. There must have been something like two or three hundred Special Reserve officers serving overseas. But except for three or four who were not directly recommended by the battalion commander, but distinguished themselves while attached to brigade or divisional staffs, or those who happened to be sent to new-army battalions or other regiments, we remained undecorated. I can only recall three exceptions. The normal proportion of awards, considering the casualties we suffered, which was about sixty or seventy killed, should have been at least ten times that amount. I myself never performed any feat for which I might conceivably have been decorated throughout my service in France.

The regimental spirit persistently survived all catastrophes. Our First Battalion, for instance, was annihilated within two months of joining the British Expeditionary Force. Young Orme, who joined straight from Sandhurst, at the crisis of the first battle of Ypres, found himself commanding a battalion reduced to only about forty rifles. With these and another small force, the remnants of the Second Battalion of the Queen's Regiment, reduced to thirty men and two officers, he helped to recapture three lines of lost trenches and was himself killed. The reconstituted battalion, after heavy fighting at Bois Grenier in December, was again all but annihilated at the Aubers Ridge and Festubert in the following May, and again at Loos in September, when the one officer-survivor of the attack was a machine-gun officer loaned from the South Staffordshire Regiment. The same sort of thing happened time after time in fighting at Fricourt, the Quadrangle, High Wood, Delville Wood, and Ginchy on the Somme in 1916, and again at Puisieux and Bullecourt in the spring fighting of 1917.[5] In the course of the war at least fifteen or twenty thousand men must have passed through each of the two line battalions, whose fighting strength was never more than eight hundred. After each catastrophe the ranks were filled up with new drafts from home, with the lightly wounded from the previous disaster returning after three or four months' absence, and with the more seriously wounded returning after nine months or a year.

In the First and Second Battalions throughout the war it was not merely the officers and non-commissioned officers who knew their regimental history. The men knew far more about Minden and Albuhera and Waterloo than they did about the fighting on the other fronts or the official causes of the war.

XII

In 1916, when on leave in England after being wounded on the Somme, I began an account of my first few months in France. Unfortunately, I wrote it as a novel and I have now to retranslate it into history. I will give one reconstituted chapter:

On arrival in France[1] we six Royal Welch Fusilier officers went to the Harfleur base-camp near Havre. Later it was to become an educational centre for trench-routine, use of bombs, trench-mortars, rifle-grenades, gas-helmets, and similar technicalities. But now we did a route-march or two through the French countryside and that was all, except for fatigues in Havre at the docks, helping the Army Service Corps unload stores from ships. The town was gay. As soon as we had arrived we were accosted by numerous little boys pimping for their sisters. 'I take you to my sister. She very nice. Very good jig-a-jig. Not much money. Very cheap. Very good. I take you now. Plenty champagne for me?' We were glad when we got orders to go up the line. But disgusted to find ourselves attached not to the Royal Welch Fusiliers, but to the Welsh Regiment.

We had heard little about the Welsh Regiment except that it was tough but rough, and that the Second Battalion, to which we were now attached, had a peculiar regimental history as the old Sixty-ninth Foot. It had originally been formed as an emergency force from pensioners and boy-recruits and sent overseas to do the work of a regular battalion – I forget in which eighteenth-century campaign. At one time it had served as marines. The Ups and Downs was the battalion's army nick-name, partly because 69 is a number which makes the same sense whichever way up it is written. The 69 was certainly upside-down when we joined it. All the company officers except two boys recently from Sandhurst and a Special Reserve captain were attached from other regiments. There were now six Royal Welch Fusiliers, two South Wales Borderers, two East Surreys, two Wiltshires, one from the Border Regiment, one from the King's Own Yorkshire Light Infantry. Even the quartermaster was an alien from the Connaught Rangers. There were perhaps four time-serving N.C.O.'s left in the battalion. Of the men, not more than fifty or so had been given more than a couple of months' training before being sent out; some had only three weeks' training; a great many had never fired a musketry course. This was because the First Division had been in constant hard fighting since the previous August; the Second Welsh had in eight months lost its full fighting strength five times over. The last occasion was the Richebourg fighting of 9th May, one of the worst disasters of the early part of the war; the division's epitaph in the official *communiqué* read: 'Meeting with considerable opposition in the direction of the Rue du Bois, our attacks were not pressed.'

The Welsh ranks had been made up first with reservists of the later categories, then with re-enlisted men, then with Special Reservists of pre-war enlistment, then with 1914 recruits of three or four months' training; but each class had in turn been exhausted. Now nothing was left to send but recruits of the spring 1915 class, and various sweepings and scourings. The First Battalion had, meanwhile, had the same heavy losses. In Cardiff they advertised: 'Enlist at the depot and get to France quick.' The recruits were principally men either over-age or under-age – a repetition of regimental history – or men who had some slight physical disability which prevented them from enlisting in regiments more particular than the Welsh. I still have the roll of my first platoon of forty men. The figures given for their ages are misleading. When they enlisted all the over-age men had put themselves in the late thirties and all the under-age men had called themselves eighteen. But once in France the over-age men did not mind adding on a few genuine years. No less than fourteen in the roll give their age as forty or over and these were not all. Fred Prosser, a painter in civil life, who admitted to forty-eight, was really fifty-six. David Davies, collier, who admitted to forty-two, and Thomas Clark, another collier who admitted to forty-five, were only one or two years junior to Prosser. James Burford, collier and fitter, was even older than these. When I first spoke to him in the trenches, he said: 'Excuse me, sir, will you explain what this here arrangement is on the side of my rifle?' 'That's the safety-catch. Didn't you do a musketry course at the depot?' 'No, sir, I was a re-enlisted man and I had only a fortnight there. The old Lee-Metford didn't have no safety-catch.' I asked him when he had last fired a rifle. 'In Egypt in 1882,' he said. 'Weren't you in the South African War?' 'I tried to re-enlist but they told me I was too old, sir. I had been an old soldier when I was in Egypt. My real age is sixty-three.' He spent all his summers as a tramp and in the bad months of the year worked as a collier, choosing a new pit every season. I heard him and David Davies one night in a dug-out opposite mine talking about the different seams of coals in Wales and tracing them from county to county and pit to pit with technical comments. It was one of the most informative conversations I ever heard.

The other half of the platoon contained the under-age section. There were five of these boys; William Bumford, collier, for instance, who gave his age as eighteen, was really only fifteen. He used to get into trouble for falling asleep on sentry duty. The official penalty for this was death, but I had observed that he could not help it. I had seen him suddenly go to sleep, on his feet, while holding a sandbag open for another fellow to fill. So we got him a job as orderly to a chaplain for a while, and a few months later all men over fifty and all boys under eighteen were combed out and sent to the base. Bumford and Burford were both sent; but neither escaped the war. Bumford was old enough to be sent back to the battalion in the later stages of the war, and was killed; Burford was killed, too, in a bombing accident at the base-camp. Or so I was told – the fate of many of my comrades in France has come to me merely as hearsay.

The troop-train consisted of forty-seven coaches and took twenty-five hours to arrive at Béthune, the rail-head. We went via St. Omer. It was about nine o'clock in the evening and we were hungry, cold and dirty. We had expected a short journey and so allowed our baggage to be put in a locked van. We played nap to keep our minds off the discomfort and I lost sixty francs, which was over two pounds at the existing rate of exchange. On the platform at Béthune a little man in filthy khaki, wearing the Welsh cap-badge, came up with a friendly touch of the cap most unlike a salute. He was to be our guide to the battalion, which was in the Cambrin trenches about ten kilometres away. He asked us to collect the draft of forty men we had with us and follow him. We marched through the unlit suburbs of the town. We were all intensely excited at the noise and flashes of the guns in the distance. The men of the draft had none of them been out before, except the sergeant in charge. They began singing. Instead of the usual music-hall songs they sang Welsh hymns, each man taking a part. The Welsh always sang when they were a bit frightened and pretending that they were not; it kept them steady. They never sang out of tune.

We marched towards the flashes and could soon see the flare-lights curving over the trenches in the distance. The noise of the guns grew louder and louder. Then we were among the batteries. From behind us on the left of the road a salvo of four shells came suddenly over our heads. The battery was only about two hundred yards away. This broke up *Aberystwyth* in the middle of a verse and set us off our balance for a few seconds; the column of fours tangled up. The shells went hissing away eastward; we could see the red flash and hear the hollow bang where they landed in German territory. The men picked up their step again and began chaffing. A lance-corporal dictated a letter home: 'Dear auntie, this leaves me in the pink. We are at present wading in blood up to our necks. Send me fags and a life-belt. This war is a booger. Love and kisses.'

The roadside cottages were now showing more and more signs of dilapidation. A German shell came over and then whoo–oo–oooooooOOO–bump–CRASH! twenty yards away from the party. We threw ourselves flat on our faces. Presently we heard a curious singing noise in the air, and then flop! flop! little pieces of shell-casing came buzzing down all around. 'They calls them the musical instruments,' said the sergeant. 'Damn them,' said Frank Jones-Bateman, who had a cut in his hand from a jagged little piece, 'the devils have started on me early'. 'Aye, they'll have a lot of fun with you before they're done, sir,' grinned the sergeant. Another shell came over. Every one threw himself down again, but it burst two hundred yards behind us. Only Sergeant Jones had remained on his feet and laughed at us. 'You're wasting yourselves, lads,' he said to the draft. 'Listen by the noise they make coming where they're going to burst.'

At Cambrin village, which was about a mile from the front trenches, we were taken into a ruined house. It had been a chemist's shop and the coloured glass lights were still in the window. It was the billet of the Welsh company quartermaster-sergeants. Here we were issued with gas-respirators and field dressings. This was the first respirator issued in France. It was a gauze-pad filled with chemically-treated cotton waste, to be tied across the mouth and nose. It seems it was useless against German gas. I never put it to the test. A week or two later came the 'smoke-helmet', a greasy grey-felt bag with a talc window to look through, but no mouth-piece. This also was probably ineffective against gas. The talc was always cracking and there were leaks where it was stitched into the helmet.

These were early days of trench-warfare, the days of the jam-tin bomb and the gas-pipe trench-mortar. It was before Lewis or Stokes guns, steel helmets, telescopic rifle-sights, gas-shells, pill-boxes, tanks, trench-raids, or any of the later improvements of trench warfare.

After a meal of bread, bacon, rum and bitter stewed

tea sickly with sugar, we went up through the broken trees to the east of the village and up a long trench to battalion headquarters. The trench was cut through red clay. I had a torch with me which I kept flashed on the ground. Hundreds of field mice and frogs were in the trench. They had fallen in and had no way out. The light dazzled them and we could not help treading on them. So I put the torch back in my pocket. We had no picture of what the trenches would be like, and were not far off the state of mind in which one young soldier joined us a week or two later. He called out very excitedly to old Burford who was cooking up a bit of stew in a dixie, apart from the others: 'Hi, mate, where's the battle? I want to do my bit.'

The trench was wet and slippery. The guide was giving hoarse directions all the time. 'Hole right.' 'Wire high.' 'Wire low.' 'Deep place here, sir.' 'Wire low.' I had never been told about the field telephone wires. They were fastened by staples to the side of the trench, and when it rained the staples were always falling out and the wire falling down and tripping people up. If it sagged too much one stretched it across the top of the trench to the other side to correct the sag, and then it would catch one's head. The holes were the sump-pits used for draining the trenches. We were now under rifle-fire. I always found rifle-fire more trying than shell-fire. The gunner was usually, I knew, firing not at people but at map-references – cross-roads, likely artillery positions, houses that suggested billets for troops, and so on. Even when an observation officer in an aeroplane or captive balloon or on a church spire was directing the gun-fire it seemed unaimed, somehow. But a rifle bullet even when fired blindly always had the effect of seeming aimed. And we could hear a shell coming and take some sort of cover, but the rifle bullet gave no warning. So though we learned not to duck to a rifle bullet, because once it was heard it must have missed, it gave us a worse feeling of danger. Rifle bullets in the open went hissing into the grass without much noise, but when we were in a trench the bullets, going over the hollow, made a tremendous crack. Bullets often struck the barbed wire in front of the trenches, which turned them and sent them spinning in a head-over-heels motion – ping! rockety-ockety-ockety-ockety into the woods behind.

Battalion headquarters was a dug-out in the reserve line about a quarter of a mile from the front companies. The colonel, a twice-wounded regular, shook hands with us and offered us the whisky bottle. He said that we were welcome, and hoped that we would soon grow to like the regiment as much as our own. It was a cosy dug-out for so early a stage of trench-warfare. (This sector had only recently been taken over from the French, who knew how to make themselves comfortable. It had been a territorial division of men in the forties who had a local armistice with the Germans opposite; there was no firing and apparently even civilian traffic through the lines.) There was an ornamental lamp, a clean cloth, and polished silver on the table. The colonel, adjutant, doctor, second-in-command, and signalling officer were at dinner. It was civilized cooking, with fresh meat and vegetables. Pictures were pasted on the walls, which were wall-papered; there were beds with spring mattresses, a gramophone, easy chairs. It was hard to reconcile this with accounts I had read of troops standing waist-deep in mud and gnawing a biscuit while shells burst all around. We were posted to our companies. I went to C Company. 'Captain

Dunn is your company commander,' said the adjutant. 'The soundest officer in the battalion. By the way, remind him that I want that list of D.C.M. recommendations for the last show sent in at once, but not more than two names, or else they won't give us any. Four is about the ration for the battalion in a dud show.'

Our guide took us up to the front line. We passed a group of men huddled over a brazier. They were wearing water-proof capes, for it had now started to rain, and cap-comforters, because the weather was cold. They were little men, daubed with mud, and they were talking quietly together in Welsh. Although they could see we were officers, they did not jump to their feet and salute. I thought that this was a convention of the trenches, and indeed I knew that it was laid down somewhere in the military textbooks that the courtesy of the salute was to be dispensed with in battle. But I was wrong; it was just slackness. We overtook a fatigue-party struggling up the trench loaded with timber lengths and bundles of sandbags, cursing plaintively as they slipped into sump-holes and entangled their burdens in the telephone wire. Fatigue-parties were always encumbered by their rifles and equipment, which it was a crime ever to have out of reach. When we had squeezed past this party we had to stand aside to let a stretcher-case past. 'Who's the poor bastard, Dai?' the guide asked the leading stretcher-bearer. 'Sergeant Gallagher,' Dai answered. 'He thought he saw a Fritz in No Man's Land near our wire, so the silly b—r takes one of them new issue percussion bombs and shoots it at 'im. Silly b—r aims too low, it hits the top of the parapet and bursts back. Deoul! man, it breaks his silly f—ing jaw and blows a great lump from his silly f—ing face, whatever. Poor silly b—r! Not worth

sweating to get him back! He's put paid to, whatever.'
The wounded man had a sandbag over his face. He was
dead when they got him back to the dressing-station. I
was tired out by the time I got to company headquarters. I was carrying a pack-valise like the men, and my
belt was hung with all the usual furnishings – revolver,
field-glasses, compass, whisky-flask, wire-cutters, periscope, and a lot more. A Christmas-tree that was
called. (These were the days in which officers went out
to France with swords and had them sharpened by the
armourer before sailing. But I had been advised to
leave my sword back in the billet where we had tea; I
never saw it again or bothered about it.) I was hot and
sweaty; my hands were sticky with the clay from the
side of the trench. C Company headquarters was a
two-roomed timber-built shelter in the side of a trench
connecting the front and support lines. Here were
tablecloth and lamp again, whisky-bottle and glasses,
shelves with books and magazines, a framed picture of
General Joffre, a large mirror, and bunks in the next
room. I reported to the company commander.

I had expected him to be a middle-aged man with a
breastful of medals, with whom I would have to be formal; but Dunn was actually two months younger than
myself. He was one of the fellowship of 'only survivors'. Captain Miller of the Black Watch in the same
division was another. Miller had only escaped from the
Rue du Bois massacre by swimming down a flooded
trench. He has carried on his surviving trade ever
since.* Only survivors have great reputations. Miller
used to be pointed at in the streets when the battalion

---

* I do not know what happened to Miller. This was written in the
summer of 1916. [RG]

was back in reserve billets. 'See that fellow. That's Jock Miller. Out from the start and hasn't got it yet.' Dunn had not let the war affect his morale at all. He greeted me very easily with: 'Well, what's the news from England? Oh sorry, first I must introduce you. This is Walker – clever chap, comes from Cambridge and fancies himself as an athlete. This is Jenkins, one of those patriotic chaps who chucked up his job to come here. This is Price, who only joined us yesterday, but we like him; he brought some damn good whisky with him. Well, how long is the war going to last and who's winning? We don't know a thing out here. And what's all this talk about war-babies? Price pretends he knows nothing about them.' I told them about the war and asked them about the trenches.

'About trenches,' said Dunn. 'Well, we don't know as much about trenches as the French do and not near as much as Fritz does. We can't expect Fritz to help, but the French might do something. They are greedy; they won't let us have the benefit of their inventions. What wouldn't we give for parachute-lights and their aerial torpedoes! But there's no connection between the two armies except when there's a battle on, and then we generally let each other down.

'When I was out here first, all that we did in the trenches was to paddle about in water and use our rifles. We didn't think of them as places to live in, they were just temporary inconveniences. Now we work all the time we are here, not only for safety but for health. Night and day. First, the fire-steps, then building traverses, improving the communication trenches, and so on; lastly, on our personal comfort-shelters and dugouts. There was a territorial battalion that used to relieve us. They were hopeless. They used to sit down in the trench and say: "Oh my God, this is the limit." They'd pull out pencil and paper and write home about it. Did no work on the traverses or on fire positions. Consequence – they lost half their men from frost-bite and rheumatism, and one day the Germans broke in and scuppered a lot more of them. They allowed the work we'd done in the trench to go to ruin and left the whole place like a sewage-farm for us to take over again. We were sick as muck. We reported them several times to brigade headquarters, but they never got any better. Slack officers, of course. Well, they got smashed, as I say, and were sent away to be lines-of-communication troops. Now we work with the First South Wales Borderers. They're all right. Awful chaps those territorial swine. Usen't to trouble about latrines at all; left food about and that encouraged rats; never filled a sandbag. I only once saw a job of work that they did. That was a steel loop-hole they put in. But they put it facing square to the front and quite unmasked, so they had two men killed at it – absolute death-trap. About our chaps. They're all right, but not as right as they ought to be. The survivors of the show ten days ago are feeling pretty low, and the big new draft doesn't know anything yet.'

'Listen,' said Walker, 'there's too much firing going on. The men have got the wind up over something. Waste of ammunition, and if Fritz knows we're jumpy he'll give us an extra bad time. I'll go up and stop them.'

Dunn went on. 'These Welshmen are peculiar. They won't stand being shouted at. They'll do anything if you explain the reason for it. They will do and die, but they have to know their reason why. The best way to make them behave is not to give them too much time to think. Work them off their feet. They are good workmen. Officers must work too, not only direct the work. Our time-table is like this. Breakfast at eight o'clock in the morning, clean trenches and inspect rifles, work all morning; lunch at twelve, work again from one till about six, when the men feed again. "Stand-to" at dusk for about an hour, work all night, "stand-to" for an hour before dawn. That's the general programme. Then there's sentry duty. The men do two-hour sentry spells, then work two hours, then sleep two hours. At night sentries are doubled, so our working parties are smaller. We officers are on duty all day and divide up the night in three-hourly watches.' He looked at his wrist watch. 'I say,' he said, 'that carrying-party must have got the R.E. stuff by now. Time we all got to work. Look here, Graves, you lie down and have a doss on that bunk. I want you to take the watch before "stand-to." I'll wake you up and show you round. Where the hell's my revolver? I don't like to go out without that. Hello, Walker, what was wrong?'

Walker laughed. 'A chap from the new draft. He had never fired his musketry course at Cardiff, and to-night he fired ball for the first time. It seemed to go to his head. He'd had a brother killed up at Ypres and he said he was going to avenge him. So he blazed off all his own ammunition at nothing, and two bandoliers out of the ammunition-box besides. They call him the Human Maxim now. His fore-sight's misty with heat. Corporal Parry should have stopped him; but he was just leaning up against the traverse and shrieking with laughter. I gave them both a good cursing. Some other new chaps started blazing away, too. Fritz retaliated with machine-guns and whizz-bangs. No casualties. I don't know why. It's all quiet now. Everybody ready?'

They went out and I rolled up in my blanket and fell asleep. Dunn woke me about one o'clock. 'Your watch,' he said. I jumped out of the bunk with a rustle of straw; my feet were sore and clammy in my boots. I was cold, too. 'Here's the rocket-pistol and a few flares. Not a bad night. It's stopped raining. Put your equipment on over your raincoat or you won't be able to get at your revolver. Got a torch? Good. About this flare business. Don't use the pistol too much. We haven't many flares, and if there's an attack we will want as many as we can get. But use it if you think that there is something doing. Fritz is always sending up flare lights, he's got as many as he wants.'

He showed me round the line. The battalion front-age was about eight hundred yards. Each company held two hundred of these with two platoons in the front line and two platoons in the support line about a hundred yards back. Dunn introduced me to the platoon sergeants, more particularly to Sergeant Eastmond of the platoon to which I was posted. He asked Sergeant Eastmond to give me any information that I wanted, then went back to sleep, telling me to wake him up at once if anything was wrong. I was left in charge of the line. Sergeant Eastmond was busy with a working-party, so I went round by myself. The men of the working-party, who were building up the traverses with sandbags (a traverse, I learned, was a safety-buttress in the trench), looked curiously at me. They were filling sandbags with earth, piling them up bricklayer fashion, with headers and stretchers alternating, then patting them flat with spades. The sentries stood on the fire-step at the corners of the traverses, stamping their feet and blowing on their fingers. Every now and then they peered over the top for a few seconds. Two parties, each of an N.C.O. and two men, were out in the company listening-posts, connected with the front trench by a sap about fifty yards long. The German front line was about three hundred yards beyond them. From berths hollowed in the sides of the trench and curtained with sandbags came the grunt of sleeping men.

I jumped up on the fire-step beside the sentry and cautiously raising my head stared over the parapet. I could see nothing except the wooden pickets supporting our protecting barbed-wire entanglement and a dark patch or two of bushes beyond. The darkness seemed to move and shake about as I looked at it; the bushes started travelling, singly at first, then both together. The pickets were doing the same. I was glad of the sentry beside me; his name, he told me, was Beaumont. 'They're quiet to-night, sir,' he said, 'a relief going on; I think so, surely.' I said: 'It's funny how those bushes seem to move.' 'Aye, they do play queer tricks. Is this your first spell in trenches, sir?' A German flare shot up, broke into bright flame, dropped slowly and went hissing into the grass just behind our trench, showing up the bushes and pickets. Instinctively I moved. 'It's bad to do that, sir,' he said, as a rifle bullet cracked and seemed to pass right between us. 'Keep still, sir, and they can't spot you. Not but what a flare is a bad thing to have fall on you. I've seen them burn a hole in a man.'

I spent the rest of my watch in acquainting myself with the geography of the trench-section, finding how easy it was to get lost among *culs de sac* and disused alleys. Twice I overshot the company frontage and wandered among the Munsters on the left. Once I tripped and fell with a splash into deep mud. At last my watch was ended with the first signs of dawn. I passed the word along the line for the company to stand-to arms. The N.C.O's whispered hoarsely into the dug-outs: 'Stand-to, stand-to,' and out the men tumbled with their rifles in their hands. As I went towards company headquarters to wake the officers I saw a man lying on his face in a machine-gun shelter. I stopped and said: 'Stand-to, there.' I flashed my torch on him and saw that his foot was bare. The machine-gunner beside him said: 'No good talking to him, sir.' I asked: 'What's wrong? What's he taken his boot and sock off for?' I was ready for anything odd in the trenches. 'Look for yourself, sir,' he said. I shook the man by the arm and noticed suddenly that the back of his head was blown out. The first corpse that I saw in France was this suicide. He had taken off his boot and sock to pull the trigger of his rifle with his toe; the muzzle was in his mouth. 'Why did he do it?' I said. 'He was in the last push, sir, and that sent him a bit queer, and on top of that he got bad news from Limerick about his girl and another chap.' He was not a Welshman, but belonged to the Munsters; their machine-guns were at the extreme left of our company. The suicide had already been reported and two Irish officers came up. 'We've had two or three of these lately,' one of them told me. Then he said to the other: 'While I remember, Callaghan, don't forget to write to his next-of-kin. Usual sort of letter, cheer them up, tell them he died a soldier's death, anything you like. I'm not going to report it as suicide.'

At stand-to rum and tea were served out. I had a look at the German trenches through a periscope – a streak of sandbags four hundred yards away. Some of these were made of coloured stuff, whether for camouflage or from a shortage of plain canvas I do not know. There was no sign of the enemy, except for a wisp or two of wood-smoke where they, too, were boiling up a hot drink. Between us and them was a flat meadow with cornflowers, marguerites and poppies growing in the long grass, a few shell holes, the bushes I had seen the night before, the wreck of an aeroplane, our barbed wire and theirs. A thousand yards away was a big ruined house, behind that a redbrick village (Auchy), poplars and haystacks, a tall chimney, another village (Haisnes). Half-right was a pithead and smaller slag-heaps. La Bassée lay half-left; the sun caught the weathervane of the church and made it twinkle.

I went off for a sleep. The time between stand-to and breakfast was the easy part of the day. The men who were not getting in a bit of extra sleep sat about talking and smoking, writing letters home, cleaning their rifles, running their thumb-nails up the seams of their shirts to kill the lice, gambling. Lice were a standing joke. Young Bumford handed me one like this. 'We was just having an argument as to whether it was best to kill the old ones or the young ones, sir. Morgan here says that if you kill the old ones, the young ones will die of grief, but Parry here, sir, he says that the young ones are easier to kill and you can catch the old ones when they come to the funeral.' He appealed to me as an arbiter. 'You've been to college, sir, haven't you?' I said: 'Yes, I had, but so had Crawshay Bailey's brother Norwich.' This was held to be a wonderfully witty answer. *Crawshay Bailey* is one of the idiotic songs of Wales. (Crawshay Bailey himself 'had an engine and he couldn't make it go', and all his relations in the song had similar shortcomings. Crawshay Bailey's brother Norwich, for instance, was fond of oatmeal porridge, and was sent to Cardiff College, for to get a bit of knowledge.) After that I had no trouble with the platoon at all.

Breakfast at company headquarters was bacon, eggs, coffee, toast and marmalade. There were three chairs and two ammunition-boxes to sit on. Accustomed to company commanders in England not taking their junior officers into their confidence, I was struck by the way that questions of the day were settled at meal-times by a sort of board-meeting with Dunn as chairman. On this first morning there was a long debate as to the best way of keeping sentries awake. Dunn finally decided to issue a company order against sentries leaning up against the traverse; it made them sleepy. Besides, when they fired their rifles the flash would come always from the same place. The Germans might fix a rifle on the spot after a time. I told Dunn of the bullet that came between Beaumont and myself. 'Sounds like a fixed rifle,' he said, 'because not one aimed shot in a hundred comes as close as that at night. And we had a chap killed in that very traverse the night we came in.' The Bavarian Guards Reserve were opposite us at the time and their shooting was good. They had complete control of the sniping situation.

Dunn began telling me the characters of the men in my platoon; also which N.C.O.'s were trustworthy and which had to be watched. He was going on to tell me just how much to expect from the men at my platoon inspection of rifles and equipment, when there was a sudden alarm. Dunn's servant came rushing in, his eyes blank with horror and excitement: 'Gas, sir, gas! They're using gas.' 'My God!' said Price. We all looked at Dunn. He said imperturbably: 'Very well, Kingdom, bring me my respirator from the other room, and another pot of marmalade.' This was only one of many gas alarms. It originated with smoke from the German trenches where breakfast was also going on; we knew the German meal-times by a slackening down of rifle-fire. Gas was a nightmare. Nobody believed in the efficacy of the respirators, though we were told that they were proof against any gas the enemy could send over. Pink army forms marked 'Urgent' were constantly arriving from headquarters to explain how to use these contrivances. They were all contradictory. First the respirators were to be kept soaking wet, then they were to be kept dry, then they were to be worn in a satchel, then, again, the satchel was not to be used.

Frank Jones-Bateman came to visit me from the company on our right. He mentioned with a false ease that he had shot a man just before breakfast: 'Sights at four hundred,' he said. He was a quiet boy of nineteen. He had just left Rugby and had a scholarship waiting for him at Clare, Cambridge. His nickname was 'Silent Night'.

XIII

Here are extracts from letters that I wrote at this time:[1]

21st May 1915. – Back in billets again at a coal-mining village called La Bourse. It is not more than three miles and a half from the trenches, but the mines are still working. As we came out of the trenches the Germans were shelling the wood by Cambrin village, searching for one of our batteries. I don't think they got it, but it was fun to see the poplar trees being lopped down like tulips when the whizz-bangs hit them square. When we marched along the *pavé* road from Cambrin the men straggled about out of step and out of fours. Their feet were sore from having had their boots on for a week – they only have one spare pair of socks issued to them. I enclose a list of their minimum load, which weighs about sixty pounds. A lot of extras get put on top of this – rations, pick or shovel, periscope, and their own souvenirs to take home on leave:

Greatcoat	1	Cardigan	1
Tin, mess	1	Cap, fatigue comforter	1
„ cover	1	Pay-book	1
Shirt	1	Disc, identity	1
Socks, pair	1	Waterproof sheet	1
Soap	1	Tin of grease	1

Towel 1	Field-service dressing 1
Housewife 1	Respirator 1
Holdall 1	Spine protector 1
Razor 1	Jack knife 1
„ case 1	Set of equipment.
Lather brush 1	Rounds ammunition 150
Comb 1	Rifle and bayonet.
Fork 1	Rifle cover 1
Knife 1	Oil bottle and pull-through.
Spoon 1	Entrenching tool 1
Tooth brush 1	Laces, pair 1

Well, anyhow, marching on cobbled roads is difficult, so when a staff-officer came by in a Rolls-Royce and cursed us for bad march-discipline I felt like throwing something at him. Trench soldiers hate the staff and the staff know it. The principal disagreement seems to be about the extent to which trench conditions should modify discipline. The La Bourse miners are old men and boys dressed in sloppy blue clothes with bulging pockets. There are shell craters all around the pit-head. I am billeted with a fatherly old man called Monsieur Hojdés, who has three marriageable daughters; one of them lifted up her skirt to show me a shell-wound on her thigh that laid her up last winter.

22nd May. – A colossal bombardment by the French at Souchez, a few miles away – continuous roar of artillery, coloured flares, shells bursting all along the ridge by Notre Dame de Lorette. I couldn't sleep. It went on all night. Instead of dying away it grew and grew till the whole air rocked and shook; the sky was lit up with huge flashes. I lay in my feather bed and sweated. This morning they tell me there was a big thunderstorm in the middle of the bombardment. But, as Walker says: 'Where the gunder ended and the thunder began was hard to say.' The men had hot baths at the mines and cleaned up generally. Their rifles are all in an advanced state of disrepair and many of their clothes are in rags, but neither can be replaced, we are told, until they are much worse. The platoon is billeted in a barn full of straw. Old Burford, who is so old that he refuses to sleep with the other men of the platoon, has found a doss in an out-building among some farm tools. In trenches he will sleep on the fire-step even in the rain rather than in a warm dug-out with the other men. He says that he remembers the C.O. when he was in long skirts. Young Bumford is the only man he'll talk to. The platoon is always ragging Bumford for his childish simplicity. Bumford plays up to it and begs them not to be too hard on 'a lad from the hills'.

23rd May. – We did company drill in the morning. Afterwards Jones-Bateman and I lay on the warm grass and watched the aeroplanes flying above the trenches pursued by a trail of white shrapnel puffs. In the evening I was detailed to take out a working-party to Vermelles les Noyelles to work on a second line of defence – trench digging and putting up barbed wire under an R.E. officer. But the ground was hard and the men were tired out when they got back about two o'clock in the morning. They sang songs all the way home. They have one about Company Quartermaster-Sergeant Finnigan:

> Coolness under fire,
> Coolness under fire,
> Mentioned in dispatches
> For pinching the company rations,
> Coolness under fire.

Now he's on the peg,
Now he's on the peg,
Mentioned in dispatches
For drinking the company rum,
Now he's on the peg.

The chorus is:

Whiter than the milky cokernuts,
Whiter than the milky cokernuts,
Wash me in the water
That you washed your dirty daughter in
And I shall be whiter than the milky cokernuts.
   Nuts,
   Nuts,
Oooooh nuts.

Finnigan doesn't mind the libel at all.

This is what happened the other day. Two young miners, in another company, disliked their sergeant, who had a down on them and gave them all the most dirty and dangerous jobs. When they were in billets he crimed them for things they hadn't done. So they decided to kill him. Later they reported at Battalion Orderly Room and asked to see the adjutant. This was irregular, because a private is not allowed to speak to an officer without an N.C.O. of his own company to act as go-between. The adjutant happened to see them and said: 'Well, what is it you want?' Smartly slapping the small-of-the-butt of their sloped rifles they said: 'We've come to report, sir, that we are very sorry but we've shot our company sergeant-major.' The adjutant said: 'Good heavens, how did that happen?' They answered: 'It was an accident, sir.' 'What do you mean? Did you mistake him for a German?' 'No, sir, we mistook him for our platoon sergeant.' So they were both shot by a firing squad of their own company against the wall of a convent at Béthune. Their last words were the battalion rallying-cry: 'Stick it, the Welsh!' (They say that a certain Captain Haggard first used it in the battle of Ypres when he was mortally wounded.) The French military governor was present at the execution and made a little speech saying how gloriously British soldiers can die.

You would be surprised at the amount of waste that goes on in trenches. Ration biscuits are in general use as fuel for boiling up dixies, because fuel is scarce. Our machine-gun crews boil their hot water by firing off belt after belt of machine-gun ammunition at no particular target, just generally spraying the German line. After several pounds' worth of ammunition has been used, the water in the guns – they are water-cooled – begins to boil. They say they make German ration and carrying parties behind the line pay for their early-morning cup of tea. But the real charge will be on income-tax after the war.

24th May. – To-morrow we return to trenches. The men are pessimistic but cheerful. They all talk about getting a 'cushy' one to send them back to 'Blitey'. Blitey is, it seems, Hindustani for 'home'. My servant, Fry, who works in a paper-bag factory at Cardiff in civil life, has been telling me stories about cushy ones. Here are two of them. 'A bloke in the Munsters once wanted a cushy, so he waves his hand above the parapet to catch Fritz's attention. Nothing doing. He waves his arms about for a couple of minutes. Nothing doing, not a shot. He puts his elbows on the fire-step, hoists his body upside down and waves his legs about till he get blood to the head. Not a shot did old Fritz fire. "Oh," says the Munster man, "I don't believe there's a damn square-head there. Where's the German army to?" He has a peek over the top – crack! he gets it in the head. Finee.' Another story: 'Bloke in the Camerons wanted a cushy bad. Fed up and far from home, he was. He puts his hand over the top and gets his trigger finger taken off, and two more beside. That done the trick. He comes laughing through our lines by the old boutillery. "See, lads," he says, "I'm aff to bony Scotland. Is it na a beauty?" But on the way down the trench to the dressing-station he forgets to stoop low where the old sniper was working. *He* gets it through the head too. Finee. We laugh fit to die.'

To get a cushy one is all that the old hands think of. Only twelve men have been with the battalion from the beginning and they are all transport men except one, Beaumont, a man in my platoon. The few old hands who went through the last fight infect the new men with pessimism; they don't believe in the war, they don't believe in the staff. But at least they would follow their officers anywhere, because the officers happen to be a decent lot. They look forward to a battle because a battle gives more chances of a cushy one, in the legs or arms, than trench warfare. In trench warfare the proportion of head wounds is much greater. Haking commands this division. He's the man who wrote the standard textbook, *Company Training*. The last shows have not been suitable ones for company commanders to profit by his directions. He's a decent man; he came round this morning to an informal inspection of the battalion and shook hands with the survivors. There were tears in his eyes. Sergeant Smith swore half-aloud: 'Bloody lot of use that is, busts up his bloody division and then weeps over what's bloody left.' Well, it was nothing to do with me; I didn't allow myself to feel either for the general or for the sergeant. It is said here that Haking has told General French that the division's *morale* has gone completely. So far as I can see that is not accurate; the division will fight all right but without any enthusiasm. It is said too that when the new army comes out the division will be withdrawn and used on lines of communication for some months at least. I don't believe it. I am sure no one will mind smashing up over and over again the divisions that are used to being smashed up. The general impression here is that the new-army divisions can't be of much military use.

28th May. – In trenches among the Cuinchy brick-stacks. Not my idea of trenches. There has been a lot of fighting hereabouts. The trenches have made themselves rather than been made, and run inconsequently in and out of the big thirty-foot high stacks of brick; it is most confusing. The parapet of one of the trenches which we do not occupy is built up with ammunition-boxes and corpses. Everything here is wet and smelly. The lines are very close. The Germans have half the brick-stacks and we have the other half. Each side snipes down from the top of its brick-stacks into the other's trenches. This is also a great place for rifle-grenades and trench-mortars. We can't reply properly to these; we have only a meagre supply of rifle-grenades and nothing to equal the German sausage mortar bomb. This morning about breakfast time, just as I came out of my dug-out, a rifle-grenade landed within six feet of me. For some reason, instead of falling on its head and exploding, it landed with its stick in the wet clay and stood there looking at me. They are difficult to see coming; they are shot from a rifle, with its butt on the ground, tilted, and go up a long way before they turn over and come down. I can't understand why this particular rifle-grenade fell as it did; the chances were impossibly against it.

Sausages are easy to see and dodge, but they make a terrible noise when they drop. We have had about ten casualties in our company to-day from them. I find that I have extraordinarily quick reactions to danger; but every one gets like that. We can sort out all the different explosions and disregard all the ones that don't concern us – the artillery duel, machine-gun fire at the next company to us, desultory rifle-fire. But the faint plop! of the mortar that sends off the sausage or the muffled rifle noise when a grenade is fired, we pick out at once. The men are much afraid, yet always joking. The company sergeant-major stands behind Number Eleven brick-stack and shoots at the sausages with a rifle as they come over; trying to explode them in the air. He says that it's better than pigeon-shooting. He hasn't hit one yet. Last night a lot of stuff was flying about, including shrapnel. I heard one shell whish-whishing towards me. I dropped flat. It burst just over the trench. My ears sang as though there were gnats in them and a bright scarlet light shone over everything. My shoulder was twisted in falling and I thought I had been hit, but I hadn't been. The vibration made my chest sing, too, in a curious way, and I lost my sense of equilibrium. I was much ashamed when the sergeant-major came along the trench and found me on all fours, because I couldn't stand up straight. It was at a place where 'Petticoat Lane' runs into 'Lowndes Square'.

There has been a dead man lying on the fire-step

waiting to be taken down to the cemetery to-night. He was a sanitary-man, killed last night in the open while burying lavatory stuff between our front and support lines. His arm was stretched out and, when he was got in, it was still stiff, so that when they put him on the fire-step his stiff arm stretched right across the trench. His comrades joke as they push it out of the way to get by. 'Out of the light, you old bastard. Do you own this bloody trench?' Or they shake hands with him famil-iarly. 'Put it there, Billy Boy.' Of course, they're miners and accustomed to death. They have a very limited morality, but they keep to it. They will, for instance, rob anyone, of anything, except a man in their own platoon; they will treat every stranger as an enemy until he is proved their friend, and then there is nothing they won't do for him. They are lecherous, the young ones at least, but without the false shame of the Eng-lish lecher. I had a letter to censor the other day written by a lance-corporal to his wife. He said that the French girls were nice to sleep with, so she mustn't worry on his account, but that he far preferred sleeping with her and missed her a great deal.

6th June. – We have been billeted in Béthune, a fair-sized town about seven miles or so behind the front line. There is everything one wants, a swimming bath, all sorts of shops, especially a cake-shop, the best I've ever met, a hotel where you can get a really good dinner, and a theatre where we have brigade 'gaffs'. I saw a notice this morning on a building by the Béthune-La Bassée canal – 'Troops are forbidden to bomb fish. By order of the Town Major.' Béthune is very little knocked about, except a part called Fau-bourg d'Arras, near the station. I am billeted with a family called Averlant Paul, in the Avenue de Bruay, people of the official class. They are refugees from Poimbert. There are two little boys and an elder sister, who is in what corresponds with the under-fifth of the local high-school. She was worried last night over her lessons and asked me to help her write out the theory of decimal division. She showed me the notes she had taken; they were full of abbreviations. I asked why she'd used abbreviations. She said: 'The lady professor talked very fast because we were much hurried.' 'Why were you hurried?' 'Oh, because part of the school is used as a billet for the troops and the Germans were shelling it, and we were always having to take shelter in the cellar, and when we came back each time there was less and less time left.'

9th June. – I am beginning to realize how lucky I was in my gentle introduction to the trenches at Cambrin. We are now in a nasty salient a little to the south of the brick-stacks, where casualties are always heavy. The company had seventeen casualties yesterday from bombs and grenades. The front trench averages thirty yards from the Germans. Today, at one part, which is only twenty yards away from an occupied German sap, I came along whistling *The Farmer's Boy*, to keep up my spirits, when suddenly I saw a group bending over a man lying at the bottom of the trench. He was making a snoring noise mixed with animal groans. At my feet was the cap he had worn, splashed with his brains. I had never seen human brains before; I had somehow regarded them as a poetical figment. One can joke with a badly-wounded man and congratulate him on being out of it. One can disregard a dead man. But even a miner can't make a joke that sounds like a joke over a man who takes three hours to die after the top part of his head has been taken off by a bullet fired at twenty yards range. Beaumont, of whom I told you in my last letter, was also killed. He was the last unwounded survivor of the original battalion, except for the transport men. He had his legs blown against his back. Every one was swearing angrily, then an R.E. officer came up and told me that there was a tunnel driven under the German front line and that if we wanted to do a bit of bombing, now was the time. So he sent the mine up – it was not a big one, he said, but it made a tremendous noise and covered us with dirt – and the chaps waited for a few seconds for the other Germans to rush up to help the wounded away and then they chucked all the bombs they had.

Beaumont had been telling me how he had won about five pounds in the sweepstake after the Rue du Bois show. It was a sweepstake of the sort that leaves no bitterness behind it. Before a show the platoon pools all its available cash and the winners, who are the survivors, divide it up afterwards. Those who are killed can't complain, the wounded would have given far more than that to escape as they have, and the unwounded regard the money as a consolation prize for still being here.

24th June. – We are billeted in the cellars of Vermelles, which was taken and re-taken eight times last October. There is not a single house undamaged in the place. I suppose it once had two or three thousand inhabitants. It is beautiful now in a fantastic way. We came up two nights ago; there was a moon shining behind the houses and the shells had broken up all the hard lines. Next morning we found the deserted gardens of the town very pleasant to walk about in; they are quite overgrown and flowers have seeded themselves about wildly. Red cabbages and roses and madonna lilies are the chief ornaments. There is one garden with currant bushes in it. I and the company sergeant-major started eating along the line towards each other without noticing each other. When we did, we both remembered our dignity, he as a company sergeant-major and I as an officer. He saluted, I acknowledged the salute, we both walked away. After a minute or two we both came back hoping the coast was clear and again, after an exchange of salutes, had to leave the currants and pretend that we were merely admiring the flowers. I don't quite know why I was feeling like that. The company sergeant-major was a regular and it was natural in him, and I suppose that it was courtesy to his scruples that made me stop. Anyhow, along came a couple of privates and stripped the bushes clean.

This afternoon we had a cricket match, officers versus sergeants, in an enclosure between some houses out of observation from the enemy. The front line is perhaps three quarters of a mile away. I made top score, twenty-four; the bat was a bit of a rafter, the ball was a piece of rag tied round with string, and the wicket was a parrot cage with the grisly remains of a parrot inside. It had evidently died of starvation when the French evacuated the town. The corpse was perfectly clean and dry and I recalled a verse of Skelton's:

> Parrot is a fair bird for a ladie.
> God of His goodness him framed and wrought.
> When parrot is dead he doth not putrify,
> Yea, all things mortal shall turn unto nought
> Save mannës soul which Christ so dear bought,

That never can die, nor never die shall.
Make much of parrot, that popajay royal.[2]

The match was broken up suddenly by machine-gun fire. It was not aimed at us; the Germans were shooting at one of our aeroplanes and the bullets falling down from a great height had a penetrative power greater than an ordinary spent bullet.

This is a very idle life except for night-digging on the reserve line. By day there is nothing to do. We can't drill because it is too near the German lines, and there is no fortification work to be done in the village. To-day two spies were shot. A civilian who had hung on in a cellar and had, apparently, been flashing news, and a German soldier disguised as an R.E. corporal who was found tampering with the telephone wires. We officers spend a lot of time practising revolver-shooting. Jenkins brought out a beautiful target from the only undestroyed living-room in our billet area. It was a glass case full of artificial fruit and flowers, so we put it up on a post at fifty yards range. He said: 'I've always wanted to smash one of these damn things. My aunt had one. It's the sort of thing that *would* survive an intense bombardment.' For a moment I felt a tender impulse to rescue it. But I smothered it. So we had five shots each, in turn. Nobody could hit it. So at last we went up to within twenty yards of it and fired a volley. Someone hit the post and that knocked it off into the grass. Jenkins said: 'Damn the thing, it must be bewitched. Let's take it back.' The glass was unbroken, but some of the fruit had come loose. Walker said: 'No, it's in pain; we must put it out of its suffering.' He gave it the *coup de grâce* from close quarters.

There is an old Norman church here, very much

broken. What is left of the tower is used as a forward observation post by the artillery. I counted eight unexploded shells sticking into it. I went in with Jenkins; the floor was littered with rubbish, broken masonry, smashed chairs, ripped canvas pictures (some of them look several hundreds of years old), bits of images and crucifixes, muddied church vestments rotting in what was once the vestry. Only a few pieces of stained glass remained fixed in the edges of the windows. I climbed up by way of the altar to the east window and found a piece about the size of a plate. I gave it to Jenkins. 'Souvenir,' I said. When he held it up to the light it was St. Peter's hand with the keys of heaven; medieval glass. 'I'm sending this home,' he said. As we went out we met two men of the Munsters. They were Irish Catholics. They thought it sacrilegious for Jenkins to be taking the glass away. One of them said: 'Shouldn't take that, sir; it will bring you no luck.'*

Walker was ragging Dunn this evening. 'I believe you'll be sorry when the war's over, skipper. Your occupation will be gone and you'll have to go back on the square at the depot for six months and learn how to form fours regimentally. You missed that little part of the show when you left Sandhurst and came straight here. You'll be a full colonel by then, of course. I'll give the sergeant-major half a crown to make you really sweat. I'll be standing in civvies at the barrack-gate laughing at you.'

There is a company commander here called Furber. His nerves are in pieces, and somebody played a dirty joke on him the other day – rolling a bomb, undetonated, of course, down the cellar steps to frighten him.

* Jenkins was killed not long after. [RG]

This was thought a great joke. Furber is the greatest pessimist out here. He's laid a bet[3] with the adjutant that the trench lines will not be more than a mile from where they are in this sector two years hence. Every one laughs at Furber, but they like him because he sings sentimental cockney songs at the brigade gaffs when we are back at Béthune.

XIV

Now as the summer advanced there came new types of
bombs and trench-mortars, heavier shelling, improved
gas-masks and a general tightening up of discipline.
We saw the first battalions of the new army and felt
like scarecrows by comparison. We went in and out of
the Cambrin and Cuinchy trenches, with billets in Béthune and the neighbouring villages. By this time I had
caught the pessimism of the division. Its spirit in the
trenches was largely defensive; the policy was not to
stir the Germans into more than their usual hostility.
But casualties were still very heavy for trench warfare.
Pessimism made everyone superstitious. I became superstitious too: I found myself believing in signs of the
most trivial nature. Sergeant Smith, my second sergeant, told me of my predecessor in command of the
platoon. 'He was a nice gentleman, sir, but very wild.
Just before the Rue du Bois show he says to me: "By
the way, sergeant, I'm going to get killed to-morrow. I
know that. And I know that you're going to be all
right. So see that my kit goes back to my people. You'll
find their address in my pocket-book. You'll find five
hundred francs there too. Now remember this, Sergeant Smith, you keep a hundred francs yourself and
divide up the rest among the chaps left." He says: "Send
my pocket-book back with my other stuff, Sergeant

Smith, but for God's sake burn my diary. They mustn't see that. I'm going to get it *here*!" He points to his forehead. And that's how it was. He got it through the forehead all right. I sent the stuff back to his parents. I divided up the money and I burnt the diary.'

One day I was walking along a trench at Cambrin when I suddenly dropped flat on my face; two seconds later a whizz-bang struck the back of the trench exactly where I had been. The sergeant who was with me, walking a few steps ahead, rushed back: 'Are you killed, sir?' The shell was fired from a battery near Auchy only a thousand yards away, so that it must have arrived before the sound of the gun. How did I know that I should throw myself on my face?

I saw a ghost at Béthune. He was a man called Private Challoner who had been at Lancaster with me and again in F Company at Wrexham. When he went out with a draft to join the First Battalion he shook my hand and said: 'I'll meet you again in France, sir.' He had been killed at Festubert in May and in June he passed by our C Company billet where we were just having a special dinner to celebrate our safe return from Cuinchy. There was fish, new potatoes, green peas, asparagus, mutton chops, strawberries and cream, and three bottles of Pommard. Challoner looked in at the window, saluted and passed on. There was no mistaking him or the cap-badge he was wearing. There was no Royal Welch battalion billeted within miles of Béthune at the time. I jumped up and looked out of the window, but saw nothing except a fag-end smoking on the pavement. Ghosts were numerous in France at the time.

There was constant mining going on in this Cambrin-Cuinchy sector. We had the prospect of being blown up at any moment. An officer of the R.E. tunnelling company was awarded the Victoria Cross while we were here. A duel of mining and counter-mining was going on. The Germans began to undermine his original boring, so he rapidly tunnelled underneath them. It was touch and go who would get the mine ready first. He won. But when he detonated it from the trench by an electric lead, nothing happened. He ran down again into the mine, retamped the charge, and was just back in time to set it off before the Germans. I had been into the upper boring on the previous day. It was about twenty feet under the German lines. At the end of the gallery I found a Welsh miner, one of our own men who had transferred to the Royal Engineers, on listening duty. He cautioned me to silence. I could distinctly hear the Germans working somewhere underneath. He whispered: 'So long as they work, I don't mind; it's when they stop.' He did his two-hour spell by candle-light. It was very stuffy. He was reading a book. The mining officer had told me that they were allowed to read; it didn't interfere with their listening. It was a paper-backed novelette called *From Mill Girl to Duchess*. The men of the tunnelling companies were notorious thieves, by the way. They would snatch things up from the trench and scurry off with them into their borings; just like mice.

After one particularly bad spell of trenches I got bad news in a letter from Charterhouse. Bad news in the trenches might affect a man in either of two ways. It might drive him to suicide (or recklessness amounting to suicide), or it might seem trivial in comparison with present experiences and be disregarded. But unless his leave was due he was helpless. A year later, when I was in trenches in the same sector, an officer of the North Staffordshire Regiment had news from home that his wife was living with another man. He went out on a raid the same night and was either killed or captured; so the men with him said. There had been a fight and they had come back without him. Two days later he was arrested at Béthune trying to board a leave-train to go home; he had intended to shoot up the wife and her lover. He was court-martialled for deserting in the face of the enemy, but the court was content to cashier him. He went as a private soldier to another regiment. I do not know what happened afterwards.

The bad news was about Dick, saying that he was not at all the innocent sort of fellow I took him for. He was as bad as anyone could be. The letter was written by a cousin of mine who was still at Charterhouse. I tried not to believe it. I remembered that he owed me a grudge and decided that this was a very cruel act of spite. Dick's letters had been my greatest stand-by all these months when I was feeling low; he wrote every week, mostly about poetry. They were something solid and clean to set off against the impermanence of trench life and the uncleanness of sex-life in billets. I was now back in Béthune. Two officers of another company had just been telling me how they had slept, in the same room, one with the mother and one with the daughter. They had tossed for the mother because the daughter was a 'yellow-looking little thing like a lizard'. And the Red Lamp, the army brothel, was round the corner in the main street. I had seen a queue of a hundred and fifty men waiting outside the door, each to have his short turn with one or the other of the three women in the house. My servant, who had been in the queue, told me that the charge was ten francs a man – about eight shillings at that time. Each woman served nearly a battalion of men every week for as long as she lasted.

The assistant provost-marshal had told me that three weeks was the usual limit, 'after which the woman retires on her earnings, pale but proud'. I was always being teased because I would not sleep even with the nicer girls. And I excused myself, not on moral grounds or on grounds of fastidiousness, but in the only way they could understand: I said that I didn't want a dose. A good deal of talk in billets was about the peculiar bed-manners of the French women. 'She was very nice and full of games. I said to her: "S'il vous plaît, ôtes-toi la chemise, ma chérie." But she wouldn't. She said, "Oh no'-non, mon lieutenant. Ce n'est pas convenable." ' I was glad when we were back in trenches. And there I had a more or less reassuring letter from Dick. He told me that I was right, that my cousin had a spite against him and me, that he had been ragging about in a silly way, but that there was not much harm to it; he was very sorry and would stop it for the sake of our friendship.

At the end of July, I and Robertson, one of the other five Royal Welch officers who had been attached to the Welsh, got orders to proceed to the Laventie sector, some miles to the north. We were to report to the Second Battalion of the Royal Welch Fusiliers. Frank Jones-Bateman and Hanmer Jones, two more of us, went to the First Battalion. The remaining two of the six had already gone back, McLellan sick and Watkin with bomb wounds that have kept him limping ever since. We were sorry to say good-bye to the men; they all crowded round to shake hands and wish us luck. And we felt a little sorry too that we had to start all over again getting to know a new company and new regimental customs. But it would be worth it, to be with our own regiment. Robertson and I agreed to take our journey as leisurely as possible. Laventie was only seventeen miles away, but our orders were to go there by train; so a mess-cart took us down to Béthune. We asked the railway transport officer what trains he had to Laventie. He told us one was going in a few minutes; we decided to miss it. There was no train after that until the next day, so we stopped the night at the Hôtel de la France. (The Prince of Wales, who was a lieutenant in the Fortieth Siege Battery, was billeted there sometimes. He was a familiar figure in Béthune. I only spoke to him once; it was in the public bath, where he and I were the only bathers one morning. He was graciously pleased to remark how emphatically cold[1] the water was and I loyally assented that he was emphatically right. We were very pink and white and did exercises on the horizontal bar afterwards. I joked to Frank about it: 'I have just met our future King in a bath.' Frank said: 'I can trump that. Two days ago I had a friendly talk with him in the A.S.C. latrines.' The Prince's favourite rendezvous was the *Globe*, a café in the Béthune market square reserved for British officers and French civilians; principally spies by the look of them. I once heard him complaining indignantly that General French had refused to let him go up into the line.)

The next day we caught our train. It took us to a junction, the name of which I forget. Here we spent a day walking about in the fields. There was no train until next day, when one took us on to Berguette, a railhead still a number of miles from Laventie, where a mess-cart was waiting for us in answer to a telegram we had sent. We finally rattled up to battalion headquarters in Laventie High Street. We had taken fifty-two hours to come seventeen miles. We saluted the adjutant smartly, gave our names, and said that we were Third Battalion officers posted to the regiment. He did not shake hands with us, offer us a drink, or give us a word of welcome. He said coldly: 'I see. Well, which of you is senior? Oh, never mind. Give your particulars to the regimental sergeant-major. Tell him to post whoever is senior to A Company and the other to B Company.' The sergeant major took our particulars. He introduced me to a young second-lieutenant of A Company, to which I was to go. He was a special reservist of the East Surrey Regiment and was known as the Surrey-man. He took me along to the company billet. As soon as we were out of earshot of battalion headquarters I asked him: 'What's wrong with the adjutant? Why didn't he shake hands or give me any sort of decent welcome?'

The Surrey-man said: 'Well, it's your regiment, not mine. They're all like that. You must realize that this is a regular battalion, one of the only four infantry battalions in France that is still more or less its old self. This is the Nineteenth Brigade, the luckiest in France. It has not been permanently part of any division, but used as army reserve to put in wherever a division has been badly knocked. So, except for the retreat, where it lost about a company, and Fromelles, where it lost half of what was left, it has been practically undamaged. A lot of the wounded have rejoined since. All our company commanders are regulars, and so are all our N.C.O.'s. The peace-time custom of taking no notice of newly-joined officers is still more or less kept up for the first six months. It's bad enough for the Sandhurst chaps, it's worse for special reservists like you and Rugg and Robertson, it's worse still for outsiders like me from another regiment.' We were going

down the village street. The men sitting about on the
door-steps jumped up smartly to attention as we passed
and saluted with a fixed stony glare. They were magnificent looking men. Their uniforms were spotless,
their equipment khaki-blancoed and their buttons and
cap-badges twinkling. We reached company headquarters, where I reported to my company commander,
Captain G. O. Thomas. He was a regular of seventeen
years' service, a well-known polo-player, and a fine soldier. This is the order that he would himself have
preferred. He shook hands without a word, waved me
to a chair, offered a cigarette and continued writing his
letter. I found later that A was the best company I
could have struck.

The Surrey-man asked me to help him censor some
company letters before going over to the battalion
mess for lunch; they were more literate than the ones in
the Welsh regiment, but duller. On the way to the mess
he told me more about the battalion. He asked me
whether it was my first time out. 'I was attached to the
Second Welsh Regiment for three months; I commanded a company there for a bit.' 'Oh, were you?
Well, I'd advise you to say nothing at all about it, then
they'll not expect too much of you. They treat us like
dirt; in a way it will be worse for you than for me
because you're a full lieutenant. They'll resent that
with your short service. There's one lieutenant here of
six years' service and second-lieutenants who have
been out here since the autumn. They have already had
two Special Reserve captains foisted on them; they're
planning to get rid of them somehow. In the mess, if
you open your mouth or make the slightest noise the
senior officers jump down your throat. Only officers of
the rank of captain are allowed to drink whisky or turn

on the gramophone. We've got to jolly well keep still and look like furniture. It's just like peace time. Mess bills are very high; the mess was in debt at Quetta last year and we are economizing now to pay that back. We get practically nothing for our money but ordinary rations and the whisky we aren't allowed to drink.

'We've even got a polo-ground here. There was a polo-match between the First and Second Battalions the other day. The First Battalion had had all their decent ponies pinched that time when they were sent up at Ypres and the cooks and transport men had to come up into the line to prevent a break through. So this battalion won easily. Can you ride? No? Well, sub-alterns who can't ride have to attend riding-school every afternoon while we're in billets. They give us hell, too. Two of us have been at it for four months and haven't passed off yet. They keep us trotting round the field, with crossed stirrups most of the time, and they give us pack-saddles instead of riding-saddles. Yesterday they called us up suddenly without giving us time to change into breeches. That reminds me, you notice everybody's wearing shorts? It's a regimental order. The battalion thinks it's still in India. They treat the French civilians just like "niggers," kick them about, talk army Hindustani at them. It makes me laugh sometimes. Well, what with a greasy pack-saddle, bare knees, crossed stirrups, and a wild new transport pony that the transport men had pinched from the French, I had a pretty thin time. The colonel, the adjutant, the senior major and the transport officer stood at the four corners of the ring and slogged at the ponies as they came round. I came off twice and got wild with anger, and nearly decided to ride the senior major down. The

funny thing is that they don't realize that they are treating us badly – it's such an honour to be serving with
the regiment. So the best thing is to pretend you don't
care what they do or say.'

I protested: 'But all this is childish. Is there a war on
here or isn't there?'

'The battalion doesn't recognize it socially,' he
answered. 'Still, in trenches I'd rather be with this battalion than in any other that I have met. The senior
officers do know their job, whatever else one says about
them, and the N.C.O.'s are absolutely trustworthy.'

The Second Battalion was peculiar in having a battalion
mess instead of company messes. The Surrey-man said
grimly: 'It's supposed to be more sociable.' This was
another peace-time survival. We went together into the
big château near the church. About fifteen officers of various ranks were sitting in chairs reading the week's
illustrated papers or (the seniors at least) talking quietly.
At the door I said: 'Good morning, gentlemen,' the new
officer's customary greeting to the mess. There was no
answer. Everybody looked at me curiously. The silence
that my entry had caused was soon broken by the gramophone, which began singing happily:

> We've been married just one year,
> And Oh, we've got the sweetest,
> And Oh, we've got the neatest,
> And Oh, we've got the cutest
> Little oil stove.

I found a chair in the background and picked up *The
Field*. The door burst open suddenly and a senior officer
with a red face and angry eye burst in. 'Who the blazes

put that record on?' he shouted to the room. 'One of the bloody warts I expect. Take it off somebody. It makes me sick. Let's have some real music. Put on the *Angelus*.' Two subalterns (in the Royal Welch a subaltern had to answer to the name of 'wart') sprang up, stopped the gramophone, and put on *When the Angelus is ringing*. The young captain who had put on *We've been married* shrugged his shoulders and went on reading, the other faces in the room were blank.

'Who was that?' I whispered to the Surrey-man.

He frowned. 'That's Buzz Off,'[2] he said.

Before the record was finished the door opened and in came the colonel; Buzz Off reappeared with him. Everybody jumped up and said in unison: 'Good morning, sir.' It was his first appearance that day. Before giving the customary greeting and asking us to sit down he turned spitefully to the gramophone: 'Who on earth puts this wretched *Angelus* on every time I come into the mess? For heaven's sake play something cheery for a change.' And with his own hands he took off the *Angelus*, wound up the gramophone and put on *We've been married just one year*. At that moment a gong rang for lunch and he abandoned it. We filed into the next room, a ball-room with mirrors and a decorated ceiling. We sat down at a long, polished table. The seniors sat at the top, the juniors competed for seats as far away from them as possible. I was unlucky enough to get a seat at the foot of the table facing the commanding officer, the adjutant and Buzz Off. There was not a word spoken down that end except for an occasional whisper for the salt or for the beer – very thin French stuff. Robertson, who had not been warned, asked the mess waiter for whisky. 'Sorry, sir,' said the mess waiter, 'it's against orders for the young officers.' Robertson was a man of forty-two, a solicitor with a large practice, and had stood for Parliament in the Yarmouth division at the previous election.

I saw Buzz Off glaring at us and busied myself with my meat and potatoes.

He nudged the adjutant. 'Who are those two funny ones down there, Charley,' he asked.

'New this morning from the militia. Answer to the names of Robertson and Graves.'

'Which is which?' asked the colonel.

'I'm Robertson, sir.'

'I wasn't asking you.'

Robertson winced, but said nothing. Then Buzz Off noticed something.

'T'other wart's wearing a wind-up tunic.' Then he bent forward and asked me loudly. 'You there, wart. Why the hell are you wearing your stars on your shoulder instead of your sleeve?'

My mouth was full and I was embarrassed. Everybody was looking at me. I swallowed the lump of meat whole and said: 'It was a regimental order in the Welsh Regiment. I understood that it was the same everywhere in France.'

The colonel turned puzzled to the adjutant: 'What on earth's the man talking about the Welsh Regiment for?' And then to me: 'As soon as you have finished your lunch you will visit the master-tailor. Report at the orderly room when you're properly dressed.'

There was a severe struggle in me between resentment and regimental loyalty. Resentment for the moment had the better of it. I said under my breath: 'You damned snobs. I'll survive you all. There'll come a time when there won't be one of you left serving in the battalion to remember battalion mess at Laventie.' This time came, exactly a year later.*[3]

We went up to the trenches that night. They were high-command trenches; because water was struck when one dug down three feet, the parapet and parados were built up man-high. I found my platoon curt and reserved. Even when on sentry-duty at night they would never talk confidentially about themselves and their families like my platoon in the Welsh Regiment. Townsend, the platoon-sergeant, was an ex-policeman who had been on the reserve when war broke out. He used to drive his men rather than lead them. 'A' Company was at Red Lamp Corner; the front trench broke off short here and started again further back on the right. A red lamp was hung at the corner, invisible to the enemy, but a warning after dark to the company on our right not to fire to the left of it. Work and duties were done with a silent soldier-like efficiency quite foreign to the Welsh.[4]

The first night I was in trenches my company commander asked me to go out on patrol; it was the regimental custom to test new officers in this way. All the time that I had been with the Welsh I had never once been out in No Man's Land, even to inspect the barbed wire. In the Welsh Regiment the condition of the wire was, I believe, the responsibility of the battalion intelligence officer. I never remember any work done on it by C Company. I think we left it to the Royal Engineers. When Hewitt, the machine-gun officer, used to go out on patrol sometimes it was regarded as a mad escapade. But with both battalions of the

* The quartermaster excepted. [RG]

Royal Welch Fusiliers it was a point of honour to be masters of No Man's Land from dusk to dawn. There was not a night at Laventie that a message did not come down the line from sentry to sentry: 'Pass the word; officer's patrol going out.' My orders for this patrol were to see whether a German sap-head was occupied by night or not.

I went out from Red Lamp Corner with Sergeant Townsend at about ten o'clock. We both had revolvers. We pulled socks, with the toes cut off, over our bare knees, to prevent them showing up in the dark and to make crawling easier. We went ten yards at a time, slowly, not on all fours, but wriggling flat along the ground. After each movement we lay and watched for about ten minutes. We crawled through our own wire entanglements and along a dry ditch; ripping our clothes on more barbed wire, glaring into the darkness till it began turning round and round (once I snatched my fingers in horror from where I had planted them on the slimy body of an old corpse), nudging each other with rapidly beating hearts at the slightest noise or suspicion, crawling, watching, crawling, shamming dead under the blinding light of enemy flares and again crawling, watching, crawling. (A Second Battalion officer who revisited these Laventie trenches after the war was over told me of the ridiculously small area of No Man's Land compared with the size it seemed on the long, painful journeys that he made over it. 'It was like the real size of the hollow in a tooth compared with the size it feels to the tongue.')

We found a gap in the German wire and came at last to within five yards of the sap-head that was our objective. We waited quite twenty minutes listening for any signs of its occupation. Then I nudged Sergeant

Townsend and, revolvers in hand, we wriggled quickly forward and slid into it. It was about three feet deep and unoccupied. On the floor were a few empty cartridges and a wicker basket containing something large and smooth and round, twice as large as a football. Very, very carefully I groped and felt all around it in the dark. I couldn't guess what it was. I was afraid that it was some sort of infernal machine. Eventually I dared to lift it out and carry it back. I had a suspicion that it might be one of the German gas-cylinders that we had heard so much about. We got back after making the journey of perhaps two hundred yards in rather more than two hours. The sentries passed along the word that we were in again. Our prize turned out to be a large glass container quarter-filled with some pale yellow liquid. This was sent down to battalion headquarters and from there sent along to the divisional intelligence office. Everybody was very interested in it. The theory was that the vessel contained a chemical for re-damping gas masks. I now believe it was the dregs of country wine mixed with rainwater. I never heard the official report. The colonel, however, told my company commander in the hearing of the Surrey-man: 'Your new wart seems to have more guts than the others.' After this I went out fairly often. I found that the only thing that the regiment respected in young officers was personal courage.

Besides, I had worked it out like this. The best way of lasting the war out was to get wounded. The best time to get wounded was at night and in the open, because a wound in a vital spot was less likely. Fire was more or less unaimed at night and the whole body was exposed. It was also convenient to be wounded when there was no rush on the dressing-station services, and when the back areas were not being heavily shelled. It was most convenient to be wounded, therefore, on a night patrol in a quiet sector. You could usually manage to crawl into a shell-hole until somebody came to the rescue. Still, patrolling had its peculiar risks. If you were wounded and a German patrol got you, they were as likely as not to cut your throat. The bowie-knife was a favourite German patrol weapon; it was silent. (At this time the British inclined more to the 'cosh', a loaded stick.) The most important information that a patrol could bring back was to what regiment and division the troops opposite belonged. So if a wounded man was found and it was impossible to get him back without danger to oneself, the thing to be done was to strip him of his badges. To do that quickly and silently it might be necessary first to cut his throat or beat in his skull.

Sir P. Mostyn, a lieutenant who was often out patrolling at Laventie, had a feud on with a German patrol on the left of the battalion frontage. (Our patrols usually consisted of an officer and one or, at the most, two men. German patrols were usually six or seven men under an N.C.O. German officers left as much as they decently could to their N.C.O.'s. They did not, as one of our sergeant-majors put it, believe in 'keeping a dog and barking themselves'.) One night Mostyn caught sight of his opponents; he had raised himself on one knee to throw a percussion bomb at them when they fired and wounded him in the arm, which immediately went numb. He caught the bomb before it hit the ground and threw it with his left hand, and in the confusion that followed managed to return to the trench.

Like every one else I had a carefully worked out formula for taking risks. We would all take any risk, even the certainty of death, to save life or to maintain an important position. To take life we would run, say, a one-in-five risk, particularly if there was some wider object than merely reducing the enemy's man-power; for instance, picking off a well-known sniper, or getting fire ascendancy in trenches where the lines were dangerously close. I only once refrained from shooting a German I saw, and that was at Cuinchy about three weeks after this. When sniping from a knoll in the support line where we had a concealed loop-hole I saw a German, about seven hundred yards away, through my telescopic sights. He was having a bath in the German third line. I somehow did not like the idea of shooting a naked man, so I handed the rifle to the sergeant who was with me and said: 'Here, take this. You're a better shot than me.' He got him, he said; but I had not stayed to watch.

About saving the lives of enemy wounded there was disagreement; the convention varied with the division. Some divisions, like the Canadians and a division of Lowland territorials, who had, they claimed, atrocities to avenge, would not only take no risks to rescue enemy wounded, but would go out of their way to finish them off. The Royal Welch Fusiliers were gentlemanly: perhaps a one-in-twenty risk to get a wounded German to safety would be considered justifiable. An important factor in taking risks was our own physical condition. When exhausted and wanting to get quickly from one point in the trenches to another without collapse, and if the enemy were not nearer than four or five hundred yards, we would sometimes take a short cut over the top. In a hurry we would take a one-in-two-hundred risk, when dead tired a one-in-fifty risk. In some battalions where the *morale* was not high, one-in-fifty risks were often taken in mere laziness or despair. The Munsters in the First Division were said by the Welsh to 'waste men wicked' by not keeping properly under cover when in the reserve lines. In the Royal Welch there was no wastage of this sort. At no time in the war did any of us allow ourselves to believe that hostilities could possibly continue more than nine months or a year more, so it seemed almost worth while taking care; there even seemed a chance of lasting until the end absolutely unhurt.

The Second Royal Welch, unlike the Second Welsh, believed themselves better trench fighters than the Germans. With the Second Welsh it was not cowardice but modesty. With the Second Royal Welch it was not vainglory but courage; as soon as they arrived in a new sector they insisted on getting fire ascendancy. Having found out from the troops they relieved all possible information as to enemy snipers, machine-guns, and patrols, they set themselves to deal with them one by one. They began with machine-guns firing at night. As soon as one started traversing down a trench the whole platoon farthest removed from its fire would open five rounds rapid at it. The machine-gun would usually stop suddenly but start again after a minute or two. Again five rounds rapid. Then it usually gave up.

The Welsh seldom answered a machine-gun. If they did, it was not with local organized fire, beginning and ending in unison, but in ragged confused protest all along the line. There was almost no firing at night in the Royal Welch, except organized fire at a machine-gun or a persistent enemy sentry, or fire at a patrol close enough to be distinguished as a German one. With all other battalions I met in France there was random popping off all the time; the sentries wanted to show their spite against the war. Flares were rarely used in the Royal Welch; most often as signals to our patrols that it was time to come back.

As soon as enemy machine-guns had been discouraged, our patrols would go out with bombs to claim possession of No Man's Land. At dawn next morning came the struggle for sniping ascendancy. The Germans, we were told, had special regimental snipers, trained in camouflaging themselves. I saw one killed once at Cuinchy who had been firing all day from a shell-hole between the lines. He had a sort of cape over his shoulders of imitation grass, his face was painted green and brown, and his rifle was also green fringed. A number of empty cartridges were found by him, and his cap with the special oak-leaf badge. Few battalions attempted to get control of the sniping situation. The Germans had the advantage of having many times more telescopic sights than we did, and steel loopholes that our bullets could not pierce. Also a system by which the snipers were kept for months in the same sector until they knew all the loopholes and shallow places in our trenches, and the tracks that our ration-parties used above-ground by night, and where our traverses came in the trench, and so on, better than we did ourselves. British snipers changed their trenches, with their battalions, every week or two, and never had time to learn the German line thoroughly. But at least we counted on getting rid of the unprofessional German sniper. Later we had an elephant-gun in the battalion that would pierce the German loopholes, and if we could not locate the loophole of a persistent sniper we did what we could to dislodge him by a volley of rifle-grenades, or even by ringing up the artillery.

It puzzled us that if a sniper were spotted and killed,

another sniper would begin again next day from the same position. The Germans probably underrated us and regarded it as an accident. The willingness of other battalions to let the Germans have sniping ascendancy helped us; enemy snipers often exposed themselves unnecessarily, even the professionals. There was, of course, one advantage of which no advance or retreat of the enemy could rob us, and that was that we were always facing more or less East; dawn broke behind the German lines, and they seldom realized that for several minutes every morning we could see them though still invisible ourselves. German night wiring-parties often stayed out too long, and we could get a man or two as they went back; sunsets were against us, but sunset was a less critical time. Sentries at night were made to stand with their head and shoulders above the trenches and their rifles in position on the parapet. This surprised me at first. But it meant greater vigilance and self-confidence in the sentry, and it put the top of his head above the level of the parapet. Enemy machine-guns were trained on this level, and it was safer to be hit in the chest or shoulders than in the top of the head. The risk of unaimed fire at night was negligible so this was really the safest plan. It often happened in battalions like the Second Welsh, where the head-and-shoulder rule was not in force and the sentry just took a peep now and then, that an enemy patrol would sneak up unseen to the British wire, throw a few bombs and get safely back. In the Royal Welch the barbed-wire entanglement was the responsibility of the company behind it. One of our first acts on taking over trenches was to inspect and repair it. We did a lot of work on the wire.

Thomas was an extremely silent man; it was not

sullenness but shyness. 'Yes' and 'no' was the limit of his usual conversation; it was difficult for us subalterns. He never took us into his confidence about company affairs, and we did not like asking him too much. His chief interests seemed to be polo and the regiment. He was most conscientious in taking his watch at night, a thing that the other company commanders did not always do. We enjoyed his food-hampers sent every week from Fortnum and Mason; we messed by companies when in the trenches. Our only complaint was that Buzz Off, who had a good nose for a hamper, used to spend more time than he would otherwise have done in the company mess. This embarrassed us. Thomas went on leave to England about this time. I heard about it accidentally. He walked about the West End astonished at the amateur militariness that he met everywhere. To be more in keeping with it he gave elaborate awkward salutes to newly-joined second-lieutenants and raised his cap to dug-out colonels and generals. It was a private joke at the expense of the war.

I used to look forward to our spells in trenches at Laventie. Billet life meant battalion mess, also riding-school, which I found rather worse than the Surrey-man had described it. Parades were carried out with peace-time punctiliousness and smartness, especially the daily battalion guard-changing which every now and then, when I was orderly officer, it was my duty to supervise. On one occasion, after the guard-changing ceremony and inspection were over and I was about to dismiss the old guard, I saw Buzz Off cross the village street from one company headquarters to another. As he crossed I called the guard to attention and saluted. I waited for a few seconds and then dismissed the guard, but he had not really gone into the billet; he had been waiting in the doorway. As soon as I dismissed the guard he dashed out with a great show of anger. 'As you were, as you were, stand fast!' he shouted to the guard. And then to me: 'Why in hell's name, Mr. Graves, didn't you ask my permission to dismiss the parade? You've read the King's Regulations, haven't you? And where the devil are your manners, anyhow?' I apologized. I said that I thought he had gone into the house. This made matters worse. He bellowed at me for arguing; then he asked me where I had learned to salute. 'At the depot, sir,' I answered. 'Then, by heaven, Mr. Graves, you'll have to learn to salute as the battalion does. You will parade every morning before breakfast for a month under Staff-sergeant Evans and do an hour's saluting drill.' Then he turned to the guard and dismissed them himself. This was not a particular act of spite against me but the general game of 'chasing the warts', at which all the senior officers played. It was honestly intended to make us better soldiers.

I had been with the Royal Welch about three weeks when the Nineteenth Brigade was moved down to the Béthune sector to fill a gap in the Second Division; the gap was made by taking out the brigade of Guards to go into the Guards Division which was then being formed. On the way down we marched past Lord Kitchener. Kitchener, we were told, commented to the brigadier on the soldier-like appearance of the leading battalion – which was ourselves – but said cynically: 'Wait until they've been a week or two in the trenches; they will lose some of that high polish.' He apparently mistook us for one of the new-army battalions.

The first trenches we went into on our arrival were the Cuinchy brick-stacks. The company I was with was on the canal-bank frontage, a few hundred yards to the left of where I had been with the Welsh Regiment at the end of May. The Germans opposite wished to be sociable. They sent messages over to us in undetonated rifle-grenades. One of these messages was evidently addressed to the Irish battalion we had relieved:

> We all German korporals wish you English korporals a good day and invite you to a good German dinner to-night with beer (ale) and cakes. You little dog ran over to us and we keep it safe; it became no food with you so it run to us. Answer in the same way, if you please.

Another message was a copy of the *Neueste Nachrichten*, a German army newspaper printed at Lille. It gave sensational details of Russian defeats around Warsaw and immense captures of prisoners and guns. But we were more interested in a full account in another column of the destruction of a German submarine by British armed trawlers; no details of the sinking of German submarines had been allowed to appear in any English papers. The battalion cared no more about the successes or reverses of our Allies than it did about the origins of the war. It never allowed itself to have any political feelings about the Germans. A professional soldier's job was to fight whomsoever the King ordered him to fight; it was as simple as that. With the King as colonel-in-chief of the regiment it was even simpler. The Christmas 1914 fraternization, in which the battalion was among the first to participate, was of the same professional simplicity; it was not an emotional hiatus but a commonplace of military tradition – an exchange of courtesies between officers of opposite armies.

Cuinchy was one of the worst places for rats. They

came up from the canal and fed on the many corpses and multiplied. When I was here with the Welsh a new officer came to the company, and, as a token of his welcome, he was given a dug-out containing a spring-bed. When he turned in that night he heard a scuffling, shone his torch on the bed, and there were two rats on his blankets tussling for the possession of a severed hand. This was thought a great joke.

The colonel called for a patrol to go out along the side of the tow-path, where we had heard suspicious sounds on the previous night, to see whether a working-party was out. I volunteered to go when it was dark. But there was a moon that night so bright and full that it dazzled the eyes to look at it. Between us and the Germans was a flat stretch of about two hundred yards, broken only by shell-craters and an occasional patch of coarse grass. I was not with my own company, but lent to B, which had two officers away on leave. Childe-Freeman, the company commander, said: 'You're not going out on patrol tonight, are you? It's almost as bright as day.' I said: 'All the more reason for going; they won't be expecting me. Will you please have everything as usual? Let the men fire an occasional rifle and send up a flare every half hour. If I go carefully they'll not see me.' But I was nervous, and while we were having supper I clumsily knocked over a cup of tea, and after that a plate. Freeman said: 'Look here, I'll 'phone through to battalion and tell them it's too bright for you to go out.' But I knew Buzz Off would accuse me of cold feet, so Sergeant Williams and I put on our crawlers and went out by way of a mine-crater at the side of the tow-path. There was no need that night for the usual staring business. We could see only too clearly. All we had to do was to wait for an opportunity to move quickly, stop dead and trust to luck, then move on quickly again. We planned our rushes from shell-hole to shell-hole; the opportunities were provided by artillery or machine-gun fire which would distract the sentries. Many of the craters contained corpses of men who had been wounded and crept in and died. Some of them were skeletons, picked clean by the rats. We got to within thirty yards of a big German working-party who were digging a trench ahead of their front line. Between them and us we could count a covering party of ten men lying on the grass in their great-coats. We had gone far enough. There was a German lying on his back about twelve yards away humming a tune. It was the 'Merry Widow' waltz. The sergeant, who was behind me, pressed my foot with his hand and showed me the revolver he was carrying. He raised his eyebrows inquiringly. I gave him the signal for 'no'. We turned to go back; it was hard not to go back too quickly. We had got about half-way back when a German machine-gun opened traversing fire along the top of our trenches. We immediately jumped to our feet; the bullets were brushing the grass, so it was safer to be standing up. We walked the rest of the way back, but moving irregularly to distract the aim of the covering party if they saw us. Back in the trench I rang up the artillery and asked them to fire as much shrapnel as they could spare fifty yards short of where the German front trench touched the tow-path; I knew that one of the night-lines of the battery supporting us was trained near enough to this point. A minute and a quarter later the shells started coming over. We heard the clash of downed tools and distant shouts and cries; we reckoned the probable casualties. The next morning at stand-to Buzz Off came up to me: 'I hear you were on patrol last night?' I said: 'Yes, sir.' He asked me for particulars. When I had told him about the covering party he cursed me for 'not scuppering them with that revolver of yours. Cold feet,' he snorted as he turned away.

One day while we were here the Royal Welch were instructed to shout across to the enemy and induce them to take part in a conversation. The object was to find out how strongly the German front trenches were manned at night. A German-speaking officer in the company among the brick-stacks was provided with a megaphone. He shouted: 'Wie gehts ihnen, kamaraden?' Somebody shouted back in delight: 'Ah, Tommee, hast du den deutsch gelernt?' Firing stopped and a conversation began across the fifty yards or so of No Man's Land. The Germans refused to say what regiment they were. They would not talk any military shop. One of them shouted out: 'Les sheunes madamoiselles de La Bassée bonnes pour coucher avec. Les madamoiselles de Béthune bonnes aussi, hein?' Our spokesman refused to discuss this. In the pause that followed he asked how the Kaiser was. They replied respectfully that he was in excellent health, thank you. 'And how is the Crown Prince?' he asked them. 'Oh, b—r the Crown Prince,' shouted somebody in English, and was immediately suppressed by his comrades. There was a confusion of angry voices and laughter. Then they all began singing the 'Wacht am Rhein'. The trench was evidently very well held indeed.

XV

This was the end of August 1915, and particulars of the coming offensive against La Bassée were beginning to leak through the young staff officers. The French civilians knew that it was coming and so, naturally, did the Germans. Every night now new batteries and lorry-trains of shells came rumbling up the Béthune-La Bassée road. There were other signs of movement: sapping forward at Vermelles and Cambrin, where the lines were too far apart for a quick rush across, to make a new front line; orders for evacuation of hospitals; the appearance of cavalry and new-army divisions. Then Royal Engineer officers supervised the digging of pits at intervals in the front line. They were sworn not to say what these were for, but we knew that they were for gas-cylinders. Scaling ladders for climbing quickly out of trenches were brought up by the lorry-load and dumped at Cambrin village. As early as September 3rd I had a bet with Robertson that our division would attack on this Cambrin-Cuinchy sector. When I went home on leave on September 9th the sense of impending events was so great that I almost wished I was not going.

Leave came round for officers about every six or eight months in ordinary times; heavy casualties shortened the period, general offensives cut off leave altogether.

There was only one officer in France who was ever said to have refused to go on leave when his turn came round – Cross of the Fifty-second Light Infantry (the Second Battalion of the Oxford and Bucks Light Infantry, which insisted on its original style as jealously as we kept our 'c' in 'Welch'). Cross is alleged to have refused leave on these grounds: 'My father fought with the regiment in the South African War and had no leave; my grandfather fought in the Crimea with the regiment and had no leave. I do not regard it in the regimental tradition to take home-leave when on active service.' Cross was a professional survivor and was commanding the battalion in 1917 when I last heard of him.

London seemed unreally itself. In spite of the number of men in uniform in the streets, the general indifference to and ignorance about the war was remarkable. Enlistment was still voluntary. The universal catchword was 'Business as usual'. My family were living in London now, at the house formerly occupied by my uncle, Robert von Ranke, the German consul. He had been forced to leave in a hurry on August 4th, 1914, and my mother had undertaken to look after it for him while the war lasted. So when Edward Marsh, then secretary to the Prime Minister, rang me up from Downing Street to arrange a meal, someone intervened and cut him off. The telephone of the German consul's sister was, of course, closely watched by the anti-espionage men of Scotland Yard. The Zeppelin scare had just begun. Some friends of the family came in one night. They knew I had been in the trenches, but were not interested. They began telling me of the air-raids, of bombs dropped only three streets off. So I said: 'Well, do you know, the other day I was asleep in a house and in the early morning an aeroplane dropped a bomb next door and killed three soldiers who were billeted there, and a woman and child.' 'Good gracious,' they said, looking at me with sudden interest, 'what did you do then?' I said: 'I went to sleep again; I was tired out. It was at a place called Beuvry, about four miles behind the trenches.' They said: 'Oh, but that was in France,' and the look of interest faded from their faces, as though I had taken them in with a stupid catch. I went up to Harlech for the rest of my leave, and walked about on the hills in an old shirt and a pair of shorts. When I got back, 'The Actor', a regular officer in A Company, asked me: 'Had a good time on leave?' I said: 'Yes.' He said: 'Go to many dances?' I said: 'Not one.' 'What shows did you go to?' 'I didn't go to any shows.' 'Hunt?' 'No!' 'Slept with any nice girls?' 'No, I didn't. Sorry to disappoint you.' 'What the hell *did* you do, then?' 'Oh, I just walked about on some hills.' 'Good God,' he said, 'chaps like you don't deserve to go on leave.'

On September 19th we relieved the Middlesex at Cambrin, and it was said that these were the trenches from which we were to attack. The preliminary bombardment had already started, a week in advance. As I led my platoon into the line I recognized with some disgust the same machine-gun shelter where I had seen the suicide on my first night in trenches. It seemed ominous. This was the first heavy bombardment that I had yet seen from our own guns. The trenches shook properly and a great cloud of drifting shell-smoke clouded the German trenches. The shells went over our heads in a steady stream; we had to shout to make our neighbours hear. Dying down a little at night, the noise began again every morning at dawn, a little louder each time. We said: 'Damn it, there can't be a living soul left in those trenches.' And still it went on. The Germans retaliated, though not very vigorously. Most of their heavy artillery had been withdrawn from this sector, we were told, and sent across to the Russian front. We had more casualties from our own shorts and from blow-backs than from German shells. Much of the ammunition that our batteries were using came from America and contained a high percentage of duds; the driving-bands were always coming off. We had fifty casualties in the ranks and three officer casualties, including Buzz Off, who was badly wounded in the head. This was before steel helmets were issued; we would not have lost nearly so many if we had had them. I had two insignificant wounds on the hand which I took as an omen on the right side. On the morning of the 23rd Thomas came back from battalion headquarters with a notebook in his hand and a map for each of us company officers. 'Listen,' he said, 'and copy out all this skite on the back of your maps. You'll have to explain it to your platoons this afternoon. Tomorrow morning we go back to Béthune to dump our blankets, packs, and greatcoats. On the next day, that's Saturday the 25th, we attack.' It was the first definite news we had been given and we looked up half startled, half relieved. I still have the map and these are the orders as I copied them down:

FIRST OBJECTIVE. – *Les Briques Farm*. – The big house plainly visible to our front, surrounded by trees. To get this it is necessary to cross three lines of enemy trenches. The first is three hundred yards distant, the second four hundred, and the third about six hundred. We then cross two railways. Behind the second railway line is a German trench called the Brick Trench. Then comes the Farm, a strong place with moat and cellars and a kitchen garden strongly staked and wired.

Second Objective. – *The Town of Auchy*. – This is also plainly visible from our trenches. It is four hundred yards beyond the Farm and defended by a first line of trench half way across, and a second line immediately in front of the town. When we have occupied the first line our direction is half-right, with the left of the battalion directed on Tall Chimney.

Third Objective. – *Village of Haisnes*. – Conspicuous by high-spired church. Our eventual line will be taken up on the railway behind this village, where we will dig in and await reinforcements.

When Thomas had reached this point the shoulders of The Actor were shaking with laughter. 'What's up?' asked Thomas irritably. The Actor asked: 'Who in God's Name is originally responsible for this little effort?' Thomas said: 'Don't know. Probably Paul the Pimp or someone like that.' (Paul the Pimp was a captain on the divisional staff, young, inexperienced and much disliked. He 'wore red tabs upon his chest, And even on his undervest.') 'Between you and me, but you youngsters be careful not to let the men know, this is what they call a subsidiary attack. We'll have no supports. We've just got to go over and keep the enemy busy while the folk on our right do the real work. You notice that the bombardment is much heavier over there. They've knocked the Hohenzollern Redoubt to bits. Personally, I don't give a damn either way. We'll get killed anyhow.' We all laughed. 'All right, laugh now, but by God on Saturday we've got to carry out this funny scheme.' I had never heard Thomas so talkative before. 'Sorry,' The Actor apologized, 'carry on with the dictation.' Thomas went on:

The attack will be preceded by forty minutes discharge of the accessory,* which will clear the path for a thousand yards, so that the two railway lines will be occupied without difficulty. Our advance will follow closely behind the accessory. Behind us are three fresh divisions and the Cavalry Corps. It is expected we shall have no difficulty in breaking through. All men will parade with their platoons; pioneers, servants, etc. to be warned. All platoons to be properly told off under N.C.O.'s. Every N.C.O. is to know exactly what is expected of him, and when to take over command in case of casualties. Men who lose touch must join up with the nearest company or regiment and push on. Owing to the strength of the accessory, men should be warned against remaining too long in captured trenches where the accessory is likely to collect, but to keep to the open and above all to push on. It is important that if smoke-helmets have to be pulled down they must be tucked in under the shirt.

The Actor interrupted again. 'Tell me, Thomas, do you believe in this funny accessory?' Thomas said: 'It's damnable. It's not soldiering to use stuff like that even though the Germans did start it. It's dirty, and it'll bring us bad luck. We're sure to bungle it. Look at those new gas-companies (sorry, excuse me this once,

---

* The gas-cylinder had by this time been put into position on the front line. A special order came round imposing severe penalties on anyone who used any word but 'accessory' in speaking of the gas. This was to keep it secret, but the French civilians knew all about it long before this. [RG]

I mean accessory-companies). Their very look makes me tremble. Chemistry-dons from London University, a few lads straight from school, one or two N.C.O.'s of the old-soldier type, trained together for three weeks, then given a job as responsible as this. Of course they'll bungle it. How could they do anything else? But let's be merry. I'm going on again:

Men of company: what they are to carry:

Two hundred rounds of ammunition (bomb-throwers fifty, and signallers one hundred and fifty rounds).

Heavy tools carried in sling by the strongest men.

Waterproof sheet in belt.

Sandbag in right coat-pocket.

Field dressing and iodine.

Emergency ration, including biscuit.

One tube-helmet, to be worn when we advance, rolled up on the head. It must be quite secure and the top part turned down. If possible each man will be provided with an elastic band.

One smoke-helmet, old pattern, to be carried for preference behind the back where it is least likely to be damaged by stray bullets, etc.

Wire-cutters, as many as possible, by wiring party and others; hedging-gloves by wire party.

Platoon screens, for artillery observation, to be carried by a man in each platoon who is not carrying a tool.

Packs, capes, greatcoats, blankets will be dumped, not carried.

No one is to carry sketches of our position or anything likely to be of service to the enemy.

'That's all. I believe we're going over first with the Middlesex in support. If we get through the German wire I'll be satisfied. Our guns don't seem to be cutting it. Perhaps they're putting that off until the intense bombardment. Any questions?'

That afternoon I repeated it all to the platoon and told them of the inevitable success attending our assault. They seemed to believe it. All except Sergeant Townsend. 'Do you say, sir, that we have three divisions and the Cavalry Corps behind us?' he asked. 'Yes,' I answered. 'Well, excuse me, sir, I'm thinking it's only those chaps on the right that'll get reinforcements. If we get half a platoon of Mons Angels,[1] that's about all we will get.' 'Sergeant Townsend,' I said, 'you are a well-known pessimist. This is going to be a good show.' The next morning we were relieved by the Middlesex and marched back to Béthune, where we dumped our spare kit at the Montmorency Barracks. The battalion officers messed together in a big house near by. This billet was claimed at the same time by the staff of a new-army division which was to take part in the fighting next day. The argument was settled in a friendly way by division and battalion messing together. It was, someone pointed out, like a caricature of The Last Supper in duplicate. In the middle of the long table sat the two pseudo-Christs, the battalion colonel and the divisional general. Everybody was drinking a lot; the subalterns were allowed whisky for a treat, and were getting rowdy. They raised their glasses with: 'Cheero, we will be messing together tomorrow night in La Bassée.' Only the company commanders were looking worried. I remember C Company commander especially, Captain A. L. Samson, biting his thumb and refusing to join in the general excitement. I think it was Childe-Freeman of B Company who said that night: 'The last time the regiment was in these parts it was under decent generalship. Old Marlborough knew better than to attack the La Bassée lines; he masked them and went round.'

The G.S.O. 1 of the new-army division, a staff-colonel, knew the adjutant well. They had played polo together in India. I happened to be sitting next to them. The G.S.O. 1 said to the adjutant, rather drunkenly: 'Charley, do you see that silly old woman over there? Calls himself General Commanding. Doesn't know where he is; doesn't know where his division is; can't read a map properly. He's marched the poor sods off their feet and left his supplies behind, God knows where. They've had to use their iron rations and what they could pick up in the villages. And to-morrow he's going to fight a battle. Doesn't know anything about battles; the men have never been in trenches before, and to-morrow's going to be a glorious balls-up, and the day after to-morrow he'll be sent home.' Then he said, quite seriously: 'Really, Charley, it's just like that, you mark my words.'

That night we marched back again to Cambrin. The men were singing. Being mostly from the Midlands they sang comic songs instead of Welsh hymns: *Slippery Sam*, *When we've Wound up the Watch on the Rhine*, and *I do like a S'nice S'mince Pie*, to concertina accompaniment. The tune of the *S'nice S'mince Pie* ran in my head all next day, and for the week following I could not get rid of it. The Second Welsh would never have sung a song like *When we've Wound up the Watch on the Rhine*. Their only songs about the war were defeatist:

I want to go home,
I want to go home,

The coal-box and shrapnel they whistle and roar,
I don't want to go to the trenches no more,
I want to go over the sea
Where the Kayser can't shoot bombs at me.
Oh, I
Don't want to die,
I want to go home.

There were several more verses in the same strain. Hewitt, the Welsh machine-gun officer, had written one in a more offensive spirit:

I want to go home,
I want to go home.
One day at Givenchy the week before last
The Allmands attacked and they nearly got past.
They pushed their way up to the keep,
Through our maxim-gun sight we did peep,
Oh my!
They let out a cry,
They never got home.

But the men would not sing it, though they all admired Hewitt.

The Béthune-La Bassée road was choked with troops, guns and transport, and we had to march miles north out of our way to get back to Cambrin. As it was we were held up two or three times by massed cavalry. Everything seemed in confusion. A casualty clearing-station had been planted astride one of the principal crossroads and was already being shelled. When we reached Cambrin we had marched about twenty miles in all that day. We were told then that the Middlesex would go over first with us in support, and to their left the Second Argyll and Sutherland Highlanders, with the Cameronians in support; the junior officers complained loudly at our not being given the honour of leading the attack. We were the senior regiment, they protested, and entitled to the 'Right of the Line'. We moved into trench sidings just in front of the village. There was about half a mile of communication trench between us and the trenches proper, known as Maison Rouge Alley. It was an hour or so past midnight. At half-past five the gas was to be discharged. We were cold, tired and sick, not at all in the mood for a battle. We tried to snatch an hour or two of sleep squatting in the trench. It had been raining for some time. Grey, watery dawn broke at last behind the German lines; the bombardment, which had been surprisingly slack all night, brisked up a little. 'Why the devil don't they send them over quicker?' asked The Actor. 'This isn't my idea of a bombardment. We're getting nothing opposite us. What little there is is going into the Hohenzollern.' 'Shell shortage. Expected it,' answered Thomas. We were told afterwards that on the 23rd a German aeroplane had bombed the Army Reserve shell-dump and sent it up. The bombardment on the 24th and on the day of the battle itself was nothing compared with that of the previous days. Thomas looked strained and ill. 'It's time they were sending that damned accessory off. I wonder what's doing.'

What happened in the next few minutes is difficult for me now to sort out. It was more difficult still at the time. All we heard back there in the sidings was a distant cheer, confused crackle of rifle-fire, yells, heavy shelling on our front line, more shouts and yells and a continuous rattle of machine-guns. After a few minutes, lightly-wounded men of the Middlesex came stumbling down Maison Rouge Alley to the dressing-station. I was at the junction of the siding and the alley. 'What's happened? What's happened?' I asked. 'Bloody balls-up' was the most detailed answer I could get. Among the wounded were a number of men yellow-faced and choking, with their buttons tarnished green; these were gas cases. Then came the stretcher cases. Maison Rouge Alley was narrow and the stretchers had difficulty in getting down. The Germans started shelling it with five-point-nines. Thomas went through the shelling to battalion headquarters to ask for orders. It was the same place that I had visited on my first night in the trenches. This group of dug-outs in the reserve line showed very plainly from the air as battalion head-quarters, and should never have been occupied on the day of a battle. Just before Thomas arrived the Germans put five shells into it. The adjutant jumped one way, the colonel another, the regimental sergeant-major a third. One shell went into the signals dug-out and destroyed the telephone. The colonel had a slight wound on his hand; he joined the stream of wounded and was carried as far as the base with it. The adjutant took charge. All this time A Company had been waiting in the siding for the rum to arrive; the tradition of every attack was a double tot of rum beforehand. All the other companies got it except ours. The Actor was cursing: 'Where the bloody hell's that storeman gone?' We fixed bayonets in readiness to go up to the attack as soon as Thomas came back with orders. The Actor sent me along the siding to the other end of the company. The stream of wounded was continuous. At last Thomas's orderly appeared, saying: 'Captain's orders, sir: A Company to move up to the front line.' It seems that at that moment the storeman appeared with the rum. He was hugging the rum-bottle, without rifle or equipment, red-faced and retching. He staggered up to The Actor and said: 'There you are, sir,' then fell on his face in the thick mud of a sump-pit at the junction of the trench and the siding. The stopper of the bottle flew out and what was left of the three gallons bubbled on the ground. The Actor said nothing. It was a crime deserving the death-penalty. He put one foot on the storeman's neck, the other in the small of his back, and trod him into the mud. Then he gave the order 'Company forward.' The company went forward with a clatter of steel over the body, and that was the last heard of the storeman.

What had happened in the front line was this. At half-past four the commander of the gas-company in the front line sent a telephone message through to divisional headquarters: 'Dead calm. Impossible discharge accessory.' The answer came back: 'Accessory to be discharged at all costs.' Thomas's estimate of the gas-company's efficiency was right enough. The spanners for unscrewing the cocks of the cylinders were found, with two or three exceptions, to be misfits. The gasmen rushed about shouting and asking each other for the loan of an adjustable spanner. They discharged one or two cylinders with the spanners that they had; the gas went whistling out, formed a thick cloud a few yards away in No Man's Land, and then gradually spread back into the trenches. The Germans had been expecting the attack. They immediately put their gas-helmets on, semi-rigid ones, better than ours. Bundles of oily cotton-waste were strewn along the German parapet and set alight as a barrier to the gas. Then their batteries opened on our lines. The confusion in the front trench was great; the shelling broke several of the gas-cylinders and the trench was soon full of gas. The gas-company dispersed.

No orders could come through because the shell in the signals dug-out at battalion headquarters had cut communication both between companies and battalion headquarters and between battalion headquarters and division. The officers in the front trench had to decide on immediate action. Two companies of the Middlesex, instead of waiting for the intense bombardment which was to follow the forty minutes of gas, charged at once and got as far as the German wire – which our artillery had not yet attempted to cut. What shelling there had been on it was shrapnel and not high explosive; shrapnel was no use against barbed wire. The Germans shot the Middlesex men down. It is said that one platoon found a gap and got into the German trench. But there were no survivors of the platoon to confirm the story. The Argyll and Sutherland Highlanders went over too, on their left. Two companies, instead of charging at once, rushed back to the support line out of the gas-filled front trench and attacked from there. It will be recalled that the front line had been pushed forward in preparation for the battle; these companies were therefore attacking from the old front line. The barbed wire entanglements in front of this trench had not been removed, so that they were caught and machine-gunned between their own front and support lines.[2] The leading companies were equally unsuccessful. When the attack started, the German N.C.O.'s had jumped up on the parapet to encourage their men. It was a Jaeger regiment and their musketry was good.

The survivors of the first two companies of the Middlesex were lying in shell-craters close to the German wire, sniping and making the Germans keep their heads down. They had bombs to throw, but these were nearly all of a new type issued for the battle; the fuses were lit on the match-and-matchbox principle and the rain had made them useless. The other two companies of the Middlesex soon followed in support. Machine-gun fire stopped them half-way. Only one German machine-gun was now in action, the others had been knocked out by rifle or trench-mortar fire. Why the single gun remained in action is a story in itself.

It starts like this. British colonial governors and high-commissioners had the privilege of nominating one or two officers from their countries to be attached in war-time to the regular British forces. Under this scheme the officers appointed began as full lieutenants. The Governor-General of Jamaica (or whatever his proper style may be) nominated the eighteen-year-old son of a rich Jamaica planter. He was sent straight from Jamaica to the First Middlesex. He was good-hearted enough but of little use in the trenches. He had never been out of the island in his life and, except for a short service with the West Indian militia, knew nothing of soldiering. His company commander took a fatherly interest in Young Jamaica, as he was called, and tried to teach him his duties. This company commander was known as The Boy. He had twenty years' service in the Middlesex, and the unusual boast of having held every rank from 'boy' to captain in the same company. His father, I believe, had been the regimental sergeant-major. The difficulty was that Jamaica was a full lieutenant and so senior to the other experienced subalterns in the company, who were only second-lieutenants. The colonel decided to shift Jamaica off on some course or extra-regimental appointment at the earliest opportunity. Somewhere about May or June he had been asked to supply an officer for the brigade trench-mortar company, and he had sent Jamaica. Trench-mortars at that time were dangerous and ineffective; so the appointment seemed suitable. At the same time the Royal Welch Fusiliers had also been asked to detail an officer, and the colonel had sent Tiley, an ex-planter from Malay, who was what is called a fine natural soldier. He had been chosen because he was attached from another regiment and had showed his resentment at the manner of his welcome somewhat too plainly. By September mortars had improved in design and become an important infantry arm; Jamaica was senior to Tiley and was therefore in the responsible position of commanding the company.

When the Middlesex made the charge, The Boy was mortally wounded as he climbed over the parapet. He fell back and began crawling down the trench to the stretcher-bearers' dug-out. He passed Jamaica's trench-mortar emplacement. Jamaica had lost his gun-team and was serving the trench-mortars himself. When he saw The Boy he forgot about his guns and ran off to get a stretcher-party. Tiley meanwhile, on the other flank, opposite Mine Point, had knocked out the machine-guns within range. He went on until his gun burst. The machine-gun in the Pope's Nose, a small salient opposite Jamaica, remained in action.

It was at this point that the Royal Welch Fusiliers came up in support. Maison Rouge Alley was a nightmare; the Germans were shelling it with five-nines bursting with a black smoke and with lachrymatory shells. This caused a continual scramble backwards and forwards. There were cries and counter-cries: 'Come on!' 'Get back, you bastards!' 'Gas turning on us!' 'Keep your heads, you men!' 'Back like hell, boys.' 'Whose orders?' 'What's happening?' 'Gas!' 'Back!' 'Come on!' 'Gas!' 'Back!' Wounded men and stretcher-bearers were still trying to squeeze past. We were alternately putting on and taking off our gas-helmets and that made things worse. In many places the trench was filled in and we had to scramble over the top. Childe-Freeman got up to the front line with only fifty men of B Company; the rest had lost their way in some abandoned trenches half-way up. The adjutant met him in the support line. 'You ready to go over, Free-man?' he asked. Freeman had to admit that he had lost most of his company. He felt this keenly as a disgrace; it was the first time that he had commanded a com-pany in battle. He decided to go over with his fifty men in support of the Middlesex. He blew his whistle and the company charged. They were stopped by machine-gun fire before they had passed our own entanglements. Freeman himself died, but of heart-failure, as he stood on the parapet. After a few minutes C Company and the remainder of B reached the front line. The gas-cylinders were still whistling and the trench full of dying men. Samson decided to go over; he would not have it said that the Royal Welch had let down the Middlesex. There was a strong comradely feeling between the Middlesex and the Royal Welch. The Royal Welch and Middlesex were drawn together in dislike of the Scots. The other three battalions in the brigade were Scottish, and the brigadier was a Scot and, unjustly no doubt, accused of favouring them. Our adjutant voiced the general opinion:[3] 'The Jocks are all the same, the trousered variety and the bare-backed variety. They're dirty in trenches, they skite too much, and they charge like hell – both ways.' The

Middlesex, who were the original Diehard battalion, had more than once, with the Royal Welch, considered themselves let down by the Jocks. So Samson with C and the rest of B Company charged. One of the officers told me later what happened to himself. It had been agreed to advance by platoon rushes with supporting fire. When his platoon had run about twenty yards he signalled them to lie down and open covering fire. The din was tremendous. He saw the platoon on the left flopping down too, so he whistled the advance again. Nobody seemed to hear. He jumped up from his shell-hole and waved and signalled 'Forward'. Nobody stirred. He shouted: 'You bloody cowards, are you leaving me to go alone?' His platoon sergeant, groaning with a broken shoulder, gasped out: 'Not cowards, sir. Willing enough. But they're all f—ing dead.' A machine-gun traversing[4] had caught them as they rose to the whistle.

Our company too had become separated by the shelling. The Surrey-man got a touch of gas and went coughing back. The Actor said he was skrim-shanking and didn't want the battle. This was unfair. The Surrey-man looked properly sick. I do not know what happened to him, but I heard that the gas was not much and that he managed, a few months later, to get back to his own regiment in France. I found myself with The Actor in a narrow trench between the front and support lines. This trench had not been built wide enough for a stretcher to pass the bends. We came on The Boy lying on his stretcher wounded in the lungs and the stomach. Jamaica was standing over him in tears, blubbering: 'Poor old Boy, poor old Boy, he's going to die; I'm sure he is. He's the only one who was decent to me.' The Actor found we could not get by.

He said to Jamaica: 'Take that poor sod out of the way, will you? I've got to get my company up. Put him into a dug-out or somewhere.' Jamaica made no answer; he seemed paralysed by the horror of the occasion. He could only repeat: 'Poor old Boy, poor old Boy.' 'Look here,' said The Actor, 'if you can't shift him into a dug-out we'll have to lift him on top of the trench. He can't live now and we're late getting up.' 'No, no,' Jamaica shouted wildly. The Actor lost his temper and shook Jamaica roughly by the shoulders. 'You're the bloody trench-mortar wallah, aren't you?' he asked fiercely. Jamaica nodded miserably. 'Well, your battery is a hundred yards from here. Why the hell aren't you using your gas-pipes on that machine-gun in the Pope's Nose? Buzz off back to them.' And he kicked him down the trench. Then he called over his shoulder: 'Sergeant Rose and Corporal Jennings, lift this stretcher up across the top of the trench. We've got to pass.' Jamaica leaned against a traverse. 'I do think you're the most heartless beast I've ever met,' he said weakly.

We went on up to the front line. It was full of dead and dying. The captain of the gas-company, who had kept his head and had a special oxygen respirator, had by now turned off the gas. Vermorel-sprayers had cleared out most of the gas, but we still had to wear our masks. We climbed up and crouched on the fire-step, where the gas was not so thick – gas was heavy stuff and kept low. Then Thomas arrived with the remainder of A Company and, with D, we waited for the whistle to follow the other two companies over. Fortunately at this moment the adjutant appeared. He told Thomas that he was now in command of the battalion and he didn't care a damn about orders; he was going to cut his losses. He said he would not send A and D over until he got definite orders from brigade. He had sent a runner back because telephone communication was cut, and we must wait. Meanwhile the intense bombardment that was to follow the forty minutes' discharge of gas began. It concentrated on the German front trench and wire. A good deal of it was short and we had further casualties in our trenches. The survivors of the Middlesex and of our B and C Companies in craters in No Man's Land suffered heavily.

My mouth was dry, my eyes out of focus, and my legs quaking under me. I found a water-bottle full of rum and drank about half a pint; it quieted me and my head remained clear. Samson was lying wounded about twenty yards away from the front trench. Several attempts were made to get him in. He was very badly hit and groaning. Three men were killed in these attempts and two officers and two men wounded. Finally his own orderly managed to crawl out to him. Samson ordered him back, saying that he was riddled and not worth rescuing; he sent his apologies to the company for making such a noise. We waited for about a couple of hours for the order to charge. The men were silent and depressed. Sergeant Townsend was making feeble, bitter jokes about the good old British army muddling through and how he thanked God we still had a navy. I shared the rest of the rum with him and he cheered up a little. Finally a runner came with a message that the attack was off for the present.

Rumours came down the trenches of a disaster similar to our own in the brick-stack area, where the Fifth Brigade had gone over, and again at Givenchy, where it was said that men of the Sixth Brigade at the Duck's Bill salient had fought their way into the enemy trenches, but had been bombed out, their own supply of bombs failing. It was said, however, that things were better on the right, where there had been a slight wind to take the gas over. There was a rumour that the First, Seventh, and Forty-seventh Divisions had broken through. My memory of that day is hazy. We spent it getting the wounded down to the dressing-station, spraying the trenches and dug-outs to get rid of the gas, and clearing away the earth where trenches were blocked. The trenches stank with a gas-blood-lyddite-latrine smell. Late in the afternoon we watched through our field-glasses the advance of the reserves towards Loos and Hill 70; it looked like a real break through. They were being heavily shelled. They were troops of the new-army division whose staff we had messed with the night before. Immediately to the right of us was the Highland Division, whose exploits on that day Ian Hay has celebrated in *The First Hundred Thousand*; I suppose that we were 'the flat caps on the left' who 'let down' his comrades-in-arms.

As soon as it was dusk we all went out to get in the wounded. Only sentries were left in the line. The first dead body I came upon was Samson's. I found that he had forced his knuckles into his mouth to stop himself crying out and attracting any more men to their death. He had been hit in seventeen places. Major Swainson, the second-in-command of the Middlesex, came crawling in from the German wire. He seemed to be wounded in the lungs, the stomach and a leg. Choate, a Middlesex second-lieutenant, appeared; he was unhurt, and together we bandaged Swainson and got him into the trench and on a stretcher. He begged me to loosen his belt; I cut it with a bowie-knife that I had bought in Béthune for use in the fighting. He said: 'I'm about done for.'* We spent all that night getting in the wounded of the Royal Welch, the Middlesex and those of the Argyll and Sutherland who had attacked from the front trench. The Germans behaved generously. I do not remember hearing a shot fired that night, and we kept on until it was nearly dawn and we could be plainly seen; then they fired a few shots in warning and we gave it up. By this time we had got in all the wounded and most of the Royal Welch dead. I was surprised at some of the attitudes in which the dead had stiffened – in the act of bandaging friends' wounds, crawling, cutting wire. The Argyll and Sutherland had seven hundred casualties, including fourteen officers killed out of the sixteen that went over; the Middlesex five hundred and fifty casualties, including eleven officers killed.

Two other Middlesex officers besides Choate were unwounded; their names were Henry and Hill, second-lieutenants who had recently come with commissions from, I think, the Artists' Rifles; their welcome in the Middlesex had been something like mine in the Royal Welch. They had been lying out in shell-holes in the rain all day, sniping and being sniped at. Henry, according to Hill, had dragged five wounded men into his shell-hole and thrown up a sort of parapet with his hands and a bowie-knife that he was carrying. Hill had his platoon sergeant with him, screaming for hours with a stomach wound, begging for morphia; he was dying, so Hill gave him five pellets. We always carried

* Major Swainson recovered quickly and was back at the Middlesex Depot after a few weeks. On the other hand, Lawrie, a Royal Welch company quartermaster-sergeant back at Cambrin, was hit in the neck that day by a spent machine-gun bullet which just pierced the skin, and died of shock a few hours later. [RG]

morphia with us for emergencies like this. When Choate, Henry and Hill arrived back in the trenches with a few stragglers they reported at the Middlesex head-quarters. Hill told me the story. The colonel and the adjutant were sitting down to a meat pie when he and Henry arrived. Henry said: 'Come to report, sir. Ourselves and about ninety men of all companies. Mr. Choate is back, unwounded, too.' They looked up dully. The colonel said: 'So you've come back, have you? Well, all the rest are dead. I suppose Mr. Choate had better command what's left of A Company, the bombing officer will command what's left of B (the bombing officer had not gone over but remained with headquarters), Mr. Henry goes to C Company, Mr. Hill to D. The Royal Welch are holding the front line. We are here in support. Let me know where to find you if I want you. Good night.' There was no offer to have a piece of meat pie or a drink of whisky, so they saluted and went miserably out. They were called back by the adjutant. 'Mr. Hill! Mr. Henry!' 'Sir?' Hill said that he expected a change of mind as to the propriety with which hospitality could be offered by a regular colonel and adjutant to temporary second-lieutenants in distress. But it was only to say: 'Mr. Hill, Mr. Henry, I saw some men in the trench just now with their shoulder-straps unbuttoned and their equipment fastened anyhow. See that this practice does not occur in future. That's all.' Henry heard the colonel from his bunk complaining that he had only two blankets and that it was a deucedly cold night. Choate arrived a few minutes later and reported; the others had told him of their reception. After he had saluted and reported that Major Swainson, who had been thought killed, was wounded and on the way down to the dressing-station, he leaned over the table, cut a large piece of meat pie and began eating it. This caused such surprise that nothing further was said. He finished his meat pie and drank a glass of whisky, saluted, and joined the others.

Meanwhile, I had been given command of the survivors of B Company. There were only six company officers left in the Royal Welch. Next morning there were only five. Thomas was killed by a sniper. He was despondently watching the return of the new-army troops on the right. They had been pushed blindly into the gap made by the advance of the Seventh and Forty-seventh Divisions on the previous afternoon; they did not know where they were or what they were supposed to do; their ration supply had broken down. So they flocked back, not in a panic, but stupidly, like a crowd coming back from a cup final. Shrapnel was bursting above them. We noticed that the officers were in groups of their own. We could scarcely believe our eyes, it was so odd. Thomas need not have been killed; but he was in the sort of mood in which he seemed not to care one way or the other. The Actor took command of A. We lumped our companies together after a couple of days for the sake of relieving each other on night watch and getting some sleep. The first night I agreed to take the first watch, waking him up at midnight. When I went to call him I could not wake him up; I tried everything. I shook him, shouted in his ear, poured water over him, banged his head against the side of the bed. Finally I threw him on the floor. I was desperate for want of sleep myself, but he was in a depth of sleep from which nothing could shake him, so I heaved him back on the bunk and had to finish the night out myself. Even 'Stand-to!' failed to arouse him. I woke him at last at nine o'clock in the morning and he was furious with me for not having waked him at midnight.

The day after the attack we spent carrying the dead down to burial and cleaning the trench up as well as we could. That night the Middlesex held the line while the Royal Welch carried all the unbroken gas-cylinders along to a position on the left flank of the brigade, where they were to be used on the following night, September 27th. This was worse than carrying the dead; the cylinders were cast-iron and very heavy and we hated them. The men cursed and sulked, but got the carrying done. Orders came that we were to attack again. Only the officers knew; the men were only to be told just beforehand. It was difficult for me to keep up appearances with the men; I felt like screaming. It was still raining, harder than ever. We knew definitely this time that ours was only a subsidiary night attack, a diversion to help a division on our right to make the real attack. The scheme was the same as before. At four p.m. the gas was to be discharged again for forty minutes, then came a quarter of an hour's bombardment, and then the attack. I broke the news to the men about three o'clock. They took it very well. The relations of officers and men, and of senior and junior officers, had been very different in the excitement of the attack. There had been no insubordination, but a greater freedom, as if everyone was drunk together. I found myself calling the adjutant Charley on one occasion; he appeared not to mind it in the least. For the next ten days my relations with my men were like those I had with the Welsh Regiment; later discipline reasserted itself and it was only occasionally that I found them intimate.

At four p.m., then, the gas went off again. There was

a strong wind and it went over well; the gasmen had brought enough spanners this time. The Germans were absolutely silent. Flares went up from the reserve lines and it seemed as though all the men in the front line were dead. The brigadier decided not to take too much for granted; after the bombardment he sent out twenty-five men and an officer of the Cameronians as a feeling-patrol. The patrol reached the German wire; there was a burst of machine-gun and rifle fire and only two wounded men regained the trench. We waited on the fire-step from four to nine o'clock, with fixed bayonets, for the order to go over. My mind was a blank except for the recurrence of 'S'nice smince spie, s'nice smince spie . . . I don't like ham, lamb or jam and I don't like roley-poley . . .' The men laughed at my singing. The sergeant who was acting company sergeant-major said to me: 'It's murder, sir.' 'Of course it's murder, you bloody fool,' I agreed. 'But there's nothing else for it, is there?' It was still raining. 'But when I see's a s'nice smince spie, I asks for a helping twice . . .' At nine o'clock we were told that the attack was put off; we were told to hold ourselves in readiness to attack at dawn.

No order came at dawn. And no more attacks were promised us after this. From the morning of September 24th to the night of October 3rd I had in all eight hours of sleep. I kept myself awake and alive by drinking about a bottle of whisky a day. I had never drank it before and have seldom drank it since; it certainly was good then. We had no blankets, greatcoats, or waterproof sheets. We had no time or material to build new shelters, and the rain continued. Every night we went out to get in the dead of the other battalions. The Germans continued to be indulgent and we had few casualties. After the first day or two the bodies swelled and stank. I vomited more than once while superintending the carrying. The ones that we could not get in from the German wire continued to swell until the wall of the stomach collapsed, either naturally or punctured by a bullet; a disgusting smell would float across. The colour of the dead faces changed from white to yellow-grey, to red, to purple, to green, to black, to slimy.

On the morning of the 27th a cry was heard from No Man's Land. It was a wounded man of the Middlesex who had recovered consciousness after two days. He was close to the German wire. Our men heard it and looked at each other. We had a lance-corporal called Baxter and he was tender-hearted. He was the man to boil up a special dixie of tea for the sentries of his section when they came off duty. When he heard the wounded man cry out he ran up and down the trench calling for a volunteer to come out with him and bring the man in. Of course no one would go; it was death to put one's head over the trench. He came running to ask me. I excused myself as the only officer in the company. I said I would come out with him at dusk, but I would not go now. So he went out himself. He jumped quickly over the parapet, then strolled across waving a handkerchief; the Germans fired at him to frighten him, but he came on, so they let him come up close. They must have heard the Middlesex man themselves. Baxter continued towards them and, when he got up to the Middlesex man, he stopped and pointed to show the Germans what he was at. Then he dressed the man's wounds, gave him a drink of rum and some biscuit that he had with him, and told him that he would come back again for him in the evening. He did come back for him with a stretcher-party and

the man eventually recovered. I recommended Baxter
for the Victoria Cross, being the only officer who had
seen the thing done; but he only got a Distinguished
Conduct Medal.

The Actor and I had decided to get into touch with
the battalion on our right. It was the Tenth Highland
Light Infantry. I went down their trench some time in
the morning of the 26th. I walked nearly a quarter of a
mile before seeing either a sentry or an officer. There
were dead men, sleeping men, wounded men, gassed
men, all lying anyhow. The trench had been used as a
latrine. Finally I met a Royal Engineer officer. He said
to me: 'If the Boche knew what an easy job it was, he'd
just walk over and take this trench.' So I came back
and told The Actor that we might expect to have our
flank in the air at any moment. We turned the communication trench that made the boundary between the
two battalions into a fire-trench facing right; a machine-
gun was mounted to put up a barrage in case they ran.
On the night of the 27th the Highlanders mistook
some of our men, who were out in No Man's Land
getting in the dead, for the enemy. They began firing
wildly. The Germans retaliated. Our men caught the
infection, but were at once told to cease fire. 'Cease
fire' went along the trench until it came to the H.L.I.,
who misheard it as 'Retire.' A panic seized them and
they came rushing back.[5] Fortunately they came down
the trench instead of over the top. They were stopped
by a sergeant of the Fifth Scottish Rifles,[6] a territorial
battalion now in support to ourselves and the Middlesex. He chased them back into their trench at the point
of the bayonet.

On the 3rd of October we were relieved. The relieving troops were a composite battalion consisting of

about a hundred men of the Second Royal Warwickshire Regiment and about seventy Royal Welch
Fusiliers, all that was left of our own First Battalion.
Hanmer Jones and Frank Jones-Bateman had both
been wounded. Frank had his thigh broken with a rifle-
bullet while stripping the equipment off a wounded
man in No Man's Land; the cartridges in the man's
pouches had been set on fire by a shot and were exploding.* We went back to Sailly la Bourse for a couple of
days, where the colonel rejoined us with his bandaged
hand, and then further back to Annezin, a little village
near Béthune, where I lodged in a two-roomed cottage
with an old woman called Adelphine Heu.

* He was recommended for a Victoria Cross but got nothing because
no officer evidence, which is a condition of award, was available.
[RG]

XVI

At Annezin we reorganized. Some of the lightly
wounded rejoined for duty and a big draft from the
Third Battalion arrived, so that in a week's time we
were nearly seven hundred strong, with a full complement of officers. Old Adelphine made me comfortable.
She used to come into my room in the morning when I
was shaving and tell me the local gossip – how stingy
her daughter-in-law was, and what a rogue the Maire
was, and about the woman at Fouquières who had just
been delivered of black twins. She said that the Kaiser
was a bitch and spat on the floor to confirm it. Her
favourite subject was the shamelessness of modern
girls. Yet she herself had been gay and beautiful and
much sought after when she was young she said. She
had been in service as lady's maid to a rich draper's
wife of Béthune, and had travelled widely with her in
the surrounding country, and even over the border into
Belgium. She asked me about the various villages in
which I had recently been billeted, and told me scandal
about the important families who used to live in each.
She asked me if I had been in La Bassée; she did not
realize that it was in the hands of the enemy. I said no,
but I had tried to visit it recently and had been detained.
'Do you know Auchy, then?' I said that I had seen it
often from a distance. 'Then perhaps you know a big

farm-house between Auchy and Cambrin called Les Briques Farm?' I said, startled, that I knew it very well, and that it was a strong place with a moat and cellars and a kitchen garden now full of barbed wire. She said: 'Then I shall tell you. I was staying there in 1870. It was the year of the other war and there was at the house a handsome young *petit-caporal* who was fond of me. So because he was a nice boy and because it was the war, we slept together and I had a baby. But God punished me and the baby died. That's a long time ago.'

She told me that all the girls in Annezin prayed every night for the war to end and for the English to go away as soon as their money was spent. She said that the clause about the money was always repeated in case God should miss it.

Troops serving in the Pas de Calais loathed the French; except for occasional members of the official class, we found them thoroughly unlikeable people, and it was difficult to sympathize with their misfortunes. They had all the shortcomings of a border people. I wrote home about this time:

'I find it very difficult to love the French here. Even when we have been billeted in villages where no troops have been before, I have not met a single case of the hospitality that one meets among the peasants of other countries. It is worse than inhospitality here, for after all we are fighting for their dirty little lives. They suck enormous quantities of money out of us too. Calculate how much has flowed into the villages around Béthune, which for many months now have been continuously housing about a hundred thousand men. Apart from the money that they get paid directly as billeting allow-ance, there is the pay that the troops spend. Every private soldier gets his five-franc note (nearly four shillings) every ten days, and spends it on eggs, coffee, and beer in the local *estaminets*; the prices are ridiculous and the stuff bad. In the brewery at Béthune, the other day, I saw barrels of already thin beer being watered from the canal with a hose-pipe. The *estaminet*-keepers water it further.' (The fortunes made in the war were consolidated after the Versailles Treaty, when every peasant in the devastated areas staked preposterous compensation claims for the loss of possessions that he had never had.) It was surprising that there were so few clashes between the British and French as there were. The Pas de Calais French hated us and were convinced that when the war was over we intended to stay and hold the Channel ports. It was impossible for us at the time to realize that it was all the same to the peasants whether they were on the German or the British side of the line – it was a foreign military occupation anyhow. They were not at all interested in the sacrifices that we were making for 'their dirty little lives'. Also, we were shocked at the severity of French national accountancy; when we were told, for instance, that every British hospital train, the locomotive and carriages of which had been imported from England, had to pay a £200 fee for use of the rails on each journey they made from railhead to base.

The fighting was still going on around Loos. We could hear the guns in the distance, but it was clear that the thrust had failed and that we were now skirmishing for local advantages. But on October 13th there was a final flare-up; the noise of the guns was so great that even the inhabitants of Annezin, accustomed to these alarms, were properly frightened, and began packing up in case the Germans broke through. Old Adelphine was in tears with fright. Early that afternoon

I was in Béthune at the *Globe* drinking champagne-cocktails with some friends who had joined from the Third Battalion, when the assistant provost-marshal put his head in the door and called out: 'Any officers of the Fifth, Sixth, or Nineteenth Brigades here?' We jumped up. 'You are to return at once to your units.' 'Oh God,' said Robertson, 'that means another show.' Robertson had been in D Company and so escaped the charge. 'We'll be pushed over the top to-night to reinforce some-one, and that'll be the end of us.'

We hurried back to Annezin and found everything in confusion. 'We're standing-to – at half an hour's notice for the trenches,' we were told. We packed up hastily and in a few minutes the whole battalion was out in the road in fighting order. We were to go up to the Hohen-zollern Redoubt and were now issued with new trench maps of it. The men were in high spirits, even the sur-vivors of the show. They were singing songs to the accompaniment of an accordion and a penny whistle. Only at one time, when a 'mad-minute' of artillery noise was reached, they stopped and looked at each other, and Sergeant Townsend said sententiously: 'That's the charge. Many good fellows going west at this moment; maybe chums of ours.' Gradually the noise died down, and a message came at last from bri-gade that we would not be needed. It had been another dud show, chiefly to be remembered for the death of Charles Sorley, a captain in the Suffolks, one of the three poets of importance killed in the war. (The other two were Isaac Rosenberg and Wilfred Owen.)

This ended the operations for 1915. Tension was relaxed. We returned to battalion mess, to company drill, and to riding-school for the young officers. It was as though there had been no battle except that the senior officers were fewer and the Special Reserve element larger. Two or three days later we were back in trenches in the same sector. In October I was gazetted a captain in the Third (Special Reserve) Battalion. Promotion in the Third Battalion was rapid for subalterns who had joined early, because the battalion had trebled its strength and so was entitled to three times as many captains as before. It was good to have my pay go up several shillings a day, with an increase of war bonus and possible gratuity and pension if I were wounded, but I did not consider that side of it much. It was rank that was effective overseas. And here I was promoted captain over the heads of officers who had longer trench service and were older and better trained than myself. I went to the adjutant and offered not to wear the badges of rank while serving with the battalion. He said not unkindly: 'No, put your stars up. It can't be helped.' I knew that he and the colonel had no use for Special Reserve captains unless they were outstandingly good, and would not hesitate to get rid of them.

A Special Reserve major and captain had been recently sent home from the First Battalion, with a confidential report of inefficiency. I was anxious to avoid any such disgrace. Nor was my anxiety unfounded; shortly after I left the Second Battalion two other Special Reserve captains, one of whom had been promoted at the same time as myself, were sent back as 'likely to be of more service in the training of troops at home'. One of them was, I know, more efficient than I was.

I was in such a depressed state of nerves now that if I had gone into the trenches as a company officer I should probably have modified my formula for taking risks. Fortunately, I had a rest from the front line, being attached to the brigade sappers. Hill of the Middlesex was also having this relief. He told me that the Middlesex colonel had made a speech to the survivors of the battalion as soon as they were back in billets, telling them that the battalion had been unfortunate but would soon be given an opportunity of avenging its dead and making a fresh and, this time he hoped, successful attack upon La Bassée. 'I know you Diehards! You will go like lions over the top.' Hill's servant had whispered confidentially to Hill: 'Not on purpose I don't, sir!' The sapping company specialized in maintaining communication and reserve trenches in good repair. I was with it for a month before being returned to ordinary company duty. My recall was a punishment for failing, one day when we were in billets, to observe a paragraph in battalion orders requiring my presence on battalion parade.

My remaining trench service with the Second Battalion this autumn was uneventful. There was no excitement left in patrolling, no horror in the continual experience of death. The single recordable incident I recall was one of purely technical interest, a new method that an officer named Owen and myself invented for dealing with machine-guns firing at night. The method was to give each sentry a piece of string about a yard long, with a cartridge tied at each end; when the machine-gun started firing, sentries who were furthest from the fire would stretch the string in the direction of the machine-gun and peg it down with the points of the cartridges. This gave a pretty accurate line on the machine-gun. When we had about thirty or more of these lines taken on a single machine-gun we fixed rifles as accurately as possible along them and waited for it; as soon as it started we opened five rounds rapid. This gave a close concentration of fire and no element of nervousness could disturb the aim, the rifles being secured between sandbags. Divisional headquarters asked us for a report of the method. There was a daily exchange of courtesies between our machine-guns and the Germans' at stand-to; by removing cartridges from the ammunition belt it was possible to rap out the rhythm of the familiar call: 'Me–et me do–wn in Pi–cca–di–ll–y,' to which the Germans would reply, though in slower tempo, because our guns were faster than theirs: 'Se–e you da–mned to He–ll first.'[1]

It was late in this October that I was sent a press-cutting from *John Bull*. Horatio Bottomley, the editor, was protesting against the unequal treatment for criminal offences meted out to commoners and aristocrats. A young man, he said, convicted in the police-court of a criminal offence was merely bound over and put in the care of a physician – because he was the grandson of an earl! An offender not belonging to the influential classes would have been given three months without the option of a fine. The article described in some detail how Dick, a sixteen-year-old boy, had made 'a certain proposal' to a corporal in a Canadian regiment stationed near 'Charterhouse College', and how the corporal had very properly given him in charge of the police. This news was nearly the end of me. I decided that Dick had been driven out of his mind by the war. There was madness in the family, I knew; he had once shown me a letter from his grandfather scrawled in circles all over the page. It would be easy to think of him as dead.

I had now been in the trenches for five months and was getting past my prime. For the first three weeks an officer was not much good in the trenches; he did not know his way about, had not learned the rules of health and safety, and was not yet accustomed to recognizing degrees of danger. Between three weeks and

four months he was at his best, unless he happened to
have any particular bad shock or sequence of shocks.
Then he began gradually to decline in usefulness as
neurasthenia developed in him. At six months he
was still more or less all right; but by nine or ten
months, unless he had a few weeks' rest on a technical
course or in hospital, he began to be a drag on the
other members of the company. After a year or fifteen
months he was often worse than useless. Officers had a
less laborious but a more nervous time than the men.
There were proportionately twice as many neurasthenic cases among officers as among men, though the
average life of a man before getting killed or wounded
was twice as long as an officer's. Officers between the
ages of twenty-three and thirty-three had a longer useful life than those older or younger. I was too young.
Men over forty, though they did not suffer from the
want of sleep so much as those under twenty, had less
resistance to the sudden alarms and shocks. Dr. W.H.R.
Rivers told me later that the action of one of the duct-
less glands – I think the thyroid – accounted for this
decline in military usefulness. It pumped its chemical
into the blood as a sedative for tortured nerves; this
process went on until the condition of the blood was
permanently affected and a man went about his tasks
in a stupid and doped way, cheated into further endurance. It has taken some ten years for my blood to run
at all clean. The unfortunates were the officers who
had two years or more continuous trench service. In
many cases they became dipsomaniacs. I knew three or
four officers who had worked up to the point of two
bottles of whisky a day before they were lucky enough
to get wounded or sent home in some other way. A
two-bottle company commander of one of our line

battalions still happens to be alive who, in three shows running, got his company needlessly destroyed because he was no longer capable of taking clear decisions.

Aside from wounds, gas, and the accidents of war, the life of the trench soldier was, for the most part, not unhealthy. Food was plentiful and hard work in the open air made up for the discomfort of wet feet and clothes and draughty billets. A continual need for alertness discouraged minor illnesses; a cold was thrown off in a few hours, an attack of indigestion was hardly noticed. This was true, at least, in a good battalion, where the men were bent on going home either with an honourable wound or not at all. In an inferior battalion the men would prefer a wound to bronchitis, but would not mind the bronchitis. In a bad battalion they did not care 'whether,' in the trench phrase, 'the cow calved or the bull broke its bloody neck.' In a really good battalion, as the Second Battalion was when I went to it first, the question of getting wounded and going home was not permitted to be raised. Such a battalion had a very small sick list. In the 1914–15 winter there were no more than four or five casualties from 'trench feet' in the Second, and the following winter no more than eight or nine; the don't-care battalions lost very heavily indeed. Trench feet was almost entirely a matter of morale, in spite of the lecture-formula that N.C.O.'s and officers used to repeat time after time to the men: 'Trench feet is caused by tight boots, tight puttees or any other clothing calculated to interfere with the circulation of blood in the legs.' Trench feet was caused rather by going to sleep with wet boots, cold feet, and depression. Wet boots, by themselves, did not matter. If the man warmed his feet at a brazier or stamped them until they were warm and then went off to sleep with a sandbag tied round them he took no harm. He might even fall asleep with cold, wet feet, and they might swell slightly owing to tightness of boots or puttees; but trench feet only came if he did not mind getting trench feet or anything else, because his battalion had lost the power of sticking things out. At Bouchavesnes on the Somme in the winter of 1916–17 a battalion of dismounted cavalry lost half its strength in two days from trench feet; our Second Battalion had just had ten days in the same trenches with no cases at all.

Autumn was melancholy in the La Bassée sector; in the big poplar forests the leaves were French yellow and the dykes were overflowing and the ground utterly sodden. Béthune was not the place it had been; the Canadians billeted there drew two or three times as much pay as our own troops and had sent the prices up. But it was still more or less intact and one could still get cream buns and fish dinners.

In November I had orders to join the First Battalion, which was reorganizing after the Loos fighting. I was delighted. I found it in billets at Locon, behind Festubert, which was only a mile or two to the north of Cambrin. The difference between the two battalions continued markedly throughout the war, however many times each battalion got broken. The difference was that the Second Battalion at the outbreak of war had just finished its eighteen years overseas tour, while the First Battalion had not been out of England since the South African War. The First Battalion was, therefore, less old-fashioned in its militarism and more human; livers were better; the men had dealings with white women and not with brown. It would have been impossible in the First Battalion to see what I once saw in the Second – a senior officer pursuing a private soldier down the street, kicking his bottom because he had been slack in saluting. The First Battalion was as efficient and as regimental, on the whole more successful in its fighting, and a much easier battalion to live in.

The battalion already had its new company commanders and I went as second-captain to young Richardson of A Company. He was from Sandhurst, and his company was one of the best that I was ever with. They were largely Welshmen of 1915 enlistment. None of the officers in the company were more than twenty-two or twenty-three years old. A day or two after I arrived I went to visit C Company, where a Third Battalion officer whom I knew was commanding. The C's greeted me in a friendly way. As we were talking I noticed a book lying on the table. It was the first book (except my Keats and Blake) that I had seen since I came to France that was not either a military text-book or a rubbish novel. It was the *Essays of Lionel Johnson*. When I had a chance I stole a look at the fly-leaf, and the name was Siegfried Sassoon. I looked round to see who could possibly be called Siegfried Sassoon and bring *Lionel Johnson* with him to the First Battalion. He was obvious, so I got into conversation with him, and a few minutes later we were walking to Béthune, being off duty until that night, and talking about poetry. Siegfried had, at the time, published nothing except a few privately-printed pastoral pieces of eighteen-ninetyish flavour and a satire on Masefield which, about halfway through, had forgotten to be a satire and was rather good Masefield. We went to the cake shop and ate cream buns. At this time I was getting my first book of poems, *Over the Brazier*, ready for the press; I had one or two drafts in my pocket-book and showed them to Siegfried. He told me that they were too realistic and that war should not be written about in a realistic way. In return he showed me some of his own poems. One of them began:

> Return to greet me, colours that were my joy,
> Not in the woeful crimson of men slain . . .[2]

This was before Siegfried had been in the trenches. I told him, in my old-soldier manner, that he would soon change his style.

That night the whole battalion went up to work at a new defence scheme at Festubert. Festubert was a nightmare, and had been so since the first fighting there in 1914, when the inmates of its lunatic asylum had been caught between two fires and broken out and run all over the countryside. The British trench line went across a stretch of ground marked on the map as 'Marsh, sometimes dry in the summer.' It consisted of islands of high-command trench, with no communication between them except at night, and was a murderous place for patrols. The battalion had been nearly wiped out here six months previously. We were set to build up a strong reserve line. It was freezing hard and we were unable to make any progress on the frozen ground. We came here night after night. We raised a couple of hundred yards of trench about two or three feet high, at the cost of several men wounded from casual shots skimming the trench in front of us. Work was resumed by other troops when the thaw came and a thick seven foot-high ramp built. We were told later that it gradually sank down into the marsh, and in the end was completely engulfed.

When I left the Second Battalion I was permitted to take my servant, Private Fahy (known as Tottie Fay, after the actress), with me. Tottie was a reservist from Birmingham who had been called up when war broke out, and had been with the Second Battalion ever since. By trade he was a silversmith and he had recently, when on leave, made a cigarette case and engraved it with my name as a present. He worked well and we liked each other. When he arrived at the First Battalion he met a Sergeant Dickens who had been his boozing chum in India seven or eight years back; so they celebrated it. The next morning I was surprised to find my buttons not polished and no hot water for shaving. I was annoyed; it made me late for breakfast. I could get no news of Tottie. On my way to rifle inspection at nine o'clock at the company billet I noticed something unusual at the corner of a farm-yard. It was Field Punishment No. 1 being carried out – my first sight of it. Tottie was the victim. He had been awarded twenty-eight days for 'drunkenness in the field'. He was spread-eagled to the wheel of a company limber, tied by the ankles and wrists in the form of an X. He remained in this position – 'Crucifixion,' they called it – for several hours a day; I forget how many, but it was a good working-day. The sentence was to be carried out for as long as the battalion remained in billets, and was to be continued after the next spell of trenches. I shall never forget the look that Tottie gave me. He was a quiet, respectful, devoted servant, and he wanted to tell me that he was sorry for having let me down. His immediate reaction was an attempt to salute; I could see him try to lift his hand to his forehead, and bring his heels together, but he could do nothing; his eyes filled with tears. The battalion police-sergeant, a fierce-looking man, had just finished knotting him up when I arrived. I told Tottie that I was sorry to see him in trouble. That drink, as it proved, did him good in the end. I had to find another servant. Old Joe, the quartermaster, knowing that Tottie was the only trained officer's servant in the battalion, took him from me when his sentence expired; he even induced the colonel to remit a few days of it. Tottie was safer in billets with Old Joe than in trenches with me. Some time in the summer of the following year his seven years' contract as a reservist expired. When their 'buckshee seven' expired, reservists were sent home for a few days and then 'deemed to have re-enlisted under the Military Service Act', and recalled to the battalion. But Tottie made good use of his leave. His brother-in-law was director of a munitions factory and took Tottie in as a skilled metal-worker. He was made a starred man – his work was so important to industry that he could not be spared for military service, so Tottie is, I hope, still alive. Good luck to him and to Birmingham. Sergeant Dickens was a different case. He was a fighter, and one of the best N.C.O.'s in either battalion of the regiment. He had been awarded the D.C.M. and Bar, the Military Medal and the French Médaille Militaire. Two or three times already he had been promoted to sergeant's rank and each time been reduced for drunkenness. He escaped field-punishment because it was considered sufficient for him to lose his stripes, and whenever there was a battle Dickens would distinguish himself so conspicuously as a leader that he would be given his stripes back again.

Early in December the rumour came that we were

going for divisional training to the back areas. I would not believe it, having heard stories of this kind too often, and was surprised when it turned out to be true. Siegfried Sassoon, in his *Memoirs of a Fox-hunting Man*, has described this battalion move. It was an even more laborious experience for our A Company than for his C Company. We got up at five o'clock one morning, breakfasted hastily, packed our kits, and marched down to the railhead three miles away. Here we had the task of entraining all the battalion stores, transport and transport-animals. This took us to the middle of the morning. We then entrained ourselves for a ten-hour journey to a junction on the Somme about twenty miles away from the front line. The officers travelled in third-class apartments, the men in closed trucks marked: 'Hommes 40, chevaux 8' – they were very stiff when they arrived. 'A' Company was called on to do the detraining job too. When we had finished, the dixies of tea prepared for us were all cold. The other companies had been resting for a couple of hours; we had only a few minutes. The march was along *pavé* roads and the rough chalk tracks of the Picardy downland. It started about midnight and finished about six o'clock next morning, the men carrying their packs and rifles. There was a competition between the companies as to which would have the fewest men falling out; A won. The village we finally arrived at was called Montagne le Fayel. No troops had been billeted here before, and its inhabitants were annoyed at being knocked up in the middle of the night by our advance-guard to provide accommodation for eight hundred men at two hours' notice. We found these Picard peasants much more likeable than the Pas de Calais people. I was billeted with an old man called Monsieur Elie Caron, a retired schoolmaster with a bright eye and white hair. He lived entirely on vegetables, and gave me a vegetarian pamphlet entitled *Comment Vivre Cent Ans*. We already knew of the coming Somme offensive, so this was a good joke.[3] He also gave me Longfellow's *Evangeline* in English. I have always been sorry for English books stranded in France, whatever their demerits; so I accepted it and later brought it home.

We were at Montagne for six weeks. The colonel, who appears in Siegfried's books as Colonel Winchell, was known in the regiment as Scatter, short for Scatter-cash, because when he first joined the regiment he had been so lavish with his allowance. Scatter put the battalion through its paces with peace-time severity. He asked us to forget the trenches and to fit ourselves for the open warfare that was bound to come once the Somme defences were pierced. Every other day was a field-day; we were back again in spirit to General Haking's *Company Training*. Even those of us who did not believe in the break-through thoroughly enjoyed these field-days. The guns could only just be heard in the distance, it was quite unspoilt country, and every man in the battalion was fit. Days that were not field-days were given up to battalion drill and musketry. This training seemed entirely unrelated to war as we had experienced it. We played a lot of games, including inter-battalion rugger; I played full-back for the battalion. Three other officers were in the team; Richardson as front-row scrum-man; Pritchard, another Sandhurst boy, who was fly-half; and David Thomas, a Third Battalion second-lieutenant, who was an inside three-quarter. David Thomas and Siegfried were the closest friends

I made while in France. David was a simple, gentle fellow and fond of reading. Siegfried, he, and I were together a lot.

One day David met me in the village street. He said: 'Did you hear the bugle? There's a hell of a row on about something. All officers and warrant-officers are to meet in the village school-room at once. Scatter's looking as black as thunder. No one knows yet what the axe is about.' We went along together and squeezed into one of the school desk-benches. When the colonel entered and the room was called to attention by the senior major, David and I hurt ourselves standing up, bench and all. Scatter told us all to be seated. The officers were in one class, the warrant-officers and non-commissioned officers in another. The colonel glared at us from the teacher's desk. He began his lecture with general accusations. He said that he had lately noticed many signs of slovenliness in the battalion – men with their pocket-flaps undone, and actually walking down the village street with their hands in their trousers-pockets – boots unpolished – sentries strolling about on their beats at company billets instead of marching up and down in a soldier-like way – rowdiness in the *estaminets* – slackness in saluting – with many other grave indications of lowered discipline. He threatened to stop all leave to the United Kingdom unless discipline improved. He promised us a saluting parade every morning before breakfast which he would attend in person. All this was general axe-ing and we knew that he had not yet reached the particular axe. It was this: 'I have here principally to tell you of a very disagreeable occurrence. As I was going out of my orderly room early this morning I came upon a group of soldiers; I will not mention their company. One of these soldiers was in conversation with a lance-corporal. You may not believe it, but it was a fact that he addressed the corporal by his Christian name; *he called him Jack*. The corporal made no protest. To think that the First Battalion has sunk to a level where it is possible for such familiarity to exist between N.C.O.'s and the men under their command! Naturally, I put the corporal under arrest, and he appeared before me at once on the charge of "conduct unbecoming to an N.C.O." He was reduced to the ranks, and the man was given field-punishment for using insubordinate language to an N.C.O. And, I warn you, if any further case of the sort comes to my notice – and I expect you officers to report the slightest instance to me at once instead of dealing with it as a company matter . . .' I tried to catch Siegfried's eye, but he was busy avoiding it, so I caught David's instead. This is one of those caricature scenes that now seem to sum up the various stages of my life.[4] There was a fresco around the walls of the class-room illustrating the evils of alcoholism. It started with the innocent boy being offered a drink by his mate, and then his down-ward path, culminating in wife-beating, murder, and *delirium tremens*.

The battalion's only complaint against Montagne was that women were not so easy to get hold of in that part of the country as around Béthune; the officers had the unfair advantage of being able to borrow horses and ride into Amiens. I remained puritanical. There was a Blue Lamp at Amiens as there was at Abbéville, Havre, Rouen, and all the big towns behind the lines. The Blue Lamp was for officers, as the Red Lamp was for men. It was most important for discipline to be maintained in this way.

In January the Seventh Division sent two company officers from each brigade to instruct troops at the base. I and a captain in the Queen's were the two who had been out longest, so we were chosen; it was a gift of two months longer life to us.

XVII

I was one of about thirty instructors at the Havre 'Bull Ring', where newly-arrived drafts were sent for technical instruction before going up the line. Most of my colleagues were specialists in musketry, machine-gun, gas, or bombs. I had no specialist training, only general experience. I was put on instructional work in trench relief and trench discipline in a model set of trenches. My principal other business was arms-drill. One day it rained, and the commandant of the Bull Ring suddenly ordered me to lecture in the big concert hall. 'There are three thousand men there waiting for you, and you're the only available officer with a loud enough voice to make himself heard.' They were Canadians, so instead of giving my usual semi-facetious lecture on 'How to be happy though in the trenches,' I paid them the compliment of telling them the story of Loos, and what a balls-up it was, and why it was a balls-up. It was the only audience that I ever held for an hour with real attention. I expected the commandant to be furious with me because the principal object of the Bull Ring was to inculcate the offensive spirit, but he took it well and I had several more concert-hall lectures put on me after this.

In the instructors' mess the chief subjects of conversation besides local and technical talk were *morale*, the reliability of various divisions in battle, the value of different training methods, and war-morality, with particular reference to atrocities. We talked more freely there than would have been possible either in England or in the trenches. We decided that about a third of the troops in the British Expeditionary Force were dependable on all occasions; these were the divisions that were always called on for the most important tasks. About a third were variable, that is, where a division contained one or two bad battalions, but could be more or less trusted. The remainder were more or less untrustworthy; being put in positions of comparative safety they had about a quarter of the casualties that the best divisions had. It was a matter of pride to belong to one of the recognized best divisions – the Seventh,[1] the Twenty-ninth, Guards', First Canadian, for instance. They were not pampered when in reserve as the German storm-troops were, but promotion, leave, and the chance of a wound came quicker in them. The mess agreed that the most dependable British troops were the Midland county regiments, industrial Yorkshire and Lancashire troops, and the Londoners. The Ulsterman, Lowland Scots and Northern English were pretty good. The Catholic Irish and the Highland Scots were not considered so good[2] – they took unnecessary risks in trenches and had unnecessary casualties, and in battle, though they usually made their objective, they too often lost it in the counter-attack; without officers they were no good. English southern county regiments varied from good to very bad. All overseas troops were good. The dependability of divisions also varied with their seniority in date of promotion.[3] The latest formed regular divisions and the second-line territorial divisions, whatever their recruiting area, were usually inferior. Their senior offi-cers and warrant-officers were not good enough.[4]

We once discussed which were the cleanest troops in trenches, taken in nationalities. We agreed on a list like this, in descending order: English and German Protes-tants; Northern Irish, Welsh and Canadians; Irish and German Catholics; Scottish;[5] Mohammedan Indians; Algerians; Portuguese; Belgians; French. The Belgians and French were put there for spite; they were not really dirtier than the Algerians or Portuguese.

Atrocities. Propaganda reports of atrocities were, we agreed, ridiculous. Atrocities against civilians were surely few. We remembered that while the Germans were in a position to commit atrocities against enemy civilians, Germany itself, except for the early Russian cavalry raid, had never had the enemy on her soil. We no longer believed accounts of unjustified German atrocities in Belgium; knowing the Belgians now at first-hand. By atrocities we meant, specifically, rape, mutilation and torture, not summary shootings of suspected spies, harbourers of spies, *francs-tireurs*, or disobedient local officials. If the atrocity list was to include the accidental-on-purpose bombing or machine-gunning of civilians from the air, the Allies were now committing as many atrocities as the Germans. French and Belgian civilians had often tried to win our sympathy and presents by exhibiting mutilations of children – stumps of hands and feet, for instance – representing them as deliberate, fiendish atrocities when they were merely the result of shell-fire, British or French shell-fire as likely as not. We did not believe that rape was any more common on the German side of the line than on the Allied side. It was unnecessary. Of course, a bully-beef diet, fear of death, and absence of wives made ample provision of women necessary in the occupied areas. No doubt the German army authorities provided brothels in the principal French towns behind the line, as did the French on the Allied side. But the voluntary system would suffice. We did not believe stories of forcible enlistment of women.

As for atrocities against soldiers. The difficulty was to say where to draw the line. For instance, the British soldier at first regarded as atrocious the use of bowie-knives by German patrols. After a time he learned to use them himself; they were cleaner killing weapons than revolvers or bombs. The Germans regarded as atrocious the British Mark VII rifle bullet, which was more apt to turn on striking than the German bullet. For true atrocities, that is, personal rather than military violations of the code of war, there were few opportunities. The most obvious opportunity was in the interval between surrender of prisoners and their arrival (or non-arrival) at headquarters. And it was an opportunity of which advantage was only too often taken. Nearly every instructor in the mess knew of specific cases when prisoners had been murdered on the way back. The commonest motives were, it seems, revenge for the death of friends or relations, jealousy of the prisoner's pleasant trip to a comfortable prison camp in England, military enthusiasm, fear of being suddenly overpowered by the prisoners or, more simply, not wanting to be bothered with the escorting job. In any of these cases the conductors would report on arrival at headquarters that a German shell had killed the prisoners; no questions would be asked. We had every reason to believe that the same thing happened on the German side, where prisoners, as useless mouths to feed in a country already on short rations, were even less welcome. We had none of us heard of prisoners being more than threatened at headquarters to get military information from them; the sort of information that trench-prisoners could give was not of sufficient importance to make torture worth while; in any case it was found that when treated kindly prisoners were anxious, in gratitude, to tell as much as they knew.

The troops that had the worst reputation for acts of violence against prisoners were the Canadians (and later the Australians). With the Canadians the motive was said to be revenge for a Canadian found crucified with bayonets through his hands and feet in a German trench; this atrocity was never substantiated, nor did we believe the story freely circulated that the Canadians crucified a German officer in revenge shortly afterwards, (Of the Australians the only thing to be said was that they were only two generations removed from the days of Ralph Rashleigh and Marcus Clarke.)[6] How far this reputation for atrocities was deserved, and how far it was due to the overseas habit of bragging and leg-pulling, we could not decide. We only knew that to have committed atrocities against prisoners was, among the overseas men, and even among some British troops, a boast, not a confession.

I heard two first-hand accounts later in the war.

A Canadian-Scot: 'I was sent back with three bloody prisoners, you see, and one was limping and groaning, so I had to keep on kicking the sod down the trench. He was an officer. It was getting dark and I was getting fed up, so I thought: "I'll have a bit of a game." I had them covered with the officer's revolver and I made 'em open their pockets. Then I dropped a Mills' bomb in each, with the pin out, and ducked behind a traverse. Bang, bang, bang! No more bloody prisoners. No good Fritzes but dead 'uns.'

An Australian: 'Well, the biggest lark I had was at Morlancourt when we took it the first time. There were a lot of Jerries in a cellar and I said to 'em: "Come out, you Camarades." So out they came, a dozen of 'em, with their hands up. "Turn out your pockets," I told 'em. They turned 'em out. Watches and gold and stuff, all dinkum. Then I said: "Now back into your cellar, you sons of bitches." For I couldn't be bothered with 'em. When they were all down I threw half a dozen Mills' bombs in after 'em. I'd got the stuff all right, and we weren't taking prisoners that day.'

The only first-hand account I heard of large-scale atrocities was from an old woman at Cardonette on the Somme, with whom I was billeted in July 1916. It was at Cardonette that a battalion of French Turcos overtook the rear guard of a German division retreating from the Marne in September 1914. The Turcos surprised the dead-weary Germans while they were still marching in column. The old woman went, with gestures, through a pantomime of slaughter, ending: 'Et enfin ces animaux leur ont arraché les oreilles et les ont mis à la poche.'[7] The presence of coloured troops in Europe was, from the German point of view, we knew, one of the chief Allied atrocities. We sympathized. Recently, at Flixécourt, one of the instructors told us, the cook of a corps headquarter-mess used to be visited at the château every morning by a Turco; he was orderly to a French liaison officer. The Turco used to say: 'Tommy, give Johnny pozzy,' and a tin of plum and apple jam used to be given him. One afternoon the corps was due to shift, so that morning the cook said to the Turco, giving him his farewell tin: 'Oh, la, la,

Johnny, napoo pozzy to-morrow.' The Turco would not believe it. 'Yes, Tommy, mate,' he said, 'pozzy for Johnny to-morrow, to-morrow, to-morrow.' To get rid of him the cook said: 'Fetch me the head of a Fritz, Johnny, to-night. I'll ask the general to give you pozzy to-morrow, to-morrow, to-morrow.' 'All right, mate,' said the Turco, 'me get Fritz head to-night, general give me pozzy to-morrow.' That evening the mess cook of the new corps that had taken over the château was surprised to find a Turco asking for him and swinging a bloody head in a sandbag. 'Here's Fritz head, mate,' said the Turco, 'general give me pozzy to-morrow, to-morrow, to-morrow.' As Flixécourt was twenty miles or more behind the line . . . He did not need to end the story, but swore it was true, because he had seen the head.

We discussed the continuity of regimental *morale*. A captain in a line battalion of one of the Surrey regiments said: 'It all depends on the reserve battalion at home.' He had had a year's service when the war broke out; the battalion, which had been good, had never recovered from the first battle of Ypres. He said: 'What's wrong with us is that we have a rotten depot. The drafts are bad and so we get a constant re-infection.' He told me one night in our sleeping hut: 'In both the last two attacks that we made I had to shoot a man of my company to get the rest out of the trench. It was so bloody awful that I couldn't stand it. It's the reason why I applied to be sent down here.' This was not the usual loose talk that one heard at the base. He was a good fellow and he was speaking the truth. I was sorrier for Phillips – that was not his name – than for any other man I met in France. He deserved a better regiment. There was never any trouble with the Royal Welch like that. The boast of every good battalion in France was that it had never lost a trench; both our battalions made it. This boast had to be understood broadly; it meant never having been forced out of a trench by an enemy attack without recapturing it before the action ended. Capturing a German trench and being unable to hold it for lack of reinforcements did not count, nor did retirement from a trench by order or when the battalion of the left or right had broken and left a flank in the air. And in the final stages of the war trenches could be honourably abandoned as being entirely obliterated by bombardment, or because not really trenches at all, but a line of selected shell-craters.

We all agreed on the value of arms-drill as a factor in *morale*. 'Arms-drill as it should be done,' someone said, 'is beautiful, especially when the company feels itself as a single being and each movement is not a movement of every man together, but a single movement of one large creature.' I used to have big bunches of Canadians to drill four or five hundred at a time. Spokesmen came forward once and asked what sense there was in sloping and ordering arms and fixing and unfixing bayonets. They said they had come to France to fight and not to guard Buckingham Palace. I told them that in every division of the four in which I had served there had been three different kinds of troops. Those that had guts but were no good at drill; those that were good at drill but had no guts; and those that had guts and were good at drill. These last fellows were, for some reason or other, much the best men in a show. I didn't know why and I didn't care. I told them that when they were better at fighting than the Guards' Division they could perhaps afford to neglect their arms-drill.

We often theorized in the mess about drill. We knew

that the best drill never came from being bawled at by a sergeant-major, that there must be perfect respect between the man who gives the order and the men that carry it through. The test of drill came, I said, when the officer gave an incorrect word of command. If the company could carry through the order intended without hesitation, or, suppose the order happened to be impossible, could stand absolutely still or continue marching without any disorder in the ranks, that was good drill. The corporate spirit that came from drilling together was regarded by some instructors as leading to loss of initiative in the men drilled. Others denied this and said it acted just the other way round. 'Suppose there is a section of men with rifles, and they are isolated from the rest of the company and have no N.C.O. in charge and meet a machine-gun. Under the stress of danger that section will have that all-one-body feeling of drill and will obey an imaginary word of command. There will be no communication between its members, but there will be a drill movement. Two men will quite naturally open fire on the machine-gun while the remainder will work round part on the left flank and part on the right, and the final rush will be simultaneous. Leadership is supposed to be the perfection for which drill has been instituted. That is wrong. Leadership is only the first stage. Perfection of drill is communal action. Drill may seem to be antiquated parade-ground stuff, but it is the foundation of tactics and musketry. It was parade-ground musketry that won all the battles in our regimental histories; this war will be won by parade-ground tactics. The simple drill tactics of small units fighting in limited spaces – fighting in noise and confusion so great that leadership is quite impossible.' In spite of variance on this point we all agreed that regimental pride was the greatest moral force that kept a battalion going as an effective fighting unit, contrasting it particularly with patriotism and religion.

Patriotism. There was no patriotism in the trenches.[8] It was too remote a sentiment, and rejected as fit only for civilians. A new arrival who talked patriotism would soon be told to cut it out. As Blighty, Great Britain was a quiet, easy place to get back to out of the present foreign misery, but as a nation it was nothing. The nation included not only the trench-soldiers themselves and those who had gone home wounded, but the staff, Army Service Corps, lines of communication troops, base units, home-service units, and then civilians down to the detested grades of journalists, profiteers, 'starred' men exempted from enlistment, conscientious objectors, members of the Government. The trench-soldier, with this carefully graded caste-system of honour, did not consider that the German trench-soldier might have exactly the same system himself. He thought of Germany as a nation in arms, a unified nation inspired with the sort of patriotism that he despised himself. He believed most newspaper reports of conditions and sentiments in Germany, though believing little or nothing of what he read about conditions and sentiments in England. His cynicism, in fact, was not confined to his own country. But he never underrated the German as a soldier. Newspaper libels on Fritz's courage and efficiency were resented by all trench-soldiers of experience.

Religion. It was said that not one soldier in a hundred was inspired by religious feeling of even the crudest kind. It would have been difficult to remain religious in the trenches though one had survived the

irreligion of the training battalion at home. A regular
sergeant at Montagne, a Second Battalion man, had
recently told me that he did not hold with religion in
time of war. He said that the niggers (meaning the Indians) were right in officially relaxing their religious
rules when they were fighting. 'And all this damn nonsense, sir – excuse me, sir – that we read in the papers,
sir, about how miraculous it is that the wayside crucifixes are always getting shot at but the figure of our
Lord Jesus somehow don't get hurt, it fairly makes me
sick, sir.' This was to explain why in giving practice
fire-orders from the hill-top he had shouted out: 'Seven
hundred, half left, bloke on cross, five rounds consec-
rate, FIRE!' His platoon, even the two men whose
letters home always had the same formal beginning:
'Dear Sister in Christ', or 'Dear Brother in Christ',
blazed away.

The troops, while ready to believe in the Kaiser as a
comic personal devil, were aware that the German soldier was, on the whole, more devout than himself in
the worship of God. In the instructors' mess we spoke
freely of God and Gott as opposed tribal deities. For
the regimental chaplains as a body we had no respect.
If the regimental chaplains had shown one tenth the
courage, endurance, and other human qualities that
the regimental doctors showed, we agreed, the British
Expeditionary Force might well have started a religious revival. But they had not. The fact is that they
were under orders not to get mixed up with the fighting, to stay behind with the transport and not to risk
their lives. No soldier could have any respect for a
chaplain who obeyed these orders, and yet there was
not in our experience one chaplain in fifty who was not
glad to obey them. Occasionally on a quiet day in a

quiet sector the chaplain would make a daring afternoon visit to the support line and distribute a few
cigarettes, and that was all. But he was always in evidence back in rest-billets. Sometimes the colonel would
summon him to come up with the rations and bury the
day's dead, and he would arrive, speak his lines, and
hastily retire. The position was made difficult by the
respect that most of the commanding officers had for
the cloth, but it was a respect that they soon outwore.
The colonel in one battalion I served with got rid of
four new chaplains in as many months. Finally he
applied for a Roman Catholic chaplain, alleging a
change of faith in the men under his command. For, as
I should have said before, the Roman Catholics were
not only permitted in posts of danger, but definitely
enjoined[9] to be wherever fighting was so that they
could give extreme unction to the dying. And we had
never heard of an R.C. chaplain who was unwilling to
do all that was expected of him and more. It was
recalled that Father Gleeson of the Munsters, when all
the officers were put out of action at the first battle of
Ypres, stripped off his black badges and, taking command of the survivors, held the line.

Anglican chaplains were remarkably out of touch
with their troops. I told how the Second Battalion
chaplain just before the Loos fighting had preached a
violent sermon on the battle against sin, and how one
old soldier behind me had grumbled: 'Christ, as if one
bloody push wasn't enough to worry about at a time.'
The Catholic padre, on the other hand, had given his
men his blessing and told them that if they died fighting for the good cause they would go straight to
Heaven, or at any rate would be excused a great many
years in Purgatory. Someone told us of the chaplain of

his battalion when he was in Mesopotamia, how on the eve of a big battle he had preached a sermon on the commutation of tithes. This was much more sensible than the battle against sin, he said; it was quite up in the air, and took the men's minds off the fighting.

I was feeling a bit better after a few weeks at the base,[10] though the knowledge that this was only temporary relief was with me all the time. One day I walked out of the mess to begin the afternoon's work on the drill ground. I had to pass by the place where bombing instruction was given. A group of men was standing around the table where the various types of bombs were set out for demonstration. There was a sudden crash. An instructor of the Royal Irish Rifles had been giving a little unofficial instruction before the proper instructor arrived. He had picked up a No. 1 percussion grenade and said: 'Now, lads, you've got to be careful with this chap. Remember that if you touch anything while you're swinging it, it will go off.' To illustrate the point he rapped it against the edge of the table. It killed him and another man and wounded twelve others more or less severely.

XVIII

I rejoined the First Battalion in March, finding it in the line again, on the Somme. It was the primrose season. We went in and out of the Fricourt trenches, with billets at Morlancourt, a country village at that time untouched by shell-fire. (Later it was knocked to pieces; the Australians and the Germans captured and recaptured it from each other several times, until there was nothing left except the site.) 'A' Company headquarters were in a farmhouse kitchen. We slept in our valises on the red-brick floor. The residents were an old lady and her daughter. The old lady was senile and paralysed; about all she could do was to shake her head and say: 'Triste, la guerre.' We called her 'Triste la Guerre'. Her daughter used to carry her about in her arms.

The Fricourt trenches were cut in chalk, which was better in wet weather than the La Bassée clay. We were unlucky in having a battalion-frontage where the lines came closer to each other than at any other point for miles. It was only recently that the British line had been extended down to the Somme. The French had been content, as they usually were, unless they definitely intended a battle, to be at peace with the Germans and not dig in too near. But here there was a slight ridge and neither side could afford to let the other hold the crest, so they shared it, after a prolonged dispute. It was used by both the Germans and ourselves as an experimental station for new types of bombs and grenades. The trenches were wide and tumbledown, too shallow in many cases, and without sufficient traverses. The French had left relics of their nonchalance – corpses buried too near the surface; and of their love of security – a number of lousy but deep dug-outs. We busied ourselves raising the front-line parapet and building traverses to limit the damage of the trench-mortar shells that were continually falling. Every night not only the companies in the front line but both support companies were hard at work all the time. It was even worse than Cuinchy for rats; they used to run about A Company mess while we were at meals. We used to eat with revolvers beside our plates and punctuate our conversation with sudden volleys at a rat rummaging at somebody's valise or crawling along the timber support of the roof above our heads. A Company officers were gay. We had all been in our school choirs except Edmund Dadd, who sang like a crow, and we used to chant church anthems and bits of cantatas whenever things were going well. Edmund insisted on joining in.

We were at dinner one day when a Welsh boy came rushing in, hysterical with terror. He shouted out to Richardson: 'Sirr, sirr, there is a trenss-mortar in my dug-out.' This in sing-song Welsh made us all shout with laughter. Richardson said: 'Cheer up, 33 Williams, how did a big thing like a trench-mortar happen to be in your dug-out?' But 33 Williams could not explain. He went on again and again: 'Sirr, sirr, there is a trenss-mortar in my dug-out!' Edmund Dadd went out to investigate. He found that a trench-mortar shell had fallen into the trench, bounced down the dug-out steps, exploded and killed five men. 33 Williams had been lying asleep and had been protected by the body of another man; he was the only one unhit.

Our greatest trial was the canister. It was a two-gallon drum with a cylinder inside containing about two pounds of an explosive called ammonal that looked like salmon paste, smelt like marzipan, and when it went off sounded like the day of judgment. The hollow around the cylinder was filled with scrap metal apparently collected by the French villagers behind the German line – rusty nails, fragments of British and French shells, spent bullets, and the screws, nuts, and bolts that heavy lorries leave behind on the road. We dissected one canister that had not exploded and found in it, among other things, the cog-wheels of a clock and half a set of false teeth. The canister was easy to hear coming and looked harmless in the air, but its shock was as shattering as the very heaviest shell. It would blow in any but the deepest dug-outs; and the false teeth and cog-wheels and so on would go flying all over the place. We could not agree how a thing of that size was fired. The problem was not solved until 1st July, when the battalion attacked from these same trenches and found one of the canister-guns with its crew. It was a wooden cannon buried in the earth and fired with a time-fuse. The crew offered to surrender, but our men refused; they had sworn for months to get the crew of that gun.

One evening I was in the trench with Richardson and David Thomas (near 'Trafalgar Square', should anyone remember that trench-junction) when we met Pritchard and the adjutant. We stopped to talk. Richardson complained what a devil of a place it was for trench-mortars. Pritchard said: 'That is where I come in.' He was the battalion trench-mortar officer and had just been given the first two Stokes mortar-guns that we had seen in France. Pritchard said: 'They're beauties. I've been trying them out and to-morrow I'm going to get some of my own back. I can put four or five shells in the air at the same time.' The adjutant said: 'About time, too. We've had three hundred casualties in the last month here. It doesn't seem so many as that because we've had no officer casualties. In fact we've had about five hundred casualties in the ranks since Loos, and not a single officer.' Then he suddenly realized that he had said something unlucky. David said: 'Touch wood.' Everybody sprang to touch wood, but it was a French trench and unriveted.[1] I pulled a pencil out of my pocket; that was wood enough for me. Richardson said: 'I'm not superstitious, anyway.'

The next evening I was leading up A Company for a working-party. B and D Companies were in the line and we overtook C, which was also going up to work. David was bringing up the rear of C. He was looking strange, worried about something. I had never seen him anything but cheerful all the time I had known him. I asked what was the matter. He said: 'Oh, I'm fed up and I've got a cold.' C Company went along to the right of the battalion frontage and we went along to the left. It was a weird kind of night, with a bright moon. A German occupied sap was only forty or fifty yards away. We were left standing on the parapet piling up the sandbags, with the moon behind us, but the German sentries ignored us – probably because they had work on hand themselves. It often happened when both sides were busy putting up proper defences that they turned a blind eye to each other's work. Sometimes, it was said, the rival wiring-parties 'as good as borrowed each other's mallets' for hammering in the pickets. The Germans were much more ready to live and let live than we were. (The only time, so far as I know, besides Christmas 1914, that both sides showed themselves in daylight without firing at each other was once at Ypres when the trenches got so flooded that there was nothing for it but for both sides to crawl out on top to avoid drowning.) There was a continual exchange of grenades and trench-mortars on our side; the canister was going over and the men found it difficult to get out of its way in the dark. But for the first time we were giving the enemy as good as they gave us. Pritchard had been using his Stokes' mortar all day and had sent over two or three hundred rounds; twice they had located his emplacement and he had had to shift hurriedly.

'A' Company worked from seven in the evening until midnight. We must have put thousands of sandbags into position, and fifty yards of front trench were beginning to look presentable. About half-past ten there was rifle-fire on the right and the sentries passed down the news 'officer hit'. Richardson at once went along to see who it was. He came back to say: 'It's young Thomas. He got a bullet through the neck, but I think he's all right; it can't have hit his spine or an artery because he's walking down to the dressing-station.' I was pleased at this news. I thought that David would be out of it long enough perhaps to escape the coming offensive and perhaps even the rest of the war. At twelve o'clock we had finished for the night. Richardson said to me: 'Von Ranke' (only he pronounced it Von Runicke – it was my regimental nickname), 'take the company down for their rum and tea, will you? They've certainly deserved it to-night. I'll be along in a few minutes. I'm going out with Corporal

Chamberlen to see what work the wiring-party's been doing all this time.' So I took the men back. When we were well started I heard a couple of shells come over somewhere behind us. I noticed them because they were the only shells fired that night; five-nines they seemed by the noise. We were nearly back at Maple Redoubt, which was the name of the support line on the reverse side of the hill, when we heard the cry 'Stretcher-bearers!' and after a while a man came running to say: 'Captain Graves is hit.' There was a general laugh and we went on; but a stretcher-party went up anyhow to see what was wrong. It was Richardson; the shells had caught him and the corporal among the wire. The corporal had his leg blown off, and died of wounds a day or two later. Richardson had been blown into a shell-hole full of water and had lain there stunned for some minutes before the sentries heard the corporal's cries and realized what had happened. He was brought down semi-conscious; he recognized us, told us he wouldn't be long away from the company, and gave us instructions about it. The doctor said that he had no wound in any vital spot, though the skin of his left side was riddled, as we had seen, with the chalky soil blown up against him. We felt a relief in his case, as in David's, that he would be out of it for a while.

Then news came that David had died.[2] The regimental doctor, a throat specialist in civil life, had told him at the dressing-station: 'You'll be all right, only don't raise your head for a bit.' David had then, it was said, taken a letter from his pocket, given it to an orderly, and said: 'Post that.' It was a letter written to a girl in Glamorgan, to be posted in case he got killed. Then the doctor saw that he was choking; he tried trachotomy, but it was too late. Edmund and I were talking together in the company headquarters at about one o'clock when the adjutant came in. He looked ghastly. He told us that Richardson had died at the dressing-station. His heart had been weakened by rowing (he had been in the Eight at Radley) and the explosion and the cold water had been too much for it. The adjutant said to me nervously: 'You know, somehow I feel, I – I feel responsible in a way for this; what I said yesterday at "Trafalgar Square." Of course, really, I don't believe in superstition, but . . .' Just at that moment there was a noise of whizz-bang shells about twenty yards off; a cry of alarm, followed by: 'Stretcher-bearers!' The adjutant turned quite white and we knew without being told what it meant. We hurried out. Pritchard, having fought his duel all night, and finally silenced the enemy, was coming off duty. A whizz-bang had caught him at the point where the communication trench reached Maple Redoubt; it was a direct hit. The casualties of that night were three officers and one corporal.

It seemed ridiculous when we returned without Richardson to A Company billets to find 'Triste La Guerre' still alive and to hear her once more quaver out 'Triste, la guerre' when her daughter explained that the *jeune capitaine* had been killed. The old woman had taken a fancy to the *jeune capitaine*; we used to chaff him about it. I felt David's death worse than any other death since I had been in France. It did not anger me as it did Siegfried. He was acting transport-officer and every night now, when he came up with the rations, he went out on patrol looking for Germans. It just made me feel empty and lost.

One of the anthems that we used to sing was: 'He that shall endure to the end, shall be savèd.' The words repeated themselves in my head like a charm whenever things were bad. 'Though thousands languish and fall beside thee, And tens of thousands around thee perish, Yet still it shall not come nigh thee.' And there was another bit: 'To an inheritance incorruptible ... Through faith unto salvation, Ready to be revealèd at the last trump.' For 'trump' we always used to sing 'crump'. 'The last crump' was the end of the war and would we ever hear it burst safely behind us? I wondered whether I could endure to the end with faith unto salvation. I knew that my breaking point was near now, unless something happened to stave it off ... It was not that I was frightened. Certainly I feared death; but I had never yet lost my head through fright, and I knew that I never would. Nor would the breakdown come as insanity; I did not have it in me. It would be a general nervous collapse, with tears and twitchings and dirtied trousers. I had seen cases like that.

The battalion was issued with a new gas-helmet, popularly known as 'the goggle-eyed b—r with the tit'. It differed from the previous models. One breathed in through the nose from inside the helmet and breathed out through a special valve held in the mouth. I found that I could not manage this. Boxing with an already broken nose had recently displaced the septum, so that I was forced to breathe through my mouth. In a gas-attack I would be unable to use the helmet and it was the only type claimed to be proof against the new German gas. The battalion doctor advised me to have an operation done as soon as I could.

These months with the First Battalion have already been twice recorded in literary history; though in both cases in a disguise of names and characters. The two books are Siegfried Sassoon's *Memoirs of a Foxhunting Man*, and *Nothing of Importance*, by Bill Adams,

the battalion sniping and intelligence officer. Adams'
book did not sell, but was as good a book as 1917 cen-
sorship allowed; it should be reprinted. Adams was
killed;[3] in fact, three out of five of the officers of the
First Battalion at that time were killed in the Somme
fighting. Scatter's dream of open warfare was not realized. He himself was very seriously wounded. Of A
Company choir there is one survivor besides myself –
C. D. Morgan, who had his thigh smashed, and was
still in hospital sometime after the war ended.

XIX

When I was given leave in April 1916[1] I went to a military hospital in London and had my nose operated on. It was a painful operation, but performed by a first-class surgeon and cost me nothing. In peace-time it would have cost me sixty guineas, and another twenty guineas in nursing-home fees. After hospital I went up to Harlech to walk on the hills. I had in mind the verse of the psalm: 'I will lift up mine eyes unto the hills, from whence cometh my help.' That was another charm against trouble.[2] I bought a small two-roomed cottage from my mother, who owned considerable cottage property in the neighbourhood. I bought it in defiance of the war, as something to look forward to when the guns stopped ('when the guns stop' was how we always thought of the end of the war). I whitewashed the cottage and put in a table, a chair, a bed and a few dishes and cooking utensils. I had decided to live there by myself on bread and butter, bacon and eggs, lettuce in season, cabbage and coffee; and to write poetry. My war-bonus would keep me for a year or two at least. The cottage was on the hillside away from the village. I put in a big window to look out over the wood below and across the Morfa to the sea. I wrote two or three poems here as a foretaste of the good life coming after the war.[3]

It was about this time, but whether before or after my operation I cannot remember, that I was taken by my father to a dinner of the Honourable Cymmrodorion Society – a Welsh literary club – where Lloyd George, then Prime Minister, and W. M. Hughes, the Australian Prime Minister, were to speak. Hughes was perky, dry and to the point; Lloyd George was up in the air on one of his 'glory of the Welsh hills' speeches. The power of his rhetoric was uncanny. I knew that the substance of what he was saying was commonplace, idle and false, but I had to fight hard against abandoning myself with the rest of the audience. The power I knew was not his; he sucked it from his hearers and threw it back at them. Afterwards I was introduced to him, and when I looked closely at his eyes they were like those of a sleep-walker.

I rejoined the Third Battalion at Litherland, near Liverpool, where it had been shifted from Wrexham as part of the Mersey defence force; I liked the Third Battalion. The senior officers were generous in not putting more work on me than I wished to undertake, and it was good to meet again three of my Wrexham contemporaries who had been severely wounded (all of them, by a coincidence, in the left thigh) and seemed to be out of it for the rest of the war – Frank Jones-Bateman and 'Father' Watkin, who had been in the Welsh Regiment with me, and Aubrey Attwater, the assistant adjutant, who had gone to the Second Battalion early in 1915 and had been hit when out on patrol. Attwater had come from Cambridge at the outbreak of war and was known as 'Brains' in the battalion. The militia majors, who were for the most part country gentlemen with estates in Wales, and had no thoughts in peacetime beyond hunting, shooting, fishing, and the control of their tenantry, were delighted with Attwater's informative talk over the port at mess. Sergeant Malley, the mess-sergeant, would go round with his 'Light or vintage, sir?' and the old majors would say to Attwater: 'Now, Brains! Tell us about Shakespeare. Is it true that Bacon wrote him?' Or, 'Well, Brains! What do you think about this chap Hilaire Belloc? Does he really know when the war's going to end?' And Attwater would humorously accept his position as combined encyclopædia and almanac. Sergeant Malley was another friend whom I was always pleased to meet again. He could pour more wine into a glass than any other man in the world; it bulged up over the top of a glass like a cap and he was never known to spill a drop.

Wednesdays were guest-nights in the mess, when the married officers who usually dined at home were expected to attend. The band played Gilbert and Sullivan music behind a curtain. In the intervals the regimental harper gave solos – Welsh melodies picked out rather uncertainly on a hand-harp. When the programme was over the band-master was invited to the senior officers' table for his complimentary glass of light or vintage. When he was gone, and the junior officers had retired, the port went round and round, and the conversation, at first very formal, became rambling and intimate. Once, I remember, a senior major laid it down axiomatically that every so-called sportsman had at one time or another committed a sin against sportsmanship. When challenged, he cross-examined each of his neighbours in turn, putting them on their honour to tell the truth. One of them, blushing, admitted that he had once shot grouse two days before the Twelfth: 'It was my last chance before I rejoined the battalion in India.' Another said that when a public-school boy, and old enough to know better, he had killed a sitting pheasant with a stone. The next one had gone out with a poacher – in his Sandhurst days – and crumbled poison-berry into a trout-stream. An even more scandalous admission came from a new-army major, a gentleman-farmer, that his estate had been overrun with foxes one year and, the headquarters of the nearest hunt being thirty miles away, he had given his bailiff permission to protect the hen-roosts with a gun. Finally it was the turn of the medical officer to be cross-examined. He said: 'Well, once when I was a student at St. Andrews a friend asked me to put ten bob for him on a horse in the Lincolnshire. I couldn't find my bookmaker in time. The horse lost and I never returned the ten bob.' At this one of the guests, an officer in the King's Own Scottish Borderers, became suddenly excited, jumped up and leant over the table, doubling his fists. 'And was not the name of the horse Strathspey? And will you not pay me my ten shillings now immediately?'

The camp was only separated by the bombing-field from Brotherton's, where a specially sensitive explosive for detonators was made. The munition makers had permanently yellow faces and hands and drew appropriately high wages. Attwater used to argue at mess sometimes what would happen if Brotherton's blew up. Most of us held that the shock would immediately kill all the three thousand men of the camp besides destroying Litherland and a large part of Bootle. He maintained that the very closeness of the camp would save it; that the vibrations would go over and strike a big munition camp about a mile away and set that off. One Sunday afternoon Attwater limped out of the mess and suddenly saw smoke rising from

Brotherton's. Part of the factory was on fire. The camp fire-brigade was immediately bugled for and managed to put the fire out before it reached a vital spot. So the argument was never decided.[4] I was at Litherland only a few weeks. On 1st July 1916 the Somme offensive started, and all available trained men and officers were sent out to replace casualties. I was disappointed to be sent back to the Second Battalion, not the First.

It was in trenches at Givenchy, just the other side of the canal from the Cuinchy brick-stacks. I arrived at the battalion on July 5th to find it in the middle of a raid. Prisoners were coming down the trench, scared and chattering to each other. They were Saxons just returned from a divisional rest and a week's leave to Germany. Their uniforms were new and their packs full of good stuff to loot. One prisoner got a good talking-to from C Company sergeant-major, a Birmingham man, who was shocked at a packet of indecent photographs found in the man's haversack. It had been a retaliatory raid. Only a few days before, the Germans had sent up the biggest mine blown on the Western front so far. It caught our B Company – the B's were proverbially unlucky. The crater, which was afterwards named Red Dragon Crater after the Royal Welch regimental badge, must have been about thirty yards across. There were few survivors of B Company. The Germans immediately came over in force to catch the other companies in confusion. Stanway, who had been a company sergeant-major on the retreat and was now an acting-major, rallied some men on the flank and drove them back. Blair, B Company commander, was buried by the mine up to his neck and for the rest of the day was constantly under fire. Though an oldish man (he had the South African ribbon),[5] he survived this experience, recovered from his wounds, and was back in the battalion a few months later.

This raid was Stanway's revenge. He organized it with the colonel;[6] the colonel was the Third Battalion adjutant who had originally sent me out to France. The raid was elaborately planned, with bombardments and smoke-screen diversions on the flanks. A barrage of shrapnel shifted forward and back from the German front line to the supports. The intention was that the Germans at the first bombardment should go down into the shell-proof dug-outs, leaving only their sentries in the trench, and reappear as soon as the barrage lifted. When it came down again they would make another dash for the dug-outs. After this had happened two or three times they would be slow in coming out at all. Then, under cover of a smoke-screen, the raid would be made and the barrage put down uninterruptedly on the support and reserve lines to prevent reinforcements. My only part in the raid, which was successful, was to write out a detailed record of it at the colonel's request. It was not the report for divisional headquarters but a page of regimental history to be sent to the depot to be filed in regimental records. In my account I noted that for the first time for two hundred years the regiment had reverted to the pike. Instead of rifle and bayonet some of the raiders had used butchers' knives secured with medical plaster to the end of broomsticks. This pike was a lighter weapon than rifle and bayonet and was useful in conjunction with bombs and revolvers.

An official journalist at headquarters also wrote an account of the raid. The battalion enjoyed the bit about how they had gone over shouting 'Remember Kitchener!' and 'Avenge the *Lusitania*!' 'What a damn silly thing to shout,' said someone. 'Old Kitchener was all right,[7] but nobody wants him back at the War Office, that I've heard. And as for the *Lusitania*, the Germans gave her full warning, and if it brings the States into the war, it's all to the good.'

There were not many officers in the Second who had been with it when I left it a month after Loos, but at any rate I expected to have a friendlier welcome than the first time I had come to the battalion at Laventie. But, as one of them recorded[8] in his diary: 'Graves had a chilly reception, which surprised me.' The reason was simple. One of the officers who had joined the Third Battalion in August 1914, and had been on the Square with me, had achieved his ambition of a regular commission in the Second Battalion. He was one of those who had been sent out to France before me as being more efficient and had been wounded before I came out. But now he was only a second-lieutenant in the Second Battalion, where promotion was slow, and I was a captain in the Third Battalion. Line-battalion feeling against the Special Reserve was always strong, and jealousy of my extra stars made him bitter. It amused him to revive the suspicion raised at Wrexham by my German name that I was a German spy. Whether he was serious or not I cannot say, probably he could not have said either; but the result was that I found myself treated with great reserve by all the officers who had not been with me in trenches before. It was unlucky that the most notorious German spy caught in England had assumed the name of Karl Graves.[9] It was put about that he was a brother of mine. My consolation was that there was obviously a battle due and that would be the end either of me or of the suspicion. I thought to myself: 'So long as there isn't an N.C.O. told off to watch me and shoot me on the slightest appearance of treachery.' Such things had been known. As a matter of fact, though I had myself had no traffic with the enemy, there was a desultory correspondence kept up between my mother and her sisters in Germany; it came through her sister, Clara von Faber du Faur, mother of my cousin Conrad, whose husband was German consul at Zurich. It was not treasonable on either side, merely a register of the deaths of relations and discreet references to the war service of the survivors. The German aunts wrote, as the Government had ordered every German with relations or friends in enemy or neutral countries to do, pointing out the righteousness of the German cause and presenting Germany as the innocent party in a war engineered by France and Russia. My mother, equally strong for the Allied cause, wrote back that they were deluded. The officers I liked in the battalion were the colonel and Captain Dunn, the battalion doctor. Doctor Dunn was what they call a hard-bitten man; he had served as a trooper in the South African War and won the D.C.M. He was far more than a doctor; living at battalion headquarters he became the right-hand man of three or four colonels in succession. When his advice was not taken this was usually afterwards regretted. On one occasion, in the autumn fighting of 1917, a shell burst among the headquarters staff, knocking out adjutant, colonel, and signals officer. Dunn had no hesitation in pulling off the red-cross armlets that he wore in a battle and becoming a temporary combatant officer of the Royal Welch, resigning his duties to the stretcher-bearer sergeant. He took command and kept things going. The men were rather afraid of him, but had more respect for him than for anyone else in the battalion.

XX

Four days after the raid we heard that we were due for the Somme. We marched through Béthune, which had been much knocked about and was nearly deserted, to Fouquières, and there entrained for the Somme. The Somme railhead was near Amiens and we marched by easy stages through Cardonette, Daours, and Buire, until we came to the original front line, close to the place where David Thomas had been killed. The fighting had moved two miles on. This was on the afternoon of 14th July. At 4 a.m. on the 15th July we moved up the Méaulte-Fricourt-Bazentin road which wound through 'Happy Valley' and found ourselves in the more recent battle area. Wounded men and prisoners came streaming past us. What struck me most was the number of dead horses and mules lying about; human corpses I was accustomed to, but it seemed wrong for animals to be dragged into the war like this. We marched by platoons, at fifty yards distance. Just beyond Fricourt we found a German shell-barrage across the road. So we left it and moved over thickly shell-pitted ground until 8 a.m., when we found ourselves on the fringe of Mametz Wood, among the dead of our new-army battalions that had been attacking Mametz Wood. We halted in thick mist. The Germans had been using lachrymatory shell and the mist held the

fumes; we coughed and swore. We tried to smoke, but
the gas had got into the cigarettes, so we threw them
away. Later we wished we had not, because it was not
the cigarettes that had been affected so much as our
own throats. The colonel called up the officers and we
pulled out our maps. We were expecting orders for an
attack. When the mist cleared we saw a German gun
with 'First Battalion Royal Welch Fusiliers' chalked on
it. It was evidently a trophy. I wondered what had happened to Siegfried and my friends of A Company. We
found the battalion quite close in bivouacs; Siegfried
was still alive, as were Edmund Dadd and two other A
Company officers. The battalion had been in heavy
fighting. In their first attack at Fricourt they had overrun our opposite number in the German army, the
Twenty-third Infantry Regiment, who were undergoing
a special disciplinary spell in the trenches because an
inspecting staff-officer, coming round, had found that
all the officers were back in Mametz village in a deep
dug-out instead of up in the trenches with their men. (It
was said that[1] throughout that bad time in March in the
German trenches opposite to us there had been no officer of higher rank than corporal.) Their next objective
had been The Quadrangle, a small copse this side of
Mametz Wood. I was told that Siegfried had then distinguished himself by taking single-handed a battalion
frontage that the Royal Irish Regiment had failed to
take the day before. He had gone over with bombs in
daylight, under covering fire from a couple of rifles, and
scared the occupants out. It was a pointless feat; instead
of reporting or signalling for reinforcements he sat
down in the German trench and began dozing over a
book of poems which he had brought with him. When

he finally went back he did not report. The colonel was furious. The attack on Mametz Wood had been delayed for two hours because it was reported that British patrols were still out. 'British-patrols' were Siegfried and his book of poems. 'It would have got you a D.S.O. if you'd only had more sense,' stormed the colonel.[2] Siegfried had been doing heroic things ever since I had left the battalion. His nickname in the Seventh Division was 'Mad Jack'. He was given a Military Cross for bringing in a wounded lance-corporal from a mine-crater close to the German lines, under heavy fire. He was one of the rare exceptions to the rule against the decoration of Third Battalion officers. I did not see Siegfried this time; he was down with the transport having a rest. So I sent him a rhymed letter,[3] by one of our own transport men, about the times that we were going to have together when the war ended; how, after a rest at Harlech, we were going for a visit to the Caucasus and Persia and China; and what good poetry we would write. It was in answer to one he had written to me from the army school at Flixécourt a few weeks previously (which appears in *The Old Huntsman*).

I went for a stroll with Edmund Dadd, who was now commanding A Company. Edmund was cursing: 'It's not fair, Robert. You remember A Company under Richardson was always the best company. Well, it's kept up its reputation, and the C.O.[4] shoves us in as the leading company of every show, and we get our objectives and hold them, and so we've got to do the same again the next time. And he says that I'm indispensable in the company, so he makes me go over every time instead of giving me a rest and letting my second-in-command take his turn. I've had five shows in just over a fortnight and I can't go on being lucky every time. The colonel's about due for his c.b. Apparently A Company is making sure of it for him.'

For the next two days we were in bivouacs outside the wood. We were in fighting kit and the nights were wet and cold. I went into the wood to find German overcoats to use as blankets. Mametz Wood was full of dead of the Prussian Guards Reserve, big men, and of Royal Welch and South Wales Borderers of the new-army battalions, little men. There was not a single tree in the wood unbroken. I got my greatcoats and came away as quickly as I could, climbing over the wreckage of green branches. Going and coming, by the only possible route, I had to pass by the corpse of a German with his back propped against a tree. He had a green face, spectacles, close shaven hair; black blood was dripping from the nose and beard. He had been there for some days and was bloated and stinking.[5] There had been bayonet fighting in the wood. There was a man of the South Wales Borderers and one of the Lehr regiment who had succeeded in bayoneting each other simultaneously. A survivor of the fighting told me later that he had seen a young soldier of the Fourteenth Royal Welch bayoneting a German in parade-ground style, automatically exclaiming as he had been taught: 'In, out, on guard.' He said that it was the oddest thing he had heard in France.

I found myself still superstitious about looting or collecting souvenirs. The greatcoats were only a loan, I told myself. Almost the only souvenir I had allowed myself to keep was a trench periscope, a little rod-shaped metal one sent me from home; when I poked it up above the parapet it offered only an inch-square target to the German snipers. Yet a sniper at Cuinchy, in May, drilled it through, exactly central, at four hundred yards range. I sent it home, but had no time to write a note of explanation. My mother, misunderstanding, and practical as usual, took it back to the makers and made them change it for a new one.

Our brigade, the Nineteenth, was the reserve brigade of the Thirty-third Division; the other brigades, the Ninety-ninth and Hundredth, had attacked Martinpuich two days previously and had been stopped with heavy losses as soon as they started. Since then we had had nothing to do but sit about in shell-holes and watch the artillery duel going on. We had never seen artillery so thick. On the 18th we moved up to a position just to the north of Bazentin le Petit to relieve the Tyneside Irish. I was with D Company. The guide who was taking us up was hysterical and had forgotten the way; we put him under arrest and found it ourselves. As we went up through the ruins of the village we were shelled. We were accustomed to that, but they were gas shells. The standing order with regard to gas shells was not to put on one's respirator but hurry on. Up to that week there had been no gas shells except lachrymatory ones; these were the first of the real kind, so we lost about half a dozen men. When at last we arrived at the trenches, which were scooped at a roadside and only about three feet deep, the company we were relieving hurried out without any of the usual formalities; they had been badly shaken. I asked their officer where the Germans were. He said he didn't know, but pointed vaguely towards Martinpuich, a mile to our front. Then I asked him where and what were the troops on our left. He didn't know. I cursed him and he went off. We got into touch with C Company behind us on the right and with the Fourth Suffolks not far off on the left. We began deepening the trenches and locating the Germans; they were in a trench-system about five hundred yards away but keeping fairly quiet.

The next day there was very heavy shelling at noon; shells were bracketing along our trench about five yards short and five yards over, but never quite getting it. We were having dinner and three times running my cup of tea was spilt by the concussion and filled with dirt. I was in a cheerful mood and only laughed. I had just had a parcel of kippers from home; they were far more important than the bombardment – I recalled with appreciation one of my mother's sayings: 'Children, remember this when you eat your kippers; kippers cost little, yet if they cost a hundred guineas a pair they would still find buyers among the millionaires.' Before the shelling had started a tame magpie had come into the trench; it had apparently belonged to the Germans who had been driven out of the village by the Gordon Highlanders a day or two before. It was looking very draggled. 'That's one for sorrow,' I said. The men swore that it spoke something in German as it came in, but I did not hear it. I was feeling tired and was off duty, so without waiting for the bombardment to stop I went to sleep in the trench. I decided that I would just as soon be killed asleep as awake. There were no dug-outs, of course. I always found it easy now to sleep through bombardments. I was conscious of the noise in my sleep, but I let it go by. Yet if anybody came to wake me for my watch or shouted 'Stand-to!' I was alert in a second. I had learned to go to sleep sitting down, standing up, marching, lying on a stone floor, or in any other position, at a moment's notice at any time of day or night. But now I had a dreadful nightmare; it was as though somebody was handling me secretly, choosing the place to drive a knife into me. Finally, he gripped me in the small of the back. I woke up with a start, shouting, and punched the small of my back where the hand was. I found that I had killed a mouse that had been frightened by the bombardment and run down my neck.

That afternoon the company got an order through from the brigade to build two cruciform strong-points at such-and-such a map reference. Moodie, the company commander, and I looked at our map and laughed. Moodie sent back a message that he would be glad to do so, but would require an artillery bombardment and strong reinforcements because the points selected, half way to Martinpuich, were occupied in force by the enemy. The colonel came up and verified this. He said that we should build the strong-point about three hundred yards forward and two hundred yards apart. So one platoon stayed behind in the trench and the other went out and started digging. A cruciform strong-point consisted of two trenches, each some thirty yards long, crossing at right angles to each other; it was wired all round, so that it looked, in diagram, like a hot-cross bun. The defenders could bring fire to bear against an attack from any direction. We were to hold each of these points with a Lewis gun and a platoon of men.

It was a bright moonlight night. My way to the strong-point on the right took me along the Bazentin-High Wood road. A German sergeant-major, wearing a pack and full equipment, was lying on his back in the middle of the road, his arms stretched out wide. He was a short, powerful man with a full black beard. He looked sinister in the moonlight; I needed a charm to get myself past him. The simplest way, I found, was to cross myself. Evidently a brigade of the Seventh Division had captured the road and the Germans had been shelling it heavily. It was a sunken road and the defenders had begun to scrape fire-positions in the north bank, facing the Germans. The work had apparently been interrupted by a counter-attack. They had done no more than scrape hollows in the lower part of the bank. To a number of these little hollows wounded men had crawled, put their heads and shoulders inside and died there. They looked as if they had tried to hide from the black beard. They were Gordon Highlanders.

I was visiting the strong-point on the right. The trench had now been dug two or three feet down and a party of Engineers had arrived with coils of barbed wire for the entanglement. I found that work had stopped. The whisper went round: 'Get your rifles ready. Here comes Fritz.' I lay down flat to see better, and about seventy yards away in the moonlight I could make out massed figures. I immediately sent a man back to the company to find Moodie and ask him for a Lewis gun and a flare-pistol. I restrained the men, who were itching to fire, telling them to wait until they came closer. I said: 'They probably don't know we're here and we'll get more of them if we let them come right up close. They may even surrender.' The Germans were wandering about irresolutely and we wondered what the game was. There had been a number of German surrenders at night recently, and this might be one on a big scale. Then Moodie came running with a Lewis gun, the flare-pistol, and a few more men with rifle-grenades. He decided to give the enemy a chance. He sent up a flare and fired a Lewis gun over their heads. A tall officer came running towards us with his hands up in surrender. He was surprised to find that we were not Germans. He said that he belonged to the Public Schools Battalion in our own brigade. Moodie

asked him what the hell he was doing. He said that
he was in command of a patrol. He was sent back for
a few more of his men, to make sure it was not a trick.
The patrol was half a company of men wandering
about aimlessly between the lines, their rifles slung
over their shoulders, and, it seemed, without the faint-
est idea where they were or what information they
were supposed to bring back. This Public Schools Battalion was one of four or five others which had been
formed some time in 1914. Their training had been
continually interrupted by large numbers of men being
withdrawn as officers for other regiments. The only
men left, in fact, seemed to be those who were unfitted
to hold commissions; yet unfitted by their education to
make good soldiers in the ranks. The other battalions
had been left behind in England as training battalions;
only this one had been sent out. It was a constant
embarrassment to the brigade.

I picked up a souvenir that night. A German gun-
team had been shelled as it was galloping out of
Bazentin towards Martinpuich. The horses and the
driver had been killed. At the back of the limber were
the gunners' treasures. Among them was a large lump
of chalk wrapped up in a piece of cloth; it had been
carved and decorated in colours with military mottos,
the flags of the Central Powers, and the names of the
various battles in which the gunner had served. I sent it
as a present to Dr. Dunn. I am glad to say that both he
and it survived the war; he is in practice at Glasgow,
and the lump of chalk is under a glass case in his consulting room. The evening of the next day, July 19th,
we were relieved. We were told that we would be
attacking High Wood, which we could see a thousand
yards away to the right at the top of a slope. High Wood

was on the main German battle-line, which ran along the ridge, with Delville Wood not far off on the German left. Two British brigades had already attempted it; in both cases the counter-attack had driven them out. Our battalion had had a large number of casualties and was now only about four hundred strong.[6]

I have kept a battalion order issued at midnight:

To O.C. B Co. 2nd R.W.F. 20.7.16.

Companies	will	move	as	under
to	same	positions	in	S14b
as	were	to	have	been
taken	over	from	Cameronians	aaa
	A Coy.	12.30 a.m.		
	B Coy.	12.45 a.m.		
	C Coy.	1 a.m.		
	D Coy.	1.15 a.m.	aaa	
	At	2 a.m.	Company	Commanders
will	meet	C.O.	at	X
Roads	S14b 99.	aaa		
Men	will	lie	down	and
get	under	cover	but	equipment
will	not	be	taken	off
aaa				

S14b 99 was a map reference for Bazentin churchyard. We lay here on the reverse slope of a slight ridge about half a mile from the wood. I attended the meeting of company commanders; the colonel told us the plan. He said: 'Look here, you fellows, we're in reserve for this attack. The Cameronians are going up to the wood first, then the Fifth Scottish Rifles; that's at five a.m. The Public Schools Battalion are in support if anything goes wrong. I don't know if we shall be called on; if we are, it will mean that the Jocks have legged it. As usual,' he added. This was an appeal to prejudice. 'The Public Schools Battalion is, well, what we know, so if we are called for, that means it will be the end of us.' He said this with a laugh and we all laughed. We were sitting on the ground protected by the road-bank; a battery of French 75's was firing rapid over our heads about twenty yards away. There was a very great concentration of guns in Happy Valley now. We could hardly hear what he was saying. He told us that if we did get orders to reinforce, we were to shake out in artillery formation; once in the wood we were to hang on like death. Then he said good-bye and good luck and we rejoined our companies.

At this juncture the usual inappropriate message came through from Division. Division could always be trusted to send through a warning about verdigris on vermorel-sprayers, or the keeping of pets in trenches, or being polite to our allies, or some other triviality, when an attack was in progress. This time it was an order for a private in C Company to report immediately to the assistant provost-marshal back at Albert, under escort of a lance-corporal. He was for a court-martial. A sergeant of the company was also ordered to report as a witness in the case. The private was charged with the murder of a French civilian in an *estaminet* at Béthune about a month previously. Apparently there had been a good deal of brandy going and the French civilian, who had a grudge against the British (it was about his wife), started to tease the private. He was reported, somewhat improbably, as having said: 'English no bon, Allmand très bon. War fineesh, napoo the English. Allmand win.' The private had immediately drawn his bayonet and run the man through. At the court martial the private was exculpated; the French civil representative commended him for having 'energetically repressed local defeatism.' So he and the two N.C.O.'s missed the battle.

What the battle that they missed was like I pieced together afterwards. The Jocks did get into the wood and the Royal Welch were not called on to reinforce until eleven o'clock in the morning. The Germans put down a barrage along the ridge where we were lying, and we lost about a third of the battalion before our show started. I was one of the casualties.

It was heavy stuff, six and eight inch. There was so much of it that we decided to move back fifty yards; it was when I was running that an eight-inch shell burst about three paces behind me. I was able to work that out afterwards by the line of my wounds. I heard the explosion and felt as though I had been punched rather hard between the shoulder-blades, but had no sensation of pain. I thought that the punch was merely the shock of the explosion; then blood started trickling into my eye and I felt faint and called to Moodie: 'I've been hit.' Then I fell down. A minute or two before I had had two very small wounds on my left hand; they were in exactly the same position as the two, on my right hand, that I had got during the preliminary bombardment at Loos. This I had taken as a sign that I would come through all right. For further security I had repeated to myself a line of Nietsche's, whose poems, in French, I had with me:

Non, tu ne peus pas me tuer.[7]

It was the poem about a man on the scaffold with the red-bearded executioner standing over him. (This copy of Nietsche, by the way, had contributed to the suspicions about me as a spy. Nietsche was execrated in the papers as the philosopher of German militarism; he was more popularly interpreted as a William le Queux mystery-man – the sinister figure behind the Kaiser.)

One piece of shell went through my left thigh, high up near the groin; I must have been at the full stretch of my stride to have escaped emasculation. The wound over the eye was nothing; it was a little chip of marble, possibly from one of the Bazentin cemetery headstones.[8] This and a finger wound, which split the bone, probably came from another shell that burst in front of me. The main wound was made by a piece of shell that went in two inches below the point of my right shoulder and came out through my chest two inches above my right nipple, in a line between it and the base of my neck.

My memory of what happened then is vague. Apparently Doctor Dunn came up through the barrage with a stretcher-party, dressed my wound, and got me down to the old German dressing-station at the north end of Mametz Wood. I just remember being put on the stretcher and winking at the stretcher-bearer sergeant who was looking at me and saying: 'Old Gravy's got it, all right.' The dressing-station was overworked that day; I was laid in a corner on a stretcher and remained unconscious for more than twenty-four hours.

It was about ten o'clock on the 20th that I was hit. Late that night the colonel came to the dressing-station; he saw me lying in the corner and was told that I was done for. The next morning, the 21st, when they were clearing away the dead, I was found to be still breathing; so they put me on an ambulance for Heilly, the nearest field-hospital. The pain of being jolted down the Happy Valley, with a shell-hole at every three or four yards of the roads, woke me for awhile. I remember screaming. But once back on the better roads I became unconscious again. That morning the colonel wrote the usual formal letters of condolence to the next-of-kin of the six or seven officers who had been killed. This was his letter to my mother:

22/7/16

Dear Mrs. Graves,

I very much regret to have to write and tell you your son has died of wounds. He was very gallant, and was doing so well and is a great loss.

He was hit by a shell and very badly wounded, and died on the way down to the base I believe. He was not in bad pain, and our doctor managed to get across and attend him at once.

We have had a very hard time, and our casualties have been large. Believe me you have all our sympathy in your loss, and we have lost a very gallant soldier.

Please write to me if I can tell you or do anything.

Yours sincerely,[9]

* * *

Later he made out the official casualty list and reported me died of wounds. It was a long casualty list, because only eighty men were left in the battalion.

Heilly was on the railway; close to the station was the hospital – marquee tents with the red cross painted prominently on the roofs to discourage air-bombing. It was fine July weather and the tents were insufferably hot. I was semi-conscious now, and realized my lung-wound by the shortness of breath. I was amused to watch the little bubbles of blood, like red soap-bubbles, that my breath made when it escaped through the hole of the wound. The doctor came over to me. I felt sorry for him; he looked as though he had not had any sleep for days. I asked him for a drink. He said: 'Would you like some tea?' I whispered: 'Not with condensed milk in it.' He said: 'I'm afraid there's no fresh milk.' Tears came to my eyes; I expected better of a hospital behind the lines. He said: 'Will you have some water?' I said: 'Not if it's boiled.' He said: 'It is boiled. And I'm afraid I can't give you anything with alcohol in it in your present condition.' I said: 'Give me some fruit then.' He said: 'I have seen no fruit for days.' But a few minutes later he came back with two rather unripe greengages. I felt so grateful that I promised him a whole orchard when I recovered.

The nights of the 22nd and 23rd were very bad. Early on the morning of the 24th, when the doctor came to see how I was, I said: 'You must send me away from here. The heat will kill me.' It was beating through the canvas on my head. He said: 'Stick it out. It's your best chance to lie here and not to be moved. You'd not reach the base alive.' I said: 'I'd like to risk the move. I'll be all right, you'll see.' Half an hour later he came back. 'Well, you're having it your way. I've just got orders to evacuate every case in the hospital. Apparently the Guards have been in it up at Delville Wood and we'll have them all coming in to-night.' I had no fears now about dying. I was content to be wounded and on the way home.

I had been given news of the battalion from a brigade-major, wounded in the leg, who was in the next bed to me. He looked at my label and said: 'I see you're in the Second Royal Welch Fusiliers. Well, I saw your High Wood show through field-glasses. The way your battalion shook out into artillery formation, company by company – with each section of four or five men in file at fifty yards interval and distance – going down into the hollow and up the slope through the barrage, was the most beautiful bit of parade-ground drill I've ever seen. Your company officers must have been superb.' I happened to know that one company at least had started without a single officer. I asked him whether they had held the wood. He said: 'They hung on at the near end. I believe what happened was that the Public Schools Battalion came away as soon as it got dark; and so did the Scotsmen. Your chaps were left there alone for some time. They steadied themselves by singing. Later, the chaplain – R.C. of course – Father McCabe, brought the Scotsmen back. They were Glasgow Catholics and would follow a priest where they wouldn't follow an officer. The middle of the wood was impossible for either the Germans or your fellows to hold. There was a terrific concentration of artillery on it. The trees were splintered to matchwood. Late that night the survivors were relieved by a brigade of the Seventh Division; your First Battalion was in it.'[10]

That evening I was put in the hospital train. They could not lift me from the stretcher to put me on a bunk, for fear of starting hæmorrhage in the lung; so they laid the stretcher on top of it, with the handles resting on the head-rail and foot-rail. I had been on the same stretcher since I was wounded. I remember the journey only as a nightmare.

My back was sagging and I could not raise my knees to relieve the cramp because the bunk above me was only a few inches away. A German officer on the other side of the carriage groaned and wept unceasingly. He had been in an aeroplane crash and had a compound fracture of the leg. The other wounded men were cursing him and telling him to stow it and be a man, but he went on, keeping every one awake. He was not delirious, only frightened and in great pain. An orderly gave me a pencil and paper and I wrote home to say that I was wounded but all right. This was July 24th, my twenty-first birthday, and it was on this day, when I arrived at Rouen, that my death officially occurred.[11] My parents got my letter two days after the letter from the colonel; mine was dated July 23rd, because I had lost count of days when I was unconscious; his was dated the 22nd.* They could not decide whether my letter had been written just before I died and misdated, or whether I had died just after writing it. 'Died of wounds' was, however, so much more circumstantial than 'killed' that they gave me up. I was in No. 8 Hospital at Rouen; an ex-château high above the town. The day after I arrived a Cooper aunt of mine, who had married a Frenchman, came up to the hospital to visit a nephew in the South Wales Borderers who had just had a leg amputated. She happened to see my name in a list on the door of the

---

* I cannot explain the discrepancy between his dating of my death and that of the published casualty list. [RG]

ward, so she wrote to my mother to reassure her. On the 30th I had a letter from the colonel:

30/7/16

DEAR VON RUNICKE,

I cannot tell you how pleased I am you are alive. I was told your number was up for certain, and a letter was supposed to have come in from Field Ambulance saying you had gone under.

Well, it's good work. We had a rotten time, and after succeeding in doing practically the impossible we collected that rotten crowd and put them in their places, but directly dark came they legged it. It was too sad.

We lost heavily. It is not fair putting brave men like ours alongside that crowd. I also wish to thank you for your good work and bravery, and only wish you could have been with them. I have read of bravery but I have never seen such magnificent and wonderful disregard for death as I saw that day. It was almost uncanny – it was so great. I once heard an old officer in the Royal Welch say the men would follow you to Hell; but these chaps would bring you back and put you in a dugout in Heaven.

Good luck and a quick recovery. I shall drink your health to-night.

* * *

I had little pain all this time, but much discomfort; the chief pain came from my finger, which had turned septic because nobody had taken the trouble to dress it, and was throbbing. And from the thigh, where the sticky medical plaster, used to hold down the dressing, pulled up the hair painfully when it was taken off each time the wound was dressed. My breath was very short still. I contrasted the pain and discomfort favourably with that of the operation on my nose of two months back; for this I had won no sympathy at all from anyone, because it was not an injury contracted in war. I was weak and petulant and muddled. The R.A.M.C. bugling outraged me. The 'Rob All My Comrades', I complained, had taken everything I had except a few papers in my tunic-pocket and a ring which was too tight on my finger to be pulled off; and now they mis-blew the Last Post flat and windily, and with the pauses in the wrong places, just to annoy me. I remember that I told an orderly to put the bugler under arrest and jump to it or I'd report him to the senior medical officer.

Next to me was a Welsh boy, named O. M. Roberts, who had joined us only a few days before he was hit. He told me about High Wood; he had reached the edge of the wood when he was wounded in the groin. He had fallen into a shell-hole. Some time in the afternoon he had recovered consciousness and seen a German officer working round the edge of the wood, killing off the wounded with an automatic pistol. Some of our lightly-wounded were, apparently, not behaving as wounded men should; they were sniping. The German worked nearer. He saw Roberts move and came towards him, fired and hit him in the arm. Roberts was very weak and tugged at his Webley. He had great difficulty in getting it out of the holster. The German fired again and missed. Roberts rested the Webley against the lip of the shell-hole and tried to pull the trigger; he was not strong enough. The German was quite close now and was going to make certain of him this time. Roberts said that he just managed to pull the trigger with the fingers of both hands when the German was only about five yards away. The shot took the top of his head off. Roberts fainted.

The doctors had been anxiously watching my lung, which was gradually filling with blood and pressing my heart too far away to the left of my body; the railway journey had restarted the hæmorrhage. They marked the gradual progress of my heart with an indelible pencil on my skin and said that when it reached a certain point they would have to aspirate me. This sounded a serious operation, but it only consisted of putting a hollow needle into my lung through the back and drawing the blood off into a vacuum flask through it. I had a local anæsthetic; it hurt no more than a vaccination, and I was reading the *Gazette de Rouen* as the blood hissed into the flask. It did not look much, perhaps half a pint. That evening I heard a sudden burst of lovely singing in the courtyard where the ambulances pulled up. I recognized the quality of the voices. I said to Roberts: 'The First Battalion have been in it again,' and asked a nurse to verify it; I was right. It was their Delville Wood show, I think, but I am uncertain now of the date.

A day or two later I was taken back to England by hospital ship.

XXI

I had sent my parents a wire that I would be arriving at Waterloo Station the next morning. The way from the hospital train to the waiting ambulances was roped off; as each stretcher case was lifted off the train a huge hysterical crowd surged up to the barrier and uttered a new roar. Flags were being waved. It seemed that the Somme battle was regarded at home as the beginning of the end of the war. As I idly looked at the crowd, one figure detached itself; it was my father, hopping about on one leg, waving an umbrella and cheering with the best of them. I was embarrassed, but was soon in the ambulance. I was on the way to Queen Alexandra's Hospital, Highgate. This was Sir Alfred Mond's big house, lent for the duration of the war, and a really good place to be in; having a private room to myself was the most unexpected luxury.

What I most disliked in the army was never being alone, forced to live and sleep with men whose company in many cases I would have run miles to avoid.

I was not long at Highgate; the lung healed up easily and my finger was saved for me. I heard here for the first time that I was supposed to be dead; the joke contributed greatly to my recovery. The people with whom I had been on the worst terms during my life wrote the most enthusiastic condolences to my parents: my house-master, for instance. I have kept a letter dated the 5th August 1916 from *The Times* advertisement department:

Captain Robert Graves.

DEAR SIR,

We have to acknowledge receipt of your letter with reference to the announcement contradicting the report of your death from wounds. Having regard, however, to the fact that we had previously published some bio-graphical details, we inserted your announcement in our issue of to-day (Saturday) under 'Court Circular' without charge, and we have much pleasure in enclos-ing herewith cutting of same.

Yours, etc.

The cutting read:

Captain Robert Graves, Royal Welch Fusiliers, offi-cially reported died of wounds, wishes to inform his friends that he is recovering from his wounds at Queen Alexandra's Hospital, Highgate, N.

* * *

Mrs. Lloyd George has left London for Criccieth.

* * *

I never saw the biographical details supplied by my father; they might have been helpful to me here. Some letters written to me in France were returned to him as my next-of-kin. They were surcharged: 'Died of wounds – present location uncertain. – P. Down, post-corporal.' The only inconvenience that my death caused me was that Cox's Bank stopped my pay and I had difficulty in persuading it to honour my cheques. I had a letter from Siegfried telling me that he was overjoyed to hear I was alive again. (I wondered whether he had been avenging me.) He was now back in England with suspected lung trouble. We agreed to take our leave together at Harlech when I was better. Siegfried wrote that he was nine parts dead from the horror of the Somme fighting.

I was able to travel early in September. We met at Paddington. Siegfried bought a copy of *The Times* at the bookstall. As usual we turned to the casualty list first; and found there the names of practically every officer in the First Battalion, either killed or wounded. Edmund Dadd was killed. His brother Julian, in Siegfried's company, wounded. (Shot through the throat, as we learned later, only able to talk in a whisper, and for months utterly prostrated. It had been at Ale Alley at Ginchy, on 3rd September. A dud show; the battalion had been outflanked in a counter-attack.) News like this in England was far more upsetting than when one was in France. I was still very weak and could not help crying all the way up to Wales. Siegfried said bitterly: 'Well, I expect the colonel got his C.B. at any rate.' England was strange to the returned soldier. He could not understand the war-madness that ran about everywhere looking for a pseudo-military outlet. Every one talked a foreign language; it was newspaper language. I found serious conversation with my parents all but impossible. A single typical memorial of this time will be enough:

A MOTHER'S ANSWER TO
'A COMMON SOLDIER'

BY A LITTLE MOTHER

A Message to the Pacifists. A Message to the Bereaved. A Message to the Trenches

Owing to the immense demand from home and from the trenches for this letter, which appeared in the 'Morning Post', the Editor found it necessary to place it in the hands of London publishers to be reprinted in pamphlet form, seventy-five thousand copies of which were sold in less than a week direct from the publisher.

Extract from a Letter from Her Majesty

'The Queen was deeply touched at the "Little Mother's" beautiful letter, and Her Majesty fully realizes what her words must mean to our soldiers in the trenches and in hospitals.'

———————

To the Editor of the 'Morning Post'

Sir, – As a mother of an only child – a son who was early and eager to do his duty – may I be permitted to reply to Tommy Atkins, whose letter appeared in your issue of the 9th inst.? Perhaps he will kindly convey to his friends in the trenches, not what the Government thinks, not what the Pacifists think, but what the mothers of the British race think of our fighting men. It is a voice which demands to be heard, seeing that we play the most important part in the history of the world, for it is we who 'mother the men' who have to uphold the honour and traditions not only of our Empire but of the whole civilized world.

To the man who pathetically calls himself a 'common soldier', may I say that we women, who demand to be heard, will tolerate no such cry as 'Peace! Peace!' where there is no peace. The corn that will wave over land watered by the blood of our brave lads shall testify to the future that their blood was not spilt in vain. We need no marble monuments to remind us. We only need that force of character behind all motives to see this monstrous world tragedy brought to a victorious ending. The blood of the dead and the dying, the blood of the 'common soldier' from his 'slight wounds' will not cry to us in vain. They have all done their share, and we, as women, will do ours without murmuring and without complaint. Send the Pacifists to us and we shall very soon show them, and show the world, that in our homes at least there shall be no 'sitting at home warm and cosy in the winter, cool and "comfy" in the summer.' There is only one temperature for the women of the British race, and that is white heat. With those who disgrace their sacred trust of motherhood we have nothing in common. Our ears are not deaf to the cry that is ever ascending from the battlefield from men of flesh and blood whose indomitable courage is borne to us, so to speak, on every blast of the wind. We women pass on the human ammunition of 'only sons' to fill up the gaps, so that when the 'common soldier' looks back before going 'over the top' he may see the women of the British race on his heels, reliable, dependent, uncomplaining.

The reinforcements of women are, therefore, behind the 'common soldier'. We gentle-nurtured, timid sex did not want the war. It is no pleasure to us to have our homes made desolate and the apple of our eye taken away. We would sooner our lovable, promising, rollicking boy stayed at school. We would have much preferred to have gone on in a light-hearted way with our amusements and our hobbies. But the bugle call came, and we have hung up the tennis racquet, we've fetched our laddie from school, we've put his cap away, and we have glanced lovingly over his last report which said 'Excellent' – we've wrapped them all in a Union Jack and locked them up, to be taken out only after the war to be looked at. A 'common soldier', perhaps, did not count on the women, but they have their part to play, and *we* have risen to our responsibility. We are proud of our men, and they in turn have to be proud of us. If the men fail, Tommy Atkins, the women won't.

> Tommy Atkins to the front,
> He has gone to bear the brunt.
> Shall 'stay-at-homes' do naught but snivel and but sigh?
> No, while your eyes are filling
> We are up and doing, willing
> To face the music with you – or to die!

Women are created for the purpose of giving life, and men to take it. Now we are giving it in a double sense. It's not likely we are going to fail Tommy. We shall not flinch one iota, but when the war is over he must not grudge us, when we hear the bugle call of 'Lights out,' a brief, very brief, space of time to withdraw into our own secret chambers and share with Rachel the Silent the lonely anguish of a bereft heart, and to look once more on the college cap, before we emerge stronger women to carry on the glorious work our men's memories have handed down to us for now and all eternity.

Yours, etc.,

A LITTLE MOTHER.

Extracts and Press Criticisms

'The widest possible circulation is of the utmost importance.' – *The Morning Post*.

'Deservedly attracting a great deal of attention, as expressing with rare eloquence and force the feelings with which the British wives and mothers have faced and are facing the supreme sacrifice.' – *The Morning Post*.

'Excites widespread interest.' – *The Gentlewoman*.

'A letter which has become celebrated.' – *The Star*.

'We would like to see it hung up in our wards.' – *Hospital Blue*.

'One of the grandest things ever written, for it combines a height of courage with a depth of tenderness which should be, and is, the stamp of all that is noblest and best in human nature.' – *A Soldier in France*.

'Florence Nightingale did great and grand things for the soldiers of her day, but no woman has done more than the "Little Mother," whose now famous letter in the *Morning Post* has spread like wild-fire from trench to trench. I hope to God it will be handed down in history, for nothing like it has ever made such an impression on our fighting men. I defy any man to feel weak-hearted after reading it . . . My God! she makes us die happy.' – *One who has Fought and Bled*.

'Worthy of far more than a passing notice; it ought to be reprinted and sent out to every man at the front. It is a masterpiece and fills one with pride, noble, level-headed, and pathetic to a degree.' – *Severely Wounded*.

'I have lost my two dear boys, but since I was shown the "Little Mother's" beautiful letter a resignation too perfect to describe has calmed all my aching sorrow, and I would now gladly give my sons twice over.' – *A Bereaved Mother*.

'The "Little Mother's" letter should reach every corner of the earth – a letter of the loftiest ideal, tempered with courage and the most sublime sacrifice.'
– *Percival H. Monkton.*

'The exquisite letter by a "Little Mother" is making us feel prouder every day. We women desire to fan the flame which she has so superbly kindled in our hearts.'
– *A British Mother of an Only Son.*

At Harlech, Siegfried and I spent the time getting our poems in order; Siegfried was at work on his *Old Huntsman*. We made a number of changes in each other's verses; I remember that I proposed amendments which he accepted in his obituary poem 'To His Dead Body' – written for me when he thought me dead. We were beginning to wonder whether it was right for the war to be continued. It was said that Asquith in the autumn of 1915 had been offered peace-terms on the basis of *status quo ante* and that he had been willing to consider them; that his colleagues had opposed him, and that this was the reason for the fall of the Liberal Government, and for the 'Win-the-War' Coalition Government of Lloyd George that superseded it. We both thought that the terms should have been accepted, though Siegfried was more vehement than I was on the subject. The view we had of the war was now non-political. We no longer saw it as a war between trade-rivals; its continuance seemed merely a sacrifice of the idealistic younger generation to the stupidity and self-protective alarm of the elder. I made a facetious marginal note on a poem I wrote about this time, called *Goliath and David* (in which the biblical legend was reversed and David was killed by Goliath):

War should be a sport for men above forty-five only, the Jesse's, not the David's. 'Well, dear father, how proud I am of you serving your country as a very gallant gentleman prepared to make even the supreme sacrifice. I only wish I were your age: how willingly would I buckle on my armour and fight those unspeakable Philistines! As it is, of course, I can't be spared; I have to stay behind at the War Office and administrate for you lucky old men.' 'What sacrifices I have made,' David would sigh when the old boys had gone off with a draft to the front singing *Tipperary*. 'There's father and my Uncle Salmon and both my grandfathers, all on active service. I must put a card in the window about it.'[1]

We defined the war in our poems by making contrasted definitions of peace. With Siegfried it was hunting and nature and music and pastoral scenes; with me it was chiefly children. When I was in France I used to spend much of my spare time playing with the French children of the villages in which I was billeted. I put them into my poems, and my own childhood at Harlech. I called my book *Fairies and Fusiliers*, and dedicated it to the regiment.

Siegfried stayed a few weeks. When he had gone I began the novel on which my earlier war chapters are based, but it remained a rough draft.

In September I went for a visit to Kent, to the house of a First Battalion friend who had recently been wounded. His elder brother had been killed in the Dardanelles,[2] and his mother kept his bedroom exactly as he had left it, with the sheets aired, his linen always freshly laundered, and flowers and cigarettes by his bedside. She was religious and went about with a vague bright look on her face. The first night I spent there my friend and I sat up talking about the war until after twelve o'clock. His mother had gone to bed early, after urging us not to get too tired. The talk excited me but I managed to fall asleep at about one o'clock. I was continually awakened by sudden rapping noises which I at first tried to disregard but which grew louder and louder. They seemed to come from everywhere. I lay in a cold sweat. About three o'clock I heard a diabolic yell and a succession of laughing, sobbing shrieks that sent me flying to the door. I collided in the passage with the mother, who, to my surprise, was fully dressed. She said: 'It's nothing. One of the maids has hysterics. I am so sorry you have been disturbed.' So I went to bed, but I could not sleep though the noises had stopped. In the morning I said to my friend: 'I'm leaving this place. It's worse than France.' He said: 'I'm sorry. I should have told you. My mother has been reading Sir Oliver Lodge's *Raymond or Life after Death*, and she sits up half the night trying to get in touch with my brother. It's pathetic, because he was not at all the person she thinks he was. The idiotic messages that she gets through from him, and believes, often make me anxious for her sanity. Still, she seems happy. The rappings are most disturbing sometimes and the maids think that the place is haunted.'[3]

In November Siegfried and I rejoined the battalion at Litherland and shared a hut together. We decided that it was no use making a protest against the war. Every one was mad; we were hardly sane ourselves. Siegfried said that we had to 'keep up the good reputation of the poets', as men of courage, he meant. The best place for us was back in France away from the more shameful madness of home service. Our function there was not to kill Germans, though that might happen, but to make things easier for the men under our command. For them the difference between being under someone whom they could count as a friend, someone who protected them as much as he could from the grosser indignities of the military system and having to study the whims of any thoughtless, petty tyrant in an officer's tunic, was all the difference in the world. By this time the ranks of both line battalions were filled with men who had enlisted for patriotic reasons and the professional-soldier tradition was hard on them ... Siegfried, for instance, on (I think) the day before the Fricourt attack. The attack had been rehearsed for a week over dummy trenches in the back areas until the whole performance was perfect, in fact almost stale. Siegfried was told to rehearse once more. Instead, he led his platoon into a wood and read to them – nothing military or literary, just the *London Mail*.[4] Though the *London Mail* was not in his line, Siegfried thought that the men would enjoy the 'Things We Want to Know' column.

Officers of the Royal Welch were honorary members of a neighbouring golf club. Siegfried and I used to go there often. He played golf and I hit a ball alongside him. I had once played at Harlech as a junior member of the Royal St. David's, but I had given it up before long because it was bad for my temper. I was afraid of taking it up again seriously, so now I limited myself to a single club. When I mishit it did not matter. I played the fool and purposely put Siegfried off his game; he was a serious golfer. It was the time of great food shortage; the submarines sank about every fourth food ship, and there was a strict meat, butter and sugar ration. But the war did not seem to have reached the links. The principal business men of Liverpool were members of the club and did not mean to go short while there was any food at all coming in at the docks. Siegfried and I went to the club-house for lunch on the day before Christmas; there was a cold buffet in the club dining-room offering hams, barons of beef, jellied tongues, cold roast turkey and chicken. A large, meaty-faced waiter presided. Siegfried satirically asked him: 'Is this all? There doesn't seem to be quite such a good spread as in previous years.' The waiter apologized: 'No, sir, this isn't quite up to the usual mark, sir, but we are expecting a more satisfactory consignment of meat on Boxing Day.' The dining-room at the club-house was always full, the links were practically deserted.

The favourite rendezvous of the officers of the Mersey garrison was the Adelphi Hotel. It had a cocktail bar and a swimming bath. The cocktail bar was generally crowded with Russian naval officers, always very drunk. One day I met a major of the King's Own Scottish Borderers there. I saluted him. He told me confidentially, taking me aside: 'It's nice of you to salute me, my boy, but I must confess that I am not what I seem. I wear a crown on my sleeve and so does a company sergeant-major; but then he's not entitled to wear these three cuff bands and the wavy border. Look at them, aren't they pretty? As I was saying, I'm not what I seem to be. I'm a sham. I've got a sergeant-major's stomach.' I was quite accustomed to drunken senior officers, so I answered respectfully: 'Really, major, and how did you come to get that?' He said: 'You think I'm drunk. Well, I am if you like, but it's true about my stomach. You see I was in that Beaumont-Hamel show and I got shot in the guts. It hurt like hell, let me tell you. They got me down to the field-hospital. I was busy dying; there was a company sergeant-major in the hospital at the time and he had got it through the head, and *he* was busy dying, too, and he did die. Well, as soon as the sergeant-major died they took out that long gut, whatever you call the thing, the thing that unwinds – they say it's as long as a cricket pitch – and they put it into me, grafted it on somehow. Wonderful chaps these medicos. They can put in spare parts as if one was a motor-car. Well, this sergeant-major seems to have been an abstemious man; the lining of the new gut is much better than my old one; so I'm celebrating it. I only wish I had his kidneys too.'

An R.A.M.C. captain was sitting by. He broke into the conversation. 'Yes, major, I know what a stomach wound's like. It's the worst of the lot. You were lucky to reach the field-ambulance alive. The best chance is to lie absolutely still. I got mine out between the lines, bandaging a fellow. I flopped into a shell-hole. My stretcher-bearers wanted to carry me back, but I wasn't having any. I kept everyone off with a revolver for forty-eight hours. That saved my life. I couldn't count on a spare gut waiting for me at the dressing-station. My only chance was to lie still and let it heal.'

In December I attended a medical board; they examined my wound and asked me how I was feeling. The president wanted to know whether I wanted a few months more home service. I said: 'No, sir, I should be much obliged if you would pass me fit for service overseas.' In January I went out again.

I went back as an old soldier; my kit and baggage proved it. I had reduced the Christmas tree that I first brought out to a pocket-torch with a fourteen-day battery in it, and a pair of insulated wire-cutters strong enough to cut German wire (the ordinary British army issue would only cut British wire). Instead of a haversack I had a pack like the ones the men carried, but lighter and waterproof. I had lost my revolver when I was wounded and had not bought another; rifle and bayonet could always be got from the battalion. (Not carrying rifle and bayonet made officers conspicuous in an attack; in most divisions now they carried them, and also wore trousers rolled down over their puttees like the men, because the Germans had been taught to recognize them by their thin knees.) Instead of the heavy blankets that I had brought out before I now had an eiderdown sleeping-bag in an oiled-silk cover. I also had Shakespeare and a Bible, both printed on india-paper, a Catullus and a Lucretius in Latin, and two light weight, folding, canvas arm-chairs, one as a present for Yates the quartermaster, the other for myself. I was wearing a very thick whipcord tunic with a neat patch above the second button and another between the shoulders; it was my only salvage from the last time out except the pair of ski-ing boots which I was wearing again, reasonably waterproof – my breeches had been cut off me in hospital.

There was a draft[5] of ten young officers with me. As Captain Charles Edmonds notes in his book *A Subaltern's War*, young officers at this time were expected to be 'roistering blades with wine and women'. These ten did their best. Three of them got venereal disease at Rouen. In each case, I believe, it was the first time that they had been with women. They were strictly brought-up Welsh boys of the professional classes and knew nothing about prophylactics. One of them was sharing a hut with me. He came in very late and very drunk one night from the *Drapeau Blanc*, a well-known blue-lamp brothel, woke me up and began telling me what a wonderful time he had had. 'He had never known before,' he said, 'what a wonderful thing sex was.' I said irritably and in some disgust: 'The *Drapeau Blanc*? Then I hope to God you washed yourself.' He was very Welsh and on his dignity. 'What do you mean, captain? I did wass my fa-ace and ha-ands.' There were no restraints in France as in England; these boys had money to spend and knew that they had a good chance of being killed within a few weeks anyhow. They did not want to die virginal. So venereal hospitals at the base were always crowded. (The troops took a lewd delight in exaggerating the proportion of army chaplains to combatant officers treated there.) The *Drapeau Blanc* saved the life of scores of them by incapacitating them for future trench service.

The instructors at the Bull Ring were full of bullet-and-bayonet enthusiasm which they tried to pass on to the drafts. The drafts were now, for the most part, either forcibly enlisted men or wounded men returning, and at this dead season of the year it was difficult for anyone to feel enthusiastic on arrival in France. The training principle had recently been revised. *Infantry Training*, 1914, had laid it down politely that the soldier's ultimate aim was to put out of action or render ineffective the armed forces of the enemy. This statement was now not considered direct enough for a war of attrition. Troops were taught instead that their duty was to HATE the Germans and KILL as many of them as possible. In bayonet-practice the men were ordered to make horrible grimaces and utter blood-curdling yells as they charged. The bayonet-fighting instructors' faces were permanently set in a ghastly grin. 'Hurt him, now! In at his belly! Tear his guts out!'

they would scream as the men charged the dummies. 'Now that upper swing at his privates with the butt. Ruin his chances for life. No more little Fritzes! . . . Naaaoh! Anyone would think that you *loved* the bloody swine, patting and stroking 'em like that. Bɪᴛᴇ ʜɪᴍ, I ꜱᴀʏ! Sᴛɪᴄᴋ ʏᴏᴜʀ ᴛᴇᴇᴛʜ ɪɴ ʜɪᴍ ᴀɴᴅ ᴡᴏʀʀʏ ʜɪᴍ! Eᴀᴛ ʜɪꜱ ʜᴇᴀʀᴛ ᴏᴜᴛ!'

Once more I was glad to be sent up to the trenches.

XXII

I was posted to the Second Battalion again. I found it near Bouchavesnes on the Somme. It was a very different Second Battalion. No riding-school, no battalion-mess, no Quetta manners. I was more warmly welcomed this time; my suspected spying activities were forgotten. But the day before I arrived the colonel[1] had been wounded while out in front of the battalion inspecting the wire. He had been shot in the thigh by one of the 'rotten crowd' of his letter, who mistook him for a German and fired without challenging; he has been in and out of nursing homes ever since. Doctor Dunn asked me with kindly disapproval what I meant by coming back so soon. I said that I could not stand England any longer. He told the acting C.O. that I was, in his opinion, unfit for trench service, so I was put in command of the headquarter company. I went to live with the transport back at Frises, where the Somme made a bend. My company consisted of regimental clerks, cooks, tailors, shoemakers, pioneers, transport men, and so on, who in an emergency could become riflemen and used as a combatant force. We were in dug-outs close to the river, which was frozen completely over except for a narrow stretch of fast water in the middle. I had never been so cold in my life; it made me shudder to think what the trenches must be like. I used to go up to them every night with the rations, the quartermaster being sick; it was about a twelve-mile walk there and back. The general commanding the Thirty-third Division had teetotal convictions on behalf of his men and stopped their issue of rum except for emergencies; the immediate result was a much heavier sick-list than the battalion had ever had. The men had always looked forward to their tot of rum at the dawn stand-to as the one bright moment of the twenty-four hours. When this was denied them, their resistance weakened. I took the rations up through Cléry, which had been a wattle and daub village of some hundreds of inhabitants. The highest part of it now standing was a short course of brick wall about three feet high; the rest was enormous overlapping shell-craters. A broken-down steam-roller by the road-side had the name of the village chalked on it as a guide to travellers. We often lost a horse or two at Cléry, which the Germans continued to shell from habit.

Our reserve billets for these Bouchavesnes trenches were at Suzanne. They were not really billets, but dug-outs and shelters. Suzanne was also in ruins. The winter was the hardest since 1894–5. The men played inter-company football matches on the river, which was now frozen two feet thick. I remember a meal here in a shelter-billet; stew and tinned tomato on metal plates. Though the food came in hot from the kitchen next door, before we had finished it there was ice on the edge of the plate. In all this area there were no French civilians, no unshelled houses, no signs of cultivation. The only living creatures that I saw except soldiers and horses and mules were a few moorhen and duck in the narrow unfrozen part of the river. There was a shortage of fodder for the horses, many of which were sick; the ration was down to three pounds a day, and they had only open standings. I have kept few records of this time, but the memory of its misery survives.

Then I had bad toothache, and there was nothing for it but to take a horse and ride twenty miles to the nearest army dental station. The dentist who attended me was under the weather like everyone else. He would do nothing at first but grumble what a fool he had been to offer his services to his country at such a low salary. 'When I think,' he said, 'of the terrible destruction to the nation's teeth that is being done by unqualified men at home, and the huge fees that they are exacting for their wicked work, it makes me boil with rage.' There followed further complaints against the way he was treated and the unwillingness of the Royal Army Medical Corps to give dentists any promotion beyond lieutenant's rank. Later he began work on my tooth. 'An abscess,' he said, 'no good tinkering about with this; must pull it out.' So he yanked at it irritably and the tooth broke off. He tried again; there was very little purchase and it broke off again. He damned the ineffective type of forceps that the Government supplied. After about half an hour he got the tooth out in sections. I rode home with lacerated gums.

I was appointed a member of a field general court-martial on an Irish sergeant charged with 'shamefully casting away his arms in the presence of the enemy'. I had heard about the case unofficially. He had been maddened by an intense bombardment, thrown down his rifle, and run with the rest of his platoon. An army order, secret and confidential, had recently instructed me that, in the case of men tried for their life on other charges, sentence might be mitigated if conduct in the field had been exemplary; but cowardice was only punishable with death and no medical excuses could be accepted. But I knew that there was nothing between sentencing the man to death and refusing to take part in the proceedings. If I chose the second course I would be court-martialled myself, and a reconstituted court would bring in the death verdict anyhow. Yet I would not sentence a man to death for an offence which I might have committed myself in the same circumstances. I was in a dilemma. I met the situation by evading it. There was one other officer in the battalion with the year's service, as a captain, which entitled him to sit on a field general court-martial. I found him willing to take my place. He was hard-boiled and glad of a trip to Amiens, and I took over his duties for him.

Executions were frequent in France. My first direct experience of official lying was when I was at the base at Havre in May 1915 and read the back-files of army orders in the officers' mess at the rest-camp. There were something like twenty reports of men shot for cowardice or desertion; yet not a week later the responsible Minister in the House of Commons, answering a question from a pacifist member, had denied that sentence of death for a military offence had been carried out in France on any member of His Majesty's forces.

The acting commanding-officer was sick and irritable; he felt the strain badly and took a lot of whisky. One spell he was too sick to be in the trenches, and came down to Frises, where he shared a dug-out with Yates the quartermaster and myself. I was sitting in my arm-chair reading the Bible and came on the text: 'The bed is too narrow to lie down therein and the coverlet too small to wrap myself therewith.'[2] 'I say, James,' I said, 'that's pretty appropriate for this place.' He raised himself on an elbow, genuinely furious. 'Look here, von Runicke,' he said, 'I am not a religious man. I've cracked a good many of the commandments since I've been in France; but while I am in command here I refuse to hear you or anyone bloody else blaspheme Holy Writ.' I liked James a lot. I had met him first on the day I arrived at Wrexham to join the regiment. He was just back from Canada and hilariously throwing chairs about in the junior ante-room of the mess. He had been driving a plough through virgin soil, he told us, and reciting Kipling to the prairie-dogs. His favourite piece was (I may be misquoting):

> Are ye there, are ye there, are ye there?
> Four points on a ninety-mile square.
> With a helio winking like fun in the sun,
> Are ye there, are ye there, are ye there?[3]

He had been with the Special Reserve a year or two before he emigrated. He cared for nobody, was most courageous, inclined to be sentimental, and probably saw longer service with the Second Battalion in the war than any officer except Yates.

A day or two later, because he was still sick and I was the senior officer of the battalion, I attended the Commanding Officers' Conference at brigade head-quarters. Opposite our trenches was a German salient and the brigadier wanted to 'bite it off' as a proof of the offensive spirit of his command. Trench soldiers could never understand the Staff's desire to bite off an enemy salient. It was not a desirable thing to be exposed to fire from both flanks; if the Germans were in a salient, our obvious duty was to keep them there as long as they could be persuaded to stay. We concluded that it was the passion for straight lines for which headquarters were well known, and that it had no strategic or tactical significance. The attack had been twice proposed and twice cancelled because of the weather. This was towards the end of February, in the thaw. I have a field-message referring to it, dated the 21st:

Please	cancel	Form 4	of	my
AA 202	units	will	draw	from
19th	brigade	B. Echelon	the	following
issue	of	rum	which	will
be	issued	to	troops	taking
part	in	the	forth	coming
operations	at	the	discretion	of
O.C.	units	2nd R.W.F.	7½	gallons.

Even this promise of special rum could not encourage the battalion. Every one agreed that the attack was unnecessary, foolish, and impossible. The company commanders assured me that to cross the three hundred yards of No Man's Land, which because of constant shelling and the thaw was a morass of mud more than knee-deep, would take even lightly-armed troops four or five minutes. It would be impossible for anyone to reach the German lines while there was a single section of Germans with rifles to defend them. The general, when I arrived, inquired in a fatherly way how old I was, and whether I was not proud to be attending a Commanding Officers' Conference at the age of twenty-one. I said that I had not examined my feelings, but that I was an old enough soldier to realize

the impossibility of the attack. The colonel of the Cameronians, who were also to be engaged, took the same
line. So the attack was finally called off.[4] That night I
went up with rations as usual; the battalion was much
relieved to hear the decision.

We had been heavily shelled on the way up, and
while I was at battalion headquarters having a drink a
message came to say that D Company limber had been
hit by a shell. As I went to inspect the damage I passed
the chaplain, who had come up with me from Frises
bend, and a group of three or four men. He was gab-
bling the burial service over a dead man lying on the
ground covered with a waterproof sheet. It was a suicide case. The misery of the weather and the knowledge
of the impending attack had been too much for him.
This was the last dead man I was to see in France, and
like the first, a suicide.

I found that the limber, which contained petrol tins
of water for the company, had had a direct hit. There
was no sign of the horses; they were highly-prized
horses, having won a prize at a divisional horse-show
some months back for the best-matched pair of the
division. So the transport sergeant and I sent the transport back and went looking for the horses in the dark.
We stumbled through miles of morass that night but
could not find them or get any news of them. We used
to boast that our transport animals were the best in
France. Our transport men were famous horse-thieves,
and no less than eighteen of our stable had been stolen
from other units at one time or another, for their good
looks. There were even two which we had 'borrowed'
from the Scots Greys. The horse I rode to the dentist
came from the French police; its only fault was that it
was the left-hand horse of the police squadron, and so

had a tendency to pull to the wrong side of the road. We had never lost a horse to any other battalion, so naturally Sergeant Meredith and I, who had started out with the rations at about four o'clock in the afternoon, kept on with the search until long after midnight. When we reached Frises at about three o'clock in the morning I was completely exhausted. I collapsed on my bunk.

The next day it was found that I had bronchitis and I went back in an ambulance to Rouen, once more to No. 8 Red Cross hospital. The major of the R.A.M.C. recognized me and said: 'What on earth are *you* doing out in France, young man? If I find you in my hospital again with those lungs of yours I'll have you court-martialled.'

The quartermaster wrote to me there that the horses had been found shortly after I had gone; they were unhurt except for grazes on their bellies and were in the possession of the machine-gun company of the Fourth Division; the machine-gunners were found disguising them with stain and trying to remove the regimental marks.

At Rouen I was asked to say where in England I would like to go to hospital. I said, at random, 'Oxford.'

XXIII

So I was sent to Oxford, to Somerville College, which, like the Examination Schools, had been converted into a hospital. It occurred to me here that I was probably through with the war, for it could not last long now. I both liked and disliked the idea. I disliked being away from the regiment in France and I liked to think that I would probably be alive when the war ended. As soon as I was passed fit Siegfried had got boarded too and tried to follow me to the Second Battalion. He was disappointed to find me gone. I felt I had somehow let him down. But he wrote that he was unspeakably relieved to know that I was back at Oxford.

I liked Oxford and wanted to stay there. I applied, on the strength of a chit from the Bull Ring commandant at Havre, for an instructional job in one of the Officer-Cadet Battalions quartered in the men's colleges. I was posted to the Wadham Company of No. 4 Battalion. These battalions had not been formed long; they had grown out of instructional schools for young officers. The cadet course was only three months (later increased to four), but it was a severe one and particularly intended to train platoon commanders in the handling of the platoon as an independent unit. About two-thirds of the cadets were men recommended for commissions by colonels in France, the remainder were public-school boys from the officers' training corps. Much of the training was drill and musketry, but the important part was tactical exercises with limited objectives. We used the army textbook S.S. 143, or '*Instructions for the training of platoons for offensive action, 1917,*' perhaps the most important War Office publication issued during the war. The author is said to have been General Solly-Flood, who wrote it after a visit to a French army school. From 1916 on the largest unit possible to control in sustained action was the platoon. Infantry training had hitherto treated the company as the chief tactical unit.

Though the quality of the officers had deteriorated from the regimental point of view (in brief, few of the new officers were now gentlemen),[1] their deficiency in manners was amply compensated for by their greater efficiency in action. The cadet-battalion system, in the next two years, saved the army in France from becoming a mere rabble. We failed about a sixth of the candidates for commissions; the failures were sometimes public-school boys without the necessary toughness, but usually men who had been recommended, from France, on compassionate grounds – rather stupid platoon sergeants and machine-gun corporals who had been out too long and were thought to need a rest. Our final selection of the right men to be officers was made by watching them play games, principally rugger and soccer. The ones who played rough but not dirty and had quick reactions were the men we wanted. We spent most of our spare time playing games with them. I had a platoon of New Zealanders, Canadians, South Africans, two men from the Fiji Island contingent, an English farm-labourer, a Welsh miner and two or three public-school boys. They were a good lot and most of them were killed later on in the war. The New Zealanders went in for rowing; the record time for the river at Oxford was made by a New Zealand eight that year. I found the work too much for my lungs, for which the climate of Oxford was unsuitable. I kept myself going for two months on a strychnine tonic and then collapsed again. I fainted and fell downstairs one evening in the dark, cutting my head open; I was taken back to Somerville. I had kept going as long as I could.

I had liked Wadham, where I was a member of the senior common-room and had access to the famous brown sherry of the college; it is specially mentioned in a Latin grace among the blessings vouchsafed to the fellows by their Creator. My commanding officer, Colonel Stenning, in better times University Professor of Hebrew, was a fellow of the college. The social system at Oxford was dislocated. The St. John's don destined to be my moral tutor when I came up was a corporal in the General Reserve; he wore grey uniform, drilled in the parks, and saluted me whenever we met. A college scout had a commission and was instructing in the other cadet battalion. There were not, I suppose, more than a hundred and fifty undergraduates at Oxford at this time; these were Rhodes scholars, Indians, and men who were unfit. I saw a good deal of Aldous Huxley, Wilfred Childe, and Thomas Earp, who were running an undergraduates' literary paper of necessarily limited circulation called *The Palatine Review*, to which I contributed. Earp had set himself the task of keeping the Oxford tradition alive through the dead years: he was president and sole member, he said, of some seventeen undergraduate social and literary societies. In 1919 he was still in residence, and handed over the minute-books to the returning university. Most of the societies were then re-formed.

I enjoyed being at Somerville. It was warm weather and the discipline of the hospital was easy. We used to lounge about in the grounds in our pyjamas and dressing-gowns, and even walk out into St. Giles' and down the Cornmarket (also in pyjamas and dressing-gowns) for a morning cup of coffee at the Cadena. And there was a V.A.D. probationer[2] with whom I fell in love. I did not tell her so at the time. This was the first time that I had fallen in love with a woman, and I had difficulty in adjusting myself to the experience. I used to meet her when I visited a friend in another ward, but we had little talk together. I wrote to her after leaving hospital. When I found that she was engaged to a sub-altern in France I stopped writing. I had seen what it felt like to be in France and have somebody else playing about with one's girl. Yet by the way she wrote reproving me for not writing she may well have been as fond of me as she was of him. I did not press the point. There was the end of it, almost before it started.

While I was with the cadet battalion I used to go out to tea nearly every Sunday to Garsington. Siegfried's friends, Philip and Lady Ottoline Morrell, lived at the manor house there. The Morrells were pacifists and it was here that I first heard that there was another side to the question of war guilt. Clive Bell was working on the manor farm; he was a conscientious objector, and had been permitted to do this, as work of national importance, instead of going into the army. Aldous Huxley, Lytton Strachey and the Hon. Bertrand Russell were frequent visitors. Aldous was unfit, otherwise he would certainly have been in the army like Osbert and Sacheverell Sitwell, Herbert Read, Siegfried, Wilfred

Owen, myself and most other young writers of the time, none of whom now believed in the war. Bertrand Russell, who was beyond the age of liability for military service but an ardent pacifist (a rare combination), turned sharply on me one afternoon and said: 'Tell me, if a company of men of your regiment were brought along to break a strike of munition makers and the munition makers refused to submit, would you order the men to fire?' I said: 'Yes, if everything else failed. It would be no worse than shooting Germans, really.' He was surprised and asked: 'Would your men obey you?' 'Of course they would,' I said; 'they loathe munition makers and would be only too glad of a chance to shoot a few. They think that they're all skrim-shankers.' 'But they realize that the war's all wicked nonsense?' 'Yes, as well as I do.' He could not understand my attitude.

Lytton Strachey was unfit, but instead of allowing himself to be rejected by the doctors he preferred to appear before a military tribunal as a conscientious objector. He told us of the extraordinary impression that was caused by an air-cushion which he inflated during the proceedings as a protest against the hardness of the benches. Asked by the chairman the usual question: 'I understand, Mr. Strachey, that you have a conscientious objection to war?' he replied (in his curious falsetto voice), 'Oh no, not at all, only to *this* war.' Better than this was his reply to the chairman's other stock question, which had previously never failed to embarrass the claimant: 'Tell me, Mr. Strachey, what would you do if you saw a German soldier trying to violate your sister?' With an air of noble virtue: 'I would try to get between them.'

In 1916 I met more well-known writers than ever

before or since. There were two unsuccessful meetings. George Moore had just written *The Brook Kerith* and my neurasthenic twitchings interrupted the calm, easy flow of his conversational periods. He told me irritably not to fidget; in return I taunted him with having introduced cactus into the Holy Land some fifteen centuries before the discovery of America, its land of origin. At the Reform Club, H. G. Wells, who was Mr. Britling in those days and full of military optimism, talked without listening. He had just been taken for a 'Cook's Tour' to France and had been shown the usual sights that royalty, prominent men of letters, and influential neutrals were shown by staff-conductors. He described his experiences at length and seemed unaware that I and the friend[3] who was with me had also seen the sights. But I liked Arnold Bennett for his kindly unpretentiousness. And I liked Augustine Birrell. I happened to correct him when he said that the Apocrypha was not read in the church services; and again when he said that Elihu the Jebusite was one of Job's comforters. He tried to override me in both points, but I called for a Bible and proved them. He said, glowering very kindly at me: 'I will say to you what Thomas Carlyle once said to a young man who caught him out in a misquotation, "Young man, you are heading straight for the pit of Hell!"'

And who else? John Galsworthy; or was my first meeting with him a year or two later? He was editor of a magazine called *Réveillé*, published under Government auspices (and was treated very ungenerously), the proceeds of which were to go to a disabled-soldier fund. I contributed. When I met him he asked me technical questions about soldier-slang – he was writing a war-play and wanted it accurate. He seemed a humble man and except for these questions listened without talking. This is, apparently, his usual practice; which explains why he is a better writer if a less forceful propagandist than Wells ... And Ivor Novello, in 1918. Then aged about twenty and already world famous as the author and composer of the patriotic song:

Keep the home fires burning
While the hearts are yearning ...

There was some talk of his setting a song of mine. I found him, wearing a silk dressing-gown, in a setting of incense, cocktails, many cushions, and a Tree or two. I felt uncomfortably military. I removed my spurs (I was a temporary field-officer at the time) out of courtesy to the pouffes. He was in the Royal Naval Air Service, but his genius was officially recognized and he was able to keep the home fires burning until the boys came home.

By this time the War Office had stopped the privilege that officers had enjoyed, after coming out of hospital, of going to their own homes for convalescence. It was found that many of them took no trouble to get well quickly and return to duty; they kept late nights, drank, and overtaxed their strength. So when I was somewhat recovered I was sent to a convalescent home for officers in the Isle of Wight. It was Osborne Palace; my bedroom had once been the royal night-nursery of King Edward VII and his brothers and sisters. This was the strawberry season and fine weather; the patients were able to take all Queen Victoria's favourite walks through the woods and along the quiet sea-shore, play billiards in the royal billiard-room, sing bawdy songs in the royal music-room, drink the Prince

Consort's favourite Rhine wines among his Winter-halters, play golf-croquet and go down to Cowes when in need of adventure. We were made honorary members of the Royal Yacht Squadron. This is another of the caricature scenes of my life; sitting in a leather chair in the smoking-room of what had been and is now again the most exclusive club in the world, drinking gin and ginger, and sweeping the Solent with a powerful telescope.

I made friends with the French Benedictine Fathers who lived near by; they had been driven from Solesmes in France by the anti-clerical laws of 1906, and had built themselves a new abbey at Quarr. The abbey had a special commission from the Vatican to collect and edit ancient church music. Hearing the fathers at their plain-song made us for the moment forget the war completely. Many of them were ex-army officers who had, I was told, turned to religion after the ardours of their campaigns or after disappointments in love. They were greatly interested in the war, which they saw as a dispensation of God for restoring France to Catholicism. They told me that the freemason element in the French army had been discredited and that the present Supreme Command was predominantly Catholic – an augury, they said, of Allied victory. The guest-master showed me the library of twenty thousand volumes, hundreds of them black-letter. The librarian was an old monk from Béthune and was interested to hear from me an accurate account of the damage to his quarter of the town. The guest-master asked me whether there were any books that I would like to read in the library. He said that there were all kinds there – history, botany, music, architecture, engineering, almost every other lay subject. I asked him whether there was a poetry section. He smiled kindly and said, no, poetry was not regarded as improving.

The Father Superior asked me whether I was a *bon catholique*. I replied no, I did not belong to the true religion. To spare him a confession of agnosticism I added that my parents were Protestants. He said: 'But if ours is the true religion why do you not become a Catholic?' He asked the question in such a simple way that I felt ashamed. But I had to put him off somehow, so I said: 'Reverend father, we have a proverb in England never to swap horses while crossing a stream. I am still in the war, you know.' I offered: 'Peut-être après la guerre.' This was a joke with myself; it was the stock answer that the Pas de Calais girls were ordered by their priests to give to Allied soldiers who asked for a 'Promenade, mademoiselle?' It was seldom given, I was told, except for the purpose of bargaining. All the same, I half-envied the Fathers their abbey on the hill, finished with wars and love affairs. I liked their kindness and seriousness; the clean whitewashed cells and the meals eaten in silence at the long oaken tables, while a novice read the *Lives of the Saints*; the food, mostly cereals, vegetables and fruit, was the best I had tasted for years – I was tired of ration beef, ration jam, ration bread and cheese. At Quarr, Catholicism ceased to be repulsive to me.

Osborne was gloomy. Many of the patients there were neurasthenic and should have been in a special neurasthenic hospital. A. A. Milne was there, as a sub-altern in the Royal Warwickshire Regiment, and in the least humorous vein. Vernon Bartlett, of the Hampshire Regiment, who had introduced me to the Quarr Fathers, decided with me that something must be started. So we founded the 'Royal Albert Society'; its

aim was to revive interest in the life and times of the
Prince Consort. I was president and my regalia consisted of a Scottish dirk, Hessian boots and a pair of
side-whiskers. Official business was not allowed to
proceed until the announcement had been duly made
that the whiskers were on the table. Membership was
open only to those who professed themselves students
of the life and works of the Prince Consort, those who
had been born in the province of Alberta in Canada,
those who had resided for six months or upwards by
the banks of the Albert Nyanza, those who held the
Albert Medal for saving life, or those who were linked
with the Prince Consort's memory in any other signal
way. The members were expected to report at each
meeting reminiscences that they had collected from old
palace-servants and Osborne cottagers, throwing light
on the human side of the Consort's life. We had about
fifteen members and ate strawberries. On one occasion
about a dozen officers came in to join the society; they
professed to have the necessary qualifications. One
said that he was the grandson of the man who had
built the Albert Memorial; one had worked at the
Albert Docks; and one actually did possess the Albert
Medal for saving life; the others were mere students.
They submitted quietly at first to the ceremonies and
business, but it was soon apparent that they were not
serious and had come to break up the society; they
were, in fact, most of them drunk. They began giving
indecent accounts of the private life of the Prince Consort, alleging that they could substantiate them with
documentary evidence. Bartlett and I got worried; it
was not that sort of society. So, as president, I rose and
told in an improved version the story which had won
the 1914 All-England Inter-regimental Competition at

Aldershot for the worst story[4] of the year. I linked it up with the Prince Consort by saying that he had been told it by John Brown, the Balmoral ghillie, in whose pawky humour Queen Victoria used to find such delight, and that it had prevented him from sleeping for three days and nights, and was a contributory cause of his premature death. The story had the intended effect; the interruptors threw up their hands in surrender and walked out. It struck me suddenly how far I had come since my first years at Charterhouse seven years back, and what a pity it was that I had not used the same technique there.

On the beach one day Bartlett and I saw an old ship's fender; the knotted ropes at the top had frayed into something that looked like hair, so Bartlett said to me: 'Poor fellow, I knew him well. He was in my platoon in the Hampshire Regiment and jumped overboard from the hospital ship.' A little farther along we found an old pair of trousers half in the water, and a coat, and then some socks and a boot. So we dressed up Bartlett's old comrade, draped sea-weed over him where necessary, and walked on. Soon after we met a coast-guard and turned back with him. We said: 'There's a dead man on the beach.' He stopped a few yards off and said, holding his nose: 'Pooh, don't he 'alf stink!' We turned again, leaving him with the dead, and the next day read in the Isle of Wight paper of a hoax that 'certain convalescent officers at Osborne' had played on the coroner. Bartlett and I were nonsensical, and changed the labels of all the pictures in the galleries. Anything to make people laugh. But it was hard work.

XXIV[1]

I used to hear from Siegfried regularly. He had written in March from the Second Battalion asking me to pull myself together and send him a letter because he was horribly low in spirits. He complained that he had not been made at all welcome. A Special Reserve officer who had transferred to the Second Battalion and was an acting-captain had gone so far as to call him a bloody wart and allude to the bloody First Battalion. He had swallowed the insult, but was trying to get transferred to the First Battalion. The Second was resting until the end of the month about two miles from Morlancourt (where we had been together in the previous March), surrounded by billows of mud slopes and muddy woods and aerodromes and fine new railroads, where he used to lollop around on the black mare of an afternoon watching the shells bursting away by the citadel. The black mare was a beautiful combative creature with a homicidal kink, only ridden by Siegfried. David Thomas and I once watched him breaking her in. His patience was wonderful. He would put the mare at a jump and she would sulk; and he would not force her but turn her around and then lead her back to it. Time after time she refused, but could not provoke his ill-temper or make him give up his intention. Finally she took the jump in mere boredom. It was

a six-footer, and she could manage higher than that.
He was in C Company now, he wrote, with a half-witted
platoon awaiting his orders to do or die, and a beast of
a stiff arm where Dr. Dunn had inoculated him, sticking his needle in and saying: 'Toughest skin of the lot,
but you're a tough character, I know.' Siegfried protested that he was not so tough as Dunn thought. He
was hoping that the battalion would get into some sort
of show soon; it would be a relief after all these weeks
of irritation and discomfort and disappointment. (That
was a feeling that one usually had in the Second Battalion.) He supposed that his *Old Huntsman* would not
be published until the autumn. He had seen the *Nation*
that week, and commented how jolly it was for him
and me to appear as a military duet singing to a pacifist
organ. 'You and me, the poets who mean to work
together some day and scandalize the jolly old Gosse's
and Strachey's.' (Re-reading this letter now I am
reminded that the occasion of the final end of our correspondence ten years later was my failure to observe
the proper literary punctilios towards the late Sir
Edmund Gosse, C.B. And, by the way, when the *Old
Huntsman* appeared, Sir Edmund severely criticized
some lines of an allegorical poem in it:

... Rapture and pale Enchantment and Romance
And many a slender sickly lord who'd filled
My soul long since with lutanies of sin
Went home because he could not stand the din.[2]

This, he considered, might be read as a libel on the
British House of Lords. The peerage, he said, had
proved itself splendidly heroic in the war.)
Siegfried had his wish; he was in heavy fighting with

the battalion in the Hindenburg Line soon after. His platoon was then lent as support to the Cameronians, and when, in a counter-attack, the Cameronians were driven out of some trenches that they had won, Siegfried, with a bombing party of six men, regained them. He was shot through the throat but continued bombing until he collapsed. The Cameronians rallied and returned, and Siegfried's name was sent in for a Victoria Cross. The recommendation was refused, however, on the ground that the operations had not been successful; for the Cameronians were later driven out again by a bombing party under some German Siegfried.

He was back in England and very ill. He told me that often when he went out he saw corpses lying about on the pavement. He had written from hospital, in April, how bloody it was about the Second Battalion. Yates had sent him a note saying that four officers were killed and seven wounded in the show at Fontaine-les-Croiselles, the same place that he had been at, and it had been a 'perfectly bloody battle'. But there had been an advance of about half a mile, which seemed to Siegfried to be some consolation. Yet, in the very next sentence, he wrote how mad it made him to think of all the good men being slaughtered that summer, and all for nothing. The bloody politicians and ditto generals with their cursed incompetent blundering and callous ideas would go on until they were tired of it or had got all the kudos they wanted. He wished he could do something to protest against it, but even if he were to shoot the Premier or Sir Douglas Haig they could only shut him up in a mad-house like Richard Dadd of glorious memory. (I recognized the allusion. Dadd was an early nineteenth-century painter who made out a list of people who deserved to be killed. The first on the list was his father. He picked him up one day in Hyde Park and carried him on his shoulders for nearly half a mile before publicly drowning him in the Serpentine.) Siegfried went on to say that if he refused to go out again as a protest they would only accuse him of being afraid of shells. He asked me whether I thought we would be any better off by the end of that summer of carnage. We would never break their line. So far, in April, we had lost more men than the Germans. The Canadians at Vimy had lost appallingly, yet the official *communiqués* were lying unblushingly about the casualties. Julian Dadd had come to see him in hospital and, like every one else, urged him not to go out again, to take a safe job at home – but he knew that it was only a beautiful dream, that he would be morally compelled to go on until he was killed. The thought of going back now was agony, just when he had got back into the light again – 'Oh life, oh sun.'[3] His wound was nearly healed and he expected to be sent for three weeks to a convalescent home. He didn't like the idea, but *anywhere* would be good enough if he could only be quiet and see no one, just watch the trees dressing up in green and feel the same himself. He was beastly weak and in a rotten state of nerves. The gramophone in the ward plagued him beyond endurance. The *Old Huntsman* had come out that spring after all, and, for a joke, he had sent a copy to Sir Douglas Haig. He couldn't be stopped doing *that* anyhow.

In June he had gone to visit the Morrells just before I left hospital at Oxford. He had no idea I was still there, but he wrote that perhaps it was as well that we didn't meet, neither of us being at our best; at least one of us should be in a normal frame of mind when we were together. I had asked what he had been writing since he came home, and he answered that five poems of his had appeared in the *Cambridge Magazine* (one of the few pacifist journals published in England at the time, the offices of which were later raided by militarist flying-cadets). He said that none of them were much good except as digs at the complacent and perfectly ——— people who thought the war ought to go on indefinitely until every one was killed except themselves. The pacifists were urging him to produce something red hot in the style of Barbusse's *Under Fire* but he couldn't do it; he had other things in his head, *not poems*. I didn't know what he meant by this but hoped that it was not a programme of assassination. He wrote that the thought of all that happened in France nearly drove him dotty sometimes. He was down in Kent, where he could hear the guns thudding all the time across the Channel, on and on, until he didn't know whether he wanted to rush back and die with the First Battalion or stay in England and do what he could to prevent the war going on. But both courses were hopeless. To go back and get killed would be only playing to the gallery – and the wrong gallery – and he could think of no way of doing any effective preventive work at home. His name had been sent in for an officer-cadet battalion appointment in England, which would keep him safe if he wanted to take it; but it seemed a dishonourable way out. Now at the end of July another letter came: it felt rather thin. I sat down to read it on the bench dedicated by Queen Victoria to John Brown ('a truer and more faithful heart never burned within human breast'). When I opened the envelope a newspaper-cutting fluttered out; it was marked in ink: '*Bradford Pioneer*, Friday, July 27, 1917.' I read the wrong side first:

THE C.O.'S MUST BE SET FREE
By Philip Frankford

The conscientious objector is a brave man. He will be remembered as one of the few noble actors in this world drama when the impartial historian of the future sums up the history of this awful war.

The C.O. is putting down militarism. He is fighting for freedom and liberty. He is making a mighty onslaught upon despotism. And, above all, he is preparing the way for the final abolition of war.

But thanks to the lying, corrupt, and dastardly capitalist Press these facts are not known to the general public, who have been taught to look upon the conscientious objectors as skunks, cowards, and shirkers.

Lately a renewed persecution of C.O.'s has taken place. In spite of the promises of 'truthful' Cabinet Ministers, some C.O.'s have been sent to France, and there sentenced to death – a sentence afterwards transferred to one of 'crucifixion' or five or ten years' hard labour. But even when allowed to remain in this country we have to chronicle the most scandalous treatment of these men – the salt of the earth. Saintly individuals like Clifford Allen, Scott Duckers, and thousands of others, no less splendid enthusiasts in the cause of anti-militarism, are in prison for no other reason than because they refuse to take life; and because they will not throw away their manhood by becoming slaves to the military machine. These men MUST BE FREED. The political 'offenders' of Ireland . . .

Then I turned over and read:

Finished with the War
A Soldier's Declaration

(This statement was made to his commanding officer by Second-Lieutenant S. L. Sassoon, Military Cross, recommended for D.S.O., Third Battalion Royal Welch Fusiliers, as explaining his grounds for refusing to serve further in the army. He enlisted on 3rd August 1914, showed distinguished valour in France, was badly wounded and would have been kept on home service if he had stayed in the army.)

I am making this statement as an act of wilful defiance of military authority, because I believe that the war is being deliberately prolonged by those who have the power to end it.

I am a soldier, convinced that I am acting on behalf of soldiers. I believe that this war, upon which I entered as a war of defence and liberation, has now become a war of aggression and conquest. I believe that the purposes for which I and my fellow-soldiers entered upon this war should have been so clearly stated as to have made it impossible to change them, and that, had this been done, the objects which actuated us would now be attainable by negotiation.

I have seen and endured the sufferings of the troops, and I can no longer be a party to prolong these sufferings for ends which I believe to be evil and unjust.

I am not protesting against the conduct of the war, but against the political errors and insincerities for which the fighting men are being sacrificed.

On behalf of those who are suffering now I make this protest against the deception which is being practised

on them; also I believe that I may help to destroy the
callous complacence with which the majority of those
at home regard the continuance of agonies which they
do not share, and which they have not sufficient imagin-
ation to realize.

July 1917.   S. SASSOON.

This filled me with anxiety and unhappiness. I entirely
agreed with Siegfried about the 'political errors and
insincerities'; I thought his action magnificently courageous. But there were more things to be considered
than the strength of our case against the politicians. In
the first place, he was not in a proper physical condition
to suffer the penalty which he was inviting, which was
to be court-martialled, cashiered and imprisoned. I
found myself most bitter with the pacifists who had
encouraged him to make this gesture. I felt that, not
being soldiers, they could not understand what it would
cost Siegfried emotionally. It was wicked that he should
attempt to face the consequences of his letter on top
of his Quadrangle and Fontaine-les-Croiselles experiences. I knew, too, that as a gesture it was inadequate.
Nobody would follow his example either in England or
in Germany. The war would obviously go on, and go
on until one side or the other cracked.

I decided to intervene. I applied to appear before the
medical board that was sitting next day; and I asked the
board to pass me fit for home service. I was not fit and
they knew it, but I asked it as a favour. I had to get out
of Osborne and attend to things. Next I wrote to the
Hon. Evan Morgan, with whom I had canoed at Oxford
a month or two previously. He was private secretary
to one of the Coalition Ministers. I asked him to do

everything he could to prevent republication of or comment on the letter in the newspapers, and to arrange that a suitable answer should be given to Mr. Lees Smith, then the leading pacifist M.P. and now Postmaster-General in the Labour Cabinet, when he brought up a question in the House about it. I explained to Morgan that I was on Siegfried's side really, but that he should not be allowed to become a martyr in his present physical condition. Next I wrote to the Third Battalion. I knew that the colonel, a South Welshman,[4] was narrowly patriotic, had never been to France, and could not possibly be expected to take a sympathetic view. But the senior-major,[5] an Irishman, was humane, so I wrote to him explaining the whole business, asking him to make the colonel see it in a reasonable light. I told him of Siegfried's recent experiences in France. I suggested that he should be medically boarded and given indefinite leave.

The next news I heard was from Siegfried, who wrote from the Exchange Hotel, Liverpool, that no doubt I was worrying about him. He had come up to Liverpool a day or two before and walked into the Third Battalion orderly room at Litherland feeling like nothing on earth, but probably looking fairly self-possessed. The senior-major was commanding, the colonel being away on holiday. (I was much relieved at this bit of luck.) The senior-major, who was nicer than anything I could imagine and made him feel an utter brute, had consulted the general commanding Mersey defences. And the general was consulting God 'or someone like that'. Meanwhile, he was staying at the hotel, having sworn not to run away to the Caucasus. He hoped, in time, to persuade them to be nasty about it, and said that he did not think that they realized that his performance would soon be given great publicity.

He hated the whole business more than ever, and knew more than ever that he was right and would never repent of what he had done. He said that things were looking better in Germany, but that Lloyd George would probably say that it was a 'plot'. The politicians seemed to him incapable of behaving like human beings.

The general consulted not God but the War Office, and the War Office was persuaded not to press the matter as a disciplinary case, but to give Siegfried a medical board. Morgan had done his part of the work well. The next task I set myself was to persuade Siegfried to take the medical board. I rejoined the battalion and met him at Liverpool. He looked very ill; he told me that he had just been down to the Formby links and thrown his Military Cross into the sea. We discussed the whole political situation; I told him that he was right enough in theory; but that every one was mad except ourselves and one or two others, and that it was hopeless to offer rightness of theory to the insane. I said that the only possible course for us to take was to keep on going out to France till we got killed. I now expected myself before long to go back for the fourth time. I reminded him of the regiment; what did he think that the First and Second Battalions would think of him? How could they be expected to understand his point of view? They would say that he was ratting, that he had cold feet, and was letting the regiment down by not acting like a gentleman. How would Old Joe, even, understand it (and he was the most understanding man in the regiment)? To whom was his letter addressed? The army could, I repeated, only understand it as cowardice, or at the best as a lapse from good form. The civilians were more mad and hopeless than the army. He would not accept this view, but I made it plain that his letter had not been given and would not be given the publicity he intended; so, because he was ill, and knew it,[6] he consented to appear before the medical board.

So far, so good. The next thing was to rig the medical board. I applied for permission to give evidence as a friend of the patient. There were three doctors on the board – a regular R.A.M.C. colonel and major, and a captain, who was obviously a 'duration of the war' man. I had not been long in the room when I realized that the colonel was patriotic and unsympathetic, that the major was reasonable but ignorant, and that the captain was a nerve-specialist, right-minded, and my only hope. I had to go through the whole story again. I was most deferential to the colonel and major, but used the captain as an ally to break down their scruples. I had to appear in the rôle of a patriot distressed by the mental collapse of a brother-in-arms, a collapse directly due to his magnificent exploits in the trenches. I mentioned Siegfried's 'hallucinations' in the matter of corpses in Piccadilly. The irony of having to argue to these mad old men that Siegfried was not sane! It was a betrayal of truth, but I was jesuitical. I was in nearly as bad a state of nerves as Siegfried myself and burst into tears three times in the course of my statement. Captain McDowall, whom I learned later to be a well-known morbid psychologist, played up well and the colonel was at last persuaded. As I went out he said to me: 'Young man, you ought to be before this board yourself.' I was most anxious that when Siegfried went into the board-room after me he should not undo my work by appearing too sane. But McDowall argued his seniors over.

Siegfried was sent to a convalescent home for neur-asthenics at Craiglockhart, near Edinburgh. I was detailed as his escort. Siegfried and I both thought this a great joke, especially when I missed the train and he reported to 'Dottyville', as he called it, without me. At Craiglockhart, Siegfried was in the care of W. H. R. Rivers, whom we now met for the first time, though we already knew of him as a neurologist, ethnologist and psychologist. He was a Cambridge professor and had made a point of taking up a new department of research every few years and incorporating it in his comprehensive anthropological scheme. He died shortly after the war[7] when he was on the point of contesting the London University parliamentary seat as an independent Labour candidate; intending to round off his scheme with a study of political psychology. He was busy at this time with morbid psychology. He had over a hundred neurasthenic cases in his care and diagnosed their condition largely through a study of their dream-life; his posthumous book *Conflict and Dream* is a record of this work at Craiglockhart. It was not the first time that I had heard of Rivers in this capacity. Dick had come under his observation after the police-court episode. Rivers had treated him, and after a time pronounced him sufficiently cured to enlist in the army. Siegfried and Rivers soon became close friends. Siegfried was interested in Rivers' diagnostic methods and Rivers in Siegfried's poems. Before I returned from Edinburgh I felt happier. Siegfried began to write the terrifying sequence of poems that appeared next year as *Counter-Attack*. Another patient at the hospital was Wilfred Owen, who had had a bad time with the Manchester Regiment in France; and, further, it had preyed on his mind that he had been accused of cowardice by his commanding officer. He was in a very shaky condition.[8] It was meeting Siegfried here that set him writing his war-poems. He was a quiet, round-faced little man.

XXV

I went back to Liverpool. The president of the medical board had been right: I should not have been back on duty. The training at the camp was intensive and I was in command of a trained-men company and did not allow myself sufficient rest. I realized how bad my nerves were when one day, marching through the streets of Litherland on a battalion route-march, I saw three men wearing gas-masks standing by an open manhole in the road. They were bending over a dead man; his clothes were sodden and stinking, and his face and hands were yellow. Waste chemicals of the munitions factory had got into the sewage system and he had been gassed when he went down to inspect. The men in masks had been down to get him up. The company did not pause in its march so I had only a glimpse of the group; but it was so like France that I all but fainted. The band music saved me.

I was detailed as a member of a court-martial which sat in the camp. The accused was a civilian alleged to have enlisted under the Derby Scheme, but not to have presented himself when his class was called to the colours. He was a rabbit, a nasty-looking little man. I tried to feel sympathetic but found it difficult, even when he proved that he had never enlisted. His solicitor handed us a letter from a corporal serving in

France, who explained that he had, while on leave, enlisted in the rabbit's name because he had heard that the rabbit had been rabbiting with his wife. This rabbiting the rabbit denied; but he showed that the colour of the eyes recorded on the enlistment-form was blue while his own were brown, so it seemed that the story was true so far. But a further question arose: why had he not enlisted under the Military Service Act, if he was a fit man? He said that he was starred, having done responsible work in a munitions factory for the necessary length of time before the Military Service Act had become law. However, we had police evidence on the table to show that his protection certificates were forged, that he had not been working on munitions before the Military Service Act, and that therefore he was in the class of those 'deemed to have enlisted', and so a deserter in any case. There was nothing for it but to sentence him to the prescribed two years' imprisonment. He broke down and squealed rabbit-fashion, and said that he had conscientious objections against war. It made me feel contemptible, as part of the story.

Large drafts were now constantly being sent off to the First, Second, Ninth, and Tenth Battalions in France, and to the Eighth Battalion in Mesopotamia. There were few absentees among the men warned for the drafts. But it was noticeable that they were always more cheerful about going in the spring and summer when there was heavy fighting on than in the winter months when things were quiet. (The regiment kept up its spirit even in the last year of the war. Attwater told me that big drafts sent off in the critical weeks of the spring of 1918, when the Germans had broken through the Fifth Army, went down to the station singing and cheering enthusiastically. He said that they might have been the reservists that he and I had seen assembling at Wrexham on 12th August 1914, to rejoin the Second Battalion just before it sailed for France.) The colonel always made the same speech to the draft. The day that I rejoined the battalion from the Isle of Wight I went via Liverpool Exchange Station and the electric railway to Litherland. Litherland Station was crowded with troops. I heard a familiar voice making a familiar speech; it was the colonel bidding Godspeed to a small draft of men who were rejoining the First Battalion. '. . . going cheerfully like British soldiers to fight the common foe . . . some of you perhaps may fall . . . Upholding the magnificent traditions of the Royal Welch Fusiliers . . .' The draft cheered vigorously; rather too vigorously, I told myself. When he had finished I went over and greeted a few old friends: 79 Davies, 33 Williams, and the Davies who was nicknamed 'Dym Bacon', which was Welsh for 'there isn't any bacon'. (He had won the nickname in his recruit days. He was the son of a Welsh farmer and accustomed to good food and so he complained about his first morning's breakfast, shouting out to the orderly-sergeant: 'Do you call this a bloody breakfast, man? Dym bacon, dym sausages, dym herrings, dym bloody anything. Nothing but bloody bread and jaaam.') There was another well-remembered First Battalion man – D.C.M. and rosette, Médaille Militaire, Military Medal, no stripe. 'Lost them again, sergeant?'[1] I asked. He grinned: 'Easy come, easy go, sir.' Then the train came in and I put out my hand with 'Good luck!' 'You'll excuse us, sir,' he said. The draft shouted with laughter and I saw why my hand had not been wrung, and also why the cheers had been so ironically vigorous. They were all in handcuffs. They had been detailed a fortnight before for a draft to Mesopotamia; but they wanted to go back to the First Battalion, so they overstayed their leave. The colonel, not understanding, put them into the guard-room to make sure of them for the next draft. So they were now going back in handcuffs under an escort of military police to the battalion of their choice. The colonel, as I have already said, had seen no active service himself; but the men bore him no ill-will for the handcuffs. He was a good-hearted man and took a personal interest in the camp kitchens, had built a cinema-hut within the camp, been reasonably mild in orderly room, and done his best not to drive returned soldiers too hard.

I decided to leave Litherland somehow. I knew what the winter would be like with the mist coming up from the Mersey and hanging about the camp full of T.N.T. fumes. When I was there the winter before I used to sit in my hut and cough and cough until I was sick. The fumes tarnished all buttons and made our eyes smart. I considered going back to France but I knew this was absurd as yet. Since 1916 the fear of gas had been an obsession; in any unusual smell that I met I smelt gas – even a sudden strong scent of flowers in a garden was enough to set me trembling. And I knew that the noise of heavy shelling would be too much for me now. The noise of a motor-tyre exploding behind me would send me flat on my face or running for cover. So I decided to go to Palestine, where gas was not known and shell-fire was said to be inconsiderable in comparison with France. Siegfried wrote from Craiglockhart in August: 'What do you think of the latest push? How splendid this attrition is! As Lord Crewe says: "We are not the least depressed."' I matched this with a remark of Lord Carson's: 'The necessary supply of heroes must be maintained at all costs.' At my next medical board I asked to be passed in the category of B2. This meant: 'Fit for garrison service at home.' I reckoned on being sent to the Third Garrison Battalion of the regiment, now under canvas at Oswestry in Wales. From there, when I felt a bit better, I would get myself passed B1, which meant: 'Fit for garrison service abroad,' and would, in due course, go to a garrison battalion of the regiment in Egypt. Once there it would be easy to get passed A1 and join the Twenty-fourth or Twenty-fifth (new-army) Battalion in Palestine.

So presently I was sent to Oswestry. A good colonel, but the material at his disposal was discouraging. The men were mostly compulsory enlistments, and the officers, with few exceptions, useless. The first task I was given was to superintend the entraining of battalion stores and transport; we were moving to Kinmel Park Camp, near Rhyl. I was given a company of one hundred and fifty men and allowed six hours for the job. I chose fifty of the stronger men and three or four N.C.O.'s who looked capable, and sent the rest away to play football. By organizing the job in the way that I had learnt in the First Battalion I got these fifty men to load the train in two hours less than the scheduled time. The colonel congratulated me. At Rhyl he gave me the job of giving 'further instruction' to the sixty or so young officers who had been sent to him from the cadet-battalions. Few officers in the battalion had seen any active service. Among the few was Howell Davies (now literary editor of the *Star*), who had had a bullet through his head and was in as nervous a condition as myself. We became friends, and discussed the war and poetry late at night in the hut; we used to argue furiously, shouting each other down.

It was at this point that I remembered Nancy Nicholson. I had first met her at Harlech, where the Nicholsons had a house, when I was on leave in April 1916 after the operation on my nose. She was sixteen then, on holiday from school. I had made friends with her brother Ben, the painter, whose asthma had kept him out of the army. When I went back to France in 1917 I had gone to say good-bye to Ben and the rest of the family on the way to Victoria Station, and the last person to say good-bye to me at that time was Nancy. I remembered her standing in the doorway in her black velvet dress. She was ignorant but independent-minded, good-natured, hard, and as sensible about the war as anybody at home could be. In the summer of 1917 (shortly after the episode with the Somerville nurse) I had seen her again and we had gone together to a revue, the first revue I had been to in my life. It was *Cheep*; Lee White was in it, singing of Black-eyed Susans, and how 'Girls must all be Farmers' Boys, off with skirts, wear corduroys,' and Nancy told me that she was now on the land herself. She showed me her paintings, illustrations to Stevenson's *Child's Garden of Verses*; my child-sentiment and hers – she had a happy childhood to look back on – answered each other. I liked all her family, particularly her mother, now dead, Mabel Nicholson, the painter, a beautiful wayward Scotch-melancholy person. William Nicholson, again 'the painter', is still among my friends. Tony, a brother, just older than Nancy, was a gunner, waiting to go to France.

I began a correspondence with Nancy about some children's rhymes of mine which she was going to illustrate. Then I found that I was in love with her, and on my next leave, in October 1917, I visited her at the

farm where she was working, at Hilton in Hunting-
donshire. I helped her to put mangolds through a slicer.
She was alone, except for her black poodle, among
farmers, farm labourers, and wounded soldiers who
had been put on land-service. I was alone too in my
Garrison Battalion. Our letters became more intimate
after this. She warned me that she was a feminist and
that I had to be very careful what I said about women;
the attitude of the Huntingdon farmers to their wives
and daughters kept her in a continual state of anger she
said.

I had been passed B1 now, but orders came for me to
proceed to Gibraltar. This was a disarrangement of my
plans. Gibraltar was a dead-end; it would be as difficult to get from there to Palestine as it would be from
England. A friend in the War Office undertook to cancel the order for me until a vacancy could be found in
the battalion in Egypt. At Rhyl I was enjoying the first
independent command I had yet had in the army. I got
it through a scare of an invasion of the north-east
coast, to follow a sortie of the German Fleet. A number
of battalions were sent across England for its defence.
All fit men of the Third Garrison Battalion were ordered
to move at twenty-four hours' notice to York. (There
was a slight error, however, in the Morse message from
War Office to Western Command. Instead of dash-dot-
dash-dash they sent dash-dot-dash-dot, so the battalion
was sent to Cork instead. Yet it was not recalled, being
needed as much in Cork as in York; Ireland was in
great unrest since the Easter rising in 1916, and Irish
troops at the depots were giving away their rifles to
Sinn Feiners.) The colonel told me that I was the only
officer he could trust to look after the remainder of the
battalion – thirty young officers and four or five hundred

men engaged in camp-duties. He left me a competent adjutant and three officers' chargers to ride. He also asked me to keep an eye on his children, whom he had to leave behind until a house was found for them at Cork; I used to play about a good deal with them. There was also a draft of two hundred trained men under orders for Gibraltar.

I got the draft off all right, and the inspecting general was so pleased with the soldier-like appearance that the adjutant and I had given them that he sent them all to the camp cinema at his own expense. This gave me a good mark with the colonel in Ireland. The climax of my good services was when I checked an attempt on the part of the camp quartermaster to make the battalion responsible for the loss of five hundred blankets. It happened like this. Suddenly one night I had three thousand three hundred leave-men from France thrown under my command; they were Irishmen, from every regiment in the army, and had been held up at Holyhead on the way home by the presence of submarines in the Irish Sea. They were rowdy and insubordinate, and for the four days that they were with me I had little rest. The five hundred missing blankets were some of the six thousand six hundred that had been issued to them, and had probably been sold in Rhyl to pay for cigarettes and beer. I was able to prove at the Court of Inquiry that the men, though attached to the battalion for purposes of discipline, had been issued with blankets direct from the camp quartermaster's stores before coming to it. The loss of the blankets might be presumed to have taken place between the time of issue and the time that the men arrived in the battalion lines. I had given no receipt to the camp quartermaster for the blankets. The Court of Inquiry was held in the camp quartermaster's private office; but I insisted that he should leave the room while evidence was being taken, because it was now no longer his private office but a Court of Inquiry. He had to go out, and his ignorance of my line of defence saved the case. This success, and the evidence that I was able to give the colonel of presents accepted by the battalion mess-president when at Rhyl, from wholesale caterers (the mess-president had tried to make me pay my mess-bill twice over and this was my retaliation), so pleased the colonel that he recommended me for the Russian Order of St. Anne, with Crossed Swords, of the Third Class. So, after all, I would not have left the army undecorated but for the October revolution,[2] which cancelled the award-list.

I saw Nancy again in December when I went to London, and we decided to get married at once. We attached no importance[3] to the ceremony. Nancy said she did not want to disappoint her father, who liked weddings and things. I was still expecting orders for Egypt and intending to go on to Palestine. Nancy's mother said that she would permit the marriage on one condition: that I should go to a London lung specialist to see whether I was fit for eventual service in Palestine. I went to Sir James Fowler, who had visited me at Rouen when I was wounded. He told me that my lungs were not so bad, though I had bronchial adhesions and my wounded lung had only a third of its proper expansion; but that my general nervous condition made it folly for me to think of active service in any theatre of war.

Nancy and I were married in January 1918 in St. James' Church, Piccadilly. She was just eighteen and I was twenty-two. George Mallory was the best man. Nancy had read the marriage-service for the first time that morning and had been horrified by it. She all but refused to go through the ceremony at all, though I had arranged for it to be modified and reduced to the shortest possible form. Another caricature scene to look back on: myself striding up the red carpet wearing field-boots, spurs, and sword; Nancy meeting me in a blue-check silk wedding dress, utterly furious; packed benches on either side of the church, full of relatives; aunts using handkerchiefs; the choir boys out of tune; Nancy savagely muttering the responses, myself shouting them out in a parade-ground voice. Then the reception. At this stage of the war, sugar was practically unobtainable; the wedding cake was in three tiers, but all the sugar icing was plaster. The Nicholsons had had to save up their sugar and butter cards for a month to make the cake taste anything like a cake at all. When the plaster case was lifted off there was a sigh of disappointment from the guests. A dozen of champagne had been got in. Champagne was another scarcity and there was a rush towards the table. Nancy said: 'Well, I'm going to get something out of this wedding, at any rate,' and grabbed a bottle. After three or four glasses she went off and changed back into her land-girl's costume of breeches and smock. My mother, who had been thoroughly enjoying the proceedings, caught hold of E. V. Lucas, who was standing next to her, and exclaimed: 'Oh dear, I wish she had not done that.' The embarrassments[4] of our wedding night were somewhat eased by an air-raid; bombs were dropping not far off and the hotel was in an uproar.

A week later she returned to her farm and I to my soldiers. It was an idle life now. I had no men on parade; they were all employed on camp duties. And I had found a lieutenant with enough experience to attend to the 'further instruction' of the young officers. My orderly room took about ten minutes a day; crime was rare, and the adjutant always had ready and in order the few documents to be signed; and I was free to ride my three chargers over the countryside for the rest of the day. I used to visit the present Archbishop of Wales frequently at his palace at St. Asaph; his son had been killed in the First Battalion. We found that we had in common a taste for the curious. I have kept a postcard from him which runs as follows:

THE PALACE, ST. ASAPH.

Hippophagist banquet held at Langham's Hotel, February 1868.

A. G. ASAPH

(I met numbers of bishops during the war but none since; except the Bishop of Oxford, in a railway carriage in 1927, who was discussing the beauties of Richardson.[5] And the Bishop of Liverpool, at Harlech, in 1923. I was making tea on the sea-shore when he came out from the sea in great pain, having been stung in the thigh by a jellyfish. He gladly accepted a cup of tea, tut-tutting miserably to himself that he had been under the impression that jellyfish only stung in foreign parts. As a record of the occasion he gave me a silver pencil which he had found in the sandhills while undressing.)

I grew tired of this idleness and arranged to be transferred to the Sixteenth Officer Cadet Battalion in another part of the same camp. It was the same sort of work that I had done at Oxford, and I was there from February 1918 until the Armistice in November. Rhyl was much healthier than Oxford and I found that I could play games without danger of another breakdown. A job was found for Nancy at a market-gardener's near the camp, so she came up to live with me. A month or two later she found that she was to have a baby and had to stop land work; she went back to her drawing.

None of my friends had liked the idea of my marriage, particularly to anyone as young as Nancy; one of them, Robbie Ross, Wilde's literary executor, whom I had met through Siegfried and who had been very good to me, had gone so far as to try to discourage me by hinting that there was negro blood in the Nicholson family, that it was possible that one of Nancy's and my children might revert to coal-black. Siegfried found it difficult to accustom himself to the idea of Nancy, whom he had not met, but he still wrote. After a few months at Craiglockhart, though he in no way renounced his pacifist views, he decided that the only possible thing to do was, after all, to go back to France. He had written to me in the previous October that seeing me again had made him more restless than ever. Hospital life was nearly unbearable; the feeling of isolation was the worst. He had had a long letter from Old Joe to say that the First Battalion had just got back to rest from Polygon Wood; the conditions and general situation were more appalling than anything he had yet seen – three miles of morasses, shell-holes and dead men and horses through which to get the rations up. Siegfried said that he would rather be anywhere than in hospital; he couldn't bear to think of poor Old Joe lying out all night in shell-holes and being shelled (several of the ration party were killed, but at least, according to Joe, 'the battalion got its rations'). If only the people who wrote leading articles for the *Morning Post* about victory could read Joe's letter![6]

It was about this time that Siegfried wrote the poem *When I'm asleep dreaming and lulled and warm*,[7] about the ghosts of the soldiers who had been killed, reproaching him in his dreams for his absence from the trenches, saying that they had been looking for him in the line from Ypres to Frise and had not found him. He told Rivers that he would go back to France if they would send him, making it quite clear that his views were exactly the same as they had been in July when he had written the letter of protest – only more so. He demanded a written guarantee that he would be sent back at once and not kept hanging about in a training battalion. He wrote reprehending me for the attitude I had taken in July, when I was reminding him that the regiment would only understand his protest as a lapse from good form and a failure to be a gentleman. It was suicidal stupidity and credulity, he said, to identify oneself in any way with good form or gentlemanliness,[8] and if I had real courage I wouldn't be acquiescing as I was. He pointed out that I admitted that the people who sacrificed the troops were callous b—s, and that the same thing was happening in all countries except parts of Russia. I forget how I answered Siegfried. I might have pointed out that when I was in France I was never such a fire-eater as he was. The amount of Germans that I had killed or caused to be killed was negligible compared with his wholesale slaughter. The fact was that the direction of Siegfried's unconquerable idealism changed with his environment; he varied between happy warrior and bitter pacifist. His poem:

To these I turn, in these I trust,
Brother Lead and Sister Steel;
To his blind power I make appeal,
I guard her beauty clean from rust . . .[9]

was originally written seriously, inspired by Colonel
Campbell, v.c.'s bloodthirsty 'Spirit of the Bayonet'
address at an army school. Later he offered it as a satire; and it is a poem that comes off whichever way you
read it. I was both more consistent and less heroic than
Siegfried.

I have forgotten how it was worked and whether I
had a hand in it, but he was sent to Palestine this time.
He seemed to like it there, and I was distressed in April
to have a letter from 'somewhere in Ephraim', that the
division was moving to France. He wrote that he would
be sorry to be in trenches, going over the top to take
Morlancourt or Méaulte. Seeing that we had recaptured Morlancourt had brought it home to him. He
said that he expected that the First and Second Battalions had about ceased to exist by now for the nth time.
I heard again from him at the end of May, from France.
He quoted Duhamel. 'It was written that you should
suffer without purpose and without hope, but I will
not let all your sufferings be lost in the abyss.'[10] Yet he
wrote the next paragraph in his happy-warrior vein,
saying that his men were the best that he'd ever served
with. He wished I could see them. I mightn't believe it,
but he was training them bloody well. He couldn't
imagine whence his flame-like ardour had come, but it
had come. His military efficiency was derived from the
admirable pamphlets that were now issued, so different from the stuff we used to get two years before. He

said that when he read my letter he began to think, damn Robert, damn every one except his company, which was the smartest turn-out ever seen, and damn Wales and damn leave and damn being wounded and damn everything except staying with his company until they were all melted away. (Limping and crawling across the shell-holes, lying very still in the afternoon sunshine in dignified desecrated attitudes.) I was to remember this mood when I saw him (*if* I saw him) worn out and smashed up again, querulous and nerve-ridden. Or when I read something in the casualty list and got a polite letter from Mr. Lousada, his solicitor. There never was such a battalion, he said, since 1916, but in six months it would have ceased to exist.

Nancy's brother, Tony, was also in France now. Nancy's mother made herself ill with worrying about him. Early in July he was due to come home on leave; I was on leave myself at the end of one of the four-months' cadet courses, staying with the rest of Nancy's family at a big Tudor house near Harlech. It was the most haunted house that I have ever been in, though the ghosts were invisible except in the mirrors. They would open and shut doors, rap on the oak panels, knock the shades off lamps, and drink the wine from the glasses at our elbows when we were not looking. The house belonged to an officer in the Second Battalion whose ancestors had most of them died of drink. There was only one visible ghost, a little yellow dog that appeared on the lawn in the early morning to announce deaths. Nancy saw it one day.

This was the time of the first Spanish influenza epidemic and Nancy's mother caught it, but she did not want to miss Tony when he came on leave. She wanted to go to theatres with him in London; they were devoted to each other. So when the doctor came she reduced her temperature with aspirin and pretended that she was all right. But she knew that the ghosts in the mirrors knew. She died in London on July 13th, a few days later. While she was dying her chief feeling was one of pleasure that Tony had got his leave prolonged on her account. (Tony was killed two months later.) Nancy's mother was a far more important person to her than I was, and I was alarmed of the effect that the shock of her death might have on the baby. A week later I heard that on the day that she had died Siegfried had been shot through the head while making a daylight patrol through long grass in No Man's Land. And he wrote me a verse letter which I cannot quote in full,[11] though I should like to do so. It is the most terrible of his war-poems:

AMERICAN RED CROSS HOSPITAL, NO. 22,
98–99 LANCASTER GATE, W.2.

24 July 1918

DEAR ROBERTO,

> I'd timed my death in action to the minute –
> (The *Nation* with my deathly verses in it) –
> The day told off – 13 – (the month July) –
> The picture planned – O Threshold of the dark!
> And then, the quivering songster failed to die
> Because the bloody Bullet missed its mark.

> Here I am; they *would* send me back –
> Kind M.O. at Base; Sassoon's morale grown slack;
> Swallowed all his proud high thoughts and acquiesced.
> O Gate of Lancaster, O Blightyland the Blessed.

No visitors allowed
Since Friends arrived in crowd –
Jabber – Gesture – Jabber – Gesture – Nerves went
      phut and failed
After the first afternoon when MarshMoonStreet-
      MeiklejohnArdoursandenduranSitwellitis
      prevailed,*
Caused complications and set my brain a-hop;
Sleeplessexasperuicide, O Jesu make it stop!

But yesterday afternoon my reasoning Rivers ran
      solemnly in.
With peace in the pools of his spectacled eyes and
      a wisely omnipotent grin;
And I fished in that steady grey stream and decided
      that I,
After all am no longer the Worm that refuses to die.
But a gallant and glorious lyrical soldjer;
    Bolder and bolder; as he gets older;
    Shouting, 'Back to the Front
    For a scrimmaging Stunt.'
    (I wish the weather wouldn't keep on getting
    colder.)

Yes, you can touch my banker when you need him.
Why keep a Jewish friend unless you bleed him?[12]

Oh yes, he's doing very well and sleeps from Two till
      Four
And there was Jolly Otterleen[13] a-knocking at the door,

* Visits from Edward Marsh, Robert Ross, Roderick Meiklejohn,
Robert Nichols, Osbert Sitwell. [RG]

But Matron says she mustn't, not however loud she
      knocks
(Though she's bags of golden Daisies and some
      Raspberries in a box),
Be admitted to the wonderful and wild and wobbly-
      witted sarcastic soldier-poet with a plaster on
      his crown,
Who pretends he doesn't know it (he's the Topic of the
      Town).[14]

My God, my God, I'm so excited; I've just had a letter
From Stable who's commanding the Twenty-fifth
      Battalion.
And my company, he tells me, doing better and better,
Pinched six Saxons after lunch,
And bagged machine-guns by the bunch.

But I – wasn't there –
O blast it isn't fair –
Because they'll all be wondering why
Dotty Captain[15] wasn't standing by
When they came marching home.

But I don't care; I made them love me
Although they didn't want to do it, and I've sent
      them a glorious Gramophone and God send
      you back to me
Over the green eviscerating sea –
And I'm ill and afraid to go back to them because those
      five-nines are so damned awful.
When you think of them all bursting and you're lying
      on your bed,
With the books you loved and longed for on the table;
      and your head

All crammed with village verses about Daffodils and
       Geese –
. . . O Jesu make it cease . . .

O Rivers please take me. And make me
Go back to the war till it break me.
Some day my brain will go BANG,
And they'll say what lovely faces were
The soldier-lads he sang

Does this break your heart? What do I care?

                        Sassons.[16]

And I went on mechanically at my cadet-battalion work. The candidates for commissions we got were no longer gentlemen in the regimental sense – mostly Manchester cotton clerks and Liverpool shipping clerks – but they were all experienced men from France and were quiet and well behaved. We failed about one in three. And the war went on and on. I was then writing a book of poems called *Country Sentiment*. Instead of children as a way of forgetting the war, I used Nancy. *Country Sentiment*, dedicated to her, was a collection of romantic poems and ballads. At the end was a group of pacifist war-poems. It contained one about the French civilians – I cannot think how I came to put so many lies in it – I even said that old Adelphine Heu of Annezin gave me a painted china plate, and that her pride was hurt when I offered to pay her. The truth is that I bought the plate from her for about fifteen shillings and that I never got it from her. Adelphine's daughter-in-law would not allow her to give it up, claiming it as her own, and I never got my money back from Adelphine.[17] This is only one of many of my early poems that contain falsities for public delectation.

In November came the Armistice. I heard at the same time news of the death of Frank Jones-Bateman, who had gone back again just before the end, and of Wilfred Owen, who often used to write to me from France, sending me his poems. Armistice-night hysteria did not touch the camp much, though some of the Canadians stationed there went down to Rhyl to celebrate in true overseas style. The news sent me out walking alone along the dyke above the marshes of Rhuddlan (an ancient battle-field, the Flodden of Wales) cursing and sobbing and thinking of the dead.[18]

XXVI

In the middle of December the cadet-battalions were wound up and the officers, after a few days' leave, were sent back to their units. The Third Battalion of the Royal Welch was now at Limerick. I decided to overstay my leave until Nancy's baby was born. She was expecting it early in January 1919, and her father had taken a house at Hove for the occasion. Jenny was born on Twelfth Night. She was neither coal-black nor affected by the shocks of the previous months. Nancy had had no foreknowledge of the experience – I assumed that she knew – and it took her years to recover from it. I went over to Limerick; the battalion was at the Castle Barracks. I lied my way out of the over-staying of leave.

Limerick was a Sinn Fein stronghold, and there were constant clashes between the troops and the young men of the town, yet little ill-feeling; Welsh and Irish got on well together, as inevitably as Welsh and Scottish disagreed. The Royal Welch had the situation well in hand; they made a joke of politics and used their entrenching-tool handles as shillelaghs. It looked like a town that had been through the war. The main streets had holes in them like shell-craters and many of the bigger houses seemed on the point of collapse. I was told by an old man at an antique shop that no new houses were now built in Limerick, that when one house fell down the survivors moved into another. He said too that everyone died of drink in Limerick except the Plymouth Brethren, who died of religious melancholia. Life did not start in the city before about a quarter past nine in the morning. At nearly nine o'clock once I walked down O'Connell Street and found it deserted. When the hour chimed, the door of a magnificent Georgian house was flung open and out came, first a shower of slops, which just missed me, then a dog, which lifted up its leg against a lamp-post, then a nearly naked child, which sat down in the gutter and rummaged in a heap of refuse for dirty pieces of bread; finally a donkey, which began to bray. Ireland was exactly as I had pictured it. I felt its charm as dangerous. Yet when I was detailed to take out a search-party in a neighbouring village for concealed rifles I asked the adjutant[1] to find a substitute; I said that I was an Irishman and did not wish to be mixed up in Irish politics.

I realized too that I had a new loyalty, to Nancy and the baby, tending to overshadow regimental loyalty now that the war was over. Once I was writing a rhymed nonsense letter to Nancy and Jenny in my quarters overlooking the barrack square:

Is there any song sweet enough
For Nancy or for Jenny?
Said Simple Simon to the Pieman:
'Indeed, I know not any.'

I have counted the miles to Babylon,
I have flown the earth like a bird,
I have ridden cock-horse to Banbury Cross,
But no such song have I heard.

At that moment some companies of the battalion returned to barracks from a route-march; the drums and fifes drew up under my window, making the panes rattle with *The British Grenadiers*. The insistent repetition of the tune and the hoarse words of command as the parade formed up in the square, company by company, challenged Banbury Cross and Babylon. *The British Grenadiers* succeeded for a moment in forcing their way into the poem:

> Some speak of Alexander,
> And some of Hercules,

but were driven out:

> But where are there any like Nancy and Jenny,
> Where are there any like these?[2]

I had ceased to be a British grenadier.[3]

So I decided to resign my commission at once. I consulted the priority list of trades for demobilization and found that agricultural workers and students were among the first classes to go. I did not particularly want to be a student again. I would rather have been an agricultural worker (Nancy and I spoke of farming when the war ended), but I had no agricultural background. And I found that I could take a two years' course at Oxford with a Government grant of two hundred pounds a year, and would be excused the intermediate examination (Mods.) on account of war-service. The preliminary examination (Smalls) I had already been excused because of a certificate examination that I had taken while still at Charterhouse. So there only remained the finals. The grant would be increased by a children's allowance. This sounded good enough. It seemed absurd at the time to suppose that university degrees would count for anything in a regenerated post-war England; but Oxford was a convenient place to mark time until I felt more like working for my living. We were all so accustomed to the war-time view, that the only possible qualification for peace-time employment would be a good record of service in the field, that we took it for granted that our scars and our commanding-officers' testimonials would get us whatever we wanted. A few of my fellow-officers did manage, as a matter of fact, to take advantage of the patriotic spirit of employers before it cooled again, sliding into jobs for which they were not properly qualified.

I wrote to a friend in the Demobilization Department of the War Office asking him to expedite my demobilization. He wrote back that he would do his best, but that I must be certified not to have had charge of Government moneys for the last six months; and I had not. But the adjutant had just decided to put me in command of a company. He said that he was short of officers whom he knew could be trusted with company accounts. The latest arrivals from the new-army battalions were a constant shame to the senior officers. Paternity-orders, stumer cheques, and drunk on parade were frequent. Not to mention table-manners, at which Sergeant Malley would stand aghast. There were now two mess ante-rooms, the junior and the senior, yet if a junior officer was regimentally a gentleman (belonged, that is, to the North Wales landed gentry or had been to Sandhurst) he was invited to use the senior ante-room and be among his own class. All this must have seemed very strange to the three line-battalion second-lieutenants captured in 1914, now promoted captain by the death

of most of their contemporaries and set free by the
terms of the Armistice.

The adjutant cancelled the intended appointment
only when I promised to help him with the battalion
theatricals that were being arranged for St. David's Day;
I undertook to play Cinna in *Julius Cæsar*. His change
of mind saved me over two hundred pounds. Next day
the senior lieutenant in the company that I was to have
taken over went off with the company cash-box, and I
would have been legally responsible. Before the war he
used to give displays at Blackpool Pier as *The Handcuff
King*; he got away safely to America.

I went out a few miles from Limerick to visit my
uncle, Robert Cooper, at Cooper's Hill. He was a farmer,
a retired naval officer, and had been having his ricks burnt
and cattle driven. He was very despondent. Through
the window he showed me distant cattle grazing beside
the Shannon. 'They have been out there all winter,' he
said, 'and I haven't had the heart to go out and look at
them these three months.' I spent the night at Cooper's
Hill and woke up with a chill. I knew that it was the
beginning of influenza. At the barracks I found that the
War Office telegram had come through for my demobilization, but that all demobilization among troops in
Ireland was to be stopped on the following day for an
indefinite period because of the troubles there. The adjutant, showing me the telegram, said: 'We're not going to
let you go. You promised to help us with those theatricals.' I protested, but he was firm. I did not intend to
have my influenza out in an Irish military hospital with
my lungs in their present state.

I had to think quickly. I decided to make a run for it.
The orderly-room sergeant had made my papers out
on receipt of the telegram. I had all my kit ready

packed. There only remained two things to get: the colonel's signature to the statement that I had handled no company moneys, and the secret code-marks which only the battalion demobilization officer could supply – but he was hand-in-glove with the adjutant, so it was no use asking him for them. The last train before demobilization ended was the six-fifteen from Limerick the same evening, February 13th. I decided to wait until the adjutant had left the orderly room and then casually ask the colonel to sign the statement, without mentioning the adjutant's objection to my going. The adjutant remained in the orderly room until five minutes past six. As soon as he was out of sight I hurried in, saluted, got the colonel's signature, saluted, hurried out to collect my baggage. I had counted on a jaunting-car at the barrack gates but none was to be seen. I had about five minutes left now and the station was a good distance away. I saw a corporal who had been with me in the First Battalion. I shouted to him: 'Corporal Summers, quick! Get a squad of men. I've got *my ticket* and I want to catch the last train back.' Summers promptly called four men; they picked up my stuff and doubled off with it, left, right, left, to the station. I tumbled into the train as it was moving out of the station and threw a pound-note to Corporal Summers. 'Good-bye, corporal, drink my health.'

But still I had not my demobilization code-marks and knew that when I reached the demobilization centre at Wimbledon they would refuse to pass me out. I did not care very much. Wimbledon was in England, and I would at least have my influenza out in an English and not an Irish hospital. My temperature was running high now and my mind was working clearly as it always does in fever. My visual imagery, which is cloudy and partial at ordinary times, becomes defined and complete. At Fishguard I bought a copy of the *South Wales Echo* and read in it that there would be a strike of London Electric Railways the next day, 14th February, if the railway directors would not meet the men's demands. So when the train steamed into Paddington and while it was still moving I jumped out, fell down, picked myself up and ran across to the station entrance, where, in spite of competition from porters – a feeble crew at this time – I caught the only taxi in the station as its fare stepped out. I had foreseen the taxi-shortage and could afford to waste no time getting to Wimbledon. I brought my taxi back to the train, where scores of stranded officers looked at me with envy. One, who had travelled down in my compartment, had been met by his wife. I said: 'Excuse me, but would you like to share my taxi anywhere? (I have influenza, I warn you.) I'm going down to Wimbledon, so I only need go as far as Waterloo; the steam-trains are still running.' They were delighted; they said that they lived out at Ealing and had no idea how to get there except by taxi. On the way to Waterloo he said to me: 'I wish there was some way of showing our gratitude. I wish there was something we could do for you.' I said: 'Well, there is only one thing in the world that I want at the moment. But you can't give it to me, I'm afraid. And that,' I said, 'is the proper code-marks to complete my demobilization papers. I've bolted from Ireland without them, and there'll be hell to pay if the Wimbledon people send me back.' He rapped on the glass of the taxi and stopped it. Then he got down his bag, opened it, and produced a satchel of army forms. He said: 'Well, I happen to be the Cork District Demobilization Officer and I've got the whole bag of tricks here.' So he filled my papers in.

At Wimbledon, instead of having to wait in a queue for nine or ten hours as I had expected, I was given priority and released at once; Ireland was officially a 'theatre of war' and demobilization from theatres of war had priority over home-service demobilization. So after a hurried visit to my parents, who were living close by, I continued to Hove, arriving at supper-time. When I came in, I had a sudden terror that made me unable to speak. I seemed to see Nancy's mother. She was looking rather plump and staid and dressed unlike herself, and did not appear to recognize me. She was sitting at the table between Nancy and her father. It was like a bad dream; I did not know what to say or do. I knew I was ill, but this was worse than illness. Then Nicholson introduced me: 'This is Nancy's Aunt Dora, just over from Canada.'

I warned them all that I had influenza; and hurried off to bed. Within a day or two everybody in the house had caught it except Nicholson and the baby and one servant who kept it off by a gipsy's charm. I think it was the leg of a lizard tied in a bag round her neck. A new epidemic as bad as the summer one had started; there was not a nurse to be had in Brighton. Nicholson at last found two ex-nurses. One was competent, but frequently drunk, and when drunk she would ransack all the wardrobes and pile the contents into her own bags; the other, sober but incompetent, would stand a dozen times a day in front of the open window, spread out her arms, and cry in a stage-voice: 'Sea, sea, give my husband back to me.' The husband, by the way, was not drowned, merely unfaithful. A doctor, found with difficulty, said that I had no chance of recovering; it was septic pneumonia now and both my lungs were affected. But I had determined that, having come through the war, I would not allow myself to succumb to Spanish influenza. This, now, was the third time in my life that I had been given up as dying, and each time because of my lungs. The first occasion was when I was seven years old and had double-pneumonia following measles.[4] Yet my lungs are naturally very sound, possibly the strongest part of me and, therefore, my danger mark. This time again I recovered and was up a few weeks later in time to see the mutiny of the Guards, when about a thousand men of all regiments marched out from Shoreham Camp and paraded through the streets of Brighton in protest against camp discipline.

The reaction against military discipline between the Armistice and the signing of peace delighted Siegfried and myself.[5] Siegfried had taken a prominent part in the General Election which Lloyd George forced immediately after the Armistice, asking for a warrant for hanging the Kaiser and making a stern peace. He had been supporting Philip Snowden's candidature on a pacifist platform and had faced a threatening civilian crowd, trusting that his three wound stripes and the mauve and white ribbon of his military cross would give him a privileged hearing. Snowden and Ramsay McDonald were perhaps the two most unpopular men in England at the end of the war. We now half hoped that there would be a general rising of ex-service men against the Coalition Government, but it was not to be. Once back in England the men were content to have a roof over their heads, civilian food, beer that was at least better than French beer, and enough blankets at night. They might find over-crowding in their homes, but this could be nothing to what they had been accustomed to; in France a derelict four-roomed cottage would provide billets for sixty men. They had won the war and they were satisfied. They left the rest to Lloyd George. The only serious outbreak was at Rhyl, where there was a two days' mutiny of Canadians with much destruction and several deaths. The signal for the outbreak was the cry: 'Come on, the Bolsheviks.'

When I was well enough to travel, Nancy, I and the baby went up to Harlech, where Nicholson had lent us his house to live in. We were there for a year. I discarded my uniform, having worn nothing else for four and a half years, and looked into my school trunk to see what I had to wear. There was only one suit that was not school uniform and I had grown out of that. I found it difficult to believe that the war was over. When I had last been a civilian I had been still at school, so I had no experience of independent civilian life. The Harlech villagers treated me with the greatest respect. At the Peace Day celebrations in the castle I was asked, as the senior of the officers present who had served overseas, to make a speech about the glorious dead. I have forgotten what I said, but it was in commendation of the Welshman as a fighting man and was loudly cheered. I was still mentally and nervously organized for war; shells used to come bursting on my bed at midnight even when Nancy was sharing it with me; strangers in day-time would assume the faces of friends who had been killed. When I was strong enough to climb the hill behind Harlech and revisit my favourite country I found that I could only see it as a prospective battlefield. I would find myself working out tactical problems, planning how I would hold the Northern Artro valley against an attack from the sea, or where I would put a Lewis-gun if I were trying to rush Dolwreiddiog farm from the brow of the hill, and what would be the best position for the rifle-grenade section. I still had the army habit of commandeering anything of uncertain ownership that I found lying about; also a difficulty in telling the truth – it was always easier for me now when overtaken in any fault to lie my way out. I applied the technique of taking over billets or trenches to a review of my present situation. Food, water supply, possible dangers, communication, sanitation, protection against the weather, fuel and lighting – each item was ticked off as satisfactory. And other loose habits of war-time survived, such as stopping passing motors for a lift, talking without embarrassment to my fellow-travellers in railway carriages, and unbuttoning by the roadside without shame, whoever was about. And I retained the technique of endurance, a brutal persistence in seeing things through, somehow, anyhow, without finesse, satisfied with the main points of any situation. But I modified my language, which had suddenly become foul on the day of Loos and had been foul ever since. The chief difference between war and peace was money. I had never had to worry about that since my first days at Wrexham; I had even put by about £150 of my pay, invested in War Bonds. Neither Nancy nor I knew the value of money and this £150 and my war-bonus of, I think, £250 and a disability pension that I was now drawing of £60 a year, and the occasional money that I got from poetry, seemed a great deal altogether. We engaged a nurse and a general servant and lived as though we had an income of about a thousand a year. Nancy spent much of her time drawing (she was illustrating some poems of mine), and I was busy getting *Country Sentiment* in order and writing reviews.

I was very thin, very nervous, and had about four years' loss of sleep to make up. I found that I was suffering from a large sort of intestinal worm which came from drinking bad water in France. I was now waiting until I should be well enough to go to Oxford with the Government educational grant; it seemed the easiest thing to do. I knew that it would be years before I was fit for anything besides a quiet country life. There was no profession that I wished to take up, though for a while I considered school-mastering. My disabilities were many; I could not use a telephone, I was sick every time I travelled in a train, and if I saw more than two new people in a single day it prevented me from sleeping. I was ashamed of myself as a drag on Nancy.[6] I had been much better when I was at Rhyl, but my recent pneumonia had set me back to my condition of 1917.

Siegfried had gone to live at Oxford as soon as he was demobilized, expecting me to join him. But after being there for a term or so he became literary editor of the newly-published *Daily Herald*. He gave me books to review for it. In these days the *Daily Herald* was not respectable. It was violent. It was anti-militarist. It was the only daily paper that protested against the Versailles Treaty and the blockade of Russia by the British Fleet. The Versailles Treaty shocked me; it seemed to lead certainly to another war and yet nobody cared. When the most critical decisions were being taken at Paris, public interest was concentrated entirely on three home-news items: Hawker's Atlantic flight and rescue, the marriage of Lady Diana Manners, and a marvellous horse called The Panther, which was the

Derby favourite and came in nowhere. The *Herald* spoilt our breakfast for us every morning. We read in it of unemployment all over the country, due to the closing of munition factories, of ex-service men refused re-instatement in the jobs that they had left in the early stages of the war, of market-rigging, lock-outs, and abortive strikes. I began to hear news, too, of my mother's relatives in Germany and the penury to which they had been reduced, particularly those who were retired officials and whose pension, by the collapse of the mark, was reduced to a few shillings a week. Nancy and I took all this to heart; we now called ourselves socialists.

The attitude of my family was doubtful.[7] I had fought gallantly for my country – indeed I was the only one of my father's five sons of military age who had seen active service – and was entitled to every consideration because of my shell-shocked condition; but my socialism and sympathy for the Bolsheviks outraged them. I once more forfeited the goodwill of my Uncle Charles. My father tried to talk me over, reminding me that my brother Philip had once been a pro-Boer and a Fenian, but had recovered from his youthful revolutionary idealism and come out all right in the end. Most of the elder members of my family were in the Near East, either married to British officials or British officials themselves. My father hoped that when I was recovered I would go to Egypt, perhaps in the consular service, where the family influence would be of great service to me, and there get over my revolutionary idealism. Socialism with Nancy was rather a means to a single end. The most important thing to her was judicial equality of the sexes; she held that all the wrong in the world was caused by male domination and narrowness.

She refused to see my experiences in the war as in any way comparable with the sufferings that millions of married women of the working-class went through. This at least had the effect of putting the war into the background for me; I was devoted to Nancy and respected her views in so far as they were impersonal. Male stupidity and callousness became an obsession with her and she found it difficult not to include me in her universal condemnation of men. It came to the point later when she could not bear a newspaper in the house. She was afraid of coming across something that would horrify her, some paragraph about the necessity of keeping up the population, or about women's intelligence, or about the modern girl, or anything at all about women written by clergymen. We became members of the newly formed Constructive Birth Control Society and distributed its literature among the village women, to the scandal of my family.

It was a great grief to my parents that Jenny was not baptized. My father wrote to Nancy's godfather, who also happened to be my publisher, asking him to use his influence with Nancy, for whose religion he had promised at the font to be responsible, to make her give the child Christian baptism. They were scandalized too that Nancy, finding that it was legal to keep her own name for all purposes, refused to allow herself to be called Mrs. Graves in any circumstances. At first I had been doubtful about this, thinking that perhaps it was not worth the trouble and suspicion that it caused; but when I saw that Nancy was now treated as being without personal validity I was converted. At that time there was no equal guardianship and the children were the sole property of the father; the mother was not legally a parent. We worked it out later that our children were to be thought of as solely hers, but that since I looked after them so much the boys should take the name of Graves – the girls taking Nicholson. This of course has always baffled my parents. Nor could they understand then the intimacy of our relations with the nurse and the maid. They were both women to whom we had given a job because they were in bad luck. One of them was a girl who had had a child during the war by a soldier to whom she was engaged, who got killed in France shortly afterwards. Generosity to a woman like this was Christian, but intimacy seemed merely eccentric.[8]

XXVII

In October 1919 I went up to Oxford at last. The lease of the Harlech house was ended and Nicholson gave us the furniture to take with us. The city was overcrowded; the lodging-house keepers, some of whom had nearly starved during the war, now had their rooms booked up terms ahead and charged accordingly. Keble College had put up army huts for its surplus students. There was not an unfurnished house to be had anywhere within the three-mile radius. I solved the difficulty by getting permission from my college authorities to live five miles out, on Boar's Hill; I pleaded my lungs. John Masefield, who liked my poetry, offered to rent us a cottage at the bottom of his garden.

The University was very quiet. The returned soldiers had little temptation to rag about, break windows, get drunk, or have tussles with the police and races with the bulldogs as before the war. The boys straight from the public schools were quiet too. They had had the war preached at them continually for four years, had been told that they must carry on loyally at home while their brothers were serving in the trenches, and must make themselves worthy of such sacrifices. The boys had been leaving for the cadet-battalions at the age of seventeen, so that the masters had it all their own way; trouble at public schools nearly always comes from the eighteen-year-olds. G. N. Clarke, a history don at Oriel, who had been up at Oxford just before the war and had meanwhile been an infantryman in France and a prisoner in Germany, told me: 'I can't make out my pupils at all. They are all "Yes, sir" and "No, sir." They seem positively to thirst for knowledge and they scribble away in their notebooks like lunatics. I can't remember a single instance of such stern endeavour in pre-war days.' The ex-service men – they included scores of captains, majors, colonels, and even a one-armed twenty-five-year-old brigadier – though not rowdy, were insistent on their rights. At St. John's they formed what they called a Soviet, demanding an entire revision of the college catering system; they won their point and an undergraduate representative was chosen to sit on the kitchen-committee. The elder dons whom I had often seen during the war trembling in fear of an invasion of Oxford, with the sacking and firing of the colleges and the rape of the Woodstock and Banbury Roads, and who had regarded all soldiers, myself included, as their noble saviours, now recovered their pre-war self-possession. I was amused at the difference in manner to me that some of them showed. My moral tutor, however, though he no longer saluted me when we met, remained a friend; he prevailed on the college to allow me to change my course from Classics to English Language and Literature and to take up my £60 Classical Exhibition notwithstanding. I was glad now that it was an exhibition, though in 1913 I had been disappointed that it was not a scholarship: college regulations permitted exhibitioners to be married, scholars had to remain single.

I used to bicycle down from Boar's Hill every morning to my lectures. On the way down I would collect

Edmund Blunden, who was attending the same course. He too had permission to live on the hill, on account of gassed lungs. I had been in correspondence with Edmund some time before he came to Oxford. Siegfried, when literary editor of the *Herald*, had been among the first to recognize him as a poet, and now I was helping him get his *Waggoner* through the press. Edmund had war-shock as badly as myself, and we would talk each other into an almost hysterical state about the trenches. We agreed that we would not be right until we got all that talk on to paper. He was first with *Undertones of War*, published in 1928.

Edmund and Mary his wife rented two rooms of a cottage belonging to Mrs. Delilah Becker, locally known as the Jubilee Murderess.[1] She was a fine-looking old lady and used to read her prayer-book and Bible aloud to herself every night, sitting at the open window. The prayer-book was out of date: she used to pray for the Prince Consort and Adelaide, the Queen Dowager. She was said to have murdered her husband. In Jubilee year she had gone away for a holiday, leaving her husband in the cottage with a half-witted servant-girl. News came to her that he had got the servant-girl into trouble. She wrote to him: 'Dear husband, if I find you in my cottage when I come back you shall be no more.' He did not believe her and she found him in the cottage, and sure enough he was no more. She told the police that he had gone away when he saw how angry with him she was; but no one had seen him go. He had even left his silver watch behind, ticking on a nail on the bedroom wall. The neighbours swore that she had buried him in the garden. Mary Blunden said that it was more probable that he was buried somewhere in their part of the cottage, which was semi-detached.

'There's an awfully funny smell about here sometimes,' she said. Old Delilah said to Mary once: 'I have often wondered what has happened to the old pepper-and-salt suit he had on when he was – when he went away.' Whenever she went out she took the carving-knife out of the drawer and laid it on the kitchen-table, where it could be seen by them when they went past her window. I liked Delilah very much and sent her a pound of tea every year until her death. Her comment on life in general was: 'Fair play's good sport, and we're all mortal worms.' She also used to say: 'While there's wind and water a man's all right.'[2]

I found the English Literature course tedious, especially eighteenth-century poets. My tutor, Mr. Percy Simpson, the editor of Ben Jonson's plays, sympathized. He said that he had once suffered for his preference for the Romantic revivalists. He had been beaten by his schoolmaster for having a Shelley in his possession. He had protested between the blows: 'Shelley is beautiful! Shelley is beautiful!' But he warned me that I must on no account disparage the eighteenth century when I sat for my final examination. It was also difficult for me, too, to concentrate on cases and genders and irregular verbs in Anglo-Saxon grammar. The Anglo-Saxon lecturer was candid about his subject. He said that it was of purely linguistic interest, that there was hardly a line of Anglo-Saxon extant of the slightest literary merit. I disagreed; *Beowulf* and *Judith* seemed good poems to me. Beowulf lying wrapped in a blanket among his platoon of drunken thanes in the Gothland billet; Judith going for a *promenade* to Holofernes's staff-tent; and *Brunanburgh* with its bayonet-and-cosh fighting – all this was closer to most of us at the time than the drawing-room and deer-park atmosphere of the eighteenth century. Edmund and I found ourselves translating everything into trench-warfare terms. The war was not yet over for us. In the middle of a lecture I would have a sudden very clear experience of men on the march up the Béthune-La Bassée road; the men would be singing and French children would be running along beside them, calling out: 'Tommee, Tommee, give me bullee beef'; and I would smell the stench of the knacker's yard just outside the town. Or I would be in Laventie High Street, passing a company billet; an N.C.O. would roar out, 'Party, 'shun!' and the Second Battalion men in shorts with brown knees and brown expressionless faces, would spring to their feet from the broken steps where they were sitting. Or I would be in a barn with my first platoon of the Welsh Regiment, watching them play nap by the light of dirty candle stumps. Or it would be a deep dug-out at Cambrin, where I was talking to a signaller; I would look up the shaft and see somebody's muddy legs coming down the steps, and there would be a crash and the tobacco-smoke in the dug-out would shake with the concussion and twist about in patterns like the marbling on books. These day-dreams persisted like an alternate life. Indeed they did not leave me until well on in 1928. I noticed that the scenes were nearly always recollections of my first four months in France; it seemed as though the emotion-recording apparatus had failed after Loos.

The eighteenth century was unpopular because it was French. Anti-French feeling among most ex-soldiers amounted almost to an obsession. Edmund, shaking with nerves, used to say at this time: 'No more wars for me at any price. Except against the French. If there's ever a war with them I'll go like a shot.'

Pro-German feeling was increasing. Now that the war was over and the German armies had been beaten, it was possible to give the German soldier credit for being the best fighting-man in Europe. I often heard it said that it was only the blockade that had beaten them; that in Haig's last push they never really broke, and that their machine-gun sections had held us up for as long as was needed to cover the withdrawal of the main forces. And even that we had been fighting on the wrong side; our natural enemies were the French.

At the end of my first term's work I attended the usual college board to give an account of myself. The spokesman coughed and said a little stiffly: 'I understand, Mr. Graves, that the essays that you write for your English tutor are, shall I say, a trifle temperamental. It appears, indeed, that you prefer some authors to others.'

There were a number of poets living on Boar's Hill; too many, Edmund and I agreed. It had become almost a tourist centre. There was the Poet Laureate,[3] with his bright eye, abrupt challenging manner, a flower in his buttonhole; he was one of the first men of letters to sign the Oxford recantation of war-time hatred against the Germans – indeed it was for the most part written by him. There was Gilbert Murray, too, gentle-voiced and with the spiritual look of the strict vegetarian, doing preliminary propaganda work for the League of Nations. Once, while I was sitting talking to him in his study about Aristotle's *Poetics*, and he was walking up and down the room, I suddenly asked him: 'Exactly what is the principle of that walk of yours? Are you trying to avoid the flowers on the rug or are you trying to keep to the squares?' I had compulsion-neuroses of this sort myself so it was easy to notice one in him. He wheeled round sharply: 'You're the first person who has caught me out,' he said. 'No, it's not the flowers or the squares; it's a habit that I have got into of doing things in sevens. I take seven steps, you see, then I change direction and go another seven steps, then I turn round. I asked Browne, the professor of Psychology, about it the other day, but he assured me it wasn't a dangerous habit. He said: "When you find it getting into multiples of seven, come to me again."'

I saw most of John Masefield, a nervous, generous person, very sensitive to criticism, who seemed to have suffered greatly in the war, when an orderly in a Red Cross Unit; he was now working at *Reynard the Fox*. He wrote in a hut in his garden surrounded by tall gorse-bushes and only appeared at meal-times. In the evening he used to read his day's work over to Mrs. Masefield and they would correct it together. Masefield was at the height of his reputation at the time, and there was a constant flow of American visitors to his door. Mrs. Masefield protected Jan.[4] She was from the North of Ireland, a careful manager, and put a necessary brake on Jan's generosity and sociability. We admired the way that she stood up for her rights where less resolute people would have shrunk back. The tale of Mrs. Masefield and the rabbit. Some neighbours of ours had a particularly stupid Airedale; they were taking it for a walk past the Masefields' house when a wild rabbit ran across the road from the Masefields' gorse plantation. The Airedale dashed at it and missed as usual. The rabbit, not giving it sufficient credit for stupidity and slowness, doubled back; but found the dog had not yet recovered from its mistake and ran right into its jaws. The dog's owners were delighted at the brilliant performance of their pet, recovered the rabbit, which was a small and inexperienced one, and took it home for the pot. Mrs. Masefield had seen the business through the plantation fence. It was not, strictly, a public road and the rabbit was, therefore, legally hers. That evening there came a knock at the door. 'Come in, oh, do come in, Mrs. Masefield.' It was Mrs. Masefield coming for the skin of her rabbit. Rabbit-skins were worth a lot in 1920. Mrs. Masefield's one extravagance was bridge; she used to play at a half-penny a hundred, to steady her play, she told us. She kept goats which used to be tethered near our cottage and which bleated. She was a good landlord to us, and advised Nancy to keep up with me intellectually if she wished to hold my affections.

Another poet on Boar's Hill was Robert Nichols, still another neurasthenic ex-soldier, with his flame-opal ring, his wide-brimmed hat, his flapping arms and 'mournful grandeur' in repose (the phrase is from a review by Sir Edmund Gosse). Nichols served only three weeks in France, in the gunners, and was in no show; but he was highly strung and the three weeks affected him more than twelve months affected some people. He was invalided out of the army and went to lecture in America for the Ministry of Information on British war-poets. He read Siegfried's and my poetry, and apparently gave some account of us. A legend was started of Siegfried, Robert and myself as the new Three Musketeers. Not only was Robert not in the Royal Welch Fusiliers with Siegfried and myself, but the three of us have never been together in the same room in our lives.

That winter George and Ruth Mallory invited Nancy and myself to go climbing with them. But Nancy could not stand heights and was having another baby; and, for myself, I realized that my climbing days were over. My nerves were bad, though possibly still good enough for an emergency, and beyond improvement. I was, however, drawn into one foolhardy experience at this time. Nancy and I were visiting my parents at Harlech. My two younger brothers were at the house. They played golf and mixed with local society. One evening they arranged a four at bridge with a young ex-airman and a Canadian colonel who was living in a house on the plain between Harlech Castle and the sea. The elder of my brothers got toothache; I said that I would take his place. The younger, still at Charterhouse, demurred. He was rather ashamed of me now as a non-golfer, a socialist, and not quite a gentleman. And my bridge might discredit him. I insisted, because at that time Canadian colonels interested me, and he made the best of it. I assured him that I would try not to wound his feelings. The colonel was about forty-five – tough, nervous, whisky-drinking, a killer. He was out of sorts; he said that his missus was upstairs with a headache and could not come down. We played three or four rubbers; I was playing steadily and not disgracing my brother. The colonel was drinking, the airman was competing. Finally the colonel said in a temper: 'By God, this is the rottenest bridge I've ever sat down to. Let's go bathing!' It was half-past ten and not warm for January, but we went bathing and afterwards dried ourselves on pocket handkerchiefs. 'We' was the colonel, myself and my brother. The airman excused himself. The bathe put the colonel in better humour. 'Let's go up to the village now and raid the concert. Let's pull some of the girls out and have a bit of fun.' The airman gigglingly agreed. My brother seemed embarrassed. The colonel said: 'And you, you bloody poet, are you on?' I said angrily: 'Not yet. You've had your treat, colonel. I went bathing with you and it was cold. Now it's my treat. I'm going to take you climbing and make you warm. I want to see whether you Canucks are all B.S. or not.' That diverted him.

I took them up the castle rock from the railway station in the dark. After the first piece, which was tricky, there would have been little climbing necessary if I had followed a zig-zag path; but I preferred to lead the colonel up several fairly stiff pitches. The others kept to the path. When we reached the top he was out of breath, a bit shaky, and most affable – almost affectionate. 'That was a damn good climb you showed us.' So I said: 'We've not reached the top yet.' 'Where are we going now?' he asked. I said: 'Up that turret.' We climbed into the castle and walked through the chapel into the north-western tower. It was pitch dark. I took them left into the turret which adjoined the tower but rose some twenty feet higher. The sky showed above, about the size of an orange. The turret had once had a spiral staircase, but the central core had been broken down after the Cromwellian siege; only an edging of stones remained on the walls. This edging did not become continuous until about the second spiral. We struck matches and I started up. The colonel swore and sweated, but followed. I showed him the trick of getting over the worst gap in the stones, which was too wide to bridge with one's stride, by crouching, throwing one's body forward and catching the next stone with one's hands; a scramble and he was there. The airman and my brother remained below. I was glad when we reached the second spiral. We climbed perhaps a hundred and twenty feet to the top.

When we were safely down again most of the whisky

was gone. So I said: 'Now let's visit the concert party.' I had heard the audience dispersing, from the top of the turret. We visited the artistes. The colonel was most courteous to the women, especially the blonde soprano, but he took a great dislike to the tenor, a Welshman, and told him that he was no bloody good as a singer. He cross-examined him on his military service and was delighted to find that he had been for some reason or other exempted. He called him a louse and a bloody skrim-shanker and a lot more until the blonde soprano, who was his wife, came to the rescue and threatened to chuck the colonel out. He went out grinning, kissing his hand to the soprano and telling the tenor to kiss the place where he wore no hat. The tenor turned courageous and shouted out something about reading the Scriptures and how morally unjustifiable it was to fight. We all laughed till we wheezed. Then the colonel said we must get a drink; he knocked up a hotel barman and even got inside the bar, but the barman refused to serve him and threatened to call the police. The colonel did not raid the shelves as he would have done half an hour before when the whisky was fiercer in him; he merely told the barman what he thought of the Welsh, broke a glass or two and walked out. 'Let's go home and have some more bridge.' He walked arm-in-arm with me down the hill and confided as one family man to another that his nerves were all in pieces because his missus was in the family way. That was why he had broken up the bridge-party. He had wanted her to have a good sleep. 'If we go back quietly now, she'll not wake up; we can bid in whispers.' So we went back and he drank silently and the airman drank silently and we played silently. I had three or four glasses myself; my brother abstained. We stopped at three-thirty in the morning. The colonel paid up and went to sleep on the sofa. I was eighteen shillings and my brother twelve shillings up at sixpence a hundred. I was sick and shaking for weeks after this.[5]

In March the second baby was born and we called him David. My mother was overjoyed. It was the first Graves grandson; my elder brothers had had only girls; here, at last, was an heir for the Graves family silver and documents. When Jenny was born my mother had con-doled with Nancy: 'Perhaps it is as well to have a girl first to practise on.' Nancy had from the first decided to have four children; they were to be like the children in her drawings and were to be girl, boy, girl, boy, in that order. She was going to get it all over quickly; she believed in young parents and families of three or four children fairly close together in age. She had the children in the order she intended and they were all like her drawings. She began to regret our marriage, as I also did. We wanted somehow to be dis-married – not by divorce, which was as bad as marriage – and able to live together without any legal or religious obligation to live together. It was about this time that I met Dick again, for the last time; I found him merely pleasant and dis-agreeable. He was at the university, about to enter the diplomatic service, and had changed so much that it seemed absurd to have ever suffered on his account. Yet the caricature likeness remained.[6]

XXVIII[1]

I met T. E. Lawrence first at a guest-night at All
Souls'.[2] Lawrence had just been given a college fellowship, and it was the first time for many years that he
had worn evening dress. The restlessness of his eyes
was the first thing about him I noticed. He told me that
he had read my poems in Egypt during one of his flying
visits from Arabia; he and my brother Philip had been
together in the Intelligence Department at Cairo,
before his part in the Arab revolt had begun, working
out the Turkish order of battle. I knew nothing about
his organization of the Arab revolt, his exploits and
sufferings in the desert, and his final entry into Damas-
cus. He was merely, to me, a fellow-soldier who had
come back to Oxford for a rest after the war. But I felt
a sudden extraordinary sympathy with him. Later,
when I was told that every one was fascinated by Lawrence, I tried to dismiss this feeling as extravagant. But
it remained. Between lectures at Oxford I now often
visited Lawrence at All Souls'. Though he never drank
himself, he used always to send his scout for a silver
goblet of audit ale for me. Audit ale was brewed in the
college; it was as soft as barley-water but of great
strength. (A prince[3] once came down to Oxford to
open a new museum and lunched at All Souls' before
the ceremony; the mildness of the audit ale deceived

him – he took it for lager – and he had to be taken back
to the station in a cab with the blinds drawn.) Nancy
and I lunched in Lawrence's rooms once with Vachel
Lindsay, the American poet, and his mother. Mrs. Lindsay was from Springfield, Illinois, and, like her son, a
prominent member of the Illinois Anti-Saloon League.
When Lawrence told his scout that Mr. Lindsay, though
a poet, was an Anti-Saloon Leaguer, he was scandalized and asked Lawrence's permission to lay on
Lindsay's place a copy of verses composed in 1661 by
a fellow of the college. One stanza was:

> The poet divine that cannot reach wine,
> Because that his money doth many times faile,
> Will hit on the vein to make a good strain,
> If he be but inspired with a pot of good ale.[4]

Mrs. Lindsay had been warned by friends to comment on nothing unusual that she met at Oxford.
Lawrence had brought out the college gold service in
her honour and this she took to be the ordinary thing
at a university luncheon-party.

His rooms were dark and oak-panelled. A large table
and a desk were the principal furniture. And there
were two heavy leather chairs, simply acquired. An
American oil-financier had come in suddenly one day
when I was visiting T. E. and said: 'I am here from the
States, Colonel Lawrence, to ask you a single question.
You are the only man who will answer it honestly. Do
Middle-Eastern conditions justify my putting any
money in South Arabian oil?' Lawrence, without rising, simply answered: 'No.' 'That's all I wanted to
know; it was worth coming for that. Thank you, and
good day!' In his brief glance about the room he had

found something missing; on his way home through London he chose the chairs and had them sent to Lawrence with his card. Other things in the room were pictures, including Augustus John's portrait of Feisul, which Lawrence, I believe, bought from John with the diamond which he had worn as a mark of honour in his Arab head-dress; his books, including a Kelmscott *Chaucer*; three prayer-rugs, the gift of Arab leaders who had fought with him, one of them with the sheen on the nap made with crushed lapis-lazuli; a station bell from the Hedjaz railway; and on the mantelpiece a four-thousand-year-old toy, a clay soldier on horseback from a child's grave at Carchemish, where Lawrence was digging before the war.

We talked most about poetry. I was working at a book of poems which appeared later under the title of *The Pier-Glass*. They were poems that reflected my haunted condition; the *Country Sentiment* mood was breaking down. Lawrence made a number of suggestions for improving these poems and I adopted most of them. He told me of two or three of his schemes for brightening All Souls' and Oxford generally. One was for improving the turf in the quadrangle, which he said was in a disgraceful condition, nearly rotting away; he had suggested at a college meeting that it should be manured or treated in some way or other, but no action had been taken. He now said that he was going to plant mushrooms on it, so that they would have to re-turf it altogether. He consulted a mushroom expert in town, but found that it was difficult to make spawn grow. He would have persisted if he had not been called away about this time to help Winston Churchill with the Middle-Eastern settlement.[5] Another scheme, in which I was to have helped, was to steal the Magdalen College deer. He was going to drive them into the small inner quadrangle of All Souls', having persuaded the college to reply, when Magdalen protested and asked for its deer back, that it was the All Souls' herd and had been pastured there from time immemorial. Great things were expected of this raid. It fell through for the same reason as the other. But a successful strike of college-servants for better pay and hours was said to have been engineered by Lawrence.

I took no part in undergraduate life, seldom visiting my college except to draw my Government grant and exhibition money; I refused to pay the college games' subscription, having little interest in St. John's and being unfit for games myself. Most of my friends were at Balliol and Queen's, and in any case Wadham had a prior claim on my loyalty. I spent as little time as possible away from Boar's Hill. At this time I had little to do with the children; they were in the hands of Nancy and the nurse – the nurse now also did the cooking and housework for us. Nancy felt that she wanted some activity besides drawing, though she could not decide what. One evening in the middle of the long vacation she suddenly said: 'I must get away somewhere out of this for a change. Let's go off on bicycles somewhere.' We packed a few things and rode off in the general direction of Devonshire. The nights were coldish and we had not brought blankets. We found that the best way was to bicycle by night and sleep by day. We went over Salisbury Plain past several deserted army camps; they had a ghostly look. There was accommodation in these camps for a million men, the number of men killed in the Imperial Forces during the war. We found ourselves near Dorchester, so we turned in there to visit Thomas Hardy, whom we had met not long before when he came up to Oxford to get his honorary doctor's degree. We found him active and gay, with none of the aphasia and wandering of attention that we had noticed in him at Oxford.

I wrote out a record of the conversation we had with him. He welcomed us as representatives of the post-war generation. He said that he lived such a quiet life at Dorchester that he feared he was altogether behind the times. He wanted, for instance, to know whether we had any sympathy with the Bolshevik regime, and whether he could trust the *Morning Post*'s account of the Red Terror. Then he was interested in Nancy's hair, which she wore short, in advance of the fashion, and in her keeping her own name. His comment on the name question was: 'Why, you *are* old-fashioned. I knew an old couple here sixty years ago that did the same. The woman was called Nanny Priddle (descendant of an ancient family, the Paradelles, long decayed into peasantry), and she would never change her name either.' Then he wanted to know why I no longer used my army rank. I said it was because I was no longer soldiering. 'But you have a right to it; I would certainly keep my rank if I had one. I should be very proud to be called Captain Hardy.'

He told us that he was now engaged in restoring a Norman font in a church near by. He had only the bowl to work upon, but enjoyed doing a bit of his old work again. Nancy mentioned that we had not baptized our children. He was interested, but not scandalized, remarking that his old mother had always said of baptism that at any rate there was no harm in it, and that she would not like her children to blame her in after-life for leaving any duty to them undone. 'I have usually found that what my old mother said was right.' He said that to his mind the new generation of clergymen were very much better men than the last . . . Though he now only went to church three times a year – one visit to each of the three neighbouring churches – he could not forget that the church was in the old days the centre of all the musical, literary and artistic education in the country village. He talked about the old string orchestras in Wessex churches, in one of which his father, grandfather, and he himself had taken part; he regretted their disappearance. He told us that the clergyman who appears as old St. Clair in *Tess of the D'Urbervilles* was the man who protested to the War Office about the Sunday brass-band performances at the Dorchester Barracks, and was the cause of headquarters no longer being sent to this once very popular station.

We had tea in the drawing-room, which, like the rest of the house, was crowded with furniture and ornaments. Hardy had an affection for old possessions, and Mrs. Hardy was too fond to suggest that anything at all should be removed. Hardy, his cup of tea in hand, began making jokes about bishops at the Athenæum Club and imitating their episcopal tones when they ordered: 'China tea and a little bread and butter (Yes, my lord!).' Apparently he considered bishops were fair game. He was soon censuring Sir Edmund Gosse,[6] who had recently stayed with them, for a breach of good taste in imitating his old friend, Henry James, eating soup. Loyalty to his friends was always a passion with Hardy.

After tea we went into the garden, and Hardy asked to see some of my recent poems. I showed him one, and he asked if he might make some suggestions. He objected to the phrase the 'scent of thyme', which he

said was one of the *clichés* which the poets of his generation studied to avoid. I replied that they had avoided
it so well that it could be used again now without
offence, and he withdrew the objection. He asked
whether I wrote easily, and I said that this poem was in
its sixth draft and would probably be finished in two
more. 'Why!' he said, 'I have never in my life taken
more than three, or perhaps four, drafts for a poem. I
am afraid of it losing its freshness.' He said that he had
been able to sit down and write novels by time-table,
but that poetry was always accidental, and perhaps it
was for that reason that he prized it more highly.

He spoke disparagingly of his novels, though admitting that there were chapters in them that he had
enjoyed writing. We were walking round the garden,
and Hardy paused at a spot near the greenhouse. He
said that he had once been pruning a tree here when an
idea suddenly had come into his head for a story, the
best story that he had ever thought of. It came complete
with characters, setting, and even some of the dialogue.
But as he had no pencil and paper with him, and was
anxious to finish pruning the tree before it rained, he
had let it go. By the time he sat down to recall it, all was
utterly gone. 'Always carry a pencil and paper,' he said.
He added: 'Of course, even if I could remember that
story now, I couldn't write it. I am past novel-writing.
But I often wonder what it was.'

At dinner that night he grew enthusiastic in praise of
cider, which he had drunk since a boy, and which, he
said, was the finest medicine he knew. I suggested that
in the *Message to the American People*, which he had
been asked to write, he might take the opportunity of
recommending cider.

He began complaining of autograph-hunters and their

persistence. He disliked leaving letters unanswered, and yet if he did not write these people pestered him the more; he had been upset that morning by a letter from an autograph-fiend which began:

> DEAR MR. HARDY, – I am interested to know why the devil you don't reply to my request . . .

He asked me for my advice, and was grateful for the suggestion that a mythical secretary should reply offering his autograph at one or two guineas, the amount to be sent to a hospital ('Swanage Children's Hospital,' put in Hardy), which would forward a receipt.

He said that he regarded professional critics as parasites no less noxious than autograph-hunters, and wished the world rid of them. He also wished that he had not listened to them when he was a young man; on their advice he had cut out dialect-words from his early poems, though they had no exact synonyms to fit the context. And still the critics were plaguing him. One of them recently complained of a poem of his where he had written 'his shape *smalled* in the distance'. Now what in the world else could he have written? Hardy then laughed a little and said that once or twice recently he had looked up a word in the dictionary for fear of being again accused of coining, and had found it there right enough – only to read on and find that the sole authority quoted was himself in a half-forgotten novel! He talked of early literary influences, and said that he had none at all for he did not come of literary stock. Then he corrected himself and said that a friend, a fellow-apprentice in the architect's office where he worked as a young man, used to lend him books. (His taste in literature was certainly most unexpected. Once

when Lawrence had ventured to say something dispar-
aging against Homer's *Iliad*, he protested: 'Oh, but I
admire the *Iliad* greatly. Why, it's in the *Marmion*
class!' Lawrence could not at first believe that Hardy
was not making a little joke.)

We went off the next day, but there was more talk at
breakfast before we went. Hardy was at the critics
again. He was complaining that they accused him of
pessimism. One man had recently singled out as an
example of gloom a poem he had written about a
woman whose house was burned down on her wedding-
night. 'Of course it is a humorous piece,' said Hardy,
'and the man must have been thick-witted not to see
that. When I read his criticism I went through my last
collection of poems with a pencil, marking them S, N,
and C, according as they were sad, neutral or cheerful.
I found them as nearly as possible in equal proportions; which nobody could call pessimism.' In his
opinion *vers libre* could come to nothing in England.
'All we can do is to write on the old themes in the old
styles, but try to do a little better than those who went
before us.' About his own poems he said that once they
were written he cared very little what happened to
them.

He told us of his work during the war, and said that
he was glad to have been chairman of the Anti-
Profiteering Committee, and to have succeeded in
bringing a number of rascally Dorchester tradesmen to
book. 'It made me unpopular, of course,' he said, 'but
it was a hundred times better than sitting on a military
tribunal and sending young men to the war who did
not want to go.'

This was the last time we saw Hardy, though we had
a standing invitation to come and visit him.

From Dorchester we bicycled to Tiverton in Devonshire, where Nancy's old nurse kept a fancy-goods shop. Nancy helped her dress the shop-window and advised her about framing the prints that she was selling. She also gave the shop a good turn-out, dusted the stock, and took her turn behind the counter. As a result of Nancy's work the week's receipts went up several shillings and continued at the improved figure for a week or two after we were gone. This gave Nancy the idea of starting a shop herself on Boar's Hill. It was a large residential district with no shop nearer than three miles away. She said that we should buy a second-hand army-hut, stock it with confectionery, groceries, tobacco, hardware, medicines, and all the other things that one finds in a village shop, run it tidily and economically and make our fortune. I undertook to help her while the vacation lasted and became quite excited about the idea myself. She decided to take a neighbour, the Hon. Mrs. Michael Howard,[7] into partnership. Neither Nancy nor Mrs. Howard had any experience of shop-management or commercial bookkeeping. But Mrs. Howard undertook to keep the books while Nancy did most of the other work. Nancy was anxious to start the shop six weeks after the original decision, but army huts were not obtainable at any reasonable price (the timber-merchants were in a ring); so it was decided to employ a local carpenter to build a shop to Nancy's design. A neighbour rented us a corner of his field close to the Masefields' house. The work was finished in time and the stock bought. The *Daily Mirror* advertised the opening on its front page with the heading 'SHOP-KEEPING ON PARNASSUS', and crowds came up from Oxford to look at us. We soon realized that it had either to be a big general shop

An Autobiography

which made Boar's Hill more or less independent of
Oxford (and of the unsatisfactory system of vans calling at the door and bringing stuff of inferior quality
with 'take it or leave it') or it had to be a small sweet
and tobacco shop making no challenge to the Oxford
tradesmen. We decided on the challenge. The building
had to be enlarged and two or three hundred pounds'
worth of stock purchased. Mrs. Howard was not able to
give much of her time to the work, having children to
look after and no nurse; most of it fell on Nancy and
myself. I used to serve in the shop several hours of the
day while she went round to the big houses for the daily
orders. The term had now begun and I was supposed to
be attending lectures in Oxford. Another caricature
scene: myself, wearing a green-baize apron this time,
with flushed face and disordered hair, selling a packet
of Bird's Eye tobacco to the Poet Laureate with one
hand and with the other weighing out half a pound of
brown sugar for Sir Arthur Evans' gardener's wife.

The gross weekly takings were now £60 a week and
Nancy, though she had given up her drawing, still had
the house and children to consider. We had no car, and
constant emergency bicycle-rides had to be made to
Oxford to get new stock from the wholesalers; we
made a point of always being able to supply whatever
was asked for. We engaged a shop-boy to call for
orders, but the work was still too heavy. Mrs. Howard
went out of partnership and Nancy and I found great
difficulty in understanding her accounts. I was fairly
good at conventional book-keeping; the keeping of
company accounts had been part of my lecture-syllabus
when I was instructing cadets. But that did not help me
with these, which were on a novel system.

The shop business finally ousted everything, not

only Nancy's painting, but my writing, my university work, and Nancy's proper supervision of the house and children. We had the custom of every resident of Boar's Hill but two or three. One of those whom we courted unsuccessfully was Mrs. Masefield. The proximity of the shop to her house did not please her. And her housekeeper, she said, preferred to deal with a provision merchant in Oxford and she could not override this arrangement.[8] However, to show that there was no ill-feeling, she used to come once a week to the shop and buy a tin of Vim and a packet of Lux, for which she paid money down from a cash-box which she carried with her. The moral problems of trade interested me. Nancy and I both found that it was very difficult at this time of fluctuating prices to be really honest; we could not resist the temptation of undercharging the poor villagers of Wootton, who were frequent customers, and recovering our money from the richer residents. Playing at Robin Hood came easily to me. Nobody ever caught us out; it was as easy as shelling peas, the shop-boy said, who also took his turn behind the counter. We found that most people bought tea by price and not by quality. If we happened to be out of the tea selling at ninepence a quarter which Mrs. So-and-so always bought, refusing the eightpenny tea, and Mrs. So-and-so asked for it in a hurry, the only thing to do was to make up a pound of the sevenpenny, which was the same colour as the ninepenny, and charge it at ninepence; the difference would not be noticed. We were sorry for the commercial travellers who came sweating up the hill with their heavy bags of samples, usually on foot, and had to be sent away without any orders. They would pitch a hard-luck tale and often we would relent and get in more stock than we needed. In gratitude they would tell us some of the tricks of the trade, advising us, for instance, never to cut cheese or bacon exactly to weight, but to make it an ounce or two more and overcharge for this extra piece. 'There's few can do the sum before you take the stuff off the scales and there's fewer still who will take the trouble to weigh up again when they get back home.'

The shop lasted six months. Nancy suddenly dismissed the nurse. Nancy had always practised the most up-to-date methods of training and feeding children, and the nurse, over-devoted to the children, had recently disobeyed her instructions. Nancy put the children before everything. She decided that there was nothing to be done but to take them and the house over herself, and to find a manager for the shop. At this point I caught influenza and took a long time to recover from it.

War horror overcame me again. The political situation in Europe seemed to be going from bad to worse. There was already trouble in Ireland, Russia and the Near East. The papers promised new and deadlier poison gases for the next war. There was a rumour that Lord Berkeley's house on Boar's Hill was to become an experimental laboratory for making them. I had bad nights. I thought that perhaps I owed it to Nancy to go to a psychiatrist to be cured; yet I was not sure. Somehow I thought that the power of writing poetry, which was more important to me than anything else I did, would disappear if I allowed myself to get cured; my *Pier-Glass* haunting would end and I would become merely a dull easy writer. It seemed to me less important to be well than to be a good poet. I also had a strong repugnance against allowing anyone to have the power over me that psychiatrists always seemed to win over their patients. I had always refused to allow myself to be hypnotized by anyone in any way.

I decided to see as few people as possible, stop all outside work, and cure myself. I would read the modern psychological books and apply them to my case. I had already learned the rudiments of morbid psychology from talks with Rivers, and from his colleague, Dr. Henry Head, the neurologist, under whose care Robert Nichols had been. I liked Head's scientific integrity. Once when he was testing a man whom he suspected of homicidal mania he had made some suggestion to him which came within the danger-area of his insanity; the man picked up a heavy knife from his consulting table and rushed threateningly at Head. Head, not at all quick on his legs and dodging round the table, exclaimed: 'Typical, typical! Capital, capital!' and, only as an afterthought: 'Help! Help!' He had great knowledge of the geography of the brain and the peculiar delusions and maladjustments that followed lesions in the different parts. He told me, at different times, exactly what was wrong with Mr. Jingle in *Pickwick Papers*, why some otherwise literate people found it impossible to spell, and why some others saw ghosts standing by their bedside. He said about the bedside ghosts: 'They always come to the same side of the bed, and if you turn the bed round you turn the ghost round with it. They come to the contrary side of the lesion.'[9]

A manager was found for the shop. But as soon as it was known that Nancy and I were no longer behind the counter the weekly receipts immediately began to fall; they were soon down to £20, and still falling steadily. The manager's salary was more than our profits. Prices were now falling, too, at the rate of about five per cent. every week, so that the stock on our shelves had depreciated greatly in value. And we had let one or two of the Wootton villagers run up bad debts. When we came to reckon things up we realized that it was wisest to cut the losses and sell out. We hoped to recoup our original expenditure and even to be in pocket on the whole transaction by selling the shop and the goodwill to a big firm of Oxford grocers that wished to buy it as a branch establishment. Unfortunately, the site was not ours and the landlord was prevailed upon by an interested neighbour not to let any ordinary business firm take over the shop from us and spoil the local amenities. No other site was available, so there was nothing to do but sell off what stock remained at bankrupt prices to the wholesalers and find a buyer for the building. Unfortunately again, the building was not made in bolted sections, and could not be sold to be put up again elsewhere; its only value was as timber, and in these six months the corner in timber had also been broken and the prices fallen to very little. We recovered twenty pounds of the two hundred that had been spent on it. Nancy and I were so disgusted that we decided to leave Boar's Hill. We were about five hundred pounds in debt to the wholesalers and others. A lawyer took the whole matter in hand, disposed of our assets for us, and the debt was finally reduced to about three hundred pounds. Nancy's father sent her a hundred-pound note (in a match-box) as his contribution, and the remainder was unexpectedly contributed by Lawrence. He gave me four chapters of *Seven Pillars of Wisdom*, his history of the Arab revolt, to sell for serial publication in the United States. It was a point of honour with him not to make any money out of the revolt even in the most indirect way; but if it could help a poet in difficulties, there seemed no harm in that.

We gave the Masefields notice that we were leaving the cottage at the end of the June quarter 1921. We had no idea where we were going or what we were going to do. We decided that we must get another cottage somewhere and live very quietly, looking after the children ourselves, and that we must try to make what money we needed by writing and drawing. Nancy, who had taken charge of everything when I was ill, now gave me the task of finding a cottage. It had to be found in about three weeks' time. I said: 'But you know that there are no cottages anywhere to be had.' She said: 'I know, but we are going to get one.' I said ironically: 'Describe it in detail; since there are no cottages we might as well have a no-cottage that we really like.' She said: 'Well, it must have six rooms, water in the house, a beamed attic, a walled-in garden, and it must be near the river. It must be in a village with shops and yet a little removed from the village. The village must be five or six miles from Oxford in the opposite direction from Boar's Hill. The church must have a tower and not a spire. And we can only afford ten shillings a week unfurnished.' There were other details that I took down about soil, sanitation, windows, stairs and kitchen sinks, and then I went off on my bicycle. I had first laid a ruler across the Oxford ordnance-map and found four or five villages that corresponded in general direction and distance and were on the river. By inquiry I found that two had shops; that, of these two, one had a towered church and the other a spired church. I therefore went to a firm of house-agents in Oxford and said: 'Have you any cottages to let unfurnished?' The house-agent laughed politely. So I said: 'What I want is a cottage at Islip with a walled garden, six rooms, water in the house, just outside the village, with a beamed attic, and rent ten shillings a week.' The house-agent said: 'Oh, you mean the World's End Cottage? But that is for sale, not for renting. It has failed to find a purchaser for two years, and I think that the owner will let it go now at five hundred pounds, which is only half what he originally asked.' So I went back and next day Nancy came with me; she looked round and said: 'Yes, this is the cottage all right, but I shall have to cut down those cypress trees and change those window-panes. We'll move in on quarter-day.' I said: 'But the money! We haven't the money.' Nancy answered: 'If we could find the exact house, surely to goodness we can find a mere lump sum of money.' She was right, for my mother was good enough to buy the cottage and rent it to us at the rate of ten shillings a week.

Islip was a name of good omen to me: it was associated with Abbot Islip, a poor boy of the village who had become Abbot of Westminster and befriended John Skelton when he took sanctuary in the Abbey from the anger of Wolsey. I had come more and more to associate myself with Skelton, discovering a curious affinity. Whenever I wanted a motto for a new book I always found exactly the right one somewhere or other in Skelton's poems. We moved into the Islip cottage and a new chapter started. I did not sit for my finals.[10]

XXIX

We were at Islip from 1921 until 1925. My mother in renting us the house had put a clause in the agreement that it was to be used only as a residence and not for the carrying on of any trade or business. She wanted to guard against any further commercial enterprise on our part; she need not have worried. Islip was an agricultural village, and far enough from Oxford not to be contaminated with the roguery for which the outskirts of a university town are usually well known. The village policeman led an easy life. During the whole time we were living there we never had a thing stolen or ever had a complaint to make against a native Islip cottager. Once by mistake I left my bicycle at the station for two days, and, when I recovered it, not only were both lamps, the pump and the repair outfit still in place, but an anonymous friend had even cleaned it.

Every Saturday in the winter months, as long as I was at Islip, I played football for the village team. There had been no football in Islip for some eighty years; the ex-soldiers had reintroduced it. The village nonogenarian complained that the game was not what it had been when he was a boy; he called it unmanly. He pointed across the fields to two aged willow trees: 'They used to be our home goals,' he said. 'T'other pair was half a mile upstream. Constable stopped our play in the end. Three men were killed in one game; one was kicked to death, t'other two drowned each other in a scrimmage. Her was a grand game.' Islip football, though not unmanly, was ladylike by comparison with the game as I had played it at Charterhouse. When playing centre-forward I was often booed now for charging the goal-keeper while he was fumbling with the shot he had saved. The cheers were reserved for my inside-left, who spent most of his time stylishly dribbling the ball in circles round and round the field until he was robbed; he seldom went anywhere near the goal-mouth. The football club was democratic. The cricket club was not. I played cricket the first season but left the club because the selection of the team was not always a selection of the best eleven men; regular players would be dropped to make room for visitors to the village who were friends of a club official, one of the gentry.

At first we had so little money that we did all the work in the house ourselves, including the washing. I did the cooking, Nancy did the mending and making the children's clothes; we shared the rest of the work. Later money improved: we found it more economical to send the washing out and get a neighbour in to do some of the heavier cleaning and scrubbing. In our last year at Islip we even had a decrepit car which Nancy drove. My part was to wind it up; the energy that I put into winding was almost equivalent to pushing it for a mile or two. The friends who gave it to us told us that its name was 'Dr. Marie', and when we asked 'Why?' we were told 'Because it's all right in theory.' One day when Nancy was driving down Foxcombe Hill, the steepest hill near Oxford, there was a slight jar. Nancy thought it advisable to stop; when we got out we found that there were only three wheels on the car. The other, with part of the axle, was retrieved nearly a mile back.

These four years I spent chiefly on housework and being nurse to the children. Catherine was born in 1922 and Sam in 1924. By the end of 1925 we had lived for eight successive years in an atmosphere of teething, minor accidents, epidemics, and perpetual washing of children's napkins. I did not dislike this sort of life except for the money difficulties. I liked my life with the children. But the strain told on Nancy. She was constantly ill, and often I had to take charge of everything. She tried occasionally to draw; but by the time she had got her materials together some alarm from the nursery would always disturb her. She said at last that she would not start again until all the children were house-trained and old enough for school. I kept on writing because the responsibility for making money rested chiefly on me, and because nothing has ever stopped me writing when I have had something to write. We kept the cottage cleaned and polished in a routine that left us little time for anything else. We had accumulated a number of brass ornaments and utensils and allowed them to become a tyranny, and our children wore five times as many clean dresses as our neighbours' children did.

I found that I had the faculty of working through constant interruptions. I could recognize the principal varieties of babies' screams – hunger, indigestion, wetness, pins, boredom, wanting to be played with – and learned to disregard all but the more important ones. But most of the books that I wrote in these years betray the conditions under which I worked; they are scrappy, not properly considered and obviously written out of reach of a proper reference-library. Only poetry did not suffer. When I was working at a poem nothing else mattered; I went on doing my mechanical tasks in a trance until I had time to sit down to write it out. At one period I only allowed myself half an hour's writing a day, but once I did write I always had too much to put down; I never sat chewing my pen. My poetry-writing has always been a painful process of continual corrections and corrections on top of corrections and persistent dissatisfaction. I have never written a poem in less than three drafts; the greatest number I recall is thirty-five (*The Troll's Nose-gay*). The average at this time was eight; it is now six or seven.

The children were all healthy and gave us little trouble. Nancy had strong views about giving them no meat or tea, putting them to bed early, making them rest in the afternoon and giving them as much fruit as they wanted. We did our best to keep them from the mistakes of our own childhood. But it was impossible for them when they went to the village school to avoid formal religion, class snobbery, political prejudice, and mystifying fairy stories about the facts of sex. I never felt any possessive feeling about them as Nancy did. To me they were close friends with the claims of friendship and liable to the accidents of friendship. We both made a point of punishing them in a disciplinary way as little as possible. If we lost our temper with them it was a different matter. Islip was as good a place as any for the happy childhood that we wanted to give them. The river was close and we had the loan of a canoe. There were fields to play about in, and animals, and plenty of children of their own age. They liked school.

After so much shifting about during the war I disliked leaving home, except to visit some well-ordered house where I could expect reasonable comfort. But

Nancy was always proposing sudden 'bursts for freedom', and I used to come with her and usually enjoy them. In 1922 we used a derelict baker's van for a caravan ride down to the south-coast. We had three children with us, Catherine as a four-months-old baby. It rained every single day for the month we were away – and the problem of washing and drying the baby's napkins whenever we camped for the night – and the problem of finding a farmer who would not mistake us for gypsies and would be willing to let us pull into his field – and then the shaft that twice dropped off when we were on hills – and twice the back of the cart flew open and a child fell out on the road – and the difficulty of getting oats for the horse (which had been five years on grass as being too old for work) on country roads organized for motor traffic – and cooking to be done in the open with usually a high wind and always rain and the primus stove sputtering and flaring up. It was near Lewes that we drew up on a strip of public land alongside the horse and van of a Mr. Hicks, a travelling showman from Brighton. He told us many tricks of the road and also the story of his life: 'Yes, I saw the Reverend Powers, Cantab. of Rodmell last week, and he, knowing my history, said: "Well, Mr. Hicks, I suppose that in addressing you I should be right in putting the letters B.A. after your name?" I said: "I have the right to it certainly, but when a man's down, you know how it is, he does not like attaching a handle to his name." For you must know, I was once a master at Ardingly College.'

'Indeed, Mr. Hicks, and where were you B.A.?'

'Didn't I just tell you, at Ardingly? I won a scholarship at the beginning and they gave me the choice of going to Oxford or Winchester or Cambridge or Eton.

And I chose Winchester. But I was only there a twelve-month. No, I couldn't stand it any longer owing to the disgraceful corruption of the junior clergy and the undergraduates – you understand, of course. I rub up a bit of the classic now and then, but I like to forget those times. The other day, though, me and a young Jew-boy who had cleaned up seventy-five pounds at the race meeting with photographing and one thing and another, had a fine lark. I got out two old mortar-boards and a couple of gowns from the box in the van where I keep them, and you should have seen us swaggering down Brighton Pier, my boy.' A few days later we stopped at a large mansion in Hampshire, rented by Sir Lionel Philips, the South African financier, whom Nancy knew. I found myself in an argument with him about socialist economics, and he told me a story which I liked even better than Mr. Hicks'. 'I visited Kimberley recently and realized what a deep hole I had made. Where, as a young man, I tore the first turf off with my bare hands, they were now mining down half a mile.'

In the end we got back safely.

I was so busy that I had no time to be ill myself. Nancy begged me not to talk about the war in her hearing, and I was ready to forget about it.[1] The villagers called me 'The Captain', otherwise I had few reminders except my yearly visit to the standing medical board. The board continued for some years to recommend me for a disability pension. The particular disability was neurasthenia; the train journey and the army railway-warrant filled out with my rank and regiment usually produced reminiscential neurasthenia by the time I reached the board. The award was at last made permanent at forty-two pounds a year. Ex-service

men were continually coming to the door selling
boot-laces and asking for cast-off shirts and socks. We
always gave them a cup of tea and money. Islip was a
convenient halt between the Chipping Norton and the
Oxford workhouses. One day an out-of-work ex-
service man, a steam-roller driver by trade, came
calling with his three children, one of them a baby.
Their mother had recently died in childbirth. We felt
very sorry for them and Nancy offered to adopt the
eldest child, Daisy, who was about thirteen years old
and her father's greatest anxiety. She undertook to
train Daisy in housework so that she would be able
later to go into service. Daisy was still of school age.
Her father shed tears of gratitude, and Daisy seemed
happy enough to be a member of the family. Nancy
made her new clothes – we cleaned her, bought her
shoes, and gave her a bedroom to herself. Daisy was
not a success. She was a big ugly girl, strong as a horse
and toughened by her three years on the roads. Her
father was most anxious for her to continue her education, which had been interrupted by their wanderings.
But Daisy hated school; she was put in the baby class
and the girls of her own age used to tease her. In return
she pulled their hair and thumped them, so they sent
her to Coventry. After a while she grew homesick for
the road. 'That was a good life,' she used to say. 'Dad
and me and my brother and the baby. The baby was a
blessing. When I fetched him along to the back doors I
nearly always won something. 'Course, I was artful. If
they tried to slam the door in my face I used to put my
foot in it and say: "This is my little orphan brother."
Then I used to look round and anything I seen I used
to ast for. I used to ast for a pram for the baby, if I seen
an old one in a shed; and I'd get it, too. Of course we

had a pram really, a good one, and then we'd sell the pram I'd won, in the next town we come to. Good beggars always ast for something particular, something they seen lying about. It's no good asking for food or money. I used to pick up a lot for my dad. I was a better beggar nor he was, he said. We used to go along together singing *On the Road to Anywhere*. And there was always the Spikes to go to when the weather was bad. The Spike at Chippy Norton was our winter home. They was very good to us there. We used to go to the movies once a week. The grub was good at Chippy Norton. We been all over the country, Wales and Devonshire, right up to Scotland, but we always come back to Chippy.' Nancy and I were shocked one day when a tramp came to the door and Daisy slammed the door in his face and told him to clear out of it, Nosey, and not to poke his ugly mug into respectable people's houses. 'I know you, Nosey Williams,' she said, 'you and your ex-service papers what you pinched from a bloke down in Salisbury, and the bigamy charge against you a-waiting down at Plymouth. Hop it now, quick, or I'll run for the cop.' Daisy told us the true histories of many of the beggars we had befriended. She said: 'There's not one decent man in ten among them bums. My dad's the only decent one of the lot. The reason most of them is on the road is the cops have something against them, so they has to keep moving. Of course my dad don't like the life; he took to it too late in life. And my mother was very respectable too. She kept us clean. Most of those bums is lousy, with nasty diseases, and they keeps out of the Spike as much as they can 'cause they don't like the carbolic baths.' Daisy was with us for a whole winter. When the spring came and the roads dried her father called for her again. He couldn't manage the little ones without her he said. That was the last we saw of Daisy, though she wrote to us once from Chipping Norton asking us for money.

My pension was our only certain source of income, neither of us having any private means of our own. The Government grant and college exhibition had ended at the time we moved to Islip. I never made more at this time than thirty pounds a year from my books of poetry and anthology fees, with an occasional couple of guineas for poems contributed to periodicals. There was another sixteen pounds a year from the rent of the Harlech cottage and an odd guinea or two from reviewing. My volumes of poetry did not sell. *Fairies and Fusiliers* had gone into two editions because it was published in the war-years when people were reading poetry as they had not done for many years. The inclusion of my work in Edward Marsh's *Georgian Poetry* had made my name well known, but after 1919, when the series ended, it was forgotten again. *Country Sentiment* was hardly noticed; the *Pier-Glass* was also a failure.[2] They were published by Martin Secker, not by Heinemann who had published *Fairies and Fusiliers* – William Heinemann, just before he died, had tried to teach me how poetry should be written and I resented it. These three books had been published in America, where my name was known since John Masefield, Robert Nichols and, finally, Siegfried Sassoon had gone to lecture about modern English poetry. But English poets slumped, and it was eight years before another book of my poems could find a publisher in America. In these days I used to take the reviews of my poetry-books seriously. I reckoned their effect on sales and so on the grocery bills. I still believed that it was possible to write poetry that was true poetry and yet could reach, say, a three or four thousand-copy sale. I expected some such success. I consorted with other poets and had a fellow-feeling for them. Beside Hardy, Siegfried, and the Boar's Hill residents, I knew Delamare,[3] W. H. Davies, T. S. Eliot, the Sitwells and many more. I liked W. H. Davies because he was from South Wales and afraid of the dark, and because once, I heard, he made out a list of poets and crossed them off one by one as he decided that they were not true poets – until only two names were left. I approved the final choice.[4] Delamare I liked too. He was gentle and I could see how hard he worked at his poems – I was always interested in the writing-technique of my contemporaries. I once told him what hours of worry he must have had over the lines:

Ah, no man knows
Through what wild centuries
Roves back the rose;[5]

and how, in the end, he had been dissatisfied. He admitted that he had been forced to leave the assonance 'Roves and rose', because no synonym for 'roves' was strong enough. I seldom saw Osbert and Sacheverell Sitwell after the war-years. When I did I always felt uncomfortably rustic in their society. Once Osbert sent me a present of a brace of grouse. They came from his country residence in Derbyshire in a bag labelled: 'With Captain Sitwell's compliments to Captain Graves.' Nancy and I could neither of us face the task of plucking and gutting and roasting the birds, so we

gave them to a neighbour. I thanked Osbert: 'Captain
Graves acknowledges with thanks Captain Sitwell's gift
of Captain Grouse.'

Our total income, counting birthday and Christmas
cheques from relatives, was about one hundred and
thirty pounds a year. As Nancy reminded me, this was
about fifty shillings a week and there were farm labourers at Islip, with more children than we had, who only
got thirty shillings a week. They had a much harder
time than we did earning it and had no one to fall back
on, as we had, in case of sudden illness or other emergency. We used to get free holidays, too, at Harlech,
when my mother would insist on paying the train-fare
as well as giving us our board free. We really had nothing to complain about. Thinking how difficult life
was for the labourers' wives kept Nancy permanently
depressed. I have omitted to mention a further source
of income – the Rupert Brooke Fund,[6] of which Edward
Marsh was the administrator. Rupert Brooke had
stated in his will that all royalties accruing from any
published work of his should be divided among needy
poets with families to support. When money was very
short we would dip into this bag.

We still called ourselves socialists, but had become
dissatisfied with Parliamentary socialism. We had
greater sympathy with communism, though not members of the Communist Party. None the less, when a
branch of the Parliamentary Labour Party was formed
in the village, we gave the use of the cottage for its
weekly meetings throughout the winter months. Islip
was a rich agricultural area; but with a reputation for
slut-farming. It did not pay the tenant farmers to farm
too well. Mr. Wise, one of our members, once heckled
a speaker in the Conservative interest about a protect-

ive duty imposed by the Conservative Government on dried currants. The speaker answered patronizingly: 'Well, surely a duty on Greek currants won't hurt you working men here at Islip? You don't grow currants in these parts, do you?' 'No, sir,' replied Mr. Wise, 'the farmers main crop hereabouts is squitch.'

I was persuaded to stand for the parish council, and was a member for a year. I wish I had taken records of the smothered antagonism of the council meetings. There were seven members of the council, with three representatives of labour and three representatives of the farmers and gentry; the chairman was a farmer, a Liberal who had Labour support as being a generous employer and the only farmer in the neighbourhood who had had a training at an agricultural college. He held the balance very fairly. We contended over a proposed application to the district council for the building of new cottages. Many returned ex-soldiers who wished to marry had nowhere to live with their wives. The Conservative members opposed this because it would mean a penny on the rates. Then there was the question of procuring a recreation ground for the village. The football team did not wish to be dependent on the generosity of one of the big farmers who rented it to us at a nominal rate. The Conservatives opposed this again in the interest of the rates, and pointed out that shortly after the Armistice the village had turned down a recreation ground scheme, preferring to spend the memorial subscription money on a cenotaph. The Labour members pointed out that the vote was taken, as at the 1918 General Election, before the soldiers had returned to express their view. Nasty innuendoes were made about farmers who had stayed at home and made their pile, while their labourers fought and bled. The chairman calmed the antagonists. Another caricature scene: myself in corduroys and a rough frieze coat, sitting in the village school-room (this time with no 'evils of alcoholism' around the wall, but with nature-drawings and mounted natural history specimens to take their place), debating as an Oxfordshire village elder whether or not Farmer So-and-so was justified in using a footpath across the allotments as a bridle-path, disregarding the decayed stile which, I urged, disproved his right.

My association with the Labour Party severed my relations with the village gentry with whom, when I first came to the village, I had been on friendly terms. My mother had been to the trouble of calling on the rector when she viewed the property. I had even been asked by the rector to speak from the chancel steps of the village church at a war memorial service. He suggested that I should read poems about the war. Instead of Rupert Brooke on the glorious dead, I read some of the more painful poems of Sassoon and Wilfred Owen about men dying of gas-poisoning and about buttocks of corpses bulging from the mud. And I suggested that the men who had fallen, destroyed as it were by the fall of the Tower of Siloam, had not been particularly virtuous or particularly wicked, but just average soldiers, and that the survivors should thank God that they were alive and do their best to avoid wars in the future. The church-party, with the exception of the rector, an intelligent man, was scandalized. But the ex-service men had not been too well treated on their return and it pleased them to be reminded that they were on equal terms with the glorious dead. They were modest men: I noticed that though obeying the King's desire to wear their campaigning medals, they kept them buttoned up inside their coats.

The leading Labour man of the village was William Beckley, senior. He had an inherited title dating from the time of Cromwell: he was known as 'Fisher' Beckley. A direct ancestor had been fishing on the Cherwell during the siege of Oxford, and had ferried Cromwell himself and a body of Parliamentary troops over the river. In return Cromwell had given him perpetual fishing-rights from Islip to the stretch of river where the Cherwell Hotel now stands. The cavalry skirmish at Islip bridge still remained in local tradition, and a cottager at the top of the hill showed me a small stone cannon-ball, fired on that occasion, that he had found sticking in his chimney-stack. But even Cromwell came late in the history of the Beckley family; the Beckleys were watermen on the river long before the seventeenth century. Indeed Fisher Beckley knew, by family tradition, the exact spot where a barge was sunk conveying stone for the building of Westminster Abbey. Islip was the birthplace of Edward the Confessor, and the Islip lands had been given by him to the Abbey; it was still Abbey property after a thousand years. The Abbey stone had been quarried from the side of the hill close to the river; our cottage was on the old slip-way down which the stone-barges had been launched. Some time in the 'seventies American weed was introduced into the river and made netting difficult; fishing finally became unprofitable. Fisher Beckley had been for many years now an agricultural labourer. His socialist views prevented him from getting employment in the village, so he had to trudge to work to a farm some miles out. But he was still Fisher Beckley and, among us cottagers, the most respected man in Islip.

XXX

My parents were most disappointed when I failed to sit
for my Oxford finals. But through the kindness of Sir
Walter Raleigh, the head of the English School, I was
excused finals as I had been excused everything else,
and allowed to proceed to the later degree of Bachelor
of Letters. Instead of estimating, at the examiners'
request, the effect of the influence of Dryden on pastoral poets of the early eighteenth century, or tracing
the development of the subplot in Elizabethan comed-
ies between the years 1583 and 1594, I was allowed
to offer a written thesis on a subject of my own choice.
Sir Walter Raleigh was a good friend to me. He agreed
to be my tutor on condition that he should not be
expected to tutor me. He liked my poetry, and suggested that we should only meet as friends. He was
engaged at the time on the official history of the war in
the air and found it necessary to have practical flying
experience for the task. The R.A.F. took him up as
often as he needed. It was on a flight out East that he
got typhoid fever and died.[1] I was so saddened by his
death that it was some time before I thought again
about my thesis, and I did not apply for another tutor.
The subject I had offered was *The Illogical Element in
English Poetry*. I had already written a prose book, *On
English Poetry*, a series of 'workshop notes' about the

writing of poetry. It contained much trivial but also much practical material, and emphasized the impossibility of writing poetry of 'universal appeal'. I regarded poetry as, first, a personal cathartic for the poet suffering from some inner conflict, and then as a cathartic for readers in a similar conflict. I made a tentative connection between poetry and dream in the light of the dream-psychology in which I was then interested as a means of curing myself.[2]

The thesis did not work out like a thesis. I found it difficult to keep to an academic style and decided to write it as if it were an ordinary book. Anyhow, I could expect no knowledge of or sympathy with modern psychology from the literature committee that would read it. I rewrote it in all nine times, and it was unsatisfactory when finished. I was trying to show the nature of the supra-logical element in poetry. It was only, I wrote, to be fully understood by close analysis of the latent associations of the words used; the obvious prose meaning was often in direct opposition to the latent content. The weakness of the book lay in its not clearly distinguishing between the supra-logical thought-processes of poetry and of pathology. Before it appeared I had published *The Meaning of Dreams*, which was intended to be a popular shillingsworth for the railway bookstall; but I went to the wrong publisher and he issued it at five shillings. Being too simply written for the informed public, and too expensive for the ignorant public to which it was addressed, it fell flat; as indeed it deserved.[3] I published a volume of poems every year between 1920 and 1925; after *The Pier-Glass*, published in 1921, I made no attempt to write for the ordinary reading public, and no longer regarded my work as being of public utility. I did not even flatter myself that I was conferring benefits on posterity; there was no reason to suppose that posterity would be more appreciative than my contemporaries. I only wrote when and because there was a poem pressing to be written. Though I assumed a reader of intelligence and sensibility and considered his possible reactions to what I wrote, I no longer identified him with contemporary readers or critics of poetry. He was no more real a person than the conventional figure put in the foreground of an architectural design to indicate the size of the building. As a result of this greater strictness of writing I was soon accused of trying to get publicity and increase my sales by a wilful clowning modernism. Of these books, *Whipperginny*, published in 1923, showed the first signs of my new psychological studies.

Mock-Beggar Hall, published in 1924, was almost wholly philosophical. As Lawrence wrote to me when I sent it to him, it was 'not the sort of book that one would put under one's pillow at night.' This philosophic interest was a result of my meeting with Basanta Mallik, when I was reading a paper to an undergraduate society. One of the results of my education was a strong prejudice, amounting to contempt, against anyone of non-European race; the Jews, though with certain exceptions such as Siegfried, were included in this prejudice. But I had none of my usual feelings with Basanta. He did not behave as a member of a subject-race – neither with excessive admiration nor with excessive hatred of all things English. Though he was a Bengali he was not given to flattery or insolence. I found on inquiry that he belonged to a family of high caste. His father had become converted to Christianity and signalized his freedom from Hindu superstition by changing his diet; meat and alcohol, untouched by his ancestors for some two thousand years, soon brought about his death. Basanta had been brought up in the care of a still unconverted grandmother, but did not have the strict Hindu education that the boy of caste is given by his male relatives. He was sent to Calcutta University and, some years before the war, after taking a law degree, was given the post of assistant tutor to the children of the Maharajah of Nepal. In Nepal he came to the notice of the Maharajah as one of the few members of the Court not concerned in a plot against his life, and was promoted to chief tutor.

The relations between Nepal and India were strained at this time. Basanta was the only man in Nepal with an up-to-date knowledge of international law. His advice ultimately enabled the Maharajah to induce the British to sign the 1923 treaty recognizing the complete independence of the country, which had for many years been threatened with British protection. Under the terms of this treaty, no foreigners might enter Nepal except at the personal invitation of the Maharajah. The Maharajah had sent Basanta over to England to study British political psychology; this knowledge might be useful in the event of future misunderstandings between Nepal and India. He had now been some eleven years in Oxford but, becoming a philosopher and making many friends, had overcome his long-standing grudge against the British.

Basanta used to come out to Islip frequently to talk philosophy with us. With him came Sam Harries, a young Balliol scholar, who soon became our closest friend. Metaphysics soon made psychology of secondary interest for me: it threatened almost to displace poetry. Basanta's philosophy was a development of

409

formal metaphysics, but with characteristically Indian insistence on ethics. He believed in no hierarchy of ultimate values or the possibility of any unifying religion or ideology. But at the same time he insisted on the necessity of strict self-discipline in the individual in meeting every possible demand made upon him from whatever quarter, and he recommended constant self-watchfulness against either dominating or being dominated by any other individual. This view of strict personal morality consistent with scepticism of social morality agreed very well with my practice. He returned to India in 1923 and considered taking an appointment in Nepal, but decided that to do so would put him in a position incompatible with his philosophy. He would have returned to Oxford but a friend had died, leaving him to support a typical large Hindu family of aunts and cousins remotely related. We missed Basanta's visits, but Sam Harries used to come out regularly. Sam was a communist, an atheist, enthusiastic about professional football (Aston Villa was his favourite team) and experimental films, and most puritanical in matters of sex.[4]

Other friends were not numerous. Edith Sitwell was one of them. It was a surprise, after reading her poems, to find her gentle, domesticated, and even devout. When she came to stay with us she spent her time sitting on the sofa and hemming handkerchiefs. She used to write to Nancy and me frequently, but 1926 ended the friendship. 1926 was yesterday, when the autobiographical part of my life was fast approaching its end.[5] I saw no more of any of my army friends, with the exception of Siegfried, and meetings with him were now only about once a year. Edmund Blunden had gone as professor of English Literature to Tokyo. Lawrence

was now in the Royal Tank Corps. He had enlisted in
the Royal Air Force when he came to the end of things
after the Middle-Eastern settlement of 1921, but had
been forced to leave it when a notice was given of a
question in the House about his presence there under
an assumed name. When Sir Walter Raleigh died I felt
my connection with Oxford University was broken,
and when Rivers died, and George Mallory on Everest,
it seemed as though the death of my friends was following me in peace-time as relentlessly as in war. Basanta
had spoken of getting an invitation from the Maharajah for us to visit Nepal with him but, when he found
it impossible to resume his work there, the idea lapsed.
Sam went to visit him in India in 1924; his reputation
as a communist followed him there. He wrote that he
was tagged by policemen wherever he went in Calcutta;
but they need not have worried. A week or two after his
arrival he died of cerebral malaria. After Sam's death
our friendship with Basanta gradually failed. India
re-absorbed him and we changed.

There came one more death among our friends; a
girl who had been a friend of Sam's at Oxford and had
married another friend at Balliol. They used to come
out together to Islip with Basanta and talk philosophy.
She died in childbirth. There had been insufficient care
in the pre-natal period and a midwife attended the case
without having sterilized her hands after attending an
infectious case. Deaths in childbirth had as particular
horror for me now as they had for Nancy. I had assisted
the midwife at the birth of Sam, our fourth child, and
could not have believed that a natural process like
birth could be so abominable in its pain and extravagant messiness. Many deaths and a feeling of bad luck
clouded these years. Islip was no longer a country refuge.

I found myself resorting to my war-time technique of getting through things somehow, anyhow, in the hope that they would mend. Nancy was in poor health and able to do less and less work. Our finances had been improved by an allowance from Nancy's father that covered the extra expense of the new children – we now had about two hundred pounds a year – but I decided that cottage life with four of them under six years old, and Nancy ill, was not good enough. I would have, after all, to take a job. Nancy and I had always sworn that we would manage somehow so that this would not be necessary.[6]

The only possible job that I could undertake was teaching. But I needed a degree, so I completed my thesis, which I published under the title of *Poetic Unreason* and handed in, when in print, to the examining board. I was most surprised when they accepted it and I had my bachelor's degree.[7] But the problem of an appointment remained. I did not want a preparatory or secondary-school job which would keep me away from home all day. Nancy did not want anyone else but myself and her looking after the children, so there seemed no solution. And then the doctor told Nancy that if she wished to regain her health she must spend the winter in Egypt. In fact, the only appointment that would be at all suitable would be a teaching job in Egypt, at a very high salary, where there was little work to do. And a week or two later (for this is the way things have always happened to me in emergencies) I was asked to offer myself as a candidate for the post of professor of English Literature at the newly-founded Egyptian University at Cairo. I had been recommended, I found out later, by two or three influential friends, among them Arnold Bennett, who has always been a good friend to me, and Lawrence, who had served in the war with Lord Lloyd, the then High Commissioner of Egypt. The salary amounted, with the passage money, to fourteen hundred pounds a year. I fortified these recommendations with others, from my neighbour, Colonel John Buchan, and from the Earl of Oxford,[8] who had taken a fatherly interest in me and often visited Islip. And so was given the appointment.

Among other books written in the Islip period were two essays on contemporary poetry. I then held the view that there was not such a thing as poetry of constant value; I regarded it as a product of its period only having relevance in a limited context. I regarded all poetry, in a philosophic sense, as of equal merit, though admitting that at any given time pragmatic distinctions could be drawn between such poems as embodied the conflicts and syntheses of the time and were therefore charged with contemporary sagacity, and such as were literary hang-overs from a preceding period and were therefore inept. I was, in fact, finding only extrinsic values for poetry. I found psychological reasons why poems of a particular sort appealed to a particular class of reader, surviving even political, economic, and religious change. I published two other books. One was waste – a ballad-opera called *John Kemp's Wager*. It marked the end of what I may call the folk-song period of my life. It was an artificial simple play for performance by village societies and has been once performed, in California. The newspaper cuttings that I was sent described it as delightfully English and quaint. A better book was *My Head, My Head*, a romance on the story of Elijah and the Shunamite woman. It was an ingenious attempt to repair the important omissions in the biblical story; but like all the other prose-books that I had written up to this time it failed in its chief object, which was to sell. During this period I was willing to undertake almost any writing job to bring in money. I wrote a series of rhymes for a big map-advertisement for Huntley & Palmer's biscuits (I was paid, but the rhymes never appeared); and silly lyrics for a light opera, *Lord Clancarty*, for which I was not paid, because the opera was never staged; and translations from Dutch and German carols; and rhymes for children's Christmas annuals; and edited three sixpenny pamphlets of verse for Benn's popular series – selections from Skelton's poems, and from my own, and a collection of the less familiar nursery rhymes. I did some verse-reviewing for the *Nation* and *Athenæum*, but by 1925 I found it more and more difficult to be patient with dud books of poetry. And they all seemed to be dud now. I had agreed to collaborate with T. S. Eliot in a book about modernist poetry to which we were each to contribute essays, but the plan fell through; and later I was glad that it had.[9]

I also made several attempts during these years to rid myself of the poison of war-memories by finishing my novel, but I had to abandon them. It was not only that they brought back neurasthenia, but that I was ashamed at having distorted my material with a plot, and yet not sure enough of myself to retranslate it into undisguised history. If my scruples had been literary and not moral I could easily have compromised, as many writers have since done, with a pretended diary stylistically disguising characters, times, and dates. I had found the same difficulty in my last year at Charterhouse with a projected novel of public-school life.

XXXI

So second-class, by P. & O. to Egypt, with a nurse for the children, a new wardrobe in the new cabin-trunks and a good-looking motor-car in the hold.[1] Lawrence had written to me:

> Egypt, being so near Europe, is not a savage country. The Egyptians . . . you need not dwell among. Indeed, it will be a miracle if an Englishman can get to know them. The bureaucrat society is exclusive, and lives smilingly unaware of the people. Partly because so many foreigners come there for pleasure, in the winter; and the other women, who live there, must be butterflies too, if they would consort with the visitors.
>
> I thought the salary attractive. It has just been raised. The work may be interesting, or may be terrible, according to whether you get keen on it, like Hearn, or hate it, like Nichols. Even if you hate it, there will be no harm done. The climate is good, the country beautiful, the things admirable, the beings curious and disgusting; and you are stable enough not to be caught broadside by a mere dislike for your job. Execute it decently, as long as you draw the pay, and enjoy your free hours (plentiful in Egypt) more freely. Lloyd will be a good friend.
>
> Roam about – Palestine. The Sahara oases. The Red Sea province. Sinai (a jolly desert). The Delta Swamps.

Wilfred Jennings Bramly's buildings in the Western Desert. The divine mosque architecture of Cairo town.

Yet, possibly, you will not dislike the job. I think the coin spins evenly. The harm to you is little, for the family will benefit by a stay in the warm (Cairo isn't warm, in winter) and the job won't drive you into frantic excesses of rage. And the money will be useful. You should save a good bit of your pay after the expense of the first six months. I recommend the iced coffee at Groppi's.

And so, my blessing.

I had a married half-brother and half-sister[2] in Cairo who had both been there since I was a little boy. My brother, a leading Government official (at a salary less than my own), and his wife viewed my coming to Egypt, I heard, with justifiable alarm. They had heard of my political opinions. My sister, to whom I was devoted, had no such suspicions and wrote a letter of most affectionate welcome. Siegfried came to see me off. He said: 'Do you know who's on board? "The Image!" He's still in the regiment, going to join the battalion in India. Last time I saw him he was sitting in the bottom of a dug-out gnawing a chunk of bully-beef like a rat.' The Image had been at my last preparatory school and had won a scholarship at the same time as myself; and we had been at Wrexham and Liverpool together; and he had been wounded with the Second Battalion at High Wood at the same time as myself; and now we were travelling out East together. A man with whom I had nothing in common; there was no natural reason why we should have been thrown so often in each other's company. The ship touched at Gibraltar, where we disembarked and bought figs and rode round the town. I remembered the cancelled War Office telegram and thought what a fool I had been to prefer Rhyl. At Port Said a friend of my sister's helped us through the Customs; I was feeling very sea-sick, but I knew that I was in the East because he began talking about Kipling and Kipling's wattles of Lichtenburg, and whether they were really wattles or some allied plant. And so to Cairo, looking out of the windows all the way, delighted at summer fields in January.

My sister-in-law advised us against the more exclusive residential suburb of Gizereh where she had just taken a flat herself, so with her help we found one at Heliopolis, a few miles east of Cairo. We found the cost of living very high, for this was the tourist season. But I was able to reduce the grocery bill by taking advantage of the more reasonable prices of the British army canteen; I presented myself as an officer on the pension list. We had two Sudanese servants, and, contrary to all that we had been warned about native servants, they were temperate, punctual, respectful, and never, to my knowledge, stole a thing beyond the remains of a single joint of mutton. It seemed queer to me not to look after the children or do housework, and almost too good to be true to have as much time as I needed for my writing.

The University was an invention of King Fuad's, who had always been anxious to be known as a patron of the arts and sciences. There had been a Cairo University before this one, but it had been nationalistic in its policy and, not being directed by European experts or supported by the Government, had soon come to an end. The new University had been planned ambitiously. There were faculties of science, medicine and letters, with a full complement of highly-paid professors; only one or two of these were Egyptian, the rest being English, Swedish, French and Belgian. The medicine and science faculties were predominantly English, but the appointments to the faculty of letters were predominantly French. They had been made in the summer months when the British High Commissioner was out of Egypt, or he would no doubt have discountenanced them. Only one of the French and Belgian professors had any knowledge of English, and none of them had any knowledge of Arabic. Of the two hundred Egyptian students, who were mostly the sons of rich merchants and landowners, fewer than twenty had more than a smattering of French – just enough for shopping purposes – though they had all learned English in the secondary schools. All official university correspondence was in Arabic. I was told that it was classical Arabic, in which no word is admitted that is of later date than Mohammed, but I could not tell the difference. The 'very learned Sheikh' Graves had to take his letters to the post office for interpretation. My twelve or thirteen French colleagues were men of the highest academic distinction. But two or three English village-schoolmasters would have been glad to have undertaken their work at one-third of their salaries and done it far better. The University building had been a harem-palace of the Khedive. It was French in style, with mirrors and gilding.

British officials at the Ministry of Education told me that I must keep the British flag flying in the faculty of letters. This embarrassed me. I had not come to Egypt as an ambassador of Empire, and yet I did not intend to let the French indulge in semi-political activities at my expense. The dean, M. Grégoire, was a Belgian, an authority on Slav poetry. He was tough, witty, and ran

his show very plausibly. He had acquired a certain sly-
ness and adaptability during the war when, as a civilian
in Belgium under German occupation, he had edited
an underground anti-German publication. The professor of French Literature had lost a leg in France. He
greeted me at first in a patronizing way: I was his young
friend rather than his dear colleague. But as soon as he
learned that I also had bled in the cause of civilization
and France I became his most esteemed chum. The
Frenchmen lectured, but with the help of Arabic interpreters, which did not make either for speed or
accuracy. I found that I was expected to give two lectures a week, but the dean soon decided that if the
students were ever to dispense with the interpreters
they must be given special instruction in French –
which reduced the time for lectures, so that I had only
one a week to give. This one was pandemonium. The
students were not hostile, merely excitable and anxious to show their regard for me and liberty and
Zaghlul Pasha and the well-being of Egypt, all at the
same time. I often had to shout at the top of my loudest
barrack-square voice to restore order. They had no
textbooks of any sort; there were no English books
in the University library, and it took months to get any
through the French librarian. This was January and
they were due for an examination in May. They were
most anxious to master Shakespeare, Byron, and
Wordsworth in that time. I had no desire to teach
Wordsworth and Byron to anyone, and I wished to
protect Shakespeare from them. I decided to lecture on
the most rudimentary forms of literature possible. I
chose the primitive ballad and its development into
epic and the drama. I thought that this would at least
teach them the meaning of the simpler literary terms.

But English was not easy for them, though they had learned it for eight years or so in the schools. Nobody, for instance, when I spoke of a ballad-maker singing to his harp, knew what a harp was. I told them it was what King David played upon, and drew a picture of it on the blackboard; at which they shouted out: 'O, *anur*.' But they thought it beneath their dignity to admit the existence of ballads in Egypt; though I had myself seen the communal ballad-group in action at the hind legs of the Sphinx, where a gang of fellaheen was clearing away the sand. One of the gang was a chanty-man: his whole job was to keep the others moving. The fellaheen did not exist for the students; they thought of them as animals. They were most anxious to be given printed notes of my lectures with which to prepare themselves for the examinations. I tried to make the clerical staff of the faculty duplicate some for me, but in spite of promises I never got them done. My lectures in the end became a dictation of lecture-notes for lectures that could not be given – this, at any rate, kept the students busy.

They were interested in my clothes. My trousers were the first Oxford trousers that they had seen in Egypt; their own were narrow at the ankles. So I set a new fashion. One evening I went to dine with the rector of the University. Two of my students, sons of Ministers, happened also to be invited. They noticed that I was wearing white silk socks with my evening dress. Later I heard from the vice-rector, Ali Bey Omar, whom I liked best of the University officials, that a day or two later he had seen the same students at a Government banquet, wearing white silk socks. When they looked round on the distinguished assembly they found that they were the only white socks present. Ali Bey

Omar gave a pantomime account of how they tried to loosen their braces surreptitiously and stroke down their trousers to hide their shame.

For some weeks I missed even my single hour a week, because the students went on strike. It was Ramadan, and they had to fast for a month between sunrise and sunset. Between sunset and sunrise they ate rather more than usual in compensation, and this dislocation of their digestive processes had a bad effect on their nerves. I have forgotten the pretext for the strike: it was some trouble about the intensive French instruction. The fact was that they wanted leisure at home to read up their notes of the earlier work of the term in preparation for the examination. The Professor of Arabic, who was one of the few Egyptians with a reputation as an orientalist, published a book calling attention to pre-Islamic sources of the Koran. His lectures, delivered in Arabic, demanded more exertion from them than any of the others, so when the examination came round most of them absented themselves from the Arabic paper on religious grounds. To an orthodox Mohammedan[3] the Koran, being dictated by God, can have no pre-Islamic sources.

I came to know only two of my students fairly well; one was a Greek, the other a Turk. The Turk was an intelligent, good-natured young man, perhaps twenty years old. He was very rich, and had a motor-car in which he twice took me for a drive to the Pyramids. He talked both French and English fluently, being about the only one (except for twelve who had attended a French Jesuit college) who could do so. He told me one day that he would not be able to attend my next lecture as he was going to be married. I asked him whether this was the first or second part of the ceremony; he said it was the first. When he returned he told me that he had not yet been allowed to see the face of his wife, because her family was orthodox; he would only see it at the second ceremony. But his sister had been at school with her and said that she was pretty and a good sort; and her father was a friend of his father's. Later, the second ceremony took place, and he confessed himself perfectly satisfied. I learned that it seldom happened that when the veil was lifted the bridegroom refused the bride, though he had the right to do so; she had a similar right. Usually the couple contrived to meet before even the first ceremony. The girl would slip the man a note saying: 'I shall be at Maison Cicurel at the hat-counter at three-thirty to-morrow afternoon if you want to see me. It will be quite in order for me to lift my veil to try on a hat. You will recognize me by my purple parasol.'

I inquired about the rights of Mohammedan women in Egypt. Apparently divorce was simple; the man only had to say in the presence of a witness: 'I divorce you, I divorce you, I divorce you,' and she was divorced. On the other hand she was entitled to take her original dowry back with her, with the interest that had accrued on it during her married life. Dowries were always heavy and divorces comparatively rare. It was considered very low-class to have more than one wife; that was a fellaheen habit. I was told a story of an Egyptian who was angry with his wife one morning because the breakfast-coffee was badly made. He shouted out: 'I divorce you, I divorce you, I divorce you.' 'Oh, my dear,' she said, 'now you've done it. The servants have heard what you said. I must go back to my father with my ten thousand pounds and my sixty camels.' He apologized for his hasty temper. 'We must be remarried,' he said, 'as soon as possible.' She reminded him that the law prevented them from marrying again unless there were an intermediate marriage. So he called in a very old man who was watering the lawn and ordered him to marry her. He was to understand that it was a marriage of form only. So the gardener married the woman and, immediately after the ceremony, returned to his watering-pot. Two days later the woman died, and the gardener inherited the money and the camels.

The Greek invited me to tea once. He had three beautiful sisters named Pallas, Aphrodite, and Artemis. They gave me tea in the garden with European cakes that they had learned to make at the American college. Next door a pale-faced man stood on a third-floor balcony addressing the world. I asked Pallas what he was saying: 'Oh,' she said, 'don't mind him; he's a millionaire, so the police leave him alone. He's quite mad. He lived ten years in England. He's saying now that they're burning him up with electricity, and he's telling the birds all his troubles. He says that his secretary accuses him of stealing five piastres from him, and it isn't true. Now he's saying that there can't be a God because God wouldn't allow the English to steal the fellaheen's camels for the war and not return them. Now he's saying that all religions are very much the same, and that Buddha is as good as Mohammed. But really,' she said, 'he's quite mad. He keeps a little dog in his house, actually in his very room, and plays with it and talks to it as though it were a human being.' (Dogs are unclean in Egypt.) She told me that in another twenty years the women of Egypt would be in control of everything. The feminist movement had just started, and as the women of Egypt were by far the most active and intelligent part of the population, great changes were to be

expected. She said that neither she nor her sisters
would stand her father's attempts to keep them in their
places. Her brother showed me his library. He was
doing the arts-course as a preliminary to law. Besides his
legal textbooks he had Voltaire, Rousseau, a number
of saucy French novels in paper covers, Shakespeare's
works and Samuel Smiles' *Self Help*, a book which I
had never met before. He asked my advice about his
career, and I advised him to go to a European university because an arts degree at Cairo would be of little
advantage to him.

I did not pay an official call at the Residency at first,
though my brother urged it as etiquette; I decided not
to until I had seen how things were at the University. I
had not realized before to what extent the British were
in power in Egypt. I had been told that Egypt was an
independent kingdom, but it seemed that my principal
allegiance was not to the King who had given me my
appointment and paid me my salary, but to the British
High Commissioner. Infantry, cavalry, and air squad-
rons were a reminder of his power. The British officials
could not understand the Egyptians' desire to be rid of
them. They considered Egypt most ungrateful for all
the painful and difficult administrative work that they
had put into it since the 'eighties, raising it from a bankrupt country to one of the richest in the world. None of
them took Egyptian nationalism seriously; there was no
Egyptian nation they said. The Greeks, Turks, Syrians,
and Armenians who called themselves Egyptians had
no more right in the country than the British. Before the
British occupation they had bled the fellaheen white.
The fellaheen were the only true Egyptians, and it was
not they who called for freedom. Freedom was mere
politics, a symptom of the growing riches of the coun-

try and the smatterings of Western education that they had brought with them.[4] The reduction of the British official class in the last few years was viewed with disgust. 'We did all the hard work and when we go everything will run down; it's running down already. And they'll have to call us back, or if not us, the dagoes, and we don't see why they should benefit.' They did not realize how much the vanity of the Egyptians – probably the vainest people in the world – was hurt by the constant sight of British uniform.

Egypt now considered itself a European nation. At the same time it attempted to take the place of Turkey as the leading power of Islam. This led to many anomalies. On the same day that the University students made the protest against the professor of Arabic's irreligious views, the students of El Azhar, the great Cairo theological college, struck against having to wear the Arab dress of kaftan and silk headdress and appeared in European dress and tarbouche. The tarbouche was the national hat; even British officials wore it. I myself had a tarbouche. Being red it attracted the heat of the sun; and it was stuffy inside and did not protect the back of the head. It would have been difficult to find a hat more unsuitable for the climate.[5]

XXXII

I did two useful pieces of educational work in Egypt. I ordered a library of standard textbooks of English literature for the Faculty Library at the University (from which I hope Mr. Bonamy Dobrée, my successor, profited). And I acted as examiner to the diploma class of the Higher Training College which provided English teachers for the primary and secondary schools. The following is the substance of a letter handed to me for information as a member of the Board of Examiners concerned:

To The Principal,
    Higher Training College, Cairo.

Sir,

In accordance with your instructions, I beg to submit the following statement of the works read by the Diploma Class for the forthcoming examination in English Literature (1580 to 1788) and in Science:

ENGLISH LITERATURE

1. Shakespeare's *Macbeth*.
2. Lobban's *The Spectator Club*, p. 39, and *Sir Roger and the Widow*, p. 51; (III) 5 Essays of Addison,

Fans, p. 64; *The Vision of Mirza*, p. 72; *Sir Roger at the Assizes*, p. 68; *Sir Roger at the Abbey*, p. 81; *Sir Roger at the Play*, p. 86.

3. Galsworthy's *Justice*.

4. Dryden:
   (a) With Class 4A, the following poems in Hales' *Longer English Poems*:
       (i) *Mac Flecknoe* (omitting lines 76–7; 83–6; 142–5; 154–5; 160–165; 170–181; 192–7).
       (ii) *The Song for St. Cecilia's Day* (Hales', p. 32).
       (iii) *Alexander's Feast* (Hales', p. 34).
   (b) With Class 4B, the extracts from *Absolam and Achitophel*, in Gwynn's *Masters of English Literature*, p. 144–5 (characters of Shaftesbury and Buckingham).

5. Pope:
   (a) With 4A, in Hales' *Longer English Poems*: *The Rape of the Lock* (omitting lines 27–104; 221–82; 449–66; 483 to the end).
   (b) With 4B, the character of 'Atticus', in Gwynn's *Masters of Eng. Lit.*, p. 181.

6. Johnson's *Vanity of Human Wishes*, in Hales', p. 65 (omitting lines 241–343).

7. Goldsmith's *Vicar of Wakefield*. (All done by 4A; but only to the end of chap. 19 in 4B.)

8. Goldsmith's *The Traveller*, in Hales', p. 91.

9. Gray's *Elegy*, in Hales', p. 79.

I regret that lack of time has prevented us from studying the works of Milton and Spenser or the prose works of Dr. Johnson.

SCIENCE

1. Episodes 1, 2, 3 and 6 of Sir Arthur Conan Doyle's *Memoirs of Sherlock Holmes*.
2. The first seven chapters of Sir Ray Lankester's *Science from an Easy Chair*.

I have the honour to be, Sir,
Your obedient servant, etc.

These are my contemporary comments, pinned to the letter:

'When some forty years ago England superseded France as the controlling European Power in Egypt, English was at first taught in the schools as an alternative to French, but gradually became dominant as the European administrative language, though French remained the chief language of commerce and culture. As a result, the young Egyptian, who now definitely claims himself a European and denies his African inheritance, has come to have two distinct minds (switched off and on casually) – the irresponsible hedonistic café and cinema mind, which leans towards French, and the grave moralizing bureaucratic mind, which leans towards English. Early English educationalists in Egypt shrewdly decided to give their students a moralistic character-forming view of English literature; and this tradition continues as a counterpoise to the boulevard view of life absorbed from translations of French yellow-back novels. But the student of 1926 is not so well-instructed in English as his predecessor of ten years ago, because the English educational staff has gradually been liquidated, and the teaching of English is now principally in the hands of Egyptians, former students, who are not born teachers or disciplinarians. The Western spirit of freedom as naively interpreted by the Egyptian student greatly hinders Egyptian education. The primary and secondary schools, not to mention the University, are always either on strike, threatening a strike, or prevented from striking by being given a holiday. So work gets more and more behindhand. Even the Higher Training College is not free from such disturbances, which possibly account for the regretted neglect of Milton, Spenser, and the prose works of Dr. Johnson. This Diploma Class consists of students who, after some twelve years' study of English, the last four or five years under English instructors, are now qualifying to teach the language and literature to their compatriots.

'The Egyptian student is embarrassingly friendly, very quick at learning by heart, disorderly, lazy, rhetorical, slow to reason, and absolutely without any curiosity for general knowledge. The most satisfactory way to treat him is with a good-humoured sarcasm, which he respects; but if he once gets politically excited nothing is any use but an affected violent loss of temper. When introduced to the simpler regions of English literature he finds himself most in sympathy with the eighteenth century; and the English instructor, if he wishes to get any results at all, must be ready to regard Shakespeare, Galsworthy and Conan Doyle as either immature or decadent figures in relation to the classical period. The *Science* referred to in the attached letter is supposed to educate the student in twentieth-century rationalism, to which he gives an eighteenth-century cast. The following essay is the work of one Mahmoud Mohammed Mahmoud of the Diploma Class, and refers principally to two chapters of Sir Ray Lankester's *Science from an Easy Chair*.'[1]

Environment as a Factor in Evolution

This is the theory of evolutions. Once it was thought that the earth's crust was caused by catastrophes, but when Darwin came into the world and had a good deal of philosophy, he said: 'All different kinds of species differ gradually as we go backwards and there is no catastrophes, and if we apply the fact upon previous predecessors we reach simpler and simpler predecessors, until we reach the Nature.' Man, also, is under the evolutions. None can deny this if he could deny the sun in daylight. A child from the beginning of his birthday possesses instincts like to suckle his food from the mamel of his mother and many others. But he is free of habits and he is weak as anything. Then he is introduced into a house and usually finds himself among parents, and his body is either cleansed or left to the dirts. This shows his environment. Superficial thinkers are apt to look on environment as (at best) a trifle motive in bringing up, but learned men believe that a child born in the presence of some women who say a bad word, this word, as believed by them, remains in the brain of the child until it ejects.

Environment quickly supplies modification. The life of mountainous goats leads them to train themselves on jumping. The camel is flat-footed with hoofs for the sand. Some kind of cattle were wild in the past but lived in plain lands and changed into gentle sheep. The frog when young has her tail and nostrils like the fish, suitable for life at sea, but changing her environment, the tail decreased. The sea is broad and changeable, so those who live at sea are changeable and mysterious. Put a cow in a dirty damp place and she will become more and more slender until she die. Also horses; horse had five fingers on his legs but now one only from running for water in the draught. Climate also affects bodily habits of the dear Europeans who live in Egypt. They who were smart and patient and strong with a skin worth the name of weatherproof become also fatigable and fond of leisure ... From the theory we learn that human beings should be improved like the beasts by creating healthy youngs and by good Freubel education.

'The next short specimen essay by Mohammed Mahmoud Mohammed is in answer to the question: "What impression do you get from Shakespeare of the character of Lady Macbeth?":'

THE CHARACTER OF LADY MACBETH

Sir, to write shortly, Lady Macbeth was brave and venturesome; but she had no tact. She says to Macbeth: 'Now the opportunity creates itself, lose it not. Where is your manlihood in these suitable circumstances? I have children and I know the love of a mother's heart. But you must know I would dash the child's head and drive away the boneless teeth which are milking me rather than to give a promise and then leave it.'

Macbeth says: 'But we may fail.'

'Fail?' says L. M. 'But stick to the point and we will not fail. Leave the rest to me. I shall put drugs in the grooms' drink and we shall ascuse them.'

Macbeth says: 'You are fit to lay men-children only.'

The impression on the reader becomes very great and feels with anger.

'And this from the hand of Mahmoud Mahmoud Mohammed, offered as a formal exercise in English composition:'

THE BEST USE OF LEISURE TIME

Leisure time is a variety to tireful affairs. God Almighty created the Universe in six days and took a rest in the seventh. He wished to teach us the necessity of leisure time. Man soon discovered by experience that 'All work and no play makes Jack a dull boy.' But this leisure time may be dangerous and ill-used if the mind will not take its handle and move it wisely to different directions. Many people love idleness. It is a great prodigality which leads to ruin. Many Egyptians spend their times in cafés longing for women and tracking them with their eyes, which corrupts and pollutes manners. They are perplexed and annoyed by the length of daytime. Others try to have rest through gumbling, which is the scourge of society and individual. But let *us* rather enjoy external nature, the beautiful leavy trees, the flourishing fields, and the vast lawns of green grass starred with myriads of flowers of greater or small size. There the birds sing and build their nests, the meandering canals flow with fresh water, and the happy peasants, toiling afar from the multitude of town life, purify the human wishes from personal stain. Also museums are instructive. It is quite wrong to keep to usual work and fatigable studies, but quite right to free our minds from the web of wordly affairs in which they are entangled.

Yes, let us with the lark leave our beds to enjoy the cool breeze before sunrise. Let us when the lasy or luxurious are snoring or sunk in their debaucheries sit under the shady trees and meditate. We can think of God, the river and the moon, and enjoy the reading of Gray's *Elegy* to perfection. We shall brush the dues on the lawn at sunrise, for,

A country life is sweat
In moderate cold and heat.

Or we may read the Best Companions, books full of honourable passions, wise moral and good pathos: reading maketh a full man, nobody will deny Bacon. Or we may easily get a musical instrument at little price. 'Every schoolboy knows' that music is a moral law which gives a soul to the universe. Criminals can be cured by the sweet power of music. The whale came up from the dark depths of the sea to carry the Greek musician because it was affected by the sweet harmonies which hold a mirror up to nature. Are we not better than the whale? Also gymnastic clubs are spread everywhere. Why do a youth not pass his leisure time in widdening his chest? Because a sound mind is in a sound body. Yet it is a physiological fact that the blacksmith cannot spend his leisure time in striking iron or the soldier in military exercises. The blacksmith may go to see the Egyptian Exhibition, and the soldier may go to the sea to practice swimming or to the mountains to know its caves in order that he may take shelter in time of war.

Milton knew the best uses of leisure time. He used to sit to his books reading, and to his music playing, and so put his name among the immortals. That was the case of Byron, Napoleon, Addison, and Palmerstone. And if a man is unhappy, says an ancient philosopher, it is his own fault. He *can* be happy if his leisure time brings profit and not disgrace.

'The Diploma Class students are supposed to be four years in advance of my own, and, not being of the moneyed class, are more interested in passing their examinations with distinction. Also, since their careers as teachers of English depend on the continuance of the British military occupation, they take the morality of this regime more seriously than the University students, who are mostly the sons of pashas. These, with few exceptions, suffer from the bankruptcy of modern Egyptian life; they are able to take neither European culture nor their own Islamic traditions seriously. So far as I can make out from talking with the more intelligent of them, what Egypt asks for is a European government and education free of European political domination, but with a European technical personnel in the key positions, which it cannot do without and will pay highly for. Egypt can never be a great independent spiritual or political force in the Near East, but because of its wealth it can become at least the commercial centre of Islamic orthodoxy. Turkey is already a modern European country; Egypt will remain for some time yet eighteenth-century in spirit – a compromise between political romanticism and religious classicism. For a generation or two yet the descendants of the land-owners enriched by European administration will continue to "spend their times in cafés longing for women," and to be "perplexed and annoyed by the length of daytime," while "the happy peasants" go on "toiling afar from the multitude of town life". And my professional successors will continue to become "fatigable and fond of leisure".[2]

For I had already decided to resign. So had the professor of Latin, my only English colleague. And the one-legged professor of French Literature, who was an honest man. The others stayed on.

The Egyptians were most hospitable. I attended one heavy banquet, at the Semiramis Hotel, given by the

Minister of Education. Tall Sudanese waiters dressed in red robes served a succession of the most magnificent dishes that I have seen anywhere, even on the films. I remember particularly a great model of the Cairo Citadel in ice, with the doors and windows filled with caviare which one scooped out with a golden Moorish spoon. I heard recently that this banquet, which must have cost thousands, has not yet been paid for. I found little to do in Egypt (since I had no intention of mixing with the British official class, joining the golf club, or paying official calls) but eat coffee-ices at Groppi's, visit the open-air cinemas and sit at home in our flat at Heliopolis and get on with writing. My sister, who lived near, continued sisterly. During the season of the Khamsin, a hot wind which sent the temperature up on one occasion to 113 degrees in the shade, I put the finishing touches to a book called *Lars Porsena, or The Future of Swearing and Improper Language*. I also worked on a study of the English ballad.

The best thing that I saw in Egypt was the noble face of old King Seti the Good unwrapped of its mummy-cloths in the Cairo Museum. Nearly all the best things in Egypt were dead. The funniest thing was a French bedroom farce played in Arabic by Syrian actors in a native theatre. The men and women of the cast had, for religious reasons, to keep on opposite sides of the stage. They sang French songs (in translation), varying the tunes with the quarter-tones and shrieks and trills of their own music. The audience talked all the time and ate peanuts, oranges, sunflower-seeds and heads of lettuces.

I went to call on Lord Lloyd just before the close of the academic year, which was at the end of May. Soon after I was invited to dine at the Residency. I won twenty piastres off him at bridge and was told to collect it from his A.D.C. He asked me how I found Egypt and I said: 'All right,' with an intonation that made him catch me up quickly. 'Only all right?' That was all that passed between us. He believed in his job more than I did in mine. He used to drive through Cairo in a powerful car, with a Union Jack flying from it, at about sixty miles an hour. He had motor-cyclist outriders to clear the way – Sir Lee Stack, the Sirdar, had been killed the year before while driving through Cairo and a traffic jam had materially helped his assassins. One day I was shown the spot near the Ministry of Education where it happened; there was a crowd at the spot which I at first took for a party of sightseers, but the attraction proved to be a naked woman lying on the pavement, laughing wildly and waving her arms. She was one of the *hashish* dope-cases that were very common in Egypt. The crowd was jeering at her; the policeman a few yards off paid no attention.

I attended a levee at the Abdin Palace, King Fuad's Cairo residence. It began early, at nine o'clock in the morning. The King gave honourable precedence to the staff of the University; it came in soon after the diplomatic corps and the Ministers of the Crown and some time before the army. While still in England I had been warned to buy suitable clothes – a morning coat and trousers – for this occasion. To be really correct my coat should have had green facings, green being the national colour of Egypt, but I was told that this would not be insisted upon. Opinions differed greatly as to what was suitable Court-dress; most of the French professors arrived in full evening dress with swallow-tail coats and white waistcoats, others wore ordinary dinner jackets. Most of them had opera-hats; they all had decorations round their necks. They looked like stragglers from an all-night fancy-dress ball. After signing my name in the two large hotel registers, one belonging to the King and the other to the Queen, I was given a refreshing rice-drink, a courtesy of the Queen's. I then went up the noble marble staircase. On every other step stood an enormous black soldier,[3] royally uniformed, with a lance in his hand. My soldier's eye commented on their somewhat listless attitudes; but, no doubt, they pulled themselves smartly to attention when the Egyptian army general staff went past. I had been warned that when I met King Fuad I must not be surprised at anything extraordinary I heard; a curious wheezing cry was apt to burst from his throat occasionally when he was nervous. When he was a child his family had been shot up by an assassin employed by interested relatives; and Fuad had taken cover under a table and, though wounded, had survived. We were moved from room to room. At last a quiet Turkish-looking gentleman of middle age, wearing regulation Court-dress, greeted us deferentially in French; I took him for the Grand Chamberlain. I bowed and said the same thing in French as the professor in front of me had said, and expected to be led next to the Throne Room. But the next stage was the cloak-room once more. I had already met King Fuad. And no Eastern magnificence or wheezing cry.

I attended a royal soiree a few days later. The chief event was a theatrical variety show. The performance was predominantly Italian. King Fuad had been educated in Italy, where he attained the rank of captain in the Italian cavalry, and had a great regard for Italian culture. (He was ignorant of English, but was a good French scholar.) The performance belonged to the 1870's. There was a discreet blonde shepherdess who did a hopping dance in ankle-length skirts, and a discreet tenor who confined his passion to his top notes; and there was a well-behaved comedian who made nice little jokes for the Queen. I clapped him, because I liked him better than the others, and everybody looked round at me; I realized that I had done the wrong thing. An official whispered to me that it was a command performance and that the actors were, therefore, entitled to no applause. Unless His Majesty was himself amused the turns must be greeted in silence. I was wearing Court-dress again but, not to be outdone by the Frenchmen, I had put on my three campaigning medals – and wished that I had that St. Anne of the Third Class with the Crossed Swords. And the refreshments! I will not attempt to describe that Arabian Night buffet; it was so splendid indeed that it has remained a mere blur in my memory. I pocketed some particularly fantastic confections to bring home to the children.

What caused me most surprise in Egypt was the great number of camels there. I had thought of them only as picture-postcard animals. I had not expected to see thousands of them in the streets of Cairo, holding up the motor traffic – in long trains, tied head to rump, with great sacks of green fodder on their backs.

Our children were a great anxiety. They had to drink boiled milk and boiled water and be watched all the time to prevent them from taking off their topees and blue veils. Then they all got measles and were carried off to an isolation hospital, where they were fed on all the things that we had been particular since their birth not to give them; and the native nurses stole their toys. They returned very thin and wretched-looking and we wondered if we should ever get them safely home. We booked our passages some time at the end of May. We had only just enough money for third-class on a small Italian boat with a cargo of onions. We disembarked at Venice and stopped a day there. After Egypt, Venice seemed like Heaven. It could never again be to me what it was that day. I had a European egg in Venice. Egyptian eggs were about the size of a pigeon's egg and always tasted strongly of the garlic which seemed to form a large part of the diet of the Egyptian fowl.

There are plenty of caricature scenes to look back on in Egypt. Among them, for instance, myself dressed in my smart yellow gaberdine suit and seated at a long, baize-covered table in the Faculty Conference Room. In front of me is a cup of Turkish coffee, a sun helmet, and a long record in French of the minutes of the last meeting. I am talking angry bad French at my Belgian and French colleagues in support of the young professor of Latin, who has just leaped to his feet, pale with hatred. He is declaring in worse French that he positively refuses to make a forced contribution of fifty piastres to a memorial wreath for one of the Frenchmen (who had just died), since he was never consulted. I am declaring that neither will I, blustering to him in English that so far as I am concerned all dead Frenchmen can go bury themselves at their own expense. The lofty, elegant room, once a harem drawing-room – a portrait of the late Khedive, with a large rent in it, hanging at a tipsy slant at one end of the room; at the other a large glass showcase, full of Egypto-Roman brass coins, all muddled together, their labels loose, in one corner. Through the window market-gardens, buffaloes, camels, countrywomen in black. Around the table my horrified, shrugging colleagues, turning to each other and saying: 'Inoui . . . Inoui . . .' And outside the rebellious shouts of our students working themselves up for another strike.

The rest makes no more than conversation – of the Government clerk who was so doubly unfortunate as to be run over by a racing-car and to find that the driver was the eldest son of the Minister of Justice; and of the rich girl in search of a husband who went as paying guest at fifteen guineas a week to the senior Government official's wife, agreeing to pay for all wines and cigars and extras when society came to dine, and who, meeting only senior Government officials and their wives, complained that she did not get her money's worth; and of my night visit to the temple of a headless monkey-god, full of bats; and of the English cotton manufacturer who defended the conditions in his factory on the ground that the population of Egypt since the British came had been increasing far too rapidly, and that pulmonary consumption was one of the few checks on it; and of the student's mother who, at the sports, said how much she regretted having put him on the mantelpiece when a baby and run off (being only twelve years old) to play with her dolls; and of 'The Limit', so named by Australians during the war, who told my three years' fortune by moonlight under the long shadow of the pyramid of Cheops – told it truly and phrased it falsely; and of the Arab cab-driver who was kind to his horses; and of my visit to Chawki Bey, the national poet of Egypt, in his Moorish mansion by the Nile, who was so like Thomas Hardy and in whose presence his sons, like good Turks, sat dutifully silent; and of the beggar in the bazaar with too many toes; and of the veiled vengeance there who tried to touch us; and of the official who, during the war, on a dream of dearth, had played Joseph, dumping half the wheat of Australia in Egypt, where it found no buyers and was at last eaten by donkeys and camels, and who told me that the whole secret of vivid writing was to use the active rather than the passive voice – to say 'Amr-ibn-el-Ass conquered Egypt,' rather than 'Egypt was conquered by Amr-ibn-el-Ass'; and of a visit to ancient dead Heliopolis with its lovely landscape of green fields, its crooked palm trees, its water-wheels turned by oxen, and its single obelisk; and of the other Heliopolis, a brand-new dead town on the desert's edge, built by a Belgian company, complete with racecourse and Luna Park, where the R.A.F. planes flew low at night among the houses, and where the bored wives of disappointed officials wrote novels which they never finished, and painted a little in water-colours; and of the little garden of our flat where I went walking on the first day among the fruit-trees and flowering shrubs, and how I came upon no less than eight lean and mangy cats dozing in the beds, and never walked there again; and of the numerous kites, their foul counterpart in the sky and in the palm trees; and, lastly, of that fabulous cross-breed between kite and cat which woke us every morning at dawn, a creature kept as a pet in a neighbouring tenement inhabited by Syrians and Greeks, whose strangled cock-a-doodle-doo was to me the dawn-cry of modern Egypt. (Empty cigar-box – no applause – and I thank you.)

So back to Islip; much to the disappointment of my parents, who thought that I had at last seen reason and settled down to an appointment suited equally to my needs and my talents; and to the undisguised relief of my sister-in-law.[4]

The story trails off here. But to end it with the return from Egypt would be to round it off too bookishly, to finish on a note of comfortable suspense, an anticipation of the endless human sequel. I am taking care to rob you of this. It is not that sort of story. From a historical point of view it must be read, rather, as one of gradual disintegration. By the summer of 1926 the disintegration was already well-advanced. Incidents of autobiographical pertinence became fewer and fewer.

When we came back Nancy's health was very much better, but none of us had any money left. There were a number of books to be sold, chiefly autographed first editions of modern poets; and Lawrence came to the rescue with a copy of his *Seven Pillars* marked, 'Please sell when read,' which fetched over three hundred pounds.

In 1927 Jonathan Cape wrote to me suggesting that I should write a book for boys about Lawrence. There was not much time to do it to have it ready for autumn publication (about two months) – and Lawrence was in India and I had to get his permission and send parts of the manuscript there for him to read and pass. Lowell Thomas anticipated me with a *Boy's Book of Colonel Lawrence*; so I decided to make mine a general book, three times the length of his, working eighteen hours a day at it. Most of those to whom I wrote for information about Lawrence, including His Majesty the King, gave me their help. The only rebuff I got was from George Bernard Shaw, who wrote me the following postcard:

EYOT ST. LAWRENCE,
WELWYN, HERTS.
8th June 1927.

A great mistake. You might as well try to write a funny book about Mark Twain. T. E. has got all out of himself that is to be got. His name will rouse expectations which you will necessarily disappoint. Cape will curse his folly for proposing such a thing, and never give you another commission. Write a book (if you must) about the dullest person you know; clerical if possible. Give yourself a chance.

G. B. S.

Just before Christmas the book was selling at the rate of ten thousand copies a week. I heard later that Shaw had mistaken me for my *Daily Mail* brother.

Shortly afterwards I had a reply, delayed for nine months, to an application that I had made, when things were bad, for an appointment as English lecturer in an Adult Education scheme. I was told that my qualifications were not considered sufficient. By this time I had lost all my academic manners and wrote wishing the entire committee in Baluchistan, to be tickled to death by wild butterflies.

In 1927, in a process of tidying-up, I published a collected book of my poems. One of the later ones began:

> This, I admit, Death is terrible to me,
> To no man more so, naturally.
> And I have disenthralled my natural terror
> Of every comfortable philosopher
> Or tall dark doctor of divinity.
> Death stands at last in his true rank and order.[5]

The book was selective rather than collective, intended as a disavowal of over half the poetry that I had so far printed. As Skelton told Fame, speaking of his regretted poem *Apollo Whirléd up his Chair*, I had done what I could to scrape out the scrolls, To erase it for ever out of her ragman's rolls. But I still permitted anthologists to print some of the rejected pieces if they paid highly enough – if they wanted them, that was their business and I was glad of the money. On the other hand I stopped contributing new poems to English and American periodicals. My critical writings I did not tidy up; but let them go out of print. In 1927 I began learning to print on a hand-press. In 1928 I continued learning to print.

On May 6th, 1929 Nancy and I suddenly parted company. I had already finished with nearly all my other leading and subsidiary characters, and dozens more whom I have not troubled to put in. I began to write my autobiography on May 23rd and write these words on July 24th, my thirty-fourth birthday; another month of final review and I shall have parted with myself for good. I have been able to draw on contemporary records for most of the facts, but in many passages memory has been the only source. My memory is good but not perfect. For instance, I can after two hearings remember the tune and words of any song that I like, and never afterwards forget them; but there are always odd discrepancies between my version and the original. So here, there must be many slight errors of one sort or another. No incidents, however, are invented or embellished. Some are, no doubt, in their wrong order; I am uncertain, for example, of the exact date and place of the megaphoned trench-conversation between the Royal Welch and the Germans, though I

444

have a contemporary record of it. I am not sure of some of the less-important names (even of Lance-corporal Baxter's, but it was at least a name like Baxter). To avoid the suggestion of libel I have disguised two names. Also, I make a general disclaimer of such opinions as I have recorded myself as holding from chapter to chapter, on education, nature, war, religion, literature, philosophy, psychology, politics, and so on. This is a story of what I was, not what I am. Wherever I have used autobiographical material in previous books and it does not tally with what I have written here, this is the story and that was literature.

I find myself wondering whether it is justified as a story. Yet I seem to have done most of the usual storybook things. I had, by the age of twenty-three, been born, initiated into a formal religion, travelled, learned to lie, loved unhappily, been married, gone to the war, taken life, procreated my kind, rejected formal religion, won fame, and been killed. At the age of thirty-four many things still remain undone. For instance, I have never been on a journey of exploration, or in a submarine, aeroplane or civil court of law (except a magistrate's court on the charge of 'riding a vehicle, to wit a bicycle, without proper illumination, to wit a rear lamp'). I have never mastered any musical instrument, starved, committed civil murder, found buried treasure, engaged in unnatural vice, slept with a prostitute, or seen a corpse that has died a natural death. On the other hand, I have ridden on a locomotive, won a prize at the Olympic Games, become a member of the senior common-room at one Oxford college before becoming a member of the junior common-room at another, been examined by the police on suspicion of attempted murder, passed at dusk in a hail-storm within half a mile of Stromboli when it was in eruption, had a statue of myself erected in my lifetime in a London park, and learned to tell the truth – nearly.

THE END

Dedicatory Epilogue
to
Laura Riding[1]

I have used your *World's End* as an introductory motto, but you will be glad to find no reference at all to yourself in the body of this book. I have not mentioned the *Survey of Modernist Poetry* and the *Pamphlet against Anthologies* as works of collaboration between you and me, though these books appear in publishers' catalogues and obviously put much of my own previous critical writing out of account. And though I have mentioned printing, I have not given details of it, or even said that it was with you, printing and publishing in partnership as The Seizin Press. Because of you the last chapters have a ghostly look.

The reason of all this is, of course, that by mentioning you as a character in my autobiography I would seem to be denying you in your true quality of one living invisibly, against kind, as dead, beyond event. And yet the silence is false if it makes the book seem to have been written forward from where I was instead of backward from where you are. If the direction of the book were forward I should still be inside the body of it, arguing morals, literature, politics, suffering violent physical experiences, falling in and out of love, making and losing friends, enduring blindly in time; instead of here outside, writing this letter to you, as one also living against kind – indeed, rather against myself.

You know the autobiography of that Lord Herbert of Cherbury whose son founded the Royal Welch Fusiliers; how he was educated as a gentleman, studied at Oxford, married young, travelled, played games, fought in Northern France and wrote books; until at last his active life ended with a sudden clap of thunder from the blue sky which did 'so comfort and cheer' him that he resolved at last, at this sign, to print his book *De Veritate*, concerning truth. If you were to appear in my *De Veritate* it could only be as 'this loud though yet gentle noise . . . one fair day in the summer, my casement being opened towards the south, the sun shining clear, and no wind stirring.'[2]

For could the story of your coming be told between an Islip Parish Council Meeting and a conference of the professors of the Faculty of Letters at Cairo University? How she and I happening by seeming accident upon your teasing *Quids*,[3] were drawn to write to you, who were in America, asking you to come to us. How, though you knew no more of us than we of you, and indeed less (for you knew me at a disadvantage, by my poems of the war), you forthwith came. And how there was thereupon a unity to which you and I pledged our faith and she her pleasure. How we went together to the land where the dead parade the streets and there met with demons and returned with the demons still treading behind. And how they drove us up and down the land.

That was the beginning of the end, and the end and after is yours. Yet I must relieve your parable of all anecdote of mine. I must tell, for instance, that in its extreme course in April last I re-lived the changes of many past years. That when I must suddenly hurry off to Ireland[4] I found myself on the very boat, from Fishguard, that had been my hospital-boat twelve years before. That at Limerick I met Old Ireland herself sitting black-shawled and mourning on the station bench and telling of the Fall. And so to the beautiful city of Sligo celebrated in song by my father. And the next train back, this time by the Wales of the Royal Welch Fusiliers. And the next day to Rouen with you and her, to recollect the hill-top where you seemed to die as the one on which I had seemed to die thirteen years before.[5] And then immediately back. And then, later in the same month, my sudden journey to Hilton in Huntingdon, to a farm with memories of her as I first knew her,[6] to burst in upon – as it happened – David Garnett[7] (whom I had never met before), gulping his vintage port and scandalizing him with my soldier's oaths as I denied him a speaking part in your parable.

After which.

After which, anecdotes of yours, travesties of the parable and so precious to me as vulgar glosses on it. How on April 27th, 1929 it was a fourth-storey window and a stone area and you were dying.[8] And how it was a joke between Harold the stretcher-bearer and myself that you did not die, but survived your dying, lucid interval.

After which.

After which, may I recall, since you would not care to do so yourself, with what professional appreciation (on May 16th) Mr. Lake is reported to have observed to those that stood by him in the operating theatre: 'It is rarely that one sees the spinal-cord exposed to view – especially at right-angles to itself.'

After which.

After which, let me also recall on my own account my story *The Shout*,[9] which, though written two years

ago, belongs here; blind and slow like all prophecies –
it has left you out entirely. And, because you are left
out, it is an anecdote of mine.

After which.

After which, even anecdotes fail. No more anecdotes.
And, of course, no more politics, religion, conversations, literature, arguments, dances, drunks, time,
crowds, games, fun, unhappiness. I no longer repeat to
myself: 'He who shall endure to the end, shall be
savèd.' It is enough now to say that I have endured. My
lung, still barometric of foul weather, speaks of endurance, as your spine, barometric of fair weather, speaks
of salvation.

Notes

Good-bye to All That was published by Jonathan Cape on 18 November 1929 in an edition of 5,000 copies. Following objections by Siegfried Sassoon to passages on pp. 290 and 341–3, notably the inclusion without permission of Sassoon's 'Letter to Robert Graves', Cape made an effort to recall unsold copies (of which an unknown number, possibly *c*.100–300, are extant). Cape then had the offending pages cut out of the book and replacement pages printed and glued in with a series of asterisks replacing the text. An objection by Edward Marsh was handled by tipping in an erratum slip between pp. 398–9. Because of high demand (the book sold 20,000 copies in the first week of publication), this first edition, first impression, second state (expurgated) was rapidly printed in a second impression with portions reset to account for the deleted text; third and fourth impressions appeared in November, and a fifth in December 1929, but no other corrections or changes were made until the second revised edition of 1957 (referred to hereafter as G57). In the 1957 edition Graves made alterations to virtually every paragraph of the text (including the removal of the hyphen from the title).

The first edition, but with a second state emendation included, was published in an annotated edition by Richard Perceval Graves (Berghahn, 1995; hereafter G95), in which he notes many of the differences between the first and second editions, lists numerous corrections that Sassoon and Blunden made to a copy of the text, and tracks the memoir's various inaccuracies as regards the events of Graves's own life. Since the differences between the 1929 and the 1957 editions are so extensive, I have included in the notes only selected changes in G57 where there are major excisions or additions; some instances where G57 adds necessary factual clarification or proper names; or where the alterations significantly affect Graves's representation of himself and others.

The first impression, first state, as recalled by Cape, is the text reprinted here, with one exception. For copyright reasons, the verse-letter by Sassoon, 'Letter to Robert Graves', is printed in its final form, not in the slightly garbled and edited version originally included by Graves.

My Dedication in an Epilogue

1. *World's End*: Riding's poem was included in *Love as Love, Death as Death*, the first book published by Graves's and Riding's Seizin Press in 1928. In later published versions of the poem the line 'Quiet in each other's arms' is revised to 'Locked in each other's arms'. The poem was removed from G57 and a short prologue by Graves added instead. In it he observes: 'I partly wrote, partly dictated, this book twenty-eight years ago during a complicated domestic crisis, and with very little time for revision. It was my bitter leave-taking of England where I had recently broken a good many conventions; quarrelled with or been disowned by most of my friends; been grilled by the police on a suspicion of attempted murder; and ceased to care what anyone thought of me. Reading *Goodbye to All That* over again, for the first time since 1929, I wonder how my publishers escaped a libel action.'

I

1. *The science of geography ... about chaps*: This verse is misquoted from Edmund Clerihew Bentley's 'Introductory Remarks' in *Biography for Beginners* (London: T. Werner Laurie, 1905): 'The Art of Biography / Is different from Geography. / Geography is about Maps, / But Biography is about Chaps.'

2. *at least ninety*: Graves's father, Alfred Perceval Graves (1846–1931), then aged eighty-four, was writing his own autobiography, *To Return to All That*, published by Jonathan Cape in 1930.

3. *The objects of this autobiography ... influential descendants*: These paragraphs are omitted in G57, which opens with 'As a proof of my readiness ...'. The 'Old Joe' anecdote is reinstated into Chapter XXV.

4. *1859*: Corrected in G57 to 1854.

5. *German relations ... Irish relations*: In G57 several rather negative references to his Irish father and lineage are revisited or cut; here he rephrases simply as 'I admire my German relatives'.

6. *Ere Bacchus ... a dale worse*: The poem is slightly misquoted, and this is the second not the opening stanza. The published version in *The Irish Poems of Alfred Perceval Graves: Countryside Songs, Songs and Ballads* (2nd edn., Dublin: Maunsel & Co, 1908), p. 64, runs:

> Before Bacchus could talk
> Or dacently walk
> Down Olympus he leaped from the arms of his nurse;
> But though three years in all
> Were consumed by the fall
> He might have gone further and fared a deal worse.

II

1. *As soon as I did, it was all over ... But what about it, anyhow*: This passage is omitted in G57.
2. *Here, for instance, is a letter ... Chatter, Poverty and Chastity*: This passage is omitted in G57.

III

1. *six preparatory schools*: G57 adds the names, in what follows, of Rokeby, Penrallt and Copthorne schools.
2. *Because of ἵστημι and ἵημι*: Ancient Greek verbs, the first of which (roughly, 'to stand') would probably have been taught to Graves as a boy as 'I make to stand', with its various forms including 'make (something) stand', 'stop' (something) or 'set (something) up'. The second, ('to release') would also be taught with at least three meanings: I send/release/let go. His difficulties with conjugation here are not unique.

IV

1. *ten miles from Munich*: 'Diesenhofen' (G57).
2. *I never heard it even questioned ... reasons for liking her*: Omitted in G57.
3. *Nancy's crude summary ... off my shoulders*: The sentence is omitted from this chapter in G57 and reinserted in Chapter XXV.

V

1. *how much more I owe ... than to my father*: Rephrased in G57 as 'how much I owe, as a writer, to

my mother', editing out the slight on Alfred Perceval
Graves.

VI

1. *a friend*: 'Nevill Barbour' (G57).
2. *my brother ... as the brother*: 'Charles' and 'John',
   respectively (G57). Graves's degree was conferred in
   November 1925, not 1926.

VIII

1. *sex feeling ... that Dr. Marie Stopes would call sacramental*: 'Sex feeling' becomes 'love' in G57, and the
   sentence about Marie Stopes (1880–1958) is omitted.
2. *one afternoon*: G57 inserts here 'having by then become
   a complete agnostic'.
3. *Call him Dick*: George Harcourt Johnstone (later 3rd
   Baron Derwent). Graves nicknamed him 'Peter' at school.

X

1. *I was at Harlech ... a day or two later*: Graves left
   school on 28 July 1914; war was declared on 4 August;
   Graves left to join his regiment, the Royal Welch Fusiliers, on 12 August (not 11th, as Graves states).
2. *the Royal Welch Fusiliers*: Graves refers most frequently in
   Good-bye to All That to the Royal Welch Battalions of the
   Regular Army: the 1st and 2nd Battalions are those in
   which he (and Sassoon) served on the Western Front; the
   3rd (Special Reserve) Battalion, headquartered in Wrexham, was a training unit which moved to Litherland in May
   1915, and was in Limerick by the end of the war. He also
   makes brief reference to the 25th Battalion, formed in Egypt

in 1917, and to others of the New Army battalions formed during the war (see Chapter XI). The Royal Welch Fusiliers comprised forty-two battalions by the end of the war.

3. *the company*: A section consisted of *c.*13 men, a platoon of *c.*50, a company of *c.*200, a battalion of *c.*1,000, a brigade of *c.*4,000 and a division of *c.*20,000.

4. *the German bands*: The itinerant musical groups that were a feature of pre-war life.

5. *Through German Eyes*: In a search of the column throughout the war years, it has not thus far proved possible to locate this incident, and it may be another instance of the unreliability of Graves's memory, given the speed with which the memoir was written.

6. *The camp staff consisted of . . . I am Wagon-Lits*: Passage omitted in G57.

7. *Private Robinson*: Private Probert (G57).

8. *those who survived Festubert . . . the following September*: G57 amends this to 'few who survived Festubert in the following May, survived Loos in the following September'.

9. *my publishers advise me not to give it here*: G57 does give the full dramatic scene concerning the soldier found 'committing excreta' in the barrack square. His defence of 'the diarrhoeas terrible baad' is countered by the Sergeant's evidence that '*it was done with a heffort, sir*!'.

10. *Bantam Battalion*: 'volunteers hitherto too short to qualify for the army' (G57).

XI

1. *punishment for losing a battle*: G57 adds '(This was a quite unhistorical libel, but we all believed it.)'.

2. *their regimental motto was*: G57 clarifies as 'we mis-quoted their regimental motto as'.

3.   *recent combinations*: G57 gives 1888, but the reference is to the army restructuring of 1881.
4.   *Quatre Bras?*: Corrected to 'in Egypt' (G57). [Aboukir Bay, 1801.]
5.   *1917*: G57 adds 'and again, and again until the Armistice'.

XII

1.   *On arrival in France*: May 1915.

XIII

1.   *at this time*: G57 adds 'I have restored the names of places, which we were forbidden to mention.' Richard Perceval Graves notes that 'The dating of letters in this chapter is unreliable' and that they have been subject to 'heavy rewriting' (G95, p. 340).
2.   *Parrot is a fair bird for a ladie . . . that popajay royal*: From John Skelton's 'Speke Parrot', lines 211–17. Graves slightly misquotes two lines: 'Except mannes soule, that Chryst so dere bought; / That never may dye, nor never dye shall.' John Skelton, *The Complete English Poems*, ed. John Scattergood (Harmondsworth: Penguin, 1983), p. 236.
3.   *He's laid a bet*: G57 notes that he won the bet.

XIV

1.   *emphatically cold*: G57 changes 'emphatically' to 'bloody' and adds that the prince was 'dressed in nothing at all'.
2.   *Buzz Off*: In G57 'the second-in-command'.
3.   *This time came, exactly a year later*: Phrase omitted in G57.
4.   *to the Welsh*: G57 clarifies this as the 'Welsh Regiment'.

XV

1. *Mons Angels*: G57 adds the explanatory note: 'According to the newspapers, a vision of angels had been seen by the British Army at Mons; but it was not vouchsafed to Sergeant Townsend, who was there, with most of "A" Company.'
2. *front and support lines*: Clarified in G57 as 'assault and support lines'.
3. *dislike of the Scots . . . voiced the general opinion*: This passage is toned down in G57: 'A strong comradely feeling bound the Middlesex and the Royal Welch . . . Our adjutant voiced the extreme non-Scottish view . . .'
4. *A machine-gun traversing*: G57 makes it clear this was the Pope's Nose machine gun of the earlier part of the story.
5. *came rushing back*: G57 rephrases as 'went rushing away'.
6. *a sergeant of the Fifth Scottish Rifles*: 'Sergeant McDonald', who 'was decorated for this feat' (G57).

XVI

1. *There was a daily exchange of courtesies . . . Se–e you da–mned to He–ll first*: G57 alters the response phrase to 'YES, with-OUT my DRAWERS ON!'. Paul Fussell points out the impossibility of this anecdote in *The Great War and Modern Memory* (Oxford: Oxford University Press, 1975), p. 207.
2. *Return to greet me . . . crimson of men slain*: Lines from Siegfried Sassoon's 'To Victory'. Sassoon's account differs, here and at numerous points, from Graves's, and the poem is dated 4 January 1916, two months after this meeting.
3. *We already knew . . . a good joke*: The foreknowledge claimed here is a point disputed by Sassoon. See G95, p. 345.

4. *stages of my life*: G57 adds: 'Myself in faultless khaki with highly polished buttons and belt, revolver at hip, whistle on cord, delicate moustache on upper lip, and stern endeavour a-glint in either eye, pretending to be a Regular Army captain; but crushed into that inky desk-bench like an over-grown school-boy.'

XVII

1. *the Seventh*: G57 adds 'the Second' here.
2. *were not considered so good*: Phrase omitted in G57.
3. *promotion*: 'formation' (G57).
4. *usually inferior ... not good enough*: Rephrased in G57 as 'ranked low because of inefficient officers and warrant-officers'.
5. *Scottish*: Qualified in G57 as 'Scots, with certain higher-ranking exceptions'.
6. *Of the Australians ... Marcus Clarke*: The reference is to Australia's history as a penal colony; this sentence was omitted in G57.
7. *Et enfin ces animaux ... à la poche*: 'And, finally, these animals ripped their ears off and put them into their pockets.'
8. *There was no patriotism in the trenches*: Softened in G57 to 'Patriotism, in the trenches, was too remote a sentiment.'
9. *enjoined*: Altered in G57 to the very differently inflected 'enjoyed'.
10. *the base*: Harfleur (G57).

XVIII

1. *unriveted*: Corrected in G57 to 'unrevetted'.
2. *David had died*: David Thomas died on 18 March 1916. He is the subject of Graves's war poem 'Goliath and David' in the 1917 collection of that title.

3. *These months with the First Battalion ... Adams was killed*: Omitted in G57.

XIX

1. *When I was given leave in April 1916*: G57 begins this chapter with a three-page account of 'the last occasion on which I ever attended a church service', Good Friday, 1916. Richard Perceval Graves notes that the additions in G57 are adapted from a piece in *But It Still Goes On* (1930) and that the incident took place in November not April, since Graves was in hospital on Good Friday 1916 (G95, p. 349).

2. *another charm against trouble*: G57 adds: 'though I have since learned that the last five words of the original Hebrew are really a question, not a relative clause'.

3. *I wrote two or three poems ... after the war*: G57 adds 'but have suppressed them all since'.

4. *never decided*: G57 here adds two paragraphs concerning Welsh complaints about blasphemous language in the army.

5. *the South African ribbon*: 'A Boer War veteran' (G57).

6. *the colonel*: Colonel 'Tibs' Crawshay in G57 (and generally throughout Chapters XX–XXII).

7. *Old Kitchener was all right*: In G57 'Kitchener served his purpose as a figure-head'.

8. *as one of them recorded*: 'Captain Dunn, the battalion doctor' (G57). Captain J. C. Dunn is author of *The War the Infantry Knew 1914–1919* (London: P. S. King Ltd, 1938).

9. *Karl Graves*: Armgaard Karl Graves had been convicted in Edinburgh in 1912 under the Official Secrets Act (1911) and sentenced to eighteen months imprisonment. He later wrote *The Secrets of the German War Office* (London: T. Werner Laurie, 1914).

XX

1. *It was said that*: In G57 'Edmund Dadd told me that . . .'
2. *stormed the colonel*: 'Colonel Stockwell, then in command' (G57).
3. *So I sent him a rhymed letter*: 'Familiar Letter to Siegfried Sassoon' in *Fairies and Fusiliers* (London: William Heinemann, 1917).
4. *the C.O.*: 'Stockpot' [Stockwell] (G57).
5. *the corpse of a German . . . bloated and stinking*: This experience inspired the poem 'A Dead Boche' in *Goliath and David* (London: Charles Whittingham & Co., 1917).
6. *four hundred strong*: G57 notes this figure includes 'transport, stretcher-bearers, cooks, and other non-combatants'.
7. *Non, tu ne peus pas me tuer*: 'No, you cannot kill me', a French translation of the line '*Sterben? Sterben kann ich nicht!*' ('Die? I cannot die!') from Friedrich Nietzsche's 1884 poem '*Yorick als Zigeuner*' ('Yorick as a Gypsy').
8. *The wound over the eye . . . cemetery headstones*: G57 adds 'Later, I had it cut out, but a smaller piece has since risen to the surface under my right eyebrow, where I keep it for a souvenir.'
9. *Yours sincerely*: The letter is signed 'C. Crawshay, Lt-Col.' (G57). The original letter (RWF Museum, Caernarfon) is dated 20. 07. 16, not the 22nd as Graves states here.
10. *They hung on at the near end . . . First Battalion was in it*: G57 qualifies and amplifies this overheard account in a paragraph beginning 'This was not altogether accurate', which notes that some Public Schools Battalion men maintained their position, and 'Nor did the Scots all behave badly.' 'Father McCabe' is corrected to 'Father McShane', and a recent letter to Graves from Captain Colbert of the Fifth Scottish Rifles is quoted at length.

11. *This was July 24th ... my death officially occurred*: Although Graves claims his twenty-first birthday as the 'official' date of his death, Colonel Crawshay had been informed that Graves, wounded on the morning of 20 July, died en route to the field hospital. He wrote a condolence letter to Graves's mother that evening (see note 9 above). Graves wrote to his parents on the 23rd; his letter arrived on the 24th; the Colonel's letter probably (and confusingly) arrived the day after. See also Richard Perceval Graves, *Robert Graves: The Assault Heroic* (London: Weidenfeld & Nicolson, 1986) pp. 155–7. *The Times* listed him as 'Died of Wounds' on 4 August 1916, p. 5.

XXI

1. *We were beginning to wonder ... a card in the window about it*: The passage is rewritten in G57 and moved to the opening of Chapter XXIII.

2. *I went for a visit to Kent ... killed in the Dardanelles*: The friend is Sassoon and they travelled together from Harlech. Sassoon's younger (not elder) brother, Hamo, had been killed at Gallipoli and buried at sea on 1 November 1915. Presumably the changes were to disguise the identity of those concerned, although as Sassoon pointed out to Graves afterwards, 'Your alterations of younger brother to "elder brother", etc., were unnecessary. Anyone who took the trouble to identify the brother officer could do so.' Sassoon to Graves (2 March 1930) in Robert Graves, *In Broken Images: Selected Letters of Robert Graves 1914–1946*, ed. Paul O'Prey (London: Hutchinson, 1982), p. 207.

3. *He said ... place is haunted*: Sassoon's objections to this passage led to its removal, and the substitution of asterisks, in the first impression second state (expurgated) text. G57 inserts here instead: 'There were thousands of

mothers like her, getting in touch with their dead sons by various spiritualistic means.'

4. *London Mail*: G57 adds 'a daring new popular weekly'.
5. *There was a draft*: 'I commanded a draft' (G57).

XXII

1. *the colonel*: Crawshay.
2. *The bed is too narrow . . . to wrap myself therewith*: Isaiah 28:20: 'For the bed is shorter than that a man can stretch himself on it: and the covering narrower than that he can wrap himself in it' (Authorized King James Version).
3. *Are ye there . . . are ye there?*: Misquoted from Rudyard Kipling's 'Chant-Pagan: English Irregular: '99–02' in *The Five Nations* (London: Methuen & Co., 1903), pp. 159–60: 'Our 'elios winkin' like fun – / Three sides of a ninety-mile square, / Over valleys as big as a shire – / *Are ye there? Are ye there? Are ye there?*'
4. *I said that I had not examined . . . finally called off*: Sassoon objected to this kind of self-aggrandizing and Graves rephrased the incident in G57 to take less credit.

XXIII

1. *few of the new officers were now gentlemen*: Phrase omitted in G57.
2. *V.A.D. probationer*: Named 'Marjorie' in G57 (Marjorie Machin), where the incident is placed after the final break with 'Dick', although (as Richard Perceval Graves shows in *Robert Graves: The Assault Heroic*) this was not the case.
3. *the friend*: 'Sassoon' (G57).
4. *worst story*: 'filthiest story' (G57).

XXIV

1. *XXIV*: This chapter, an account of the famous incident of Sassoon's 'Declaration', contains chronological flaws which are corrected, as far as possible, in Richard Perceval Graves's *Robert Graves: The Assault Heroic*, Book 4, Chapters 13–14. Some of the (mis)representations here also account, in part, for the breakdown of relations between Graves and Sassoon in 1930.

2. *Rapture and pale Enchantment ... not stand the din*: Lines from Sassoon's 'Conscripts'. There are slight textual variants here from the poem as published in *The War Poems of Siegfried Sassoon*, ed. Rupert Hart-Davis (London: Faber, 1983), p. 69.

3. *Oh life, oh sun*: An allusion to Graves's 'Escape' in *Goliath and David*, a poem about his own 'death' in 1916, which closes with 'O Life! O Sun!'

4. *the colonel, a South Welshman*: Colonel Jones-Williams (G57).

5. *the senior-major*: Major Macartney-Filgate (G57).

6. *because he was ill, and knew it*: Sassoon complained that Graves here 'omitted the crucial fact, that I only consented to take the Medical Board (after refusing the first one) because you swore on the Bible that nothing would induce the authorities to court-martial me. (What might or might not have happened if I'd held out doesn't matter. But *my reason for giving way* was surely part of the story.)' Sassoon to Graves (7 February 1930), *In Broken Images*, p. 199.

7. *died shortly after the war*: Rivers died on 4 June 1922.

8. *had been accused of cowardice ... very shaky condition*: This potential slight on Owen's reputation caused concern, Sassoon writing to Graves: 'What is your authority for laying so much stress (by saying nothing else!) on the "cowardice" story? Two days ago,

Mrs. Owen has written to me . . . and she complains bitterly about your reference to Wilfred. As far as I know,
you only saw O. twice . . . I saw him every day for about
3 months and can assure you that he was not "in a very
shaky condition", and said so little about being accused
of "cold feet" that I always regarded it as a negligible
affair, and had no recollection of it until it was clumsily
revived by Scott-Moncrieff in an article on O.'s poems
(in 1921). Was it fair on O. to put that in and say nothing else?' Sassoon to Graves (2 March 1930), *In Broken
Images*, pp. 206–207. G57 omits the phrase 'He was in
a very shaky condition' and alters 'had been accused of
cowardice' to 'unjustly accused'.

XXV

1. *Lost them again, sergeant*: Sergeant Dickens (G57).
2. *October revolution*: Bolshevik revolution (G57).
3. *We attached no importance*: Rephrased in G57 as
   'Though attaching no importance to the ceremony, Nancy
   did not want to disappoint her father.'
4. *The embarrassments*: G57 inserts 'Nancy and I being
   both virgins'.
5. *Richardson*: Samuel Richardson (G57).
6. *read Joe's letter*: G57 inserts material about Old Joe
   from the opening two pages of the first edition.
7. *When I'm asleep dreaming and lulled and warm*: Published as 'Death's Brotherhood' in 1918 and later retitled
   'Sick Leave' in *The War Poems of Siegfried Sassoon*, p. 94.
8. *gentleman . . . gentlemanliness*: G57 omits these two
   terms and more explicitly states 'the regiment would
   either think him a coward or regard his protest as a
   lapse from good form'.
9. *To these I turn . . . clean from rust*: From Sassoon's 'The
   Kiss' (April 1916).

10. *It was written ... lost in the abyss*: Georges Duhamel, *The New Book of Martyrs*, trans. Florence Simmonds (New York: George H. Doran, 1918), p. 40.

11. *I cannot quote in full*: As it transpired, Graves could not quote it at all and the entire poem was removed. The version he originally quoted was garbled, particularly in its layout (thereby destroying its rhyming structure); he also edited content and omitted lines. The complete version, as printed here, entitled 'Letter to Robert Graves', is in *The War Poems of Siegfried Sassoon*, pp. 130–33. Graves's alterations to the poem as it was printed in the first state 1929 (withdrawn) edition are detailed in notes 12–16 below.

12. *Yes, you can touch my banker ... unless you bleed him*: Graves omitted this couplet.

13. *Jolly Otterleen*: Graves replaced 'Jolly Otterleen' (Lady Ottoline Morrell) with 'Thingumbob'.

14. *Who pretends he doesn't ... Topic of the Town*: Graves omitted this line.

15. *Dotty Captain*: Graves replaced this with 'Captain Sassons'.

16. *O Rivers please take me ... Sassons*: Graves omitted the final six lines of the poem.

17. *Instead of children ... back from Adelphine*: Graves omits this passage in G57 and replaces it with the brief sentence: 'To forget about the war, I was writing *Country Sentiment*, a book of romantic poems and ballads.'

18. *thinking of the dead*: In G57 Graves then adds (marring the dramatic close of this chapter):

Siegfried's famous poem celebrating the Armistice began:

> Everybody suddenly burst out singing,
> And I was filled with such delight
> As prisoned birds must find in freedom ...

But 'everybody' did not include me.

He misquotes the 'famous poem', since Sassoon's 'Everyone Sang' begins: 'Everyone suddenly burst out singing.'

XXVI

1. *the adjutant*: Attwater (G57).
2. *Is there any song sweet enough . . . Where are there any
   like these?*: 'A Song for Two Children' in *Country Sentiment* (London: Martin Secker, 1920), p. 13. Graves
   slightly misquotes himself in the lines 'Is there any song
   sweet enough / For Nancy and for Jenny?' and 'I've
   counted the miles to Babylon, / I've flown the earth like a
   bird.' The poem was subsequently rewritten, with 'Nancy'
   replaced by 'Davey'. See *Robert Graves: Complete Poems*,
   ed. Beryl Graves and Dunstan Ward (Penguin, 2003) p. 62.
3. *I had ceased to be a British grenadier*: Rephrased in G57 as
   a question: 'Had I ceased to be a British grenadier?'
4. *following measles*: The remainder of this paragraph is
   rewritten in G57, Graves pointing out that while ill he
   'focused attention on a poem, "The Troll's Nosegay",
   which was giving me trouble; I had taken it through
   thirty drafts and still it would not come right. The
   thirty-fifth draft passed scrutiny, I felt better . . .'
5. *Siegfried and myself*: In G57 'and myself' is omitted,
   attributing the sentiments here only to Sassoon.
6. *drag on Nancy*: G57 continues: 'but had sworn on the
   very day of my demobilization never to be under anyone's orders for the rest of my life. Somehow I must live
   by writing.' Given his devotion (and subservience) to
   Laura Riding in 1929, it is improbable Graves could
   have uttered such a sentiment in the first edition.
7. *The attitude of my family was doubtful*: In G57: 'My
   family . . . did not know quite how to treat me.'
8. *We worked it out later . . . seemed merely eccentric*:
   Passage omitted in G57.

XXVII

1. *Mrs. Delilah Becker ... known as the Jubilee Murderess*: Edmund Blunden points out that her real name was Mrs. Angel Heavens and 'the Jubilee Murderess' was not an established nickname. See G95, p. 369.

2. *I used to bicycle down from Boar's Hill ... wind and water a man's all right*: Most of these two paragraphs are omitted in G57, although he does still (erroneously) describe Blunden as permitted to live on Boar's Hill only 'because of gassed lungs'.

3. *the Poet Laureate*: 'Robert Bridges' (G57).

4. *Jan*: Mrs. Masefield's name for John, clarified by inverted commas in G57.

5. *My nerves were bad ... shaking for weeks after this*: Graves omits these three paragraphs in G57, substituting (ironically enough, given the defenestration events of 1929) the brief comment 'I could never again now deliberately take chances with my life.'

6. *merely pleasant ... caricature likeness remained*: Rephrased in G57 as 'I ... found him disagreeably pleasant' and 'Yet the caricature likeness to the boy I had loved persisted.'

XXVIII

1. *XXVIII*: In the preface to G57, Graves notes that he has replaced this T. E. Lawrence chapter 'with a longer one written five years later'. The new chapter in G57 adds several passages about Lawrence's relations to poets and poetry.

2. *I met T. E. Lawrence first at a guest-night at All Souls'*: Graves met T. E. Lawrence in November 1919. G57 incorrectly adds 'February or March 1920'.

3. *A prince*: Prince Albert, Duke of Schleswig-Holstein (G57).

4. *The poet divine . . . a pot of good ale*: From 'The Ex-Ale-tation of Ale' in *An Antidote Against Melancholy: Made up in Pills* (London: Mer. Melancholicus, 1661), p. 5.

5. *Middle Eastern settlement*: '1922' (G57).

6. *censuring Sir Edmund Gosse*: Sassoon takes issue with this, writing to Graves that: '. . . Mrs. Hardy tells me that it was she, and not T. H. who repeated the story about Gosse imitating Henry James. "T. H. would never have criticized Gosse before a young man, almost a stranger . . . I very much dislike that way of describing T. H. as a rather comic old gentleman."' Sassoon to Graves (7 February 1930), *In Broken Images*, p. 198. Graves counters this in reply: 'Gosse imitating James: Florence Hardy was wrong; I took a précis of the conversation at the time.' Graves to Sassoon (20 February 1930), *In Broken Images*, p. 201.

7. *Mrs. Michael Howard*: G57 omits all references to her.

8. *One of those whom we courted . . . override this arrangement*: G57 omits these negative phrases, simply stating 'Even Mrs. Masefield used to visit us once a week.'

9. *War horror overcame me again . . . contrary side of the lesion*: G57 omits these two paragraphs concerning Graves's mental health.

10. *Islip was a name . . . sit for my finals*: G57 omits this final paragraph.

XXIX

1. *After so much shifting about . . . I was ready to forget about it*: G57 omits this section.

2. *I never made more at this time . . . Pier-Glass was also a failure*: In G57 he omits the story of his poetry's lack of

success, and moves most of the remainder of this paragraph to Chapter XXX.

3. *Delamare*: Amended to 'Walter de la Mare' in G57.
4. *I approved the final choice*: In G57 he explains that the
    'two names' were 'his own and mine!'.
5. *Ah, no man knows . . . Roves back the rose*: Walter de
    la Mare, 'All That's Past', *Collected Poems* (London:
    Faber, 1942), p. 167. Graves slightly misquotes the first
    line here, which is 'Oh, no man knows.'
6. *the Rupert Brooke Fund*: No such fund existed and, fol-
    lowing Marsh's objections, Cape inserted an erratum
    slip which read: 'Since this paragraph was printed, I
    have heard from Mr. Marsh that the facts are not quite
    as I have stated them, and that there is not really any
    "Rupert Brooke Fund" administered by Mr. Marsh. I
    much regret this error which arose from an imperfect
    recollection. R.G.'

XXX

1. *typhoid fever and died*: Sir Walter Raleigh died on
    13 May 1922.
2. *I had already written a prose book . . . means of curing
    myself*: G57 omits this passage about *On English Poetry*
    (London: William Heinemann, 1922).
3. *Before it appeared . . . indeed it deserved*: G57 omits
    this passage about *The Meaning of Dreams* (London:
    Cecil Palmer, 1924).
4. *Mock-Beggar Hall . . . puritanical in matters of sex*:
    G57 omits these paragraphs, and all references to the
    Indian philosopher Basanta Mallik (1879–1958), who
    was nevertheless an important influence on some of
    Graves's poetry from this period.
5. *1926 was yesterday . . . approaching its end*: This sen-
    tence, which pre-empts his arguments in the Dedicatory
    Epilogue to Laura Riding, was therefore omitted in G57.

6. *There came one more death . . . would not be necessary*: G57 omits or rewrites most of this material, notably cutting out all the references to the fears surrounding childbirth.

7. *Poetic Unreason . . . my bachelor's degree*: *Poetic Unreason* was published by Cecil Palmer in February 1925 and Graves viva-ed for his B.Litt in June. The degree was conferred in November 1925, not 1926 (cf. p. 57).

8. *the Earl of Oxford*: Asquith (G57). Herbert Henry Asquith, 1st Earl of Oxford and Asquith (1852–1928) had been Prime Minister from 1908 to 1916.

9. *Among other books . . . glad that it had*: This paragraph, which gives considerable insight into Graves's writing activities at the time, is omitted in G57.

XXXI

1. *So second-class . . . in the hold*: The notable omission from this sentence is that they were also accompanied by a 'lady secretary' – in fact, the American poet Laura Riding (1901–91). From this point forward, her absence from the text distorts the 'truth' of Graves's 'autobiography'.

2. *half-brother and half-sister*: 'My elder brother Dick, and my elder sister Mollie' (G57).

3. *Mohammedan*: Altered (and throughout) to 'Moslem' in G57.

4. *Freedom was mere politics . . . they had brought with them*: This sentence was rewritten in G57 as: 'Nationalism, a creed derived from the new smatterings of Western education we were giving the upper classes, should be disregarded as merely a symptom of the country's growing wealth.'

5. *more unsuitable for the climate*: G57 then adds a warm and affectionate paragraph about his half-brother Dick and half-sister Mollie, beginning 'My brother Dick behaved beautifully to me, as he has always done; and

so did my romantic sister Mollie, who is a water-diviner and, by my advice, always wears a beauty-patch on her right cheek-bone.'

XXXII

1. *The following is the substance of a letter ... Science from an Easy Chair*: Both this letter and Graves's contemporary comments on it are omitted in G57.

2. *The Diploma Class ... fatigable and fond of leisure*: These contemporary comments are omitted in G57, although the three sample essays are still included.

3. *black soldier*: 'Nubian soldier' (G57).

4. *relief of my sister-in-law*: G57 adds a short paragraph here to conclude the book and omits the remainder of this chapter, from 'The story trails off' until 'THE END'. The concluding paragraph in G57 does not accurately represent events:

    > The remainder of this story, from 1926 until today, is dramatic but unpublishable. Health and money both improved, marriage wore thin. New characters appeared on the stage. Nancy and I said unforgivable things to each other. We parted on May 6th, 1929. She, of course, insisted on keeping the children. So I went abroad, resolved never to make England my home again; which explains the 'Goodbye to All That' of this title.

5. *This, I admit, Death is terrible ... in his true rank and order*: 'Pure Death' from *Poems 1914–26* (London: William Heinemann, 1927), pp. 214–15. Graves slightly misquotes the last line here from its then-published version: 'Death stands again in his true rank and order.' The poem was later rewritten to begin: 'We looked, we loved, and therewith instantly / Death became terrible to

you and me. / By love we disenthralled our natural terror / From every comfortable philosopher / Or tall, grey doctor of divinity: / Death stood at last in his true rank and order.' (*Robert Graves: Complete Poems*, p. 282.)

DEDICATORY EPILOGUE TO LAURA RIDING

1. *Dedicatory Epilogue to Laura Riding*: This epilogue was removed from G57 and replaced by a new 'Epilogue' that offers some brief, selective autobiographical updates and reflections on the text from the perspective of Graves's later middle age. It begins with the (misleading) sentence: 'Though often asked to publish a continuation of this autobiography, which I wrote in 1929 at the age of thirty-three, I am always glad to report that little of outstanding autobiographical interest has happened since.'

2. *You know the autobiography . . . and no wind stirring*: In the context of the quotations, it is clear that Laura Riding is here treated as a divine being: Herbert, praying to God for a 'sign from heaven', is granted it in 'a loud though yet gentle voice'. See Sidney L. Lee, *The Autobiography of Edward, Lord Herbert of Cherbury, with Introduction, Notes, Appendices and a Continuation of the Life* (London, 1886), pp. 248–9.

3. *How she and I . . . your teasing Quids*: 'She' is Nancy. 'The Quids' is one of four poems by Laura Riding Gottschalk (as she was then) published in *The Fugitive* 3.1 (February 1924), pp. 9–14.

4. *That when I must suddenly hurry off to Ireland*: Graves went to Sligo at Laura Riding's behest to try and retrieve Geoffrey Phibbs (who was not there). The incident inspired the poem 'Return Fare' in *Poems 1929* (London: Seizin Press, 1929). Phibbs, an Irish poet who began corresponding with Riding in 1928, left Ireland in February 1929 (on Riding's invitation) to join the 'three-life' or 'trinity' of Nancy, Graves and Riding, thereby turning it

into a 'four-life'. He experienced a change of heart on Easter Monday, 1 April 1929, and left again.

5. *And the next day . . . die thirteen years before*: Graves, Riding and Nancy then travelled to France on a further quest to find Phibbs, who had rejoined his wife, Norah McGuinness. Phibbs refused to return with them to London, prompting a hysterical fit on Riding's part, which, according to Norah, took place not on a 'hilltop' but in the public lounge of their hotel. See Richard Perceval Graves, *Robert Graves: The Years with Laura 1926–40* (London: Weidenfeld & Nicolson, 1990), p. 81.

6. *her as I first knew her*: 'Her' is Nancy, who had been courted by Graves in Hilton.

7. *David Garnett*: Phibbs later visited his wife's former lover, David Garnett, in Hilton, and Graves was sent again, successfully this time, to bring him back to London on 26 April 1929.

8. *How on 27th April . . . and you were dying*: Following the collapse of relations between Riding and Phibbs, who made it clear he would not rejoin her 'circle', Riding first drank disinfectant (Lysol), then, in the early hours of 27 April, threw herself from the fourth-floor window of the flat in Hammersmith, while Graves, Phibbs and Nancy looked on. Graves jumped after her from the floor below and was uninjured. Suspicions of attempted murder were followed by investigations of attempted suicide, for which Riding narrowly escaped prosecution, largely through the intervention of Edward Marsh. Following these events, from May to July 1929, Graves wrote (partly dictated) *Good-bye to All That*. Graves and Riding left for Majorca in the autumn of 1929; Phibbs and Nancy settled together in England. For a full account of the complex series of events elliptically sketched in the Dedicatory Epilogue, see vol. 2 of Richard Perceval Graves's biography, *Robert Graves: The Years With Laura*, pp. 76–91.

9. *The Shout*: According to Graves, in the introduction to his *Collected Short Stories* (Harmondsworth: Penguin, 1968), 'The Shout' was written in 1924; Richard Perceval Graves dates it as 1926 or 1927 (G95, p. 382). The story may be read as uncannily anticipating some of the ménage à trois (or quatre) trauma of 1929, and Riding's not-quite-death cry when falling from the window.